A GENERAL HISTORY OF EUROPE

EDITED BY DENYS HAY

EUROPE IN THE
EIGHTEENTH CENTURY
1713–1783

Second edition

M. S. ANDERSON

LONGMAN

LONGMAN GROUP LIMITED
Longman House
Burnt Mill, Harlow, Essex, U.K.
Published in the United States of America
by Longman Inc., New York
© M. S. Anderson 1961
This edition © Longman Group Limited 1976
First published 1961
First issued in paperback 1970
Second edition 1976
Fourth impression 1981
ISBN 0 582 48671 8 (cased)
ISBN 0 582 48672 6 (paper)

Library of Congress Cataloging in Publication Data
Anderson, Matthew Smith
Europe in the eighteenth century, 1713–1783
(A General history of Europe)
Bibliography
Includes index
1. Europe—History—18th century. I. Title
D.286.A5 1976   940.2'5   76–7427
ISBN 0–582–48671–8
ISBN 0–582–48672–6 pbk.

Printed in Singapore by
Huntsmen Offset Printing Pte Ltd

Contents

Maps

Preface

The writing of a book as wide in scope as this one is a difficult though rewarding task. In my case its burdens have been lightened and its attractions increased by the help of a number of friends and colleagues. I am grateful to Professor D. B. Horn of the University of Edinburgh, to Dr. J. H. Western of the University of Manchester, and to my colleagues at the London School of Economics, Dr. R. M. Hatton, Mr. A. Davies, and Dr. D. C. Coleman, who have all read parts of the book in typescript and made valuable suggestions for its improvement. My wife typed over half of it at a period when she had many other calls on her time, and has also given me useful advice and comments on a number of points. For the errors and other inadequacies which a work of this kind can scarcely hope to escape the responsibility is entirely mine.

M. S. ANDERSON

LONDON, *May, 1961*

Preface to the second edition

The years since the first appearance of this book have seen the publication, notably in France, of a considerable number of works which make new and important contributions to our knowledge of eighteenth-century Europe. I have tried in this second edition to take account wherever necessary of these, and have also corrected a number of errors of fact and emphasis. This has involved not merely alteration but extensive rewriting. In addition to many minor changes and additions to the text a large amount of new matter has been incorporated in Chapters III–VI, XIV and XVI, while the discussion of the Enlightenment and of political and social ideas in general, which now seems to me inadequate as it stands in the first edition, has been expanded into an entirely new Chapter XV. I have three important debts to acknowledge. The first is to my publishers, who have been willing to allow such extensive changes. The second is to the secretarial staff of the International History Department of the London School of Economics, and in particular to Mrs. N. J. Smith, for the help they have so cheerfully given. The third and greatest is to the British Library of Political and Economic Science, which for a quarter of a century has been an unfailing source of intellectual nourishment and support.

M. S. ANDERSON

LONDON, *December, 1975*

I

Introduction[1]

The period from the early 1680s to about 1713 acts, in far more than a merely chronological sense, as a bridge between the seventeenth and eighteenth centuries. It has a distinct character of its own; but if a choice must be made, it belongs rather to the former than to the latter.

In international relations it begins with the rise to its highest pitch of the influence of Louis XIV and the failure of the Turkish attack on Vienna in 1683; while its end is marked even more clearly by the Treaties of Utrecht and Rastadt in 1713–14 and by Louis's death in 1715. In this sphere it is dominated in Western Europe by the threat of French hegemony and in the East by the beginnings of the rise of Russia. Of these two factors the former bulked much the larger in the eyes of most contemporaries. France, with her, by the standards of the age, huge population of over twenty million, her armies of a size no other State could match, her efficient commanders and subtle diplomats, seemed more than once during these decades to threaten all Western Europe with servitude. The aggressive and casually brutal way in which her strength was sometimes used, as in the seizure of Strasbourg in 1681 or the devastation of the Palatinate in 1688, increased the fears of her neighbours. Little seemed beyond Louis's power in the 1680s. He might secure his election, or that of a member of the Bourbon family, as Holy Roman Emperor. He might permanently reduce the States of West and South Germany to the position of French satellites. Above all he might secure most or all of the Spanish Empire for himself or his descendants on the death of the sickly Charles II of Spain. Such a success would mean not merely a union of the French and Spanish crowns but also French dominance of the western Mediterranean, an increased French threat to the security

[1] A list of some of the more important general works dealing with the period covered by this book will be found in Appendix I.

of England and the United Provinces, and the transformation of Spain's enormously wealthy American possessions into a French commercial preserve.

Thus until the end of the struggle over the Spanish inheritance in 1713 there were few international questions of any importance which were not influenced, and often dominated, by France and her ruler. Throughout this period Louis's policies and intentions were the object of anxious speculation in the capitals of Europe. This fear of France was to some extent exaggerated: the poor communications and the inefficient administrations of the period made it impossible for Louis to exert to the full his enormous material superiority to his neighbours. It was nevertheless a natural and inevitable fear; and even the victories of Marlborough and the death of the *roi soleil* could not completely dissipate it.

The rise of Russia to the status of a great European power was by contrast slow. To a large extent it was ignored by governments and public opinion in Western Europe during this period. Until her victory over the Swedes at Poltava in 1709, she impressed foreign observers by her military and administrative weaknesses rather than by her potential strength. Even after the crisis of the Great Northern War had been passed it was some time before the implications of her new status became clearly visible. The rise in her international importance, in other words, was an eighteenth-century phenomenon, though some of its foundations had been laid in previous generations. As such it falls within the scope of this volume.

For the European States, with one or two important exceptions, the transitional generation which began in the 1680s was in internal politics a period of despotism. The significant point is that almost all the despotisms of this period looked back rather than forward. They were still heavily dependent on religious sanctions. Monarchy was still a divinely ordained institution. Kings still wielded their powers as the vicegerents of God. They remained, almost if not quite as much as in previous generations, remote, awe-inspiring and essentially mysterious personages to the majority of their subjects. The theories of 'enlightened despotism' which were to be so widely diffused over much of Europe in the later eighteenth century, and which sometimes (though less frequently than historians have often thought) inspired the policies of rulers, were only hinted at in the age of Louis XIV. In this respect also Europe, down to the great King's death, was still living in the seventeenth century. The generation 1685–1715 was, in its political thought, more in tune with seventeenth- or even sixteenth-century apologists for divine right than with the critical and utilitarian attitudes which were to mark much eighteenth-century thinking. Already, however, Locke had laid in England many of the foundations of the eighteenth century's attitude to human psychology, and hence indirectly to questions of political right and obligation. His ideas were beginning to have some influence outside his own country even before the death of Louis XIV; we shall see them bear generous fruit in the middle and later decades of the period covered by this book.

In economic life the last generation of Louis's reign was essentially a period of stability in Western Europe. We can, none the less, easily detect in it the beginnings of changes which were to become more marked in the eighteenth century. The economic, or at least the commercial and financial, importance of England was now increasing. Less visibly to contemporaries, that of the United Provinces was entering on a long though slow decline. The economies of some of the greatest West European States were beginning, at the end of the seventeenth century, to be profoundly influenced for the first time by trade with the extra-European world. Only then were the pattern and value of England's seaborne commerce radically altered by the products and markets supplied by her possessions overseas, while a corresponding trans-formation of French trade was still slower to show itself.

In intellectual life this generation was in some very important respects a period of change. It was the age of Newton and Locke, the last stage in that wonderful burst of scientific and philosophical activity which in the seventeenth century accumulated a capital of basic ideas upon which the modern world is still living. Old certainties, received opinions, conventional attitudes, were holding their ground with increasing difficulty against the attacks of sceptics and the still more dangerous erosion produced by geographical and anthropological discoveries. Newton and his followers did not shake the religious or political faith of their contemporaries, and never intended to do so. Throughout the eighteenth century the development of the physical sciences, though it had revolutionary implications, had no really revolutionary effects. On the other hand the description, on a scale and with a detail hitherto unprecedented, of non-European peoples and civilizations, which is one of the features of the period c. 1680–1715, had much more serious results. The discovery by the reading public of noble Iroquois, virtuous Hindus and philosophic Chinese, could not but shake the Europe-centred and Christendom-centred attitudes inherited from the past.

This interest in the non-European world, and the greater width of outlook and flexibility of judgement which resulted from it, grew steadily in the eighteenth century. They confront us on almost every page written by Montesquieu and Voltaire. They were coupled with an equally important development of historical method, seen above all in Jean Mabillon's great textbook of palaeography, *De Re Diplomatica* (1681), and consequently of historical scepticism. The difficulties of writing reliable history were now more clearly understood and more frequently stated than ever before. Moreover rationalistic criticism of religious tradition and even of the Bible itself, exemplified by the *Dictionnaire Historique et Critique* of Pierre Bayle (1697) and by the work of the great French biblical critic, Richard Simon, was beginning to shake in a still more fundamental way traditional certainties inherited from the past. It was above all in this growth in some spheres of intellectual life of a critical, sometimes aggressively critical, spirit, in this developing taste for change and for rejection of the past, that the dynamism of the generation before 1715 lay. To say, as one leading historian of ideas has done, that 'virtually all the intellectual views and ideas which as a whole were to culminate in the French Revolution had already taken shape even before the reign of Louis XIV had ended',[1] is perhaps an exaggeration. But it is not a very gross one.

This generation thus shows, as any comparable period must, the interaction of conflicting tendencies. Intellectually in some ways an age of radical innovations and challenges, it saw little fundamental advance in economic life over much of the continent. During it armies came into being which in efficiency, size and cost surpassed any known for many centuries. Yet they were used, in the main, in struggles for European territorial prizes which had already been many times contested—the Rhineland, northern Italy or the southern Netherlands. Political ideas and attitudes still looked largely to the past, and were still in the main rooted in religion. Yet they were already feeling the effect of new currents of thought which were eventually to transmute them, at least in their more extreme forms, into something quite unrecognizable to seventeenth-century theorists such as Filmer or Bossuet.

On this foundation, in some parts solid and relatively unchanging, in others flimsy and unstable, the history of eighteenth-century Europe was to be built.

---

[1] P. Hazard, *The European Mind* (*see* App. I), pp. 445–6.

4

II

The Sources

The extent to which the history of any age can be known depends on
the fullness and reliability of the records left by it. These may take a
great variety of forms. The buildings, furniture, painting and sculpture
of a period are all illustrations of its activities, illustrations of a peculiarly
immediate and tangible kind. They are often the best of all guides to its
spirit, ideas and assumptions. In the main, however, the historian,
especially if he is concerned with modern history, must rely upon the
books and documents left by the period which he wishes to study. The
eighteenth century has bequeathed to scholars a varied and formidably
large legacy of this kind, although it is much smaller than that left by
the century which followed, and minute by comparison with the one
we are now accumulating for the use of posterity. The population of
Europe was much less during the period with which this book is concerned than it was to be even a few decades later. The States between
which the continent was divided and the administrative systems which

BIBLIOGRAPHY. Critical discussions of the different types of material available
for the study of the eighteenth century (as distinct from bibliographies or
critical editions of individual texts) are very rare. The following touch in
varying detail and with varying degrees of closeness upon some of the points
made in this chapter: F. Fueter, *Geschichte der neueren Historiographie* (Munich,
1936); J. W. Thompson, *A History of Historical Writing* (New York, 1942),
vol. II; R. N. Stromberg, 'History in the eighteenth century', *Journal of the
History of Ideas*, vol. XII (1951); H. Trevor-Roper, 'The historical philosophy
of the Enlightenment', *Studies on Voltaire and the Eighteenth Century*, vol. XXVII
(1963); J. H. Brumfitt, *Voltaire Historian* (Oxford, 1958); E. Weis, *Geschichts-
schreibung und Staatsauffassung in der französischen Enzyklopedie* (Wiesbaden,
1956); C. Ledré, *Histoire de la presse* (Paris, 1958); C. Bellanger and others,
Histoire générale de la presse française, vol. I (Paris, 1967); L. Hanson, *Government
and the Press, 1695–1763* (Oxford, 1936); K. Schottenloher, *Flugblatt und Zeitung*
(Berlin, 1922).

Guides to the various national archives and to manuscript collections in great
libraries are too numerous to mention here. D. H. Thomas and L. M. Case
(eds.), *Guide to the Diplomatic Archives of Western Europe* (Philadelphia, 1959),
deserves attention, however, as an up-to-date and useful though sometimes
rather summary introduction to one important class of material.

controlled them were primitive by comparison with their successors. Europeans were less literate, less aware of their history and its implications and hence less self-conscious, than they were soon to become. Thus the output in the eighteenth century of books and documents, of those traces of the past without which it can never be adequately reconstructed, was not great by modern standards. It was nevertheless very large by those of any comparable preceding period.

To the majority of eighteenth-century Europeans the State was not an entity with which they felt a very intimate relationship. It impinged on the life of the individual as a rule in a purely negative though important way, exacting tax payments, military service and sometimes forced labour, and usually doing little for him in return. Nevertheless a large portion of the material which the historian of this period has at his disposal was the product of the States, of the courts of their rulers, of their judicial systems and their administrative machinery. The eighteenth century saw over the greater part of Europe a movement towards the creation of more efficient and more centralized bureaucracies. These, as both a condition and a result of their increasing efficiency, produced a growing bulk of reports, memoranda, statistics, legislative projects and correspondence of all kinds. Documents of this essentially governmental or legal kind are available in great quantities. They can provide answers to a wide variety of questions, many of which have, at least superficially, no connexion with administrative or legal problems. They give the scholar not only an immense amount of information but also very valuable insights into the economic activity, the society and even the intellectual life of the age. Thus for example the best account of life and society in London during this period, M. Dorothy George, *London Life in the Eighteenth Century* (London, 1925), is based to a considerable extent on the records of the Petty Sessions held at the Guildhall and for the County of Middlesex. On a larger scale the reports sent to Paris by officials in the provinces during the reigns of Louis XV and Louis XVI provide not merely information important to the historian of French administrative methods but also a remarkably complete picture of the life of the areas concerned.

On the other hand materials of this legal and administrative kind have certain limitations. With few exceptions they were accumulated by men struggling with immediate and concrete problems. How can an inefficient and irrational system of taxation be made to yield more revenue? How can recruits for the army be most easily obtained from a recalcitrant population to which the idea of public spirit is almost incomprehensible? How can an archaic and often brutal judicial system be best used in the maintenance of public order? These were typical preoccupations of the eighteenth-century administrator, and the documents he produced were intended to help him answer questions of this kind. They were not meant to supply information for its own sake, much less for the convenience of scholars in the future.

The questions asked by the twentieth-century historian are, however, quite different from those which faced the eighteenth-century bureaucrat. In particular many scholars are now increasingly interested in the accurate determination of aggregate quantities—the population, imports and exports, and agricultural and industrial production of a given State or geographical area. Increasingly knowledge, however incomplete, of such quantities is being used to explain economic growth (or its absence) and social and political change. Eighteenth-century administrations were not in general equipped with reliable information of this type. What mattered to them was the number of taxable individuals and households in a State or a province rather than its total population, the yield of customs duties rather than the real quantities or values of the goods imported or exported, whether hunger was so widespread as to threaten riots and revolt rather than exactly how much grain or meat was being produced. Though many of them made during this period increasingly effective efforts to collect statistical information of various kinds (see pp. 96–7) it remained from their point of view an administrative tool and nothing more.

What attempts were made to obtain figures of the kind sought by the present-day historian, also, were often stultified by the laziness, ignorance, or venality of the officials charged with their collection. Thus the usefulness of the trade statistics which began to be collected in England in 1696 by the Inspector-General of Imports and Exports is considerably reduced by the fact that they continued throughout this period to be based on arbitrary official values for the commodities concerned. These values were realistic in 1696 but soon became quite notional, a mere bureaucratic fiction. Moreover efforts to collect quantitative information of this type were often made still more difficult by the almost universal and often justified suspicion that they were the prelude to new taxation. A clear illustration is the enumeration of peasant households over most of Russia begun on the orders of Peter I in 1718–19 to provide a basis for the new poll tax. This was carried out with considerable difficulty and in the face of much popular opposition. As a result the total number of households given by the inquiry was clearly too low. The same weaknesses continued to a lessening extent to affect the similar censuses of 'taxable souls' which were carried out later in the century. Yet the results of these inquiries, in default of anything better, remain the basis for all estimates of the population of Russia in this period.

It must also be remembered that conditions might vary very widely between different parts of the same State. Food and drink, dress, dialects, methods of land tenure, of taxation, of agriculture, might differ strikingly even in neighbouring districts of what was politically a unit. French or Prussian provinces such as Brittany or Brandenburg might have very little in common with other French or Prussian provinces such as Dauphiné or Cleves. The historian who wishes to study many aspects of the century, above all its economic and social life, on more than a local or provincial scale, must therefore cast his net as widely as possible. He must beware of taking the particular for the general, the local for the national. This warning obviously applies to a great many types of material other than administrative documents.

The extent to which sources of this kind have been printed varies very considerably between different States. In Britain the quantity of administrative and governmental documents in print relating to this period is small by comparison with that available for the sixteenth and seventeenth centuries. (The most important collections are the *Calendar of State Papers, Colonial Series, America and West Indies* (London, 1866–   ) which has as yet reached only the year 1738; the *Journal of the Commissioners for Trade and Plantations from . . . 1704 to . . . 1782* (London, 1920–38) which also deals mainly with colonial matters; and the four volumes of the *Calendar of Home Office Papers* (London, 1878–99) which contain a good deal of miscellaneous information for the years 1760–75.) In France a vast amount of work has been done on this type of material, but its results have been embodied in monographs rather than in collections of printed documents. Prussia by contrast has produced in the *Acta Borussica. Denkmaler der Preussischen Staatsverwaltung im 18 Jahrhundert*, published by the Königliche Akademie der Wissenschaften from 1892 onwards, the most complete collection of printed administrative documents available to illustrate the history of any eighteenth-century State. For Russia there is much material of this type scattered throughout the 148 volumes of the *Sbornik Imperatorskogo Russkogo Istoricheskogo Obshchestva* (St. Petersburg, 1867–1916) and in smaller collections of which *Zakonodatelnie Akty Pyotra I*, vol. I, ed. N. A. Voskresenskii (Moscow-Leningrad, 1945) is probably the most important.

In general diplomatic documents are those which the historian finds easiest to use. They are also relatively abundant and accessible for this period. They are sometimes difficult to interpret and evaluate accurately: what statesmen and monarchs said about their foreign policies in the eighteenth century is no more to be implicitly relied on than similar pronouncements today. But however complex the gradations and local variations in the economic and social life of the States of this period they had as a rule unified and reasonably coherent foreign policies which can be followed in detail from the material available. There are exceptions to the generalization; but on the whole international relations, conceived in a narrow diplomatic sense as a narrative of negotiations and agreements between States, is one of the simpler aspects of the history of the century. It is, moreover, a subject on which a relatively large amount of information is available in the form of collections of printed documents, such as the twenty-nine volumes of the *Recueil des Instructions donneés aux Ambassadeurs et Ministres de France depuis les Traités de Westphalie jusqu'à la Révolution Francaise* (Paris, 1884–1969) and the seven volumes of *British Diplomatic Instructions, 1689–1789* published by the Royal Historical Society in 1922–34. Most important of all, the *Sbornik Imperatorskogo Russkogo Istoricheskogo Obshchestva*, which has already been mentioned, contains a great amount of diplomatic correspondence drawn from British, French, Prussian and Saxon archives as well as Russian ones, which it prints in the original languages. Eighteenth-century publicists also produced a number of important collections of this kind, of which J. Rousset de Missy's *Recueil historique d'Actes, Négociations, Mémoires et Traitéz* covering the period 1713–48 in twenty-one volumes (The Hague–Amsterdam–Leipzig, 1728–54) is a good example.

Government was carried on, policies formulated and new trends in economic and intellectual life originated, in the eighteenth century as at any other time, by individuals as well as institutions. This means that our knowledge of many aspects of this period must be derived largely from private papers and correspondence. Where the individual concerned was a monarch controlling personally the fate of the State he ruled, the line dividing a private letter from a public document can become a very fine one indeed. Thus the great *Politische Correspondenz Friedrichs des Grossen* (forty-six volumes: Berlin, 1879–1939) is in form a collection of Frederick II's personal correspondence but in fact a great corpus of official documents, many of them of the highest importance. The same is true of the papers of Peter I of Russia (*Pisma i Bumagi Pyotra Velikogo* (St. Petersburg-Moscow, 1887–   ): the collection has as yet reached only the year 1711); of the *Correspondence of King George the Third from 1760 to December 1783*, ed. Sir J. Fortescue (London, 1927–28); and to varying extents of nearly all the letters of monarchs and statesmen during this period. It must be remembered, moreover, that it was quite normal for a minister, on leaving office, to take with him large quantities of documents which he regarded as his private correspondence but which to modern eyes seem important State papers. This practice seems to have been particularly common where foreign policy was concerned, above all in countries where monarchical and bureaucratic centralization had not developed very far. It was notably widespread in Great Britain, whose great libraries are therefore particularly rich in material of this kind, both printed and unprinted, for the eighteenth century. Many efforts were made to prevent the retention in private hands of documents of public importance. Victor Amadeus II of Savoy even went so far as to order in 1720 that the houses of high-ranking officials should be searched after their deaths to recover materials of this kind. Such precautions, however, could not prevent a steady leakage in almost all the States of Europe of public or semi-public documents into private hands.

Personal papers are therefore useful because they often supplement the material available from purely governmental and administrative sources. They can perform a still more important function, however, by showing how policies were evolved, how they emerged in some States from the conflicting attitudes of the ministers, diplomats and officials concerned, while in others they were merely the fiat of an all-powerful monarch. It is above all through material of this kind that the individual enters the historian's picture of the eighteenth-century States and their activities.

Collections of private papers of a different and more intimate type can also throw much light on the social, intellectual, artistic and economic life of the age. Thus, to take one of the best-known examples, the vast correspondence of Horace Walpole covering the period 1731–97 can be made to yield a great deal of information about many aspects of life in eighteenth-century England. (The best edition is that in course of publication at Yale of which thirty-nine volumes have now appeared.) The same is true of the most famous biography of the century, indeed the most famous in the English language, James Boswell's *Life of Samuel Johnson*, of which the best edition is that by G. Birkbeck Hill and L. F. Powell (Oxford, 1934–50). The letters of some of the great authors of this period—large collections of those of Voltaire, Rousseau, Hume and Gibbon, amongst others, have been published—are also one of the best avenues of approach to its intellectual life. However materials of this kind, no matter how eminent their authors, illuminate very unevenly the various aspects of eighteenth-century Europe. This is mainly because large collections of private papers dealing with economic life are much rarer than those concerned with politics, society and the world of ideas. A number of great economic institutions of a public or semi-public kind, above all trading companies and banks, have preserved substantial collections of papers relating to their activities in this period. Of these, in a few cases, parts have been published. But the papers of individual merchants or industrialists, the ledgers, accounts and commercial correspondence which would be of so much value to the historian, have very often been lost or destroyed. Of the material of this kind known to exist, moreover, only a small proportion has been printed. As a result discussion of the economic history of this period has until recently been based, to a degree which all historians would now agree is undesirable, mainly on series of official documents which are usually more complete and more accessible than the relevant private papers. Economic histories of the eighteenth century have therefore tended to be histories of economic policy, of what governments or their agents did or tried to do, as much as of economic activity, which was the result of a multitude of individual decisions.

During the last generation this position has changed markedly for the better. The papers of individual entrepreneurs and business firms (though these are inevitably more fragmentary than those of government departments and official bodies) have been used by historians with increasing effect. They have helped to paint a picture of economic life, at least in parts of Western Europe, more detailed and realistic than any available before. In one very important way in particular there has been a successful effort, notably in France, to found discussion on more certain foundations. Historical demography, the study of the growth of population in the eighteenth century, is now more securely based than ever before. The riches of the raw material available in France for work of this type has allowed the technique of 'family reconstitution' (the reconstruction of families, normally on the basis of mention of their members in parish registers and similar documents) to be used as a tool with which the historian can come to grips as never before with the demographic, and therefore to a large extent social, realities of past ages.[1] In other parts of Europe less abundant documentation makes the use of such methods more difficult; but almost everywhere they have largely unexplored and often great potentialities.

Allied to private papers and correspondence, possessing some of the same virtues but suffering in many cases from defects of their own, are the memoirs and autobiographies which the century produced in such profusion. Like private correspondence these are an important vehicle for the transmission to posterity of the thoughts and feelings of individuals. They are one of the means by which the historian can most easily 'think himself back' into the eighteenth century. Some of them, such as the *Journal et mémoires* of the Marquis d'Argenson (ed. J. B. Rathéry, Paris, 1859–67) or the more famous *Mémoires* of the Duc de Saint-Simon (ed. A. de Boislisle, Paris, 1923–28) contain important information about political matters not available elsewhere. Others such as the *Journal Historique . . . du Règne de Louis XV* of E. J. F. Barbier (Paris, 1847–56) illustrate many aspects of the social and intellectual life of the age. In a few cases (the most obvious is the *Autobiography* of Edward Gibbon, of which the best edition is that published in London in 1896) they are works of literary art in their own right. They remain today one of the few types of historical material which can be easily enjoyed by the layman. From the viewpoint of the historian, however, they often suffer from serious defects. In some cases they are quite spurious, the work of hack journalists rather than of their alleged authors. Thus the so-called *Testament politique du Cardinal Jules Alberoni* (Lausanne, 1753) is really the work of a French publicist. When genuine they are in many cases apologies rather than impartial statements of facts and intended, consciously or unconsciously, to influence posterity in favour of the writer. Such are the *Mémoiries du Duc de Choiseul* (Paris, 1904) and the *Mémoires et lettres du Cardinal de Bernis*, ed. F. Masson (Paris, 1903). More important in many ways, they are a literary form which flourished mainly in Western Europe, above all in France, and which is poorly represented in the eastern and even the central parts of the continent. Also, like the collections of private correspondence referred to above, they reflect in the main the interests

[1] Family reconstruction was first illustrated on a significant scale in E. Gautier and L. Henry, *La Population de Crulai, paroisse normande: étude historique* (Paris, 1958).

and outlook of a small privileged ruling class. Memoirs and auto-biographies written by merchants, by professional men, even by squires and farmers, do exist. One example of the latter, the *Pameti Frantiska J. Vavaka* (ed. P. J. Skopec, Prague, 1914–16) is the most important printed source of information about peasant life in Bohemia in the later eighteenth century. In general, however, the voice of the common man finds little expression in material of this type—less than in some classes of administrative documents.

The eighteenth century was a great age of travel. It was also an age in which the reading public displayed a voracious appetite for informa-tion about foreign countries. It thus saw the publication by many travellers of descriptions of their experiences. These accounts, some of them very voluminous, vary greatly in quality. As a whole, however, they provide the historian with a vast amount of information, above all about the economic and social life of Europe during this period. Often the comments of an observant but unsophisticated foreigner, shocked by the sight of habits and tastes different from those to which he is accustomed, illustrate more forcibly and convincingly than any-thing else the very real psychological and intellectual barriers which still existed between the various parts of Europe. Thus an English traveller complaining that in Russia 'it is the genious [*sic*] of this country to be everything or nothing: a middle state such as happy England boasts is not understood';[1] or that in Spain 'the children in this country seem neither to play nor to work; it is nearly impossible to buy either toys or books';[2] or a German visitor annoyed by his English landlady's refusal to allow him to play the flute on Sundays, can sometimes bring contrasts of this kind home to the reader more forcibly than pages of statistics or abstract description.

Descriptive accounts of this type have none the less considerable weaknesses. Side by side with substantial works of lasting value can be found vast numbers of books of a popular and quite ephemeral kind. Their authors were often interested in externals—clothing, food and drink, the cleanliness or otherwise of the inns in which they slept—rather than in political, economic or social questions. For this it is unfair to blame them. After all, in a great many cases they were travel-

[1] *The Russian Journals of Catherine and Maria Wilmot, 1803–08*, ed. H. Montgomery Hyde (London, 1934), p. 55.
[2] *The Journal and Correspondence of William, Lord Auckland* (London, 1861–62), vol. II, p. 84.

ling for pleasure. Moreover, like the volume of memoirs or autobiography, the book of travels was in the eighteenth century essentially
a product of Western Europe. Many were written by Englishmen and
Frenchmen, an appreciable number by Germans, Italians, Dutchmen
and Scandinavians, hardly any by Russians, Poles, Hungarians, Greeks
or Turks (and for that matter few by Spaniards or Portuguese). The
picture which they paint, therefore, is one coloured by the assumptions
which dominated the relatively wealthy and highly educated societies
of the West, one in which the viewpoint of the poorer and more backward parts of Eastern and Central Europe finds little expression.
Distance, the difficulty of travel and ignorance of the languages concerned, also meant that few of the authors of this type of book travelled
in Eastern or even Central Europe. Their works deal above all with the
cities of France and Italy, increasingly frequented by tourists, and to a
lesser extent with the Netherlands, western Germany and Spain. By
contrast Russia, Poland and the Habsburg territories attracted little
attention, and the Balkans very little indeed.

Besides this great travel literature the eighteenth century also produced a good deal of writing on the events of its own day. Some of these
semi-historical, semi-journalistic accounts are of real importance. They
are often voluminous, providing the historian with substantial bodies of
facts conveniently assembled (usually in a chronological sequence).
Examples of this type of work, selected almost at random, are John
Entick, *The General History of the Late War* (London, 1763–64), John
Andrews, *The History of the War with America, France, Spain and
Holland* (London, 1785–86), and on a larger scale the *État Politique de
l'Europe* (The Hague, 1742–49) of J. Rousset de Missy. (The last is
really a very detailed history, including many printed documents, of
the years 1734–43.) More important, such books, written by authors
who may have been eye-witnesses of some of the events they describe,
often preserve and transmit to the reader the 'feel' of the period in a
way which the 'scientific' historian, writing years later, cannot hope
to do.

Against these advantages, however, must be placed once more
considerable defects. In the first place there is often an element of
plagiarism about works of this kind. In an age when the idea of copy-
right was still new and very hard to enforce by law it was quite common
for a writer to embody in a book of his own considerable portions of
one written by someone else, and to pass the result off as his own work.
This is particularly noticeable in West European writing on distant and

little-known parts of the continent such as Russia. It is seen most clearly of all in the great commercial encyclopedias which were one of the features of the age (Malachy Postlethwayt's *Universal Dictionary of Trade and Commerce* (London, 1751–53) is the best English example) and which provide the historian with vast quantities of information whose reliability is often hard to determine. More important, the eighteenth century took, by modern standards, a rather limited view of history. The characters of kings, the intrigues of ministers, the convolutions of diplomacy, the movements of armies, attracted the attention of writers and bulked large in works on contemporary or near-contemporary events. By comparison the progress of some aspects of economic life, the introduction of new administrative methods, the development of education, even the growth of new religious sects, aroused little interest. When therefore an eighteenth-century writer attempted to narrate on a large scale the events of his own day he usually confined himself to political, military and diplomatic history and consequently produced a somewhat unbalanced picture. This is true even of so well-known a work as Voltaire's *Précis du siècle de Louis XV* (Paris, 1769) one of the best and most intelligently written examples of this *genre*. The lopsidedness of so many of these books is of course in itself a fact of historical importance. 'At any time, the conception of what is remarkable or worthy of record is a function of the whole body of current ideas, and what the writer sets down represents not merely his private judgment, but that of the community of which he forms a part.'[1] Nevertheless it clearly limits their value to the historian. Even on this semi-journalistic level, moreover, contemporary discussion of the events of the eighteenth century was influenced, usually for the worse, by prevailing ideas about the nature and functions of historical writing. It was still possible to believe, or claim to believe, that accuracy and reliability in the writing of history was unattainable, that it could never be more than a fable distorted by the ignorance or prejudices of the writer. 'O! do not read history', exclaimed the British statesman Sir Robert Walpole (an excellent eighteenth-century example of a pragmatic lack of interest in the past and its lessons), 'for that I know must be false.'[2] More important was the fact that to many of the most important writers of the period on history and historiography history

[1] F. J. Teggart, *Prolegomena to History*, University of California Publications in History, vol. IV, No. 3 (Berkeley, 1916), p. 179.

[2] W. Coxe, *Memoirs . . . of Sir Robert Walpole* (London, 1798), vol. I, p. 762.

seemed a vehicle for the exposition of ideas or the teaching of morality rather than a disinterested enquiry into the facts of the past. Boling-broke's pronouncement that it was 'philosophy teaching by example', made in 1735, set the tone for much of the historiography of the century. 'To me it appears', wrote an intelligent author at the end of the century, 'that to write history without drawing moral or political rules from it, is little better than writing a romance.'[1] Throughout this period, therefore, writers were strongly tempted to extract moral judge-ments from the events which they described. Sometimes they might even manipulate or suppress evidence in order to vindicate some pre-conceived theory or prejudice. These tendencies are perhaps most noticeable in works dealing with classical or medieval history; and there were great writers such as Hume and Gibbon who resisted them to a large extent. But writing on contemporary or near-contemporary events, especially if it aspired to the rank of literature rather than mere journalism, was often heavily influenced by them. Thus Voltaire's *Histoire de Charles XII* (Paris, 1731) and *Histoire de l'Empire de Russie sous Pierre le Grand* (Paris, 1759–63), both of which had con-siderable popularity and influence, were not works of history in the modern sense of the term. The author took considerable pains in col-lecting the information on which they were based; but they were not intended to be accumulations of accurate facts established by research. They were in part conscious works of art (in this they belong to a tradition tracing back to the Renaissance) and in part edifying stories designed to illustrate the responsibilities of rulers and thus help them to improve their judgement and act correctly in moments of crisis. When a Swedish historian, Nordberg, published in 1740 another account of the reign of Charles XII, he took the opportunity to point out a number of errors in Voltaire's book. The Frenchman replied by attacking Nordberg's work as excessively preoccupied with factual accuracy, pedantic and boring. Voltaire had the better of the ex-change, but his victory does not affect the fact that Nordberg's is the more useful book of the two to the modern scholar. It is worth noting, moreover, that in the eighteenth century as today writers of real eminence were sometimes unwilling to concern themselves with the history of their own times, regarding it as a rather second-rate subject. 'I should shrink with terror', wrote Gibbon in an autobiographical fragment of 1762, more than two years before he conceived the idea of

[1] Sir John Dalrymple, *Memoirs of Great Britain and Ireland* (London, 1788), vol. II, p. 177.

his *Decline and Fall of the Roman Empire*, 'from the modern history of England, where every character is a problem, and every reader a friend or an enemy; where a writer is supposed to hoist a flag of party, and is devoted to damnation by the adverse faction.' At a lower level, the factual and essentially journalistic level of works such as those of Entick, Andrews and a host of other writers, eighteenth-century discussion of eighteenth-century events does not as a rule suffer severely from the desire of its authors to import morality into their subjects. As it rises in the literary scale, however, it tends to become increasingly selective and moralizing. This makes it interesting to the historian of ideas but reduces its value to the scholar in search of accurate factual information.

During this period two classes of raw material for the historian begin to be produced in unprecedented quantities. Newspapers and periodicals are the first of these. Ancestors of the modern newspaper, brief, intermittently appearing and usually short-lived news-sheets, had been published from early in the seventeenth century. As it drew to a close it was becoming clear that at least in some parts of Western Europe, above all in England and the United Provinces, a demand for serious and well-informed journalism was developing on a hitherto unknown scale. Thus Courtilz de Sandras, a very voluminous writer on contemporary politics, founded in 1686 at The Hague the *Mercure Historique et Politique*, the first political monthly. The earliest English daily paper, the *Daily Courant*, came into existence in 1702. A few years later the phenomenal success and widespread imitation of the *Spectator* showed that there now also existed a considerable public demand for a non-political periodical of this kind, a journal of ideas rather than of information, and for the attractive blend of morality and entertainment which it purveyed. The development of the Press in Europe during the middle decades of the century was relatively slow, but its last years saw a very rapid growth of newspapers and periodicals over much of the continent. Eighteen newspapers were published in London in 1782; forty-two were appearing a decade later. Against the thirty-five newspapers and periodicals of all kinds published in Paris in 1779 must be placed the 169 available at the outbreak of the Revolution. In the 1770s and 1780s the French bookseller Panckouke, by acquiring control of a number of these, created what was probably the first newspaper empire in European history. In the Dutch Republic, which had pioneered the development of newspapers and had still, even in the middle and later eighteenth century, great prestige as a centre of journalism, a similar development can be seen in the emergence of important new papers such as *Le Politique Hollandais* and the *Post van der Neder Rhijn*. (The latter, soon after its foundation in 1781, had no less than 24,000 subscribers.) Even in Spain periodicals such as the *Gaceta de Madrid* and the *Espiritù de los mejores Diarios* played a significant role as vehicles of 'enlightened' thought in the later eighteenth century. To the historian these newspapers and periodicals have inevitably certain defects. In the first place, like so many of the more literary and consciously-created types of evidence available to him—memoirs, books of travels, works of contemporary history—they were a product of Western Europe and took root only slowly in the east and even the centre of the continent. Political journalism in particular could flourish only in countries where some degree of political and intellectual freedom existed, above all in Great Britain and the United Provinces. Even France had no daily paper till 1777, when the *Journal de Paris* began to appear, so that during most of this period the reading public there depended for much of its information on current affairs on newspapers published in the Netherlands, or in small neighbouring States such as Berne, Liège and Cologne. In Germany, where the despotic governments of the numerous small States tended to hamper the growth of the Press, it was not until the 1780s that serious discussion by it of political questions began to be possible. Even then this discussion was often timid compared to that in Britain or the Netherlands. In Russia the time-lag in this respect as compared to some parts of Western Europe was especially noticeable. Peter I had founded in 1703 what is usually regarded as the first Russian newspaper, the *Vedomosti*. This however was merely a government propaganda organ, appearing very irregularly, with a small circulation, and containing little but praise of the Tsar's policies and news of his victories. Though there was under Catherine II a very considerable production of literary periodicals which often took the *Spectator* or *Tatler* for their model, Russia never possessed during this period a newspaper which could comment with any degree of freedom on current politics. In other words the Press, or at least the political Press, provides more, and more important, information for the historian interested in some parts of Western Europe than for scholars whose interests lie farther east.

Even in Great Britain or the United Provinces eighteenth-century newspapers suffer, as raw materials for the writing of history, from considerable defects. Many of them were purely advertising organs which carried no news or editorial comment at all. Even in those which were newspapers in the true sense of the word advertisements bulked larger than is normal today. This advertising matter is of considerable interest from some points of view. It is in particular an important source of information about many aspects of social life, though one which is difficult to use and which has never been thoroughly exploited. But its prominence naturally tended to reduce the amount of space which could be given to news. In particular (as was to be expected in an era when communications were still slow and difficult) few journals or magazines were well-informed about events in foreign countries.

Moreover the Press was never, in any major European State, free from government influence and official pressure during this period. In France at the outbreak of the Seven Years War the government, using the journalist J.-N. Moreau as its agent, published a newspaper which it hoped to send abroad and also distribute in Paris in order to combat the anti-French arguments being put forward by the British Press. A few years later two of the most important French statesmen of the century, the Duc de Choiseul and the Comte de Vergennes, attempted to win over the Press to support their policies (notably that of intervention in 1778 in the War of American Independence). Frederick II of Prussia went much farther in this direction. He established in Cleves, one of his Rhenish provinces, a newspaper, the *Courier du Bas-Rhin*, designed to influence European opinion in his favour; paid the *Gazette de Berne* for the same purpose; and even had the editor of the hostile *Gazette de Cologne* beaten up by his agents. In Britain, where the more rapid development and greater importance of the Press made it even more worthy of the government's attentions, the politicians in power consistently attempted to influence it in their favour during most of the first half of the century. Thus in 1722 the government bought, on terms which are not precisely known, the support of the *London Journal*, its most bitter critic during the preceding three or four years. In 1731 an opposition paper alleged, probably without great exaggeration, that the ministry was spending £20,000 a year on subsidies to the Press and bribes and pensions to journalists. It is true that government influence of this kind declined from the later 1730s onwards and that by the 1750s a subsidized ministerial Press had ceased to exist. Efforts to influence newspapers in support of official policy seem however to have revived somewhat at the end of this period: in 1791 nine London newspapers were receiving regular (though relatively small) payments from secret service funds.

The pressures of this kind under which newspapers and periodicals laboured are of importance to the historian because this type of source has been used by him hitherto mainly as raw material for studies of public opinion. It is quite clear that a public opinion of a modern kind was emerging and assuming political importance by the end of this period in some parts of Europe, above all in Great Britain. It is clear also that the Press was the most important channel through which it could find expression. But to say with certainty how far any particular newspaper or periodical was expressing at any particular moment a real current of popular feeling, and how far it was merely responding to government or party pressure or the prejudices of its owners, is often very difficult indeed. It is true, of course, that the Press has always been, and is today, exposed to external influences of this kind. There were however a number of factors—the small circulations and financial weakness of nearly all newspapers, the feeling still prevalent everywhere that a free Press was a danger to political stability, the resulting existence in most countries of a system of censorship—which made the eighteenth-century Press peculiarly vulnerable in this respect.

With all these defects the newspapers and periodicals of the eighteenth century provide the historian with important (and hitherto not very systematically exploited) sources of information. The newspapers give him, as has been seen, very important material for the study of public opinion in some parts of Western Europe. They may also, on occasion, supply him with items of political information not easily accessible elsewhere. Periodicals of an unspecialized kind, such as the *Gentleman's Magazine* which began publication in 1731, provide an illuminating commentary on many aspects of the age and sometimes contain material of political importance. Journals such as C. F. Nicolai's *Briefe, die neueste Litteratur betreffend,* founded in 1759; C. F. Wieland's *Deutsche Merkur,* founded in 1773; or E. C. Fréron's *Année Littéraire,* which began publication in 1754, are of great interest for any serious study of the literature of the period.

As well as seeing the first important growth of newspapers and periodicals the eighteenth century was also the greatest age of the pamphlet. Like so many of the types of historical material discussed above, this also was predominantly a product of Western Europe, of Great Britain and the Netherlands, to a lesser extent of Germany and France. It is therefore of great potential value to the historian of some of the Western States, of relatively little to those of the eastern or even the central parts of the Continent. Pamphlets, moreover, present peculiar difficulties to the scholar who seeks to use them. They were produced in great numbers (in Britain at least in thousands during this period), have not attracted as much attention from bibliographers as might have been expected, and are frequently hard to trace in library catalogues. Apart from these purely mechanical difficulties, the historian has also to face the fact that many of them are anonymous and that, like the newspapers of the period, they were often produced to serve the purposes of some powerful individual or interest group and cannot be accepted without question as impartial examinations of the subjects with which they deal. The question of authorship can often be answered and is sometimes not very important. It is usually more necessary and often more difficult to find out whose arguments are in fact being expressed in any particular pamphlet. Thus for example *The Northern Crisis, or Reflections on the Policies of the Tsar* (London, 1716), one of the better-known of those published in England during this period, has sometimes been quoted as an illustration of the hostility then felt there to the Baltic ambitions of Peter I of Russia.[1] In fact, however, this pamphlet is not English at all. It was written by Count Gyllenborg, the Swedish minister in London, in an effort to mobilize opinion in Britain in favour of his country, which was then struggling for survival in a great war with Russia. It is clear from other sources that its arguments won considerable support in Britain. But in itself the pamphlet is evidence of nothing but the desire of the Swedes for British support.

Knowledge of the true authorship and inspiration of eighteenth-century pamphlets is important to the historian because they, like the newspapers of the period, have hitherto been used largely in studies of public opinion and in efforts to show how it influenced the development of government policy on various issues. They were, in fact, like many newspapers, intended to persuade rather than to inform their readers. Almost everywhere in Europe, until near the end of this period, they were the most effective means of mobilizing opinion on the great issues of the day. Pamphlets, especially when they deal with some limited or local issue, may contain factual information not available anywhere else. Many, notably on economic questions, were the work of experts whose views must carry considerable weight. But the highly polemical character of much of this type of writing, almost irrespective of its subject, must always be allowed for.

Finally, of course, the imaginative literature of the period—its poetry, its plays, above all its novels—is in itself a part of its history. This means that it is of interest not merely to the historian of literature but also to

[1] Karl Marx, among others, used it for this purpose in his *Secret Diplomatic History of the Eighteenth Century* (London, 1899), pp. 25ff.

the student of eighteenth-century society, ideas, and to a lesser extent economic and political life. Thus the importance of satire as a literary form during the first half of the century, of which the works of Pope and Voltaire are the greatest examples, may be seen as an expression of the analytical and rationalistic tendencies which were then in some ways the most dynamic elements in its intellectual life. In the same way the success of the moralizing novels of Richardson or plays of Lessing in the middle years of the century was largely a result of the emergence, in the wealthier parts of Western Europe, of a new and important middle-class novel-reading and play-going public with new and middle-class tastes. The primitivism and exoticism which affected most branches of literature so powerfully in the last years of this period also represents the influx into European life of powerful currents of new ideas. Nor was prose literature at least, during much of this period, seriously restricted by considerations of social class or 'suitable' subjects. Indeed a good deal of it shows, by comparison with that of the age which followed, a remarkable readiness to discuss without sentimentality or even emotion the lives of the poor, and of the criminals and potential criminals who were so numerous in all great European cities. A historian who wished to study poverty and crime in London or the *demi-monde* in Paris in the early decades of the eighteenth century could do worse than start by reading Defoe's *Colonel Jack* or Prévost's *Manon Lescaut*.

On the other hand imaginative literature, like all the more self-conscious types of historical material produced during this period, was in the main a product of Western Europe. It throws considerable light, from a number of different angles, on the history of England and France, and to a lesser extent perhaps on that of Italy and Germany. To the historian interested in Eastern Europe, or even in Spain or Portugal, it has much less to offer. Moreover it was, as any more or less sophisticated literature must be, the product and reflection of an essentially urban society. Eighteenth-century writing was the offspring of cities, of courts, of universities, of centres in which the theatre, the *salon* and the coffee-house could flourish. It might often use natural objects as a peg on which to hang its philosophizings and displays of emotion, especially in poetry. It might sometimes idealize or sentimentalize over the peasant and the labourer. It might even (as in some of Fielding's novels) occasionally draw a realistic picture of the farmer or the squire. But it was not really concerned with, and in general had not much understanding of, the rural society in which the great majority of Europeans still passed their lives. This inevitably limits its value to the historian. The studies of almanacs, chapbooks and other ephemera, the reading of the poor and the semi-educated, which have in recent years been made in France (see p. 351) may in time do something to fill this gap and deepen our understanding of mass psychologies and popular climates of feeling.[1] But however much we try to compensate for it we can never escape the fact that virtually all our sources for the study of this period, and especially the more literary and self-conscious ones, heavily over-represent the urban, educated, well-to-do parts of society everywhere in Europe as against the more backward and rural ones.

The student of the eighteenth century thus has at his disposal a wide range of sources, a series of great quarries from which he may extract virtually unlimited amounts of information and even an occasional idea. Of these sources the most important is the great mass of official papers, of reports and correspondence of all kinds, which was produced in every European State of any significance during this period. For the historian of administration, of military affairs, of diplomacy, of colonial expansion and even of many aspects of economic life, there is no substitute for material of this type. It can and should, however, be supplemented by private papers of all kinds, by memoirs and diaries, by pamphlets and newspapers. For the historian of ideas, of culture, of society, the range of relevant material is even wider. He may acquire valuable insights not merely from all these sources but from the imaginative literature of the age, from almanacs and chapbooks, from accounts of travels, from ballads and folklore, from the whole material legacy of the age in its art and architecture, and for that matter in its furniture, clothing and cookery.

[1] Bibliographical information about material of this kind can be found in C. Nisard, *Histoire des livres populaires, ou de la litterature de colportage* (Paris, 1854), and in J. Grand-Carteret, *Les Almanachs françaises* (Paris, 1896).

III

The Structure of Society

Over most of Europe during the eighteenth century society, though slowly changing, was still in essentials what it had been for generations. There are at least three obvious illustrations of this fact.

The first is the overwhelming importance of the family rather than the individual at every level of society and the fact that the family continued, at least until well into the second half of the century and even in the more advanced parts of Western Europe, to be thought of in essentially traditional terms. It was seen, in other words, through the eyes of medieval realism rather than through those of nineteenth-century sentiment. It remained, therefore, a patriarchal institution in which women and children had a definitely inferior status. It was also an institution based on continuity, on the perpetuation of the family name and the ownership of family property, rather than on the rights or sensibilities of individuals. In the upper ranks of society in particular the idea of the family as a 'house', a collectivity with imperative demands of its own rather than an association of freely interacting individuals, was still enormously powerful. The continuing widespread indifference to young children, at least until late in the century, was inevitable in the demographic conditions of the period. When so high a proportion died in the first years, even the first weeks or months, of life, it was impossible and undesirable to make a heavy emotional investment in each one as it was born. It was necessary to have many children in order to keep a few; the harshness of this demographic imperative was hostile to any growth of modern 'child-centred' attitudes. There is a good deal of evidence, in fact, to suggest that the greater value which began to be attached to children in many parts of Europe in the later decades of the

BIBLIOGRAPHY. It is difficult to find satisfactory studies of European society as a whole. However D. Gerhard, 'Regionalism and corporate order as a basic theme of European history', *Studies in Diplomatic History: essays in memory of David Bayne Horn*, ed. Ragnhild Hatton and M. S. Anderson (London, 1970) century was the result largely of a slow improvement in health and a corresponding tendency for infant mortality to fall.[1] Even among adults the continual closeness of death, far more often than today sudden and unpredictable, the result of some epidemic against which there was no defence, made it less emotionally important than it is today. Since the family, not the individual, was the fundamental building-block of society, it must, when weakened by the death of a father or mother, have its strength restored as soon as possible by remarriage. This explains the remarkable speed with which men in particular at all social levels often remarried after the loss of a wife.

[1] This is strongly suggested on a local scale by F. Lebrun, *Les Hommes et la mort en Anjou aux 17ᵉ et 18ᵉ siècles: essai de démographie et de psychologie historiques* (Paris–The Hague, 1971), p. 425.

deserves mention as a remarkable effort at a comparative study, though it is not easy reading and does not confine itself to the eighteenth century. J. O. Lindsay, 'The social classes and the foundations of the State', *New Cambridge Modern History*, vol. VII, chap. iii is less searching. *The European Nobility in the Eighteenth Century*, a collection of essays edited by A. Goodwin (London, 1953) is almost unique as an effort to study a social class against different national backgrounds. Much has been written about eighteenth-century society in France. P. Sagnac, *La Formation de la société française moderne* (2 vols., Paris, 1945–46) is a standard work which has now been to a considerable extent superseded by A. Soboul, *La Civilisation et la Révolution française*: vol. I, *La Crise de l'Ancien Régime* (Paris, 1970), and above all by the remarkable book of P. Goubert, *L'Ancien Régime*: vol I, *La Société* (Paris, 1969). F. Olivier-Martin, *L'Organisation corporative de la France d'ancien régime* (Paris, 1938) studies, from a largely legal point of view, the corporate bodies which retained such significance in the French life of this period; while C. A. B. Behrens, *The Ancien Régime* (London, 1967), is a stimulating introduction to the subject. The last fifteen years have also seen the production of a number of extremely important studies of different regions and provinces of France. Parts of P. Goubert, *Beauvais et le Beauvaisis de 1600 à 1730* (Paris, 1960) and E. Le Roy Ladurie, *Les Paysans de Languedoc* (2 vols., Paris, 1966) are relevant to the subject of this chapter; while A. Poitrineau, *La Vie rurale en Basse-Auvergne au XVIIIᵉ siècle (1726–1789)* (2 vols., Paris, 1965) and M. Agulhon, *La Vie sociale en Provence intérieure au lendemain de la Révolution* (Paris, 1970) both contain a great deal of interesting information. J. Meyer, *La Noblesse bretonne au XVIIIᵉ siècle* (2 vols., Paris, 1966) is a work of great learning, and on a smaller scale R. Forster, *The Nobility of Toulouse in the Eighteenth Century* (Baltimore, 1960) is a book of importance. There are several important recent studies of French towns: F. L. Ford, *Strasbourg in Transition, 1648–1789* (Cambridge, Mass., 1958); Olwen H. Hufton, *Bayeux in the later Eighteenth Century: a social study* (Oxford, 1967); and F.-G. Pariset (ed.) *Bordeaux au XVIIIᵉ siècle* (Bordeaux, 1968). For other

These traditional attitudes were, at least in the second half of the century and in some parts of Western Europe, slowly altering. In France and England particularly, the position of women began to improve. Hitherto they had been significant in two ways above all—through their physical indispensability as mothers, and through their theological status as occasions of sin. Now as never before they began to be regarded as true persons, individuals with feelings, abilities and rights of their own. In France this change of attitude can be seen not merely in the upper strata of society but reflected in the almanacs and other ephemeral literature which was the only reading matter of the masses.[1]

[1] Geneviève Bollême, *Les Almanachs populaires aux XVIIe et XVIIIe siècles: essai d'histoire sociale* (Paris–The Hague, 1969), p. 112.

parts of Europe there is nothing approaching the wealth of detailed studies which now exists for France. However for Great Britain M. Dorothy George, *London Life in the Eighteenth Century* (London, 1925) remains important; while W. E. Minchinton, 'The merchants in England in the eighteenth century', in *The Entrepreneur; Papers presented at the Annual Conference of the Economic History Society . . . April, 1957*, provides a brief account of an important though rather heterogeneous group, and E. Hughes, *North Country Life in the Eighteenth Century* (2 vols., London, 1952–65) is a substantial regional study. There is a very large Russian literature on that country's social structure and problems in this period. Three important works in western languages are: the relevant chapters of J. Blum, *Lord and Peasant in Russia from the Ninth to the Nineteenth Century* (Princeton, 1961); M. Confino, *Domaines et seigneurs en Russie vers la fin du XVIIIe siècle* (Paris, 1963); and M. Raeff, *Origins of the Russian Intelligentsia: the eighteenth-century nobility* (New York, 1966). For Germany and Central Europe W. H. Bruford, *Germany in the Eighteenth Century: the social background of the literary revival* (Cambridge, 1935) and W. E. Wright, *Serf, Seigneur and Sovereign: agrarian reform in eighteenth-century Bohemia* (Minneapolis, 1966) are useful; and the older works of H. Marczali, *Hungary in the Eighteenth Century* (Cambridge, 1910) and R. Kerner, *Bohemia in the Eighteenth Century* (New York, 1932) are still worth consulting. For Spain the most significant work is A. Dominguez Ortiz, *La Sociedad espanola en el siglo XVIII* (Madrid, 1955); there is useful material in the early chapters of J. Sarrailh, *L'Espagne éclairée de la seconde moitié du XVIIIe siècle* (Paris, 1954). M. Berengo, *La Società veneta alla fine del Settecento* (Florence, 1956) is an excellent study; P. Villani, *Feudalità, riforme, capitalismo agrario: panorama di storia sociale italiano tra Sette e Ottocento* (Bari, 1968) presents a synoptic view of writing on the subject so far as Italy is concerned. Family structure and relationships, an aspect of social history which is now attracting increasing attention, are treated in P. Ariès, *Centuries of Childhood: a social history of family life* (New York, 1962), a translation of a French original which is concerned only with France. A recent English study of interest is J. H. Plumb, 'The new world of children in eighteenth-century England', *Past and Present*, No. 67 (May, 1975).

26

The extent of the change, outside a small intellectual minority, should not be exaggerated. As in the past the unmarried woman, even in the most developed parts of Europe, was still hardly regarded as a person in her own right. 'The only category of women which counted', writes a modern author, 'which was truly part of the world, was that of married women.'[1] The marriage of girls (and almost as much that of young men) continued to be subject to strict parental control and often to take place very early in life, while in Catholic countries it was still common for a daughter to be compelled, in the interest of the family as whole, to take the veil. Change of a liberating kind, however slow and partial, there none the less was.

In both the great West European states, moreover, attitudes to children were altering. Much more clearly than ever before, childhood was now seen as a distinct phase in the development of a human being, with its own characteristics and requirements. The child was ceasing to be regarded as merely an immature and incompetent adult, a change symbolized in a highly significant way by the new practice of dressing children (boys more than girls) in relatively informal and comfortable clothes different from those worn by their parents. (The emergence for the first time in history of specialized shops selling only clothes for children is a good illustration of this development.) Attacks on primogeniture, on the grounds that all children had an equal right to their parents' affection and support and that the firstborn son should not be favoured as against his brothers and sisters, mark an important step away from the traditional view of the family and towards the more emotionally charged nineteenth-century one. So does the increasing emphasis, in the later decades of the century, on the duty of women to breastfeed their children after birth and not allow them to be dependent on wet-nurses. In a few parts of Europe at least parents by the end of this period saw more of their children than ever before, played with them more and took greater pains over their education. It is significant that some of the most popular children's toys and games originated, or at least were developed, in the later eighteenth century (the outstanding example is the invention of the jigsaw puzzle in England in the 1760s) and that books designed specially for children were produced in unprecedented numbers.

Yet it would be quite misleading to imagine that this picture of change was typical of Europe in general. To it two enormous qualifications

[1] Comte de Luppé, *Les Jeunes filles à la fin du XVIIIe siècle* (Paris, 1925), p. 11.

must be made. The more liberal and modern attitudes to the family and to women and children which have just been described were confined almost entirely to the upper, or in England the middle, ranks of society. They were also limited in the main to parts of Western Europe. The peasantry, the overwhelming numerical majority of society almost everywhere, remained untouched by such changing ideas. For most Europeans, therefore, tradition and habit continued to hold sway over family life as over all other aspects of existence.

The second great illustration of the conservatism of eighteenth-century society is the way in which it continued, as in the past, to be dominated by division into 'orders'. Social classes in the modern sense of the term, socio-economic groups defined above all by wealth and economic status, were still unimportant over the greater part of Europe. Their place was taken by traditional 'orders', broad groupings essentially hereditary in character, each of which united people of a particular 'quality'. Wealth as a determinant of social status, though certainly growing in importance, was still very far from decisive, even in the more economically advanced parts of Europe. What mattered most was the social esteem and the combination of rights and duties traditionally attributed to the different groups which made up society. Except to some extent in Great Britain and the Netherlands, Europe before the French Revolution was a largely closed society of orders and groups. It is misleading to analyse it in the class terms which become truly applicable only after the political and economic upheavals which began in the 1780s had done their work.[1]

This society was bolstered by tradition and by the fact that over much of Europe it still corresponded reasonably well to the economic realities of a largely pre-industrial age. It was also powerfully supported by traditional Christian teaching. This stressed heavily the need for each individual to fulfil as completely as possible the duties and responsibilities of his station in life, a station which was divinely ordained. For a man to try to change it, or to blur the distinctions between different stations, was more than merely socially disruptive: it was impious. Inequality was decreed by Providence. It was thus divinely ordained and unalterable. Without it society could not exist. For a man to fulfil

---

[1] For an important discussion of this point with regard to France see R. Mousnier, 'Problèmes de methode dans l'étude des structures sociales des XVIe, XVIIe, XVIIIe siècles', in the collection of his essays *La Plume, la faucille et le marteau* (Paris, 1970), pp. 14–19.

the obligations of the social order in which God had placed him was to perform a religious duty. 'True piety', wrote the great Catholic preacher Massillon early in the century, 'is the order of society. Religion disavows the most saintly works which one might substitute for duties; and a man is nothing before God when he is not what he is supposed to be.'[1] The same viewpoint, the same emphasis on tradition and refusal to contemplate change in the structure or workings of society, could also be expressed in more secular terms. 'A reasonable man', wrote a commentator in the middle of the century, 'is always happy if he has what is necessary for him according to his condition [i.e. his place in the social order], that is to say, if he has the protection of the laws, and can live as his father lived before him: so that one of the essential things to the good of a nation is being governed in one constant and uniform manner.'[2]

Ideas of this kind and the whole concept of immutable social orders were being slowly but steadily undermined in the eighteenth century. The Enlightenment[3] was by implication hostile to them (though many of its leading figures, notably Voltaire, were in practice deeply unwilling to disturb a social structure from which they personally benefited). More important, economic change was making traditional attitudes more difficult to sustain and traditional social distinctions a barrier to progress. Nevertheless their vitality was marked. In Central Europe, an economically stagnant area, this was especially so. The most striking illustration of this is the absolute prohibition in the Prussian law code of 1794 of marriage between nobles and middle-class women unless with special governmental permission. Without this the woman concerned was, in the eyes of the law, merely a concubine, and her children illegitimate. This was social conservatism with a vengeance; for even in backward Russia such a marriage was recognized as valid and as conferring noble status on the wife. Nowhere in Europe, again, was a clinging to traditional social distinctions more marked than in the cities of Western Germany. In Frankfurt-on-Main, for example, the burghers were divided into five groups. Members of each, by medieval regulations confirmed as late as 1731, were obliged (the regulation was not in fact enforced) to wear a special dress which made their social status immedi-

[1] Quoted in B. Groethuysen, *The Bourgeois: Catholicism versus capitalism in eighteenth-century France* (London, 1968), p. 229.
[2] Abbé le Blanc, *Letters on the English and French Nations* (London, 1747), vol. II, pp. 404–5.
[3] See below, Chap. XV.

ately visible. In the same way in Strasbourg an ordinance of 1628 had divided the city's population into six classes (two of which were further subdivided) and prescribed dress regulatons for each: though these were also of little practical importance by the eighteenth century the attitude underlying them was still dominant in the city. Sumptuary legislation of this kind existed, at least on paper, in such intellectually advanced areas as France and the city-state of Geneva. Even in England there were proposals for its introduction; and the revival there in 1687 of the High Court of Chivalry, dormant since 1640, was a sign that the most advanced of all the major European states was not immune to prevailing assumptions about how society should be structured. In 1732 the King's Advocate exhibited in this court a complaint against the widow of a merchant for using at his funeral 'ensigns of honour not belonging to his condition'; and a good many similar cases had been heard in previous years.[1] Though the court ceased to function in 1737, after only half a century of intermittent life, its mere existence is a reminder of the continuing strength of social conservatism in eighteenth-century Europe. Nor were regulations regarding dress and outward appearances confined in their operation to the middle and lower ranks of society; the nobility also was often affected by them. Thus in Venice in 1710 nobles who appeared in public without wearing the *vesta patrizia*, a special dress which was a sign of their status, were threatened with fines and imprisonment; while in Russia the Table of Ranks of 1722 specified the clothes and equipage appropriate to each of the many ranks of the Russian *dvoryanstvo*. It should be remembered, moreover, that even without any element of legal compulsion the persistence of a wide variety of traditional and regional costumes meant that different social groups were still distinguished almost everywhere by the clothes they wore with a clarity which would be inconceivable and repugnant today. Such clear-cut external distinctions were slowly beginning to disappear. Trousers (originally worn by seamen) began during this period to be a kind of uniform of artisans and urban workers in Western Europe. Their adoption during the later decades of the century as the dress of upper- and middle-class boys in Britain and France was the first step towards the uniformity of appearance between the different parts of society which we now take for granted. But this development was limited in scope, a mere forerunner of those to come.

The third great proof of the traditional character of society is the

[1] G. D. Squibb, *The High Court of Chivalry* (Oxford, 1959), p. 110.

extent to which it continued to be an amalgam of small, well-defined and closely-knit groups—parishes, manors, guilds, municipalities, at the most provinces—each with an outlook, interests and traditions of its own. To the ordinary man in Western and Central Europe the continent was divided not merely into conflicting States and rival religious confessions, but into these much smaller and more intimate units, which were of far greater practical importance to him so far as his daily life was concerned. 'Civil society', proclaimed the Prussian law code of 1794, 'consists of many small societies and estates, connected to each other by nature and law, or by both together.' This type of traditionalism, this atomization of society, was strengthened by the persistence everywhere of local and regional differences of all kinds so numerous and varied as to defy adequate description. The ordinary man lived his life within narrow geographical boundaries: at any moment in the eighteenth century a high proportion of Europeans could have said with certainty in which churchyard they would be buried. The importance therefore, so far as most people were concerned, of local rivalries, local grievances and local ambitions can scarcely be overstated. Much of the political life of the continent at the grass-roots level was in future generations to be powerfully influenced by a heritage of this kind.[1] Local dialects, often confined to surprisingly small areas and difficult to understand outside them, still retained an importance of which only the developments of the next century in transport and mass education were to rob them. Thus a local official at Riom, in the Auvergne, had to abandon an attempt to interrogate a young beggar from the little town of Courpière, little more than twenty-five kilometres away, because 'the speech of Courpière differs considerably from that of Riom'[2] This intensely local nature of reality in the eighteenth century so far as most people were concerned should never be forgotten.

Even in countries where strong centralized monarchies had emerged, the new political and administrative structure was normally superimposed on the traditional form of society without modifying it in essentials. In France, for instance, the number of guilds was con-

---

[1] It is notable, for example, that traditional rivalries were often far more important than ideologies or economic interests in explaining the way in which different villages and towns took sides in France during the Revolution. Thus in Provence, for reasons of this kind, Le Luc was Jacobin, Le Cannet hostile to the Terror; Grasse was radical and Antibes moderate Agulhon (*see* **Bibliography**, p. 25), pp. 228–9).

[2] Poitrineau (*see* Bibliography, p. 25), vol. I, p. 117.

siderably increased by Colbert's reforms in the 1660s and 1670s: the city of Poitiers had three times as many in the eighteenth century as in the fourteenth. Not until the 1750s did Vincent de Gournay, followed by his pupil Turgot, launch a systematic attack on French corporate bodies of this kind, and then with rather moderate success. Indeed where administrative efficiency and social traditions conflicted the forces of conservatism, so deeply embedded in society, very often proved the stronger. As a rule habit and prejudice set limits to the activities of rulers and bureaucracies rather than vice versa. The political failure and personal tragedy of the last years of the Emperor Joseph II (see pp. 170–1) are only the most striking of many illustrations of this fact.

Very few eighteenth-century monarchs or statesmen, however, seriously contemplated really fundamental social changes. To a man like Frederick II of Prussia society as it stood was something given, the work of time and nature, buttressed by a vast structure of rights and privileges (the two words very often meant the same thing) and rooted in the essentially conservative idea of natural law. Its structure might occasionally be modified somewhat if the interests of the State required it. Frederick's efforts in 1763 to abolish serfdom in Pomerania, its abolition in Lorraine in 1719 and in Savoy half a century later, are obvious examples of such modifications. It could not, however, be invaded or disregarded wholesale. The conception of society as, in a sense, a work of art, something which can and should be moulded and reshaped in the interests of justice, reason, or even efficiency, can of course be found in the works of a good many eighteenth-century thinkers. But this idea, and the hostility to group privileges and traditional and local peculiarities which it implied, were still confined to a small intellectual class. It had never a dominant influence on government during this period anywhere in Europe except in the Habsburg Empire under Joseph II, and perhaps on a smaller scale in the Grand Duchy of Tuscany under his brother Leopold. Provided they could maintain a minimum standard of public order and extract from their subjects enough money and recruits to maintain their courts and armed forces, monarchs as a rule showed little interest in the lack of logic and symmetry in the social organization of their subjects.

This acceptance of traditional rights and local peculiarities is shown clearly in the treatment by all European States of territories which they conquered and annexed. The idea that the newly-acquired areas should be completely assimilated by the conquering State, except as the result of a long and almost unconscious process of absorption, or that their institutions should be forcibly modified in order to speed up this process of assimilation, was almost unknown. Rapid and forcible integration of conquered territory with that of its conqueror at any level, religious, economic or social, was exceptional. Certain political and fiscal obligations had of course to be accepted by the newly acquired area, but they did not as a rule involve any drastic change in its social organization. Thus, for example, the conquest by Russia during the Great Northern War (1700–21) of the Swedish provinces of Livonia and Esthonia had little influence on society in these areas. The traditional ruling class of largely German landowners, the 'Baltic barons', suffered no loss of influence or infringement of their rights by the change. Indeed their position was strengthened, since they had now no fear of the revival of the policy of 'reductions' (resumptions of alienated Crown lands) pursued by the Swedish government in the later seventeenth century. The towns such as Riga and Dorpat, again largely German, continued to be administered very much as before except that they were now garrisoned by Russian instead of Swedish troops. The peasantry continued to be one of the most miserable and depressed in Europe. Hardly anything had changed.

So much did governments respect existing rights, so little did they value social change or administrative uniformity for their own sake, that a conquered territory was often allowed to retain privileges and institutions which clearly reduced its value to the conqueror and made more difficult its eventual assimilation by him. One of the most striking examples of this is the treatment of Strasbourg after its annexation by Louis XIV in 1681. The city had to accept a French garrison and a number of French officials and to transfer the cathedral from Lutheran to Catholic control. On the other hand down to 1789 its citizens did no militia service, could be sued in the first instance only in the municipal courts, and paid taxes only to the municipal authorities, who then negotiated with the royal treasury on the payments the city should make to it. Above all Strasbourg retained unaltered its very complex traditional constitution. It had its own system of censorship and was granted a relatively high degree of religious toleration for its Lutheran inhabitants.[1]

Parallels to these privileges existed in many of the States of Europe. The Basque provinces of Spain, to give only one instance, collected and spent public money on their own account, paying to the Spanish Crown

[1] Ford (see Bibliography, p. 25), passim, especially pp. 98–9.

only specified sums which they had agreed to provide. Concessions of this kind were sometimes a result of the weakness of the government concerned. It might well be convenient for it to delegate responsibilities in this way (see p. 103). Very often, however, they were also the product of a profound unwillingness to interfere with established institutions or practices unless it were essential to do so.

Such a position was obviously very hard to reconcile with the creation of modern centralized States. The unity of nearly all the countries of Europe was weakened by the survival of a vast structure of local and traditional rights and institutions; and these were now so deeply ingrained in the fabric of European life that only a cataclysm as great as the French Revolution could begin the work of dislodging them. Even the Revolution and the series of liberalizing movements which followed it—for the abolition of slavery and the slave trade, for the removal of the age-long disabilities imposed on Jews, for freedom of trade—did not completely defeat the conservative and traditionalist forces embodied in the idea of the sanctity of ancient institutions and inherited rights.

The success with which European society resisted the forces of change meant that it remained throughout this period extremely varied and heterogeneous. This lack of symmetry and regularity can be found at every social level. It is most marked in the landowning class and the peasantry, rather less so in the case of the towns. The extent, importance and ubiquity of these local variations and peculiarities in social structure can scarcely be exaggerated. The feelings of local patriotism and local selfconsciousness which they helped to breed often meant that areas politically united by allegiance to a single ruler none the less regarded each other with indifference or even hostility. Thus a Basque and a Castilian, a Catalan and an Andalusian, a Breton and a Gascon, might feel themselves to be fellow-subjects; fellow-citizens they could not be. In a State such as Prussia, which was an artificial creation and whose provinces were not united by a common history or bound together by natural frontiers, this position was still more acute. Until at least the middle of the century most of the subjects of the kings of Prussia probably drew no real distinction between the Prussian provinces other than their own and the possessions of foreign rulers. This parochialism underlies and vitiates the blanket terms—French, Prussian, Spanish, peasantry, bourgeoisie, nobility—which the historian must use for convenience and for want of anything better.

Nevertheless, eighteenth-century social structure, like the eighteenth-century family, was not completely dominated by conservatism and tradition or completely immune to the forces of change. To the description of it as static and traditional important qualifications must be made. In the first place the old groupings of the parish, the guild or the manor had decreasing meaning or relevance in the great cities which now occupied an increasingly large part of the social landscape. Traditional ideals and responsibilities were hard to maintain in such an environment. Increasingly though slowly, they were being drained of reality by the growth of large-scale industry, which brought with it social contrasts and cleavages of a new and often unmanageable type. It was possible for the old structure of society to retain much of its vitality in Frankfurt, which in the early decades of the century had a population of about 32,000, and where economic life centred around trade and banking rather than industry. It was even possible for it to do so, to a lesser extent, in Strasbourg, which had by 1789 a population of about 50,000 and which was also not an important industrial centre. But in London, Paris and Vienna, or even in Bristol, Lyons or Bordeaux, it could not hold out indefinitely against the forces of size and economic change and the new impersonality in social relations which they brought with them. In a truly new city such as Liverpool, which was not even a parish in its own right till 1699, a society of the traditional type never really existed.

Secondly, the conservative backward-looking social structure which still dominated Western and Central Europe in the first half of the eighteenth century was becoming noticeably weaker in its later decades. On the intellectual level it was increasingly undermined by the rationalizing influence of the Enlightenment, by its contempt for survivals of the Middle Ages and its generalizing and deductive tendencies. By 1791 intellectuals almost everywhere were prepared to give an enthusiastic welcome to the Declaration of the Rights of Man, that supreme rejection of the idea of society as a mere network of communities, interests and traditions. As the century progressed the privileges of guilds, towns, provincial assemblies, manorial courts and a host of other survivals from the past seemed increasingly opposed to the interests of the community as a whole. The assaults of the Physiocrats (see p. 95) on what seemed to them obstructive and irrational relics of feudalism, which culminated in Turgot's unsuccessful attack on guild privileges in France in 1776, were merely the most obvious example of this attitude.

Finally, this traditional type of social structure never really existed in Russia, whose rise to the status of a great power is the most important political fact in the history of this period. The reasons why medieval

Russia failed to develop a society based on groups, corporations and orders, as Western and most of Central Europe did, are far from clear. Whether the failure was caused by the country's lack of natural boundaries, great area and relatively scanty population (since it is hard to imagine a social organization of this type unless population has reached a certain minimum density); whether it was simply a result of the crushing by its rulers of any social institution which might act as a focus of opposition; or whether it was caused by some other factor or combination of factors, is difficult to say. The fact is, however, that in the eighteenth century the power of the central government in Russia was limited mainly by the sheer physical difficulty of enforcing its commands over such a vast area. Except in a few regions such as the Baltic provinces there were hardly any institutions intermediate between the individual and the State with rights which the latter had to respect.

In Western Europe the towns clung tenaciously to their privileges. In Russia by contrast no city in the seventeenth or eighteenth centuries was able to act as an effective obstacle to the exercise of monarchical power, or to exercise rights comparable to those of France, Spain or West Germany. Indeed even if they had possessed the pride and self-confidence of many Western European towns it is doubtful whether those of Russia could have done much to modify the autocratic character of the State: as late as 1785 there were only five in the whole empire with populations of over 30,000.

Moreover the only approach to a central representative institution which Russia had hitherto possessed, the *Zemskii Sobor* (Assembly of the Land), had ceased to function by the middle of the seventeenth century. Although the country was unified in much the same manner as France, by the accretion of provinces round the central nucleus of the Grand Duchy of Muscovy, it never possessed local representative bodies comparable to the French provincial estates or the *cortes* of the Spanish kingdoms. Moreover, the privileged landowning class which took shape in Russia in the early eighteenth century, the *dvoryanstvo*, never acquired the self-consciousness and corporate pride which were characteristic of most of the nobilities of Western and Central Europe. The clearest indication of this is the fact that, unlike their counterparts in nearly all Western countries, Russian landowners made no attempt to assert the principle of the indivisibility of their estates. The *mayorazgo* in Spain, the entail or 'strict settlement' in England, the *Fideikommis* in the Habsburg hereditary provinces, were all means by which the lands of a nobleman could be preserved intact after his death and thus the standing of his family maintained. When, however, Peter I attempted in 1714 to prevent by legislation the customary division of landed estates in Russia among all the sons of the owner the innovation was furiously opposed. In 1731 it had to be abandoned. Moreover, partly because the *dvoryanstvo* had not originated as an essentially military caste, the West European idea of 'honour' was quite foreign to it. Until the promulgation by Catherine II of her Charter to the Nobility in 1785 its members continued to be subject to the corporal punishment which was so severe and so widespread throughout the country. The Charter has been interpreted as an attempt by the Empress to create what Russia had failed to produce spontaneous-ly, a *noblesse* of the Western type. Like Peter I, she was trying, in an effort to westernize the country, to establish institutions which, if they took root, might tend in the long run to limit the autocratic power of the ruler. In Russia, in other words, social groupings were in general not native growths fortified by the prestige of generations of un-interrupted existence, as in the West, but artificial creations imposed from above with shallow roots in the national life. It is significant that there, apart from one or two really old families descended from in-dependent or appanage princes of the Middle Ages, such as the Golitsyns or the Odoevskiis, very few Russian noblemen took their names from those of their estates or neighbourhood, as was so common in Western Europe. It is not a great exaggeration to say that in Russia society was a creation of the State, its structure a reflection of State needs and State pressures. In Western and much of Central Europe the opposite was the case. This meant that, paradoxical as it may seem, relations between rulers and ruled were in some respects more 'modern' in backward and undeveloped Russia than in the relatively progressive countries of the West.

In almost every eighteenth-century State society was still in the main rural, and the workers on the land (who may be conveniently if not altogether accurately referred to as 'peasants') were the largest social group. The peasant's economic and social status, his standard of living and the degree of personal freedom he enjoyed, varied enormously be-tween different areas. They depended on whether he was a free man or a serf, on the way in which he held his land, on whether that land was adequate to maintain him and his family, and on a host of other factors. From the social (though not necessarily the economic) point of view the critical distinction was that between the peasant who was personally free and his fellow who was a serf. This was largely a distinction between the western and eastern halves of the continent. In the British Isles, the Iberian peninsula and Italy, legal serfdom no longer existed. (Though how far a labourer in Connaught or Calabria was a free man in any real sense of the term is quite another matter.) In France it was a serious factor only in a few eastern areas (in 1750 there were in all about 950,000 serfs in the country). In Germany the position varied from that in the south-west, where serfdom was comparatively rare and what existed was of a mild type, through that in Bavaria and Saxony, to that in Pomerania and East Prussia. In the latter great estates were dominant, the powers of the lords very extensive, and serfdom of an often highly oppressive kind the lot of the majority of the population. In Poland political chaos and the complete domination of the government by the privileged landowning class, the *szlachta*, made the status of the peasant almost comparable to that of a Negro slave in the West Indies. In Russia the unfree status which the strains of the seventeenth century and the policies of Peter I had riveted on a great part of the agrarian population was extended still more widely by Catherine II.

Very broadly speaking then, the contrast between a peasantry of serfs and one composed of men at least nominally free was a contrast between Eastern and Western Europe. This East West contrast cannot be applied too mechanically: the temptation to make easy—and to Western feelings flattering—comparisons of this kind should be resisted. In Denmark, for example, an edict of 1702 which attempted to abolish serfdom in Seeland, Laaland and the neighbouring islands remained a dead letter. There the position of the peasantry in fact deteriorated in the eighteenth century, largely because of extensive sales of Crown lands to speculators in 1765–76. By contrast, over a great area of North Russia with its poor soil and scanty population peasant labour services to a lord were unknown. Holstein, which can hardly be regarded as part of Eastern Europe, had one of the most oppressive agrarian régimes to be found anywhere on the continent; while the subjection of the peasantry which was so notable a feature of society in Livonia was the result of German and Catholic conquest in the Middle Ages.

Serfdom in eastern and northern Germany and in Russia differed essentially from that in France and western Germany. In the latter it was a medieval institution surviving with increasing difficulty in a changing social and economic climate, of little apparent value to the State and more and more the target for the criticisms of reformers.

This period saw its legal abolition in Lorraine, Savoy and Baden. East of the Elbe, on the other hand, it was a relatively new institution which had developed rapidly in the seventeenth century. In Brandenburg and Saxony its spread was accelerated by the devastation of the Thirty Years War, and above all by the critical shortage of labour which the war had produced. This, coupled with a growing demand for grain both for export and for distilling, led the landowners of these areas to extend and intensify their control over the peasant population. As well as being obliged to provide labour services, the peasant thus lost in many parts of eastern Germany the right to choose his employment, to work outside the lord's estate without the latter's consent, or even to marry without the payment to him of a small tax. His subjection was facilitated by a growing tendency towards the union in the hands of the land-owning class of landownership (*Grundherrschaft*) and rights of juris-diction (*Gerichtsherrschaft*). This meant that in the eighteenth century the landlord was usually a judicial and administrative official, and often an army officer as well. Against this concentration of authority, and still more against the power given the landowner by the dependence on him of the Prussian administration and army for their efficient functioning, the peasant was almost helpless. In both Prussia and Saxony, moreover, there had emerged after the Thirty Years War the system of *Gesinde-dienst* or *Gesindezwangsdienst* by which young peasants had to serve their lord, normally on his estate, for prescribed periods at fixed (and of course usually low) wages. A similar system prevailed in parts of the Habsburg Empire, where peasant boys who had reached the age of fourteen were regularly mustered for service in the lord's house or on his domain. Those required for such purposes normally served for three years, but might have to do so for as long as seven. The working of this system of forced labour, which was consolidated in Saxony as late as 1766, was safeguarded by efforts in many States to prevent the spread of industry to the countryside, since there it would inevitably compete with agriculture for the still limited labour force available. In Saxony there were even proposals that all children, on reaching the age of fourteen, be obliged by law to work for four years on the land.

In Russia serfdom had originated in a somewhat different way. There it arose from the efforts of the government, from the second half of the sixteenth century onwards, to pin down a scanty and shifting population in a vast undeveloped country and extract from it the money and services required for State purposes. This process was completed in the reign of Peter I by the introduction of a system of military conscription from

1705 onwards, and above all by the imposition on the Russian peasantry in 1719 of the poll-tax (literally 'soul tax', *podushnaya podat'*). Peter made the landowner responsible for the collection of this tax and for the supply of recruits from his estates. By so doing he greatly increased the lord's authority over his serfs. The nature of serfdom in Russia was thus fundamentally changed. From being primarily an attachment to the soil, as it had been under the legislation of the sixteenth and seventeenth centuries, it became increasingly one to the person of the landlord, and hence approximated to slavery. This was emphasized in 1762, when Peter III gave the lords the power to transfer serfs from one estate to another, thus depriving the serf of his traditional attachment to the land he cultivated. The abolition of slavery as a recognized legal status in 1723 thus indicated a decline in the position of the serf rather than a rise in that of the slave. Russia indeed was the one European State in which the legal position of the serf changed clearly and decisively for the worse in this period. In 1760 landowners were granted the right to exile to Siberia lazy or rebellious serfs: twelve years later there were in eastern Siberia alone over 20,000 peasants who had been sent there by their masters. The attitude to serfdom of Catherine II, after her accession in 1762, was complex and ambiguous (see p. 161) and she was certainly aware of the extent to which it now hampered the social and economic development of Russia. But she was unable, and probably unwilling, to do anything effective to restrict its growth.

The complete absence of any attempt by the rulers of Russia to protect the serf is all the more marked by contrast with the efforts of this kind, however ineffective, which were made by the governments of Prussia and the Habsburg dominions. Thus the Austrian government made a series of attempts in 1680, 1716 and 1738, to set limits to the labour services exacted from the peasants of Silesia, Bohemia and Moravia. These efforts culminated in the great reforms introduced by Joseph II in the early 1780s (see pp. 168-9). In the same way in Prussia an attempt was made in 1723 to limit the control hitherto exercised by the Junkers over the marriage of the peasant girls on their estates; and in 1763, as one of his agrarian reforms of that year, Frederick II attempted without much success to give the peasantry of Upper Silesia greater security of tenure. In no part of Europe except Poland and perhaps Hungary was the peasant quite so completely abandoned to the mercies of his master as in Russia.

Serfdom was also becoming the lot of an increasingly large proportion of the Russian people. In the far north, where the population was scanty and the soil poor, it was never of much importance. In Central Russia, on the other hand, its prevalence steadily increased, while the territorial expansion of the later decades of the century extended it to the steppe and 'black earth' regions of the south. Its establishment in the Ukraine, made final in 1783, was followed at the end of 1796, immediately after the death of Catherine II, by its extension to the Caucasus, the Crimea and the Don region. Nowhere in European Russia was now exempt from its influence. Moreover from the reign of Peter I onwards social groups hitherto free were beginning, under the pressure of taxation and conscription, to sink into serfdom. Increasingly the population of much of the country was tending to divide, apart from churchmen and a small merchant class, into a minority of landlords and a huge mass of 'bonded people' (*krepostnie lyudi*). Thus during this period rural society in Russia, though not exactly un-European, was developing along lines which had been abandoned or were being modified over most of the rest of the continent.

Areas such as the Habsburg provinces, Poland and Russia, where serfdom was onerous and the authority of the central government hard to enforce, were the natural breeding-ground of peasant revolts. All of them suffered during this period from disturbances of this type. In Bohemia there was a serious rising in 1775, and another broke out in Transylvania in 1784. In the Polish Ukraine there was a very savage revolt, provoked by the antagonism between an Orthodox and Uniate peasantry and a mainly Catholic landowning class, in the 1730s. In Russia above all agrarian discontent and disorder were endemic throughout the century, especially in its second half. Seventy-three peasant risings, most of them of purely local importance, are known to have taken place in 1762-69; and the widespread rural disorder which marked the early years of the reign of Catherine II culminated in the revolt led by the Cossack Pugachev which broke out in 1773 and was not completely suppressed till 1775. This was the greatest outburst of social protest anywhere in Europe during this period. In the Baltic provinces there was serious rural unrest in 1778 and 1783; and in another great wave of discontent in 1796-97 in Central Russia 278 separate outbreaks were recorded.

None of these revolts, however, in Russia or elsewhere, had any real programme beyond that of removing some or all of the burdens which weighed so heavily on the peasant. Most of them were little more than inarticulate outbursts of hatred and resentment. Occurring as nearly all of them did in areas where towns were few and small they were deprived of the urban leadership which alone might have brought them some degree of success. In the same way the flight of peasants to foreign States or thinly populated border areas, though it sometimes reached considerable proportions—200,000 cases of this kind were officially recorded in Russia in 1719–27 and there must have been many more which escaped official notice—could not seriously menace the social system from which they fled.

Almost everywhere in Europe village communities played an important and sometimes surprisingly independent role in the life of the countryside. Autonomous or semi-autonomous villages reached their highest pitch of development in the poorer and more remote mountain areas of the Alps, Pyrenees and Appenines. They could be found, however, enjoying varying degrees of self-government, in most European countries. Hooton Pagnell in Yorkshire, one of the few English villages about which detailed information is available, provides an example of such a community still organized, and in its own way efficiently organized, along medieval lines. Twice a year the manorial court, divided into a Court Baron which dealt with freeholders' land and a Court Leet which punished a wide range of petty offences, met at the hall of the local squire. It also elected various manorial officers; and though by the eighteenth century its functions were becoming more purely agricultural than hitherto and its legal and administrative importance was declining, it remained a very real factor in the life of the village.[1] Hooton Pagnell was typical in the autonomy it enjoyed of many similar communities in Western Europe.

In France the majority of villages, at least until late in the century, retained a high degree of self-government—more indeed than most French towns. 'Each community among us', wrote the *Parlement* of Provence to Louis XV in 1774, 'is a family which governs itself, which draws up its own laws and looks after its own interests; its municipal officer is its father.'[2] Paternalism and localism, two basic ideas of the century, are tellingly combined in this claim. Village assemblies in France, meeting periodically on Sundays after Mass, continued to regulate a wide variety of local affairs. They elected their own syndics (except for a short interval in 1702–17, when the government created

[1] A. G. Ruston and D. Witney, *Hooton Pagnell, the agricultural evolution of a Yorkshire village* (London, 1934), *passim.*
[2] C. de Ribbe, *Les Familles et la société en France avant la Révolution* (4th ed.; Tours, 1879), vol. 1, p. 92.

perpetual syndics for each parish in order to be able to sell the office and thus raise funds). They often appointed a variety of minor officials, notably the village schoolmaster. They controlled sales, purchases and rentals of common lands. Sometimes they fixed the conditions of the wine harvest, the prices of basic commodities and even rates of pay for day-labourers. As time went on their control of communal property and funds tended to be increasingly supervised by the provincial estates and by government officials such as the *intendant* and the *sub-délégué*; but the system seems to have worked reasonably well to judge by the fewness of complaints about it in the *cahiers* of 1789. It is noteworthy, moreover, that priests and *seigneurs* had to contribute in proportion to their means to communal taxation, and were often compelled to do so, if they made difficulties, by royal officials. One historian has claimed, with some exaggeration, that 'the equality of taxation which was proclaimed in 1789 had long existed with regard to communal contributions'.[1]

In north-western Germany, again, the village community (*Gemeinde*) was important and largely democratic in its structure. Like its equivalent in France it supervised communal property, safeguarded public order, and maintained the roads and bridges of its own locality. Its position was strengthened by the fact that in this area the rights of jurisdiction enjoyed by the nobility in the Middle Ages had been largely taken over by the governments of the various States.

These village communities should not be idealized, nor their defects lost sight of. They expressed the inveterate localism, the ingrained narrowness of view, the deep-rooted distrust of all change, which dominated the lives of so high a proportion of Europeans in this period. The tenacious and widespread peasant resistance to new crops such as potatoes or maize, or to novelties such as inoculation against smallpox, is a good illustration of this. The same attitudes emerge clearly in the hostility with which villages so often greeted well-meant attempts by reforming officials or governments to help them, or even to acquire more accurate knowledge of agrarian problems. In the Auvergne in 1770, for example, the efforts of the *intendant* to take a census of needy families to make easier the distribution to them of official supplies of food was resisted because of fears that the families concerned were to be forcibly deported to French Guiana. In the same area surveyors making a cartographic survey were stoned by the local peasants as sorcerers

---

[1] A. Babeau, *Le Village sous l'ancien régime* (Paris, 1878), p. 95.

likely to attract hail which would damage the crops.[1] The village community undoubtedly stood, in a limited way, for freedom in an age of despotism but it was a freedom usually marked by ignorance, prejudice and deep and irrational conservatism.

The structure, numbers and influence of the landowning class (the term 'nobility', though its use cannot always be avoided, is too narrow to be really accurate) varied enormously in different parts of Europe. Almost everywhere, except in Britain and the United Provinces, it enjoyed important legal privileges—rights of jurisdiction, immunity from certain forms of particularly severe or degrading punishment or from some types of taxation. In many States legal barriers were opposed to the acquisition by commoners of 'noble land'. In the eastern and central parts of the continent in particular the legal superiority of the landlords to other social groups was marked. Thus in Poland they retained until 1768 powers of life and death over their serfs, and in Hungary succeeded in 1731 in asserting their right to pay no taxes at all. In many countries the landowning class was tending, as the century progressed, to become more self-conscious, more jealous of its rights and more anxious to prevent commoners achieving privileged status. This is perhaps seen most clearly in Sweden, where the constitution of 1720 severely limited the ruler's right to ennoble commoners.

In most parts of Europe it had originated as a knightly class with important military functions; and military traditions and ambitions still counted for much in the outlook of many of its members in the eighteenth century. Its real military effectiveness, however, had now shrunk to very small proportions. No European army in the eighteenth century could afford to base its organization entirely on a single class or to exclude commoners completely from its commissioned ranks. This created, in many States, an implicit conflict between military efficiency and what many members of the privileged class, especially many of its poorer members, thought of as their right to monopolize commissions (see p. 184). To some extent this conflict could be resolved by the grant of privileged status to able commoners who had reached a certain level of military rank, or whose families had established some hereditary connexion with the army. This was done most notably in Russia by Peter I in the Table of Ranks which he issued in 1722. This divided the bureaucracy, as well as the commissioned ranks of the army

---

[1] Poitrineau (see Bibliography, p. 25), vol. 1, p. 117.

and navy, into fourteen distinct grades. Membership of the highest grades in the case of bureaucrats, and of all in that of army and navy officers, conferred on the holder the hereditary privileged status of a member of the landowning class. In a rather different way something of the same sort was attempted in France. There an edict of 1750 granted nobility to commoners who had reached the rank of general (of whom there were of course very few indeed) and also to all families whose male members for three generations had served in the army in commissioned ranks lower than that of general. In this way some 125 officers were ennobled in 1766–90. Besides this about 150 others were granted nobility in the forty years before 1789, though their families had not provided the required three generations of service. These figures merely show, however, how tiny was the change brought about by such measures in the composition of the French nobility, whose numbers ran into hundred of thousands. Not until after the Revolution was it possible to envisage the taking-over on a large scale of its military functions by other classes.

The landowning class had more than merely military importance in the eighteenth century. It not only provided the bulk of the officers for the armies (and to a lesser extent the navies) of nearly all European States, but played a large, sometimes an indispensable, part in the running of their administrative machines. In Prussia, where the Junkers were being transformed in the later seventeenth and early eighteenth centuries into a class of hereditary State servants, the whole administration increasingly reflected their virtues and vices. A very similar position was to be found in Russia. There Peter I had succeeded, in the face of much opposition, in asserting the principle that every landowner was bound, as a condition of holding his land, to serve the State for an unlimited period in the armed forces or the civil administration. In this way alone could the officers and administrators needed for the creation of powerful armed forces and a centralized bureaucracy be found, and Russia be enabled to play the role of a great power in Europe. The onerous obligations he thus imposed on them were naturally resented by the landlords, and under his weaker successors they succeeded in having them considerably reduced. Thus for example in 1736 the period of compulsory service was fixed at twenty-five years, so that if a child were inscribed for service very young, as was frequently done, he might become free of further obligations by the age of about thirty. In 1762 Peter III completed this process by liberating the *dvoryanstvo* from all legal obligation to serve the State, so that from this date onward it ceased to be a service class in the strict sense of the term. Nevertheless it continued to dominate both the commissioned ranks of the army and the administrative machine, and to retain for many years much of the outlook of a class of hereditary State servants. It was only with the issue by Catherine II in 1785 of her Charter to the Nobility that it began to be something approximating to a *noblesse* of the normal West European type. This document, the last and greatest grant of privileges by any ruler of Russia to the landowning class, created permanent and official assemblies of the nobility at provincial and district level, which were to have the right to make submissions to the provincial governors and in certain circumstances even to the ruler. This was a deliberate effort to endow the Russian ruling class with greater self-consciousness and self-confidence, to foster greater initiative and independence in it and make it a more creative element in Russian society. Henceforth members of the *dvoryanstvo* were to be exempt from corporal punishment and were to be deprived of their rank, property or lives only after trial by their peers. This was a long step away from the harsh and demanding attitude of Peter I and a real if limited effort to break with the tradition of autocracy and arbitrary power which was now so deeply ingrained in Russia. The Russian nobility by the end of Catherine's reign was still in many ways a distinctively Russian phenomenon, but in terms of its status and rights it was now more 'westernized' than ever before.

In France the position was very different. There, as the old military and landed nobility, the *noblesse de l'épée*, showed itself less and less able to administer a State dominated by complex social and financial problems, it was supplemented and to some extent replaced by a new administrative nobility, the *noblesse de la robe*. This class, of comparatively recent origin and led by the holders of a number of great legal offices, was now growing in wealth and influence. It provided many of the Secretaries of State who controlled during this period the workings of most of the different departments of the central administration—Chauvelin, Maurepas, Machault, the d'Argenson brothers. Equally important, it dominated the *parlements*—great, conservative and largely hereditary legal corporations, twelve in number, which could possess great political importance. On the other hand, since it was composed mainly of bourgeois who had purchased government offices carrying with them the privileges of nobility, or their descendants, the *noblesse de la robe* tended to be looked down on by the older noble families and has sometimes been considered by historians as merely the highest stratum of the French bourgeoisie. Nor had it much access to or influence at the court, or within the charmed circle immediately surrounding the royal family. Its very abilities, indeed, to some extent told against it; for learning or genuine intellectual interests seemed to many Frenchmen the qualities of a commoner, qualities with which a true nobleman could dispense. Nevertheless it was one of the most important elements in French society during this period. The passage of time and the wealth of the great *robe* families did something to lessen the condescension with which it was regarded by the older nobility, so that by the middle of the century it had largely thrown off the stigma of its middle-class origins and could see itself as part of a united *noblesse*. Able, conservative and self-interested, it had become by the years before 1789 perhaps the greatest of all obstacles to the radical overhaul of the governmental system which was now clearly needed.

In Britain also the influence of the aristocracy and squirearchy on the government and administrative system was profound. Throughout the century the House of Lords retained a political influence and popular esteem little if at all inferior to those possessed by the House of Commons. The latter in any case consisted overwhelmingly of landowners: its members were very often related to those of the upper house and owed their seats to the money and influence of some peer. Moreover to the end of this period and long after the Cabinet remained a predominantly aristocratic body. The younger Pitt, when he took office as Prime Minister in 1783, was the only member of his own Cabinet who sat in the Commons; and as late as 1830 that of Lord Grey contained thirteen peers or sons of peers, a baronet, and only one untitled commoner. In English local government also the dominance of the landowning class through the Justices of the Peace (see p. 128) was the central fact of this period.

A control by landlords of the life of their own localities as complete as that in England or Prussia can be seen in many other parts of Europe. In Hungary and Poland this control was absolute, unchallenged and unchallengeable. In the Two Sicilies also the local influence of the nobility, based on their jurisdictional and economic rights over the peasants and their possession of bodyguards of armed retainers, was enormous. In spite of the efforts in the 1730s and 1740s of Charles IV and his ministers to reduce these outmoded and dangerous powers (mainly by making the decisions of feudal courts subject to appeal in royal ones, and by limiting the number of armed followers a noble might possess) it remained very great throughout the century. In

Sweden, again, the nobility enjoyed great political importance. Not until 1809 was government office there made legally accessible to members of all classes.

The use of the words 'nobility' or 'landowning class' must not be taken as implying that a homogeneous social group is being discussed. There were vast differences between the 'nobilities' of different countries. The Polish and Hungarian squires exacting directly or through manorial officials labour services from their peasants had not much resemblance to the aristocrats of England or Sweden, whose lands were for the most part leased to tenant farmers over whom they had relatively little control. The service nobilities of Russia and Prussia had little in common with the increasingly functionless aristocrats of Spain and Italy. There were also important distinctions between the different sections and subdivisions of each national 'nobility'. In England, where the peerage was a small and relatively homogeneous body separated by a clear line of division from non-noble landowners however wealthy, the position was comparatively straightforward. In most other countries, however, the number of people who could lay claim to the privileges of nobility was very large, and the disparities between them in wealth, education and political power might be very great.

Thus in France, where the *noblesse* towards the end of this period numbered in all perhaps some 250,000 people, there were probably as few as 4,000 noble families which had any share, however small, in the life of the court, or any direct access to the monarch. That access was now being more narrowly restricted than ever before. From 1732 onwards the grant of the *honneurs de la Cour* (presentation of female members of a family to the Queen and the permitting of its male members to ride in the King's coach) presupposed that convincing proofs of nobility had been given. From 1759 it required, at least in theory, that the family in question should have been noble since before the year 1400.[1] Between a great noble who could obtain for himself and his protégés the appointments, honours and pensions which only court influence could secure, and the poor provincial squire, the *hobereau*, who might live and work in conditions no better than those enjoyed by many peasants, the gulf was wide indeed. Only in a purely legal sense can they be regarded as belonging to the same social class. The distinction between rich and poor nobles, between metropolitan and provincial, was in practice much more important than that between those of the

[1] F. Bluche, *Les Honneurs de la Cour* (Paris, 1957), vol. I, p. 3.

'robe' and the 'sword'. Even the degree of influence which the French nobility could exercise over the provincial representative bodies, the estates, in the areas where these existed, varied widely in different provinces. In Brittany perhaps as many as 3,000 *gentilshommes* had the right to attend meetings of the estates; and it was normal for several hundred (many of them very poor) to put in an appearance. In Languedoc, by contrast, only twenty-three nobles, nearly all of them much wealthier than the Breton gentry, were members of the estates.

Similarly in Spain, where in the census of 1787 half a million people (about 5 per cent of the total population) claimed to be of noble status, the difference between the poor *hidalgos* who made up the vast majority of this total and the tiny group of great landowners at the apex of the social pyramid, such as the Dukes of Infantado and Medina-Sidonia, was immense. Within these major divisions of the Spanish privileged class, moreover, there were further subdivisions: the grandees, the highest stratum of the nobility numbering little more than a hundred in all, were classified, at least in theory, in three distinct groups. Contrasts of this type were equally sharp in Poland. There the privileged class, the *szlachta*, was before the partitions an enormous group of almost a million people, the vast majority of whom were poor and many of whom owned little or no land. Many of them, to the casual observer, were distinguishable from peasants only by their possession of the right to wear a particular type of dress and by the fact that special seats were reserved for them in church. Between 'barefoot *szlachta*' of this type and the two dozen or so really great magnates who ruled the country (in so far as it was ruled at all before the partitions) there could be no real equality. A Prince Radziwill, owning lands greater in extent than many of the German States, or a member of one of the other great Polish families, the Czartoryskis, the Potockis, the Sapiehas, was a different being from the ignorant and impoverished squires who followed and depended on him. In the same way in Hungary, where legal privileges were also very widely diffused (it was said in 1787 to have three times as many 'noble' families as France though its population was only a quarter as large) the Esterhazys, Palffys, and other great families, wealthy, cultured, and influential at Vienna, moved in a different world from the semi-educated and bitterly conservative petty landlords of the Danube valley. Similar distinctions can be seen in Russia. There as early as the 1690s Prince M. Ya. Cherkasskii, the greatest secular landholder in the country, possessed over 9,000 peasant households, while eleven other landowners each possessed over a thousand. Even eighty years later, by contrast, in spite of the great growth of population and considerable extension of serfdom in the intervening period, three-fifths of all landowners in the Great Russian provinces still owned less than twenty male serfs. Even in a State as small as Venice distinctions of a different kind can be found between impoverished ancient noble families (*Barnabotti*) and *nouveaux riches* whose names had been inscribed in the Golden Book and who had thus acquired nobility. Only in a few areas whose nobilities were limited in numbers and relatively homogeneous in character, such as Sweden and Lombardy, could violent contrasts of this type be avoided.

The social importance of the towns also differed enormously in different parts of Europe. In the West they were not merely more numerous and as a rule larger than in Eastern Europe, but also enjoyed a far higher degree of effective autonomy. In Russia, Prussia and Poland they were for the most part small and, more important, timid. There centuries of dominance by autocratic government or the power of great nobles had robbed them of self-confidence and desire for autonomy. In 1699 Peter I had offered the Russian towns a degree of self-government in return for the payment of higher taxes; the proposal was rejected. In 1785 Catherine II attempted to strengthen their position and make them a more autonomous element in society by a charter (the 'city statute') which gave each of them a common council, meeting weekly, which was elected by all city-dwellers. This was an important constructive step; but it could not compensate for the effects of generations of weakness and subjection. In Western Europe, by contrast, municipal self-government had been for centuries a political and social reality. There municipal privileges in regard to such things as taxation set genuine limits to the powers of central governments. Quite apart from the imperial cities of Germany, which were independent States, or pseudostates, the towns of France, Spain and England enjoyed a significant degree of real independence in the conduct of their own affairs. In France this was symbolized by the fact that until late in the seventeenth century many towns retained fortifications and artillery of their own; Paris indeed still possessed its own cannon in the eighteenth century and had them recast in 1732. Except in a few areas—the Dutch Republic, England, some parts of Italy—townsfolk made up only a small fraction of the total population. Even at the end of the old regime only about a sixth of all Frenchmen lived in towns of over 2,000 people, while Paris itself accounted for only about two per cent of the total. Nevertheless this urban minority often had an importance out of all proportion to its mere numerical size; and there was a widespread consciousness of the differences between town and countryside and often considerable mutual dislike and mistrust. The peasant frequently resented what he saw as exploitation by the town, a feeling intensified by the considerable purchases of land by wealthy townspeople which can be seen in some parts of Europe in the later eighteenth century. The townsman for his part often felt a scarcely-suppressed fear and contempt for the semi-civilized peasant majority who surrounded him. In 1789, for example, some French towns showed themselves uneasy lest the peasantry and their grievances should be too effectively represented in the States-General when it met. Probably the widespread introduction in the second half of the century, at least in Western Europe and in the larger towns, of such urban amenities as street lighting, the numbering of houses in each street, and more or less modern fire-fighting organizations, accentuated the distinctions between town and country and hence the possibility of bad feeling between them.

In a few cities of Western Europe a small social segment of merchants, bankers or financiers was now becoming very important. In the United Provinces the patriciate of Amsterdam had long been a dominant group, enjoying great political influence as well as great wealth. In England a somewhat similar development was visible before the end of the seventeenth century; during the two generations or more which followed great London bankers, financiers or merchants, such as Samson Gideon or Sir Joshua Vanneck, had on occasion very real influence on the development of government policy. In the realm of public finance, in particular, ministers normally depended heavily on the support, and were compelled to pay attention to the advice, of a small number of great capitalists. Many of these were of Jewish, Dutch or Huguenot extraction. Moreover there was a strong tendency for this group, by marriage or by purchase of land, to become closely connected with and eventually assimilated to, the greater English landowners. (Though to the end of this period there was a strong prejudice against the grant of titles, and of the position of Justice of the Peace, to men whose money had been made in trade, industry or financial dealings, and whose property was not mainly in land.) The emergence of a similar class, even smaller in numbers but in some ways equally important, can be seen almost simultaneously in France. There the last years of the seventeenth century and beginning of the eighteenth saw the rise to positions of real though often unacknowledged power of such people as the banker Samuel Bernard, the merchant and financier Antoine Crozat (who in 1712 secured a monopoly of trade with Louisiana) or the merchant Mesnager of Rouen (who more than once represented his country in commercial negotiations with other States). Above all the Pâris family, the foundations of whose fortune were laid by a series of army contracts in the 1690s, was able to assume in the first half of the eighteenth century a position of great and sometimes decisive influence over French financial policy.

The growth of an *haute bourgeoisie* was encouraged in France (and elsewhere in Europe) by the system of tax-farming, which undoubtedly brought vast profits to a small number of wealthy families and individuals. However, the French farmers-general constituted a relatively open and fluid group. On the one hand it was constantly being strengthened by new recruits from non-noble families with interests in trade or finance; but on the other the sons of its members tended to use their parents' wealth as a means of entering the *noblesse de la robe* or of obtaining commissions in the army. There were few dynasties of tax farmers. More important in the creation of a wealthy merchant class was the immense expansion of French trade with the West Indies and the Levant which followed the peace of 1763 with Britain. This founded the fortunes of an increasing number of great trading families such as the Gradis and Bonaffé of Bordeaux and the Roux of Marseilles. Throughout Western Europe, in Britain, France or the United Provinces, a very wealthy urban class was almost entirely the product of trade, above all overseas trade, and of banking or financial dealings (tax-farming or trading in government securities). Industry, by comparison, was only beginning by the 1770s or 1780s to produce comparable fortunes; and the social status of the successful industrialist was lower than that of the successful merchant or financier. Even in England an Arkwright, a Boulton or a Wilkinson lacked the standing of a great banker or merchant. In France the century saw the emergence of only two industrial dynasties of more than local importance; the De Wendels with their great interests in the iron industry, and the Van Robais textile magnates.

On a smaller scale the growth of a commercial and financial upper middle class similar to that of Britain and France can be seen in a few other areas of Europe—Tuscany, Genoa, some West German cities. Elsewhere it was almost entirely lacking. Overwhelmingly agrarian countries with few towns, small merchant marines and little capital, such as Prussia, the Habsburg territories, Poland and Russia, could produce little of this kind. Thus although in the middle of the century the number of towns in Russia was reckoned, for tax purposes, at just over two hundred, in 1762 only sixteen of these had municipal budgets of over 1,000 roubles per annum (about £150 at the then prevailing rate of exchange). The position was similar in Poland, where in 1772 there were only five towns with populations of over 20,000, and also in Hungary. In both the influence of the urban population was further reduced by the fact that it was largely composed of aliens— Jews or Germans in Poland, Greeks or Rumanians in Hungary. All over Eastern and much of Central Europe, moreover, the position of the towns was weakened by the fact that landowners, using the raw materials produced by their estates and the forced labour of their serfs, often set up in the countryside industrial establishments which competed with urban factories and workshops.

It would, however, be a great mistake to assume that the urban population anywhere in Europe was composed of, or even normally dominated by, wealthy merchants, bankers or financiers. Everywhere small traders and artisans, and even more small landowners, were numerically and often politically of far greater importance in its makeup. Moreover it should be remembered how much in some areas the middle class (it is difficult to avoid using this somewhat anachronistic term) depended on governments for employment and economic opportunities. This was especially notable in France, where there were enormous numbers of holders of minor government offices and owners of government securities (*rentes*). It was people of this kind who were the most important element in the population of many French towns during the eighteenth century and who helped to ensure that the entrepreneurial spirit, as opposed to the legalistic, office-holding and *rentier* one, was relatively unimportant in French urban life. 'In France', wrote a contemporary, 'we have not a due regard for merchants . . . from whence it comes to pass, that the son prefers the exercise of an office that ruins him, to commerce that enrich'd his father.'[1] The greatest statistician of the century, the Abbé d'Expilly, estimated in 1763 that 60,000 French families lived from *emplois de finance* (minor offices connected with the system of taxation) and 100,000 from judicial offices, royal or seigneurial. By comparison, he calculated, bankers and merchants made up only

[1] Abbé le Blanc, *Letters*, vol. II, p. 122.

10,000 familes. At the outbreak of the revolution about eighty per cent of all privately owned property in France was 'proprietary' wealth in the form of land, buildings, government offices and annuities. Even in such great trading centres as Bordeaux and Rouen small landowners, officials and holders of government securities considerably outnumbered merchants and manufacturers. This meant that investment in industry was still, by the standards of the nineteenth century, far less the twentieth, very small.

Not only was the patrician element of great bankers and merchants confined to a few great cities in Western Europe: it was often unable to dominate even these. Thus in London the smaller merchants, traders and craftsmen, who controlled the Common Council and elected the City's four Members of Parliament, tended as a rule to be hostile to the urban magnates whose close connexions with the government and the aristocracy they distrusted and envied. A still more striking example of this tension between a wealthy oligarchy and an envious or frustrated body of smaller merchants and artisans is to be found in the city-state of Geneva. Its history throughout this period was punctuated by demands that power be more widely shared among the citizens, demands which culminated in 1768 and 1782 in serious outbreaks of violence. Essentially the same struggle, though in a less violent form, can be seen also in several of the cities of West Germany. In Cologne during the 1780s, for example, control of the city was contested between the *Magistrat* (the ruling oligarchy) and the *Bürgerschaft* (a much wider body of all full citizens, made up of house owners, master-craftsmen and a few professional men). Discontented urban groups of this kind often came increasingly, as the century progressed, to feel themselves excluded and discriminated against by the essentially aristocratic political systems of their countries. Resentments of this kind are most clearly visible in Britain and the United Provinces; but they can also be seen to a lesser extent in France and West Germany. In London this feeling made a large part of the population hostile to landlords, aristocrats and all social institutions which recalled the 'feudal' past. As a result the city tended to be sympathetic to the reforms advocated in the 1770s and 1780s by many radical writers and politicians, such as more frequent parliamentary elections and a reduction of the standing army.

The position in the great cities of France was different but not totally dissimilar. France was in the later eighteenth century the one European country in which a fairly well-to-do and fairly well-educated urban bourgeoisie was both large enough to be a significant element in society and at the same time completely excluded from political power. In the United Provinces the government had long ceased to be dominated by the nobility, though the great merchant families of Amsterdam and a few other cities formed a kind of aristocracy which aroused a good deal of envy and bad feeling in those a little further down the social scale. In Britain a bourgeois, if he were wealthy enough, would eventually be accepted, or at least secure the acceptance of his children, on equal terms by the landed gentry. The great cities and the interests which dominated them could always make their voices heard in the House of Commons. In France, by contrast, society and the political structure were still overwhelmingly aristocratic in tone, and the safety-valves for bourgeois envy and resentment which existed in Britain (and were by no means completely effective there) were much less adequate. It was not unheard-of for a French merchant, banker or even industrialist to be ennobled, even without his buying a government office which conferred nobility on the holder. In 1767 the government promised that henceforth rights almost equivalent to those of nobility should be granted each year to two important merchants, provided that their fathers and grandfathers had also been merchants. This, however, was a very half-hearted attack on a difficult problem. The obstacles in the way of the urban middle class, however well-to-do, attaining nobility are illustrated by the fact that in Brittany, a province which possessed such substantial ports as Brest and l'Orient, only twenty-two businessmen were ennobled in the three generations before 1789.

Too much, however, can be made of the gulf which separated noble and bourgeois in France in the last decades of the old regime. Whether, as used to be widely believed, the eighteenth century really saw a growth of self-consciousness and exclusiveness on the part of the French nobility as a whole now seems at least questionable. The claims which the *parlements* were putting forward more and more vociferously (see pp. 146–7) were after all, in form and even to some extent in substance, those of the nation and not merely of the nobility. Neither the *intendant* and other great officials nor the upper ranks of the Church seem to have been, as a group, more aristocratic in the later eighteenth century than they had been a hundred years earlier. The decree of 1781 which attempted to prevent the granting of army commissions to non-nobles allowed many exceptions and had in any case been foreshadowed by earlier legislation of this kind in 1718 and 1727. The *parlements*, undoubtedly, were becoming more socially exclusive and increasingly refusing to accept non-nobles as members (the *Parlement* of Dauphiné, for example, declared itself a closed group in 1762). Nevertheless in the later eighteenth century, as nobles, or at least the wealthier ones, increasingly invested in new economic enterprises, notably mining, and as the wealthy non-noble townsman increasingly bought estates and feudal rights, the distinction between the nobility and the upper bourgeoisie tended to lose some of its clarity. As a traditional society composed of 'orders' was slowly eroded by the coming of one in which status depended more and more on money it became easier to bridge social chasms which had hitherto seemed very difficult to cross. Nevertheless when all this has been said it is impossible to deny that, as the progress of the Revolution was to show very clearly, there was discontent and readiness for change at least among some sections of the French urban society in the later eighteenth century. The fact that educational standards were rising fairly rapidly was one element in this. Another was the steadily growing importance of new professional groups, small in numbers but self-conscious, well-educated and accessible to new ideas and political ambitions. These groups, such as doctors and journalists, were more ready to envisage drastic social and political changes than older and much better established ones such as lawyers.

The fact that in many West European States during this period the towns, even if not independent as the German imperial cities and the Italian city-states were, enjoyed a considerable degree of autonomy, meant that their internal organization was of real political and economic importance. That organization varied enormously, but was almost always complex, often extremely so. Municipal rights and privileges varied moreover, as might be expected, in a highly complicated and irrational way. The extraordinary variety of franchises by which members representing boroughs were elected to the House of Commons in Britain, or the distinction in Scotland between 'royal burghs', founded by charter from the King, and mere 'burghs of barony', are obvious examples of these variations. So is the legal distinction which was often drawn in France between the original city, enclosed by its medieval boundaries, and the *faubourgs* which had grown up around it. Certain characteristics, however, were common to most European towns during this period. In the majority of them an important role in government was played by the guilds. In Strasbourg, for example, the twenty guilds each elected fifteen members of the Council of Three Hundred and, of more practical importance, one member of the Senate. In most French towns indeed the ruling body was composed mainly or entirely of representatives of the craft and merchant guilds. Though there were some important German cities (Frankfurt for instance) in whose government guild influence was slight, here too it was usually powerful and often dominant. In practice, however, every West European town during this period, whatever its constitution, tended to be ruled by an oligarchy of its wealthier citizens, an oligarchy which was usually largely hereditary. Thus in Berne, where the hereditary element was unusually strong, there were only about 250 families which were classified as capable of ruling (*regimentsfähig*): of these about seventy really controlled the city. In many other towns the same names can be seen recurring for generation after generation in the membership of the ruling bodies—the Dietrichs and Wenckers in Strasbourg for example. In Nuremberg a list of families whose members were alone eligible to hold all the leading municipal offices had been drawn up and given legal effect as early as 1521; and in Frankfurt a patriciate of this kind successfully defended its position in a long series of constitutional struggles in 1705–32. Nor should it be assumed that rule of this kind was necessarily hostile to many forms of progress. The greatest achievement of urban renewal and town planning during the second half of the century, the building of the New Town in Edinburgh, was the work of a city council which was an oligarchy of the narrowest kind.

Eighteenth-century cities were able to retain their inherited social and administrative structure because few of them, at least until late in the century, were predominantly industrial. Nowhere in Europe even at the end of this period, except in a few restricted areas such as the textile-producing parts of Lancashire or the metal-working region around Liège and Dinant, could there be found large towns whose populations included considerable numbers of industrial workers of a modern type. A proletariat in the Marxist sense was coming into existence in many of the cities of Europe, one which often suffered great hardship and oppression. A family of this kind, living normally at little more than subsistence level and unable to make savings or accumulate reserves of any sort, was intensely vulnerable to sickness and unemployment. So, for that matter, were very many self-employed artisans.[1] This was a proletariat still organized in terms of workshops far more than of factories, and one still lacking any sense of class unity or any feeling that its position might be bettered by conscious action on its own part. It was also a social group largely ignored by eighteenth-century writers on

[1] For a good short discussion of working-class wages and standards of life in France see Soboul (*see* Bibliography, p. 25), pp. 426–31.

social and economic problems, who were usually far more interested in artisans and craftsmen of the traditional type than in industrial wage-earners. The fact that many of such large-scale industrial enterprises as existed—the Ural ironworks in Russia are a leading example—were geographically remote from any large town also helped urban life to retain its predominantly mercantile and handicraft character almost everywhere to the end of this period.

The still largely traditional and static society described in this chapter was doomed to rapid decay. The network of communities, orders, privileges, peculiarities and exemptions, of which it was composed, could not hope to withstand indefinitely the forces of change which were growing stronger throughout this period. From the middle of the century at latest it was being steadily though very slowly eroded by the demands of governments for larger revenues and greater administrative efficiency. It was also being undermined, more rapidly and perhaps more fundamentally, by the development of Europe's economic life. For a society based on customs and traditions which were everywhere different was slowly being substituted one based on ideas and economic pressures which were everywhere the same. Yet it would be a great mistake to describe eighteenth-century society entirely or even mainly in terms of 'progressive' forces. Like so many other aspects of the continent's life during this period, it must be studied with an eye to the past as much as to the future.

IV

Economic Life

The eighteenth century saw a good deal of economic progress in Europe, but progress which was uneven geographically, in speed, and in its effect on different types of activity. It saw a considerable development of banking and public finance in Britain and to a lesser extent in France and the Netherlands. It saw a great expansion of seaborne trade, which was again most marked in the case of Britain. Industry on the other hand developed with relative slowness until the industrial revolution began to affect Britain and to a much less extent France in the very last years of this period; and the methods and productivity of agriculture showed comparatively little change throughout the century except in a few favoured areas of Western Europe. Geographically the rapid progress of Britain and the continued high level of achievement of the Netherlands contrasted with the relative backwardness of much of Germany, Central Europe, Italy and Spain. In some parts of Poland and the

BIBLIOGRAPHY. J. M. Kulischer, *Allgemeine Wirtschaftsgeschichte*, vol. II (Munich-Berlin, 1929) is in some ways the most satisfactory single volume on the economic history of the period, while H. Heaton, *Economic History of Europe* (revised edition, London, 1948) is a well-known and reliable English introduction. W. Sombart, *Der moderne Kapitalismus* (4th ed. Munich, 1921) is a vast assembly of information and references, sometimes stimulating but uncritical and often biased. Three outstanding national economic histories are E. F. Hecksher, *An Economic History of Sweden* (Cambridge, Mass., 1954); T. S. Ashton, *An Economic History of England: the eighteenth century* (London, 1955); and E. Labrousse, P. Leon and others, *Histoire économique et sociale de la France*, vol. II, *Des derniers temps de l'age seigneuriale aux préludes de l'age industriel (1660-1789)* (Paris, 1970). B. Gille, *Histoire économique et sociale de la Russie* (Paris, 1949), is a useful short book; and on a little-studied area T. Stoianovich, 'The conquering Balkan Orthodox merchant', *Journal of Economic History*, vol. XX (1960) is considerably wider in scope than its title suggests. On population questions H. Gille, 'The demographic history of the northern European countries in the eighteenth century', *Population Studies*, vol. III

Ottoman Empire there may have been a fall, mainly because of political upheavals, in the already very low standards of productivity and consumption which prevailed at the beginning of the eighteenth century. In Russia on the other hand Peter I and his successors fostered an impressive though unbalanced development of industry and even of trade. The first decades of this period were a time of economic stagnation over most of the continent, while after the middle of the century the pace of advance perceptibly quickened in many areas.

Underlying and partly explaining this slow and uneven advance was a tendency for population, especially urban population, to increase almost everywhere. This tendency operated with varying effect in different countries; but every European State had a larger population at the end of this period than at its beginning. Thus England and Wales, which had about 5 million inhabitants in the reign of Queen Anne, could boast nearly 9 million by the end of the century. France, where this growth was less marked, had about 18 million at the death of Louis XIV and about 26 million in 1789. In Italy the population increased from perhaps 11 million in 1700 to over 16 million in 1770, while in parts of Spain the growth, though much less studied by historians, may have been as rapid as in England—from 5 or 6 million to 1700 to some 11 million a century later. In European Russia, which had about 18 million inhabitants at the death of Peter I in 1725, there were nearly 27 million by 1780; but gains of territory from Sweden, Turkey and above all Poland account for a good deal of this increase. Europe as a

(1949–50), and H. J. Habbakuk, 'English population in the eighteenth century', *Economic History Review*, vol. VI (1953) are important discussions. J. T. Krause, 'Some implications of recent work in historical demography', *Comparative Studies in Society and History*, vol. I (1958–59) is suggestive, and has full and useful references. There is a lack of good studies of European agriculture: H. See, *Esquisse d'une histoire du régime agraire en Europe aux XVIIIe et XIXe siècles* (Paris, 1921) is probably the best. Much information on the growth of industry is available in the general works on economic history mentioned above, while J. Kulischer, 'La grande industrie aux XVIIe et XVIIIe siècles', in *Annales d'Histoire Economique et Sociale*, vol. II (1931) is a suggestive sketch. R. Portal, *L'Oural au XVIIIe siècle* (Paris, 1951) is an excellent account of the greatest industrial achievement of any European State during this period. Good introductory discussions of the development of European trade (mainly maritime trade) can be found in L. B. Packard, *The Commercial Revolution, 1400–1776* (New York, 1927) and *Histoire du Commerce*, ed. J. Lacour-Gayet (Paris, 1950–55), vol. IV. R. Davis, *A Commercial Revolution: English overseas trade in the seventeenth and eighteenth centuries* (Historical Association Pamphlet; London, 1967) is a useful brief account of its subject. For financial developments in general *The History of the Principal Public Banks*, a collection of essays in whole, which had a population of perhaps 118 million in 1700, had one of about 140 million in 1750 and about 187 million in 1800.

The reasons for this remarkable demographic change are still far from clear. It seems certain that in Western Europe a slow improvement in nutrition, which made absolute starvation less likely than in the past, played a considerable part. Thus in 1709 France saw large-scale famine (as distinct from mere scarcity, however acute) for the last time. After that terrible year very sharp rises in the price of food as the result of bad harvests became less common than they had been in the seventeenth century: the doubling or more of the price of bread within a few months, not abnormal in previous generations, now became exceptional. For France, where the history of food prices has been more intensively studied than anywhere else in Europe, the crucial decade was probably that of the 1740s and the last really intense food shortage that of 1741–2. Though similar crises were to reappear later in the century (for example in the early 1770s and in 1788–89) their intensity was notably less than in the past. Some of the great killing epidemic diseases which had ravaged Europe for centuries were in any case becoming less lethal in the early decades of the century as the predominant strains of the disease-causing organisms involved became less virulent. Improved feeding,

different languages edited by J. G. Van Dillen (The Hague, 1934) remains the best source of information and C. Wilson, *Anglo-Dutch Commerce and Finance in the Eighteenth Century* (Cambridge, 1941) is also useful, as is the very detailed P. G. M. Dickson, *The Financial Revolution in England* (London, 1967). E. A. J. Johnson, *The Predecessors of Adam Smith* (London, 1937), H. Higgs, *The Physiocrats* (London, 1897), and A. W. Small, *The Cameralists: the pioneers of German social polity* (Chicago, 1909) cover between them the main trends in the economic thought of the age. The literature on mercantilism is large, but perhaps it is sufficient here to mention D. C. Coleman (ed.), *Revisions in Mercantilism* (London, 1969), which brings together a number of recent and very useful articles on the subject. *A History of Technology*, ed. C. Singer and others (Oxford, 1954–58), vols. III–IV, deal with this aspect of the period with remarkable completeness and are lavishly illustrated. Two famous pioneering works by C.-E. Labrousse in the field of price studies are *Esquisse du mouvement des prix et des revenus en France au XVIIIe siècle* (2 vols., Paris, 1933); and *La Crise de l'économie française a la fin de l'ancien régime et au début de la Révolution*, vol. I (Paris, 1944). On the origins and early stages of the Industrial Revolution in Britain there are interesting ideas in R. M. Hartwell (ed.), *The Causes of the Industrial Revolution in England* (London, 1967) and W. W. Rostow, 'The beginnings of modern growth in Europe: an essay in synthesis', *Journal of Economic History*, vol. XXXIII (1973); while T. S. Ashton, *The Industrial Revolution, 1760–1830* (London, 1958) and Phyllis Deane, *The First Industrial Revolution* (Cambridge, 1965) are standard works.

which increased resistance to infection, combined with this factor to reduce markedly the hitherto often terrible effects of epidemics. In Germany, for example, the plague of 1709–11 was the last great outbreak of the disease, so devastating in previous centuries; and after the 1720s it ceased to be a significant factor in the demographic picture of Western Europe. Infant mortality in particular fell in many areas in the second half of the eighteenth century.[1] This, coupled with a continuing high birth-rate (it differed greatly from one area to another, perhaps from 30 to 60 per thousand of total population) was the main determinant in the growth in the sheer number of Europeans during this period.

In a few areas population growth may have been accelerated by rather more sophisticated factors. In Britain particularly industrialization may have helped slightly by stimulating the demand for labour, making children profitable and thus encouraging earlier and more prolific marriages. But it should be emphasized that all over Europe the ordinary man was at the mercy of natural forces, in the extent to which he reproduced himself as in almost every other respect, to an extent hard to grasp completely today. A bad harvest or an epidemic, natural disasters against which there was little defence, could still very quickly have drastic effects upon an entire population (though it is also true that in many parts of the continent greater resilience than in the past was being shown in rapid recovery from such disasters). Over much of Europe also, religious feeling and tradition had considerable demographic effects. They meant that in Catholic areas at least marriages in Advent and Lent were notably fewer than at other times of the Christian year, while there tended to be a seasonal peak of conceptions in May and June. Certainly the significance of medical and sanitary improvements—inoculation against smallpox, the founding of hospitals, higher standards of personal cleanliness aided by the wider use of washable cotton clothing, improved water supplies—should not be exaggerated. Great parts of Europe were in the 1780s still virtually untouched by such developments. Medicine was still a compound of empiricism and tradition; trained doctors were still few and over large areas almost non-existent; hospitals were still of little importance outside a fairly small number of large towns, and in any case probably killed more people through cross-infections than they helped to cure.

[1] See the figures for the Beauvaisis and other areas in France in Goubert, *Beauvais* (*see* Bibliography, p. 25), pp. 61–2: these show a marked drop in mortality during the first years of life during the first quarter of the eighteenth century as compared with the last quarter of the preceding one.

Whatever the causes of this unprecedented increase in the number of Europeans, the economic importance of the phenomenon is beyond question. A rising population meant an increasing consumption of food and raw materials. This in its turn meant either a considerable improvement in agricultural methods, as in Great Britain, or a large extension of the area under cultivation, as in Russia, or some combination of the two. It created both a labour supply for the new forms of industrial production which were beginning to emerge in the last years of this period and a need for increased employment, above all urban employment, if some parts of Europe were not to become overpopulated rural slums (as Ireland and parts of Spain and Italy were showing signs of doing by the end of the century). In some areas, such as Scotland and Switzerland, it provided a considerable incentive to emigration; while in countries where numbers were increasing really rapidly the existence of a high proportion of young people in the population may have had important though unmeasurable psychological effects.

Except in a few geographically restricted areas agriculture was by far the most important form of economic activity in eighteenth-century Europe. On its efficiency and productivity, on systems of land tenure, and above all in the short term on the state of the harvest, depended overwhelmingly the economic well-being of society. This was mainly because the agricultural sector was almost everywhere very much bigger than any other part of the economy. Also movements in agricultural prices were as a rule much sharper than those in the prices of manufactured goods. Agricultural fluctuations thus determined the direction and amplitude of economic fluctuations in general. A crop failure meant inevitably a rapid rise in grain prices. Since cereals and above all bread made up, far more than today, the overwhelming bulk of the food intake of almost all Europeans, this inflicted immediate and often savage hardship on many people, above all on the poorest. A bad harvest also meant a reduction in the amount of seasonal work available in reaping and threshing, and often the dismissal of workers whom the farmer or the better-off peasant could no longer afford to feed; this happened, moreover, just when more and more labour was being forced on to the market by the need to stay alive in the face of rising prices. An economic crisis of this type, in a traditional agrarian economy, therefore involved a devastating mixture of falling wages, rising unemployment and rising food prices. Such a combination, apart from its purely economic results, could have dangerous social and even political ones. Some groups—rich farmers who could afford to hold stocks of food while prices rose, landlords receiving rent in the form of a share of the crop—obviously benefited; for them the time of highest prices was also that of highest return. The spectacle of a privileged minority benefiting in this way from the sufferings of the majority could stimulate acute bitterness; and it has been argued in great detail that these indirect consequences of agricultural fluctuations provided an essential part of the background and preparation for the outbreak of the Revolution in France.[1]

The organization, methods and productivity of agriculture differed greatly in different parts of Europe. In the West there were considerable areas in which technology was relatively advanced, capital for agricultural improvement not too hard to come by, and the population dense enough to encourage the development of intensive cultivation. Much of the Netherlands, a good deal of the south-east and Midlands of England, later in the century parts of the Lowlands of Scotland and some favoured areas of France, were in this position. In these areas productivity was high and increasing, interest in new methods relatively easy to arouse, and the agricultural community generally prosperous.

In the Netherlands, or at least in densely populated areas such as Flanders, West Brabant, Zeeland and South Holland, many farmers were specializing even in the seventeenth century in the production of purely commercial crops (flax, madder, woad, hops and tobacco). They had abandoned the mainly subsistence agriculture which was still dominant over a great part of the continent. Market-gardening and the cultivation of fruit had also been developed there to a degree equalled perhaps only in a few small areas of Italy, and a considerable technical literature on agricultural questions was beginning to emerge. In the eighteenth century, though they were eventually surpassed in this as in other respects by Great Britain, the Netherlands remained one of the most advanced agricultural areas in Europe. In them originated the Brabant plough which, first recorded early in the century, is generally regarded as the prototype of the modern plough. During the second half of this period they became one of the first parts of Europe to cultivate the potato on a large scale. As late as 1802 a German observer, after careful study, concluded that agricultural productivity in the Austrian Netherlands was still about 30 per cent higher than in England.

In the latter the period 1600–1750 saw a remarkably large output of

[1] See in particular the works of Labrousse (Bibliography, p. 61).

technical works on agriculture, many of which pointed the way towards improvements which were later to become generally accepted. Thus the first English treatise on the cultivation of clover appeared in 1663, and the first on the potato in the following year. By the 1680s as advanced an idea as that of the compilation of soil-maps was beginning to be put forward, while in 1749 (a surprisingly late date) the first English work on sheep-rearing made its appearance. Already in the 1720s turnips and clover were being cultivated on a considerable scale in Norfolk, and stock-breeding and land drainage were being improved. Later in the century these and other improvements in agricultural techniques were carried still further by such people as Robert Bakewell, and systematically utilized by great farmers such as Thomas Coke (afterwards Earl of Leicester). Simultaneously farms were growing larger, calling for greater amounts of capital and making more efficient use of the division of labour. The smaller squires tended slowly to give way to great landowners, and small freeholders to leaseholders who cultivated on a more extensive scale. Throughout the century moreover, and above all in its last decades, the process of 'enclosure' was going on (perhaps 5 million acres in all were enclosed in 1760–1800). The scattered holdings which had hitherto been typical of the Midlands and much of the south were now being consolidated and fenced, and common rights in meadow, waste and woodland extinguished. The effects of this movement (which undoubtedly increased the efficiency of English agriculture) on the smaller cultivators are still the subject of controversy. It seems clear, however, that the number of smaller independent farmers did not decline sharply until after the end of the great struggle with France in 1815. Nor, though enclosure could on occasion cause real suffering, is there much evidence that the cottagers and squatters, the lowest strata of eighteenth-century agrarian society in England, were driven forcibly from the land in large numbers or suffered from very serious unemployment.

The relative modernity and prosperity of agriculture in Britain and the Netherlands contrasted sharply with the poverty and backwardness of some other parts of agrarian Europe. In Sicily a dense population, a soil often poor and hard to work, primitive techniques and a social and administrative system almost unequalled in harshness, made the peasantry one of the most wretched in Europe. Though the island still exported wheat it had lost the position which it had held in the sixteenth and early seventeenth centuries as the granary of all southern Europe; in 1763–64 a famine, one of the worst of this period, and the disease which inevitably followed, killed 30,000 of its inhabitants. In Andalusia similarly a harsh geographical environment and the prevalence of great but poorly cultivated estates led to depopulation, very low productivity, and the emergence of a large class of landless labourers. In other Spanish provinces such as La Mancha and Valladolid conditions were almost as bad. In Poland and Livonia also the position of the peasantry was wretched. 'The Country People', reported an observer at the end of the seventeenth century, 'are poor and miserable and are masters of nothing they have, but are subject to their Lords, who treat them as tyrannically as Galley-Slaves.'[1] In Russia the peasant was increasingly oppressed and exploited in many ways (see pp. 40–1), though the area under cultivation and perhaps the productivity of his labour increased during this period.

Between these extremes of progress and stagnation, between the Netherlands on the one hand and Sicily and Andalusia on the other, lay great areas of Europe in which, although techniques were almost stagnant and the economic and legal position of the cultivator very vulnerable, absolute starvation and large-scale agrarian revolts were comparatively rare. These included France, much of western and central Germany, northern Spain, northern Italy and Scandinavia. In them the life of the peasant was of course hard, limited and insecure to an extent difficult to imagine today. As late as 1770, 150,000 people are said to have died of hunger in Saxony and 80,000 in Bohemia (though these figures, contemporary guesses, are certainly too high). Even in France, where total agricultural production was greater than in any other European State, techniques in general were very backward. An active school of writers during the second half of the century advocated constructive change and the introduction of new crops, machinery and methods. Henri Bertin, who for a considerable period in the 1760s and 1770s acted in effect as a kind of Minister of Agriculture, encouraged improvement of many kinds. Yet the practical effect of all this was very limited. In 1788 the great scientist Lavoisier estimated that the productivity of agriculture in Britain was on average 2·7 times that in France. The social stresses generated by an inadequate agriculture are reflected in the constant presence in Paris during the reign of Louis XV of an army of around 30,000 beggars. Many of these were ruined peasants, or landless labourers produced by the combination of a rising population and a stagnant agrarian economy. People such as these, like their predecessors

[1] *The Ancient and Present State of Poland* (London, 1697), p. 13.

for generations, flocked to the city for the succour which the countryside could not or would not provide. The same tensions are seen in France in the growth of vagrancy, with all the dangers to public order which it involved, of which complaints in the *cahiers* of 1789 provide plentiful evidence. Britain, almost alone among the states of Europe, had by the later decades of the century little fear of such developments. With an agriculture which was rapidly developing and, at least in some parts of the country, highly productive by the standards of the age; with a great merchant marine and foreign trade and hence excellent facilities for importing grain in times of shortage; with industries which were, by the end of this period, offering in a few areas employment of a new kind on a new scale, she had no fear of famine. She was thus able to go further than any other great State in abandoning, in practice if not in theory, efforts to fix the price and control the export of food.

Accurate generalization about agrarian conditions in eighteenth-century Europe is thus very difficult. The poorness of communications, the persistence of a vast structure of local peculiarities and traditional rights and privileges, meant that they varied enormously even between different parts of the same State. Thus the *latifundia* of Andalusia contrasted sharply not only with the scientifically run and highly capitalized estates of Norfolk, but also with the independent peasant holdings of the Basque provinces, Catalonia and to a lesser extent some parts of Aragon. Normandy, where enclosures were permitted by customary law and where techniques of cultivation were relatively advanced, contrasted almost as sharply with backward Lorraine, with barren and poverty-stricken Brittany, and even with the Île-de-France. The obligation of individual peasants to follow a traditional system of crop rotation, so onerous and hard to escape in eastern France, was generally much lighter and less well enforced south of the Loire. Marked divergences could occur within the same province or even within a smaller area. Thus in Brittany remnants of feudalism were much more important in Basse-Bretagne than in Haute-Bretagne, while the share of total agricultural production which went to the nobility was less in the area around Rennes, the provincial capital, than in most others. In the German States similar contrasts are visible. (For example the position of the peasantry was notably better in Lower Silesia than in most other parts of the Prussian monarchy.)

It follows therefore that there was no such thing as a European peasantry in the eighteenth century, in the sense of a more or less homogeneous class whose rights and obligations were similar in different areas of the continent. The fundamental legal and social distinction between different groups of cultivators, that which divided serfs from free men, has already been mentioned (see pp. 37-8). There were, however, other and more purely economic differences between the farmers and peasants of the various parts of Europe. The Basque farmer cultivating his own land was a different being from the Sicilian or Irish tenant paying rent through a middleman to a landlord he might never have set eyes on. In France the *laboureur* who owned a plough-team had not, as a rule, the same interests and fears as the *manœuvrier* who had no source of livelihood but his own hands. In Germany the vine-grower of the Neckar valley, and the peasant of the Erzgebirge or Thuringerwald who had an ancillary source of income in handicrafts and domestic work, had little in common with the serf of Pomerania or Holstein. These contrasts could be multiplied indefinitely. Throughout Europe the cultivators of the land showed certain common or at least widespread characteristics—technical conservatism, attachment to traditional forms of religion, hostility to great landlords and their claims—but they were not a class in any genuine sense of the term.

In international trade, as in every other aspect of economic life, development was more rapid during this period in some areas of Western Europe than in other parts of the continent. Foreign trade was still, as far as most countries were concerned, much less important than it was to become in the generations which followed the industrial revolution. As in the seventeenth century, the United Provinces and Norway were perhaps the only countries whose life depended on their ability to obtain essential imports, above all of food, in return for exports. Nevertheless commercial questions bulked very large, indeed misleadingly large, in the abundant economic literature of the period (partly because a high proportion of the writers who produced it were themselves merchants). Trade rivalry between States remained as keen and jealous as ever before. 'Almost every corner of Europe, in our age,' wrote a contemporary, 'strives to gain some part of the commercial advantages which they clearly observe to contribute so much to the enrichment and the exaltation of nations.'[1] Another asserted that commerce 'should be the great object of public attention in all national movements, and in every negotiation we enter into with foreign powers'.[2]

In this competition for trade Britain was on the whole decidedly more

[1] D. Macpherson, *Annals of Commerce* (London, 1805), vol. III, p. 292.
[2] *Mercator's Letters on Portugal and its Commerce* (London, 1754), p. 5.

successful than her rivals. Though it is impossible to provide really reliable quantitative estimates of her exports and imports at any particular date, it is clear that both increased rapidly, particularly in the last decades of the century. The growth of her overseas trade is reflected in that of her merchant fleet. From 3,300 ships with a total tonnage of 260,000 in 1702, it grew to over 8,100 with a tonnage of 590,000 in 1764, and 9,400 with a tonnage of over 695,000 in 1776. In the last years of the century its growth was even more rapid: by 1800 its carrying capacity was perhaps five or six times as great as it had been a hundred years earlier. The development of a modern system of mercantile law, above all during the years (1756–88) when Lord Mansfield was Lord Chief Justice, was also a reflection of the increasing importance of trade in the country's life; while as suppliers of raw materials, capital, and even markets, merchants played a significant part in the early stages of the industrial revolution in Britain.

Throughout this period the visible balance of Britain's trade was in her favour, sometimes heavily so. It is true that the official figures of her imports and exports which the historian has to take as his starting-point over-estimated the real strength of her position. Interest charges on the capital she imported from abroad (notably from the Netherlands), the cost of maintaining armies in Europe and paying subsidies to European allies in time of war, the fact that great though unknown quantities of foreign goods were smuggled into the country and thus did not appear in the official returns at all—these and a number of less important factors meant that the balance of payments was much less in her favour than would appear at first sight. Nevertheless her commercial position throughout this period was strong; and it was becoming still stronger as the century drew to its close. The protected market provided by her colonies, the power of her navy, and above all the industrial and technological progress which allowed her increasingly to undersell rival producers of manufactured goods, were the foundations of a commercial growth which was not only rapid but also soundly-based. This growth of her trade, moreover, as contemporaries realized, immensely strengthened her international position. In particular it helped her to emerge victorious from the crucially important colonial struggles of the age. 'What has enabled England to Support this expensive War so long,' asked the economist Charles Davenant as early as 1696, 'but the great Wealth which for Thirty Years has been flowing into us from Our Commerce Abroad?'[1]

[1] *An Essay upon the East India Trade* (London, 1696), p. 7.

About Britain's trade with America, Africa, and the East something is said elsewhere in this book (see pp. 320ff.). Her trade with Europe, though it grew less rapidly than that with the other continents, nevertheless expanded considerably. From the Baltic, above all Russia, she drew great quantities of the naval stores—masts, hemp, tar and cordage —which she could not produce herself in sufficient quantities and on which her whole position as a maritime Power depended. As a result Russia was one of the few countries with which her trade balance was heavily and continuously unfavourable. From both Sweden and Russia she drew great quantities of iron, which she was forced to import by the steady rise, for a number of reasons, in the price of charcoal for use in smelting her own iron ore. Not until the 1780s, with the increasing use of coke for smelting and the development of the puddling process, did she begin to make herself independent of the Swedish and Russian ironmasters who had for so long profited from her weakness in this respect. With the Netherlands her trade, though its relative importance was declining, remained very extensive and active. With France, until the commercial treaty of 1786, it was restricted by war, by traditional hostility and distrust, and by numerous restrictions and prohibitions imposed on both sides of the Channel. (Though a large but indefinite amount of smuggling and contraband trade went on between the two countries throughout the century.) With Spain Britain drove a thriving trade in salt fish, textiles and other manufactured goods, receiving in exchange wool, wine, vegetable oils, fruit, and of course bullion from South America. By the last years of the century she was playing a greater role than any other country in Spain's foreign trade. In Portugal British merchants and British goods enjoyed a position of almost complete dominance during the first half of this period. The Methuen Treaty of 1703 is usually taken as marking the definitive establishment of Britain's leading position in the Portuguese market; for the next fifty years a steady stream of British manufactured goods flowed to Lisbon and Oporto in exchange for the wine of Portugal and the gold of Brazil. One contemporary claimed, apparently without contradiction, that the treaty had quintupled British exports to Portugal. During the quarter of a century (1750–1777) in which he dominated Portuguese life as chief minister of King Joseph I, the Marques de Pombal made strenuous efforts to reduce this, as it seemed to him, humiliating dependence on Britain. He could do little, however, to endow Portugal with the industries and the spirit of enterprise which alone could have enabled her to escape foreign tutelage. With Italy also

British trade, based once more largely on the export of salt fish and woollen goods and on the import of silk, grew in a satisfactory though far from spectacular manner during this period. Trade with the Levant alone declined during much of the eighteenth century. Relatively flourishing until the 1730s, it then fell off rapidly, mainly because of French competition, political upheavals in Persia which disrupted the silk trade with Smyrna and Aleppo, and the lack of enterprise shown by the Levant Company. From this decline it did not begin to recover until the last years of the century.

In France this period opened with a reaction against the strict government control of foreign trade which had marked the last decades of the seventeenth century and which is associated with the name of Colbert. The *Conseil du Commerce* which was set up in 1700 and which included representatives of eleven of the main towns showed itself anti-Colbertist in outlook; and in 1697–1713 a series of important commercial treaties were negotiated with the Netherlands, Prussia, Denmark and the Hanse towns. This movement towards a more liberal system of trade regulation was short-lived. The period of the Regency and the régime of Cardinal Fleury (1726–41) were marked by a reversion to the regimentation and highly protectionist outlook of the later seventeenth century. This return to the past was challenged or criticized by many French writers on economic affairs—Saint-Pierre, Melon, d'Argenson —and also by many of the merchants whom it affected. Thus the Marseilles Chamber of Commerce, in letters to Maurepas, the Secretary for the Navy, argued in 1723 and 1742 in favour of some freeing of French trade. Not until the 1750s, however, did the prohibitions and regulations which had for so long dominated and often hampered the development of the country's economic life begin to be dismantled; and then only very slowly. This tentative movement towards greater economic liberty was accentuated and accelerated by the development of 'Physiocratic' ideas on economic questions. It contributed to the remarkable development of French overseas trade, above all colonial trade, which marked the quarter-century after the end of the Seven Years War in 1763. From 120 million livres in 1716 the value of the country's exports rose to 500 million in 1789; and the greater part of this increase took place in the last decades of the period. During the same two generations or more the value of France's imports increased six-fold.

The geographical pattern of French commerce varied notably from that visible in the case of Britain. With the Baltic France never traded

71

directly on a significant scale during the eighteenth century. British and Dutch competition; the caution and conservatism of her own merchants; the political antagonisms which divided her from Russia during much of the period; lack of sufficient capital to maintain a trade which often required heavy investment and the ability to wait some time for returns —all these made her throughout this period a minor factor in the commercial life of northern Europe. (Though great quantities of her wine, brandy, silks and colonial produce filtered into the area through Dutch or Hamburg merchants.) With Spain on the other hand her trade, encouraged by geographical proximity and political alliance, was very important. The accession of Philip V to the Spanish throne in 1700 was followed by the immigration on a considerable scale of French technicians and skilled workers. French commercial influences remained very important there throughout the century, much to the disgust of many Spaniards: by 1789 France was exporting to Spain over four times as much as she imported from her. Italy also proved a fertile field for her trade, though the establishment of a branch of the Bourbon dynasty on the throne of the Two Sicilies in 1735 never gave her quite the commercial predominance in the southern part of the peninsula for which some Frenchmen had hoped. The most striking expansion of French trade in Europe during this period was seen, however, in the Levant. The activity of the merchants of Marseilles, the encouragement given them by the French government, and perhaps the diversion to the eastern Mediterranean of energies stultified by Britain's victories in North America and India, had made France by the later decades of the century the dominant force in Europe's commerce with the Near East. In the years just before 1789 it seemed that she was about to extend her influence to the Black Sea, now for the first time for centuries opening to European trade. Only the great cycle of wars which broke out in 1792 prevented the whole eastern basin of the Mediterranean from falling under her commercial dominance.

The trading importance of the two greatest States of Western Europe was thus increasing during this period, and particularly during its last decades. That of the United Provinces, still in many ways the most economically advanced area in Europe, was by contrast stagnant or even declining. By 1739 it was believed in Amsterdam that twice as many ships unloaded their cargoes at London as at the great Dutch port. Some loss of the dominant position which the United Provinces had occupied in the commercial life of seventeenth-century Europe was inevitable as the other parts of the continent developed their merchant fleets and began to trade directly with one another, thus robbing the Dutch of their old position as the centre *par excellence* of entrepôt trade. This more than any other factor explains the fall in their commercial importance. Their decline in this respect was probably accentuated by the rigidity of their commercial policy (for example by the failure in 1738 and 1751 of proposals to make Amsterdam a free port). It was certainly accelerated by the inability of the United Provinces, partly through sheer lack of physical resources, to develop industry on any really substantial scale. The quite important industries which they possessed at the beginning of the century suffered severely during this period from foreign competition. Calico-printing and sugar-refining, for example, were badly injured by competition from Hamburg, Bremen and the Austrian Netherlands. Of the eighty cloth factories in Leyden in 1735 more than half had disappeared only sixteen years later. Developments of this kind could hardly fail to have a considerable influence on Dutch seaborne trade.

Elsewhere in northern Europe there were States with appreciable merchant navies. Sweden in 1787 possessed over 1,200 merchantmen, Prussia at the same period nearly a thousand, Hamburg perhaps 150, and Bremen something over a hundred. But the majority of these ships were small (the average Prussian merchantman had a crew of only seven men) and the part played by such States in international trade, though not negligible, was far less significant than that of Britain, France or the United Provinces.

In the Mediterranean Venice, formerly so important in the commercial life of Europe, was now sinking into irreparable decay. The city was still a trading centre of some importance. In 1703 it was claimed that it earned 10 million ducats a year through its activity in marine insurance. In 1759 nearly 1,800 ships touched there. However its own merchant marine was small and declining; and its growth was hampered by the rapidly increasing competition of Trieste and Ancona and by the hostility which existed for much of the century between Venice and the Barbary States of North Africa. Leghorn, in the Grand Duchy of Tuscany, was by contrast one of the greatest commercial centres of Europe during this period. The city was a free port with admirable quarantine arrangements (a factor of real importance where trade with the disease-ridden Levant was concerned) and considerable colonies of the Greeks, Jews and Armenians who played so large a part in the commercial life of the eastern and even the western Mediterranean. An English writer claimed in 1744 that there were 'greater numbers of [British] Ship Tonnage employed in the Trade to the free Port of Leghorn only than by the three chartered companies [i.e. the East India, South Sea and Levant Companies] all together'.[1] The Tuscan merchant marine nevertheless was completely negligible; and Leghorn depended for its importance entirely on the British, French, Dutch and Genoese ships which called there. The Kingdom of the Two Sicilies, the largest of the Italian States, was also an almost completely passive factor in the trade of Europe. The salt, grain and other commodities she exported, the manufactured goods she imported, were carried in French, British, Genoese or Ragusan ships, not in her own.

Finally the Ottoman Empire, almost the largest of European States, was commercially one of the most inert. The contempt which most Turks felt for commerce, their ignorance and mental inflexibility, and the essentially military character they had given their empire, made it impossible for them to play any real part in its foreign trade. Nor were the Jews, Greeks and Armenians who controlled almost the whole of the empire's internal trade able to play quite so important a role in its commerce with Western Europe. The result was that this was dominated by Europeans, above all Frenchmen, and that at every port in the Ottoman Empire—Salonica, Constantinople, Smyrna, Aleppo—small but very important colonies of Western merchants were to be found.

Europe was thus divided, from the standpoint of international trade, into two somewhat unequal parts. A small number of States in the West, which conducted and financed by far the greater part of the continent's commerce, existed side by side with a much larger area which provided markets and commodities for export but depended on foreign ships and merchants to supply its imports and dispose of its products. The superiority of the more advanced parts of Western Europe in commercial and financial expertise can be seen in the role which British, French, or Dutch merchants and adventurers played in stimulating the economic development of the rest of the continent. Thus the Ostend Company, through which the Emperor Charles VI hoped to obtain for the Habsburg dominions a share in Europe's trade with the East, was founded in 1722 largely on the initiative of a Scottish adventurer, Ker of Kersland; and the Swedish East India Company which came into

[1] M. Decker, *Essay on the Causes of the Decline of the Foreign Trade* (London, 1744), p. 25. The number of British ships entering the port each year in the period 1724-53 is to be found in Public Record Office, S.P. 105/301. The best year was 1734, when 446 ships flying the British flag did so.

existence some years later was founded and managed by Englishmen. The two most important merchant houses in Sweden in the last decades of the century had also been founded by Englishmen, while a Frenchman was mainly responsible for the creation in 1782 of the Bank of St. Charles in Spain.

The great expansion of seaborne trade which marked the eighteenth century was not paralleled by any comparable increase in that by land. The seas were becoming safer with the suppression of piracy and the development of marine insurance; ships were slowly increasing in size and port facilities were being improved; but the conditions under which goods had to be transported on land changed only slightly. It was possible for areas widely separated geographically to be closely united economically by the bond of seaborne trade. Comparable areas much closer together physically, if they were connected only by land communications, might live in virtual isolation from one another. A good illustration of this is the French province of Brittany. Throughout the century it looked overseas, towards the British Isles, Spain, Holland and the French colonies, rather than towards the rest of France, from which it was largely cut off, even in the later years of this period, by marsh and forest. The marked concentration of the population of the province around the coast and the barrenness and depopulation of large inland areas reflect to a considerable extent this lack of balance between communication by sea and by land, an imbalance which had profound effects everywhere. Except a few areas, parts of France and to a lesser extent England and some German states such as Hesse and Baden-Durlach, roads improved little until late in the century. In many parts of Europe the poorness of land communications was the greatest of all obstacles not merely to the growth of trade but to the development of economic life in general. In Spain, for example, serious efforts to improve the road system (or rather to create a road system) began only in 1777. Until then almost the only real roads in the country were those connecting Madrid with the various royal residences. In Sicily, in many ways the most backward and neglected part of all Western and Mediterranean Europe, the position was even worse. There even the journey between the island's two main cities, Palermo and Messina, was normally made by sea; and even in the early years of our own century there were still many Sicilian peasants who had never seen a wheeled cart, so bad or even non-existent were the roads. It is true that the cost of land transport, at least in England and France, tended to fall during the eighteenth century; but it was never possible anywhere to move heavy or bulky goods by land nearly so easily or cheaply as by water. At the beginning of this period Marshal Vauban, the great French soldier and writer on economic questions, asserted that by using a boat of the normal size on a navigable river six men and four horses could transport goods which required the use of two hundred men and four hundred horses on ordinary roads. This striking equation still, by and large, held good at its end.

Customs barriers moreover continued to impede the flow of trade along its traditional routes, notably along the great rivers. Thus there were thirty such barriers on the Rhine between Kehl and the frontier of the United Provinces, and nine between Bruges and Coblenz. Also the political units into which Europe was divided were in many cases far from being economic ones. Often they were subdivided by internal customs barriers and by differing systems of weights, measures and currency. This was the position in France, where tolls were very frequent on all the main arteries of trade and where, as one of the *cahiers* of 1789 complained, 'the infinite number of weights and measures passes the imagination'. In Spain there was a customs barrier between Castile and Valencia till 1717, while Andalusia retained its own customs system till 1778. The country also suffered from a bewildering variety of monetary systems: until 1718, when Castilian coins were for the first time made legal tender in the other provinces, she could scarcely be said to have a national currency at all. In the same way as Russia, politically united to most of the Ukraine since the 1650s, was not economically united with it till the reign of Catherine II.

The effects of the decline in the relative importance of overland trade during this period are best seen in the failure of the towns of West and South Germany to recover their former leading place in the economy of Europe. Like many of the Italian cities they were the victims of fundamental changes in the geography and techniques of European commerce. Like these cities and the United Provinces they lacked the territorial and industrial resources which might otherwise have compensated them for their commercial losses. Thus Cologne and Mainz, Nuremberg and Trier, play in eighteenth-century economic history a role of second- or even third-rate importance. The rise of Basle and Zürich (perhaps accelerated by the welcome which they gave to religious refugees from France and the Archbishopric of Salzburg) showed that the historic German cities were not necessarily condemned to stagnation and decline. Some—Augsburg and above all Frankfurt-on-Main—were able to establish themselves as important financial centres and thus recoup to a certain extent the loss of their former commercial position. These, however, were the exception rather than the rule. The complete unimportance of the Hanse (the league of North German cities so powerful in the later Middle Ages) was symbolized by the closing in 1763 of the trading depot which it had for centuries maintained at Bergen in Norway. Indeed as early as 1669 its membership had been reduced to the three cities of Lübeck, Hamburg and Bremen. So low had the reputation of Germany for material prosperity sunk by the end of the century that in 1789 a traveller in France met a respectable Frenchman who was astonished to be told that the Germans wore the same kind of clothes as the French and other peoples of Western Europe.

This period saw no spectacular industrial advance so far as most of Europe was concerned. The one important exception to this generalization (and it was to be a supremely important one) is the wonderful growth of industry, and of industry of a new kind, which was beginning to show itself in Great Britain in the last decades of the century. Accompanying this growth both as causes and results came a whole series of far-reaching economic changes: a rapid and sustained growth of population and in particular an unprecedented rise in the proportion of that population which lived in large towns; a sharp increase in the use of sometimes quite complex machines; a tendency, though a less marked one, for units of industrial production to grow larger. Perhaps the most fundamental change of all was one still in its infancy even in the 1780s— the movement in the most rapidly growing sector of British industry, cotton textiles, towards modern flow rather than traditional batch production, and thus towards a new labour discipline and organization, stricter and more rigid than any in the past. By the 1780s, as a result of this great series of interlinked changes, Britain was showing the rest of the world that self-sustaining and accelerating economic growth of a kind new in history was now within the reach of at least a few advanced areas of Western Europe. These changes were social and organizational as much as technological. Nevertheless it was the new technology more than any other aspect of what was happening which impressed contemporaries. By the 1780s the manufacure of cotton textiles in Britain had been revolutionized by a series of new machines—the spinning jenny, the water-frame, the mule—while the country's production of iron, stagnant for most of the century, was about to be vastly expanded by the large-scale use of coke for smelting. Simultaneously the power needed to drive new machines of all kinds was beginning to be provided

by James Watt's steam-engine, which had far greater economic potentialities than the expensive and inefficient 'atmospheric' engines which
preceded it. The full implications of this technological leap forward
were hidden from contemporaries. But the new machines and techniques,
and also the striking development of communications through the
building of canals and turnpike roads, were signs, clearly visible, that
Britain was moving into a new age of wealth and productivity.

The 'Industrial Revolution' did not take shape suddenly and without
warning in the 1760s, in the early 1780s, or at any other date. There had
even, some historians have argued, been earlier industrial changes which
could be reasonably described as revolutionary under the Tudors and
early Stuarts, perhaps even in the twelfth century. Certainly the foundations of the growth of industry which marked the last quarter of the
eighteenth century in Britain had been laid earlier by improvements in
agriculture; by the growing population which these made possible; by a
rapid expansion of overseas trade; and by the emergence of a government more stable and a society more free than any part of continental
Europe could boast. Yet what was happening in Britain by the 1780s was
an economic change so rapid and far-reaching that no word weaker than
'revolution' is adequate to describe it.

The reasons for this great change, the explanation of why it took place
when it did, are complex and still debated. Some of these reasons certainly were not economic ones. It seems clear, for example, that the
development of the physical sciences formed an important part of the
background to the great industrial changes. Technological advance, as
has often been pointed out, was sometimes the work of artisans with
little formal education. But this was not so frequently the case as used
to be thought; and in the second half of the century scientific knowledge
and scientific attitudes penetrated deeply into industrial society in
Britain.[1] Yet an explanation of the Industrial Revolution in these terms
has only limited usefulness. More scientific work, both pure and applied,
was done in France than in Britain during the eighteenth century; but
this did not prevent Britain from achieving by the 1780s, and probably
earlier, a clear lead over her neighbour in industrial technology. Again
the economic advantages to Britain of her relatively free society, with the
opportunities it gave for able men to rise in the social scale and the
relatively high social status which it offered to at least certain types of

---

[1] A. E. Musson and E. Robinson, 'Science and industry in the late eighteenth
century', *Economic History Review*, 2nd ser., vol. XIII (1960), pp. 222–44.

business activity, probably did a good deal to help economic growth. Yet how much and in what way are difficult to prove. As yet we simply do not know enough about the relationship between social structure and economic change in eighteenth-century Britain to do more than assume some general causal connection.

Even if intellectual and social factors are left out of the picture, and attention is concentrated merely on economic ones, it is hard to produce any simple and generally acceptable explanation of the origins of the Industrial Revolution. The eighteenth century saw a great expansion of Britain's overseas trade, above all with America (see p. 320), and this, it has frequently been argued, provided the indispensable foundation of industrial advance. Commercial profits were the source of the capital needed to finance investment in new machines and processes. Growing overseas markets meant increased demand for British goods and intensified pressure towards large-scale production of them. Certainly this line of argument, long a favourite one of many economic historians, has some validity. Yet it can easily be pushed too far. The most recent study of the subject suggests strongly that even in the three crucial decades 1760–90 only about 6 to 8 per cent of all capital formation in Britain resulted from the profits of overseas trade, and that the maximum effect of this trade during the century as a whole was to increase Britain's total productive power only by somewhere between 5 and 11 per cent.[1] An increasing population, a rise in real wages and a series of good harvests after about 1730 clearly did more to enrich Britain than trade with the outside world. Other explanations of Britain's industrial growth in purely economic terms have been offered. It has been argued, for example, that it was powerfully stimulated in periods when interest rates were low; the enclosure of common lands, the building of canals and turnpikes, investment in new machinery, even the taking out of patents for new inventions, were all encouraged by the ability to borrow cheaply. Certainly, moreover, the long-term trend of interest rates in Britain during this period was downwards. Another suggested explanation is that for much of the century the rise in industrial wages was less than that in the prices of manufactured goods. This, it is claimed, meant large windfall profits for the capitalist and hence large investment in new factories and machines. But the second of these hypotheses is now discredited (at least so far as Britain is concerned) in

[1] P. Bairoch, 'Commerce international et genèse de la révolution industrielle anglaise', *Annales*, 28ᵉ année, No. 2 (March–April, 1973), pp. 541–71.

terms both of historical fact and economic theory; and the first is very much open to question, for there seems no reason to suppose that interest rates were more important than other costs in the making of business decisions in eighteenth-century Britain.

In other words no explanation of the origins of the Industrial Revolution wholly or mainly in terms of a single factor can be satisfactory. The picture at present available is that of a process of balanced and relatively slow economic growth, with its roots deep in the past, which lasted until the 1760s or even the 1780s. This growth was the product of many factors, some of them not economic in any strict sense—changing social attitudes and the extension of education; widening overseas markets; accumulating capital for investment and a growing population to provide both workers and consumers; technical innovation and improving transport facilities. In the last decades of the century it accelerated and became increasingly unbalanced as some sectors of production (iron and still more cotton textiles) developed explosively. This very rapid lopsided growth then stimulated other branches of industry and gave new strength to the pressures making for change in the economy as a whole.

It must be emphasized, however, that really spectacular and rapid industrial growth, even in Britain, came only at the very end of the period covered by this book. Until late in the century it was rare for any industrial enterprise there to use steam-power on a considerable scale. A well-informed observer in 1752 thought there were then not more than a hundred 'fire-engines' in the country,[1] and even in 1800 all the Watt engines in use in England developed between them only about 5,000 horsepower. (For purposes of comparison, the great pumping installation built at Marly in 1681–85 to supply water for the gardens at Versailles, which was regarded as one of the technical marvels of that age, had an effective output of about eighty horsepower —roughly that of a fair-sized modern lorry.) To the very end of this period the availability of water-power was the most important factor determining the growth and location of most British industries. Industrial activity still depended on the weather, and thus could be disrupted by either drought or flood, to a degree hard to grasp today. Outside Britain, except to some extent in France and the Austrian Netherlands, the industrial revolution had not even begun to develop by the early 1780s. (In Germany the first Watt steam-engine was installed only in 1785.) Nowhere were large factories staffed by hundreds of workmen

[1] Josiah Tucker, *Reflections relating to Arts and Commerce* (London, 1752) p. 66.

and containing relatively elaborate and expensive machinery more than very exceptional features of the industrial landscape. Throughout the century the greatest cities of Europe—London, Paris, Constantinople, Moscow, St. Petersburg, Amsterdam, Naples—were capitals or sea-ports, or both, not primarily industrial centres.

This did not mean that great industrial enterprises were unknown. In France the Anzin coal-mining company, founded in the 1750s, was employing 4,000 men in the years before 1789. The Van Robais textile factory at Abbeville, one of the industrial showpieces of the age, contained within its walls during much of the century some 3,000 workers, while many hundreds more spun yarn for it in their own homes. In Britain the silk-mill set up by Thomas Lombe at Derby in 1717–21 employed over 300 work-people and contained machinery with 26,000 wheels; while two generations later the great ironmaster John Wilkinson provided one of the first important examples of 'vertical concentration' of an industry, owning his own iron-mines, coal-mines and foundries. Nevertheless the factory, in the modern sense of the term, was still in its infancy. It was small in size: an official survey of 1764 in the Austrian Netherlands, one of the most economically advanced areas of Europe, showed that there industrial enterprises with as many as forty-five workmen were exceptionally large. It was conservative in technique, dominated by ideas and traditions derived from handicraft production. Often it confined its activities only to the finishing processes in its particular industry.

Where large numbers of workers were concentrated under effective discipline and supervision in a single enterprise, it was often because they were given no choice in the matter. Every European State attempted, with varying success, to conscript for forced labour in industry the sections of its population which it regarded as unproductive and socially dangerous. Criminals, vagabonds, prostitutes, orphans, foundlings and quite often soldiers were utilized in this way in work-houses, orphanages and barracks. Thus in Bohemia in the early eigh-teenth century beggars and vagrants were systematically rounded up twice a year by the authorities, children of up to fourteen being sent to homes for foundlings and adults to forced labour. In Berlin at the same period a large lace factory was established in an orphanage, while under Frederick William I soldiers were employed in spinning wool and cotton on a considerable scale and every barracks became a kind of industrial establishment. The description of the prisons and hospitals of Europe provided by the Quaker John Howard at the end of this period shows how widespread practices of this kind still were in such institutions. Much more important were the great enterprises which it was possible to create in parts of eastern and central Europe by making use of serf labour. The supreme example of this, one of importance for the economy of the whole continent, was the development of the iron industry in Russia. In the same way the remarkable growth of the textile industry in Bohemia, which involved the creation of numbers of relatively large unified factories for the bleaching and dyeing of cloth, was made possible by the way in which serfdom allowed the landowning nobility to mobilize large amounts of unfree labour. It is not surprising therefore to find in both these countries (more particularly in Bohemia) the landowning and serf-owning class playing an unusually important rôle in industrial development. The most important type of publicly owned enterprise, organized on a very large scale, was the arsenals and dockyards of the great powers. Establishments such as those at Chatham, Brest and Kronstadt ranked high among the largest and most elaborately organized productive enterprises in Europe, almost as high as the famous arsenal at Venice had done in previous centuries. It was also quite common, particularly in central and eastern Europe, for industrial undertakings to be created by a combination of government and private initiative, or to alternate between government and private control. Thus an arms factory at Spandau, near Berlin, was set up in 1722 jointly by the Prussian government and a private banking firm. The mirror factory at Neuhaus in Austria originated in 1701 as a private concern with considerable State support, lost that support two years later, and was finally taken over completely by the State in 1720.

Over most of the continent the most usual method of industrial production was the 'domestic system'. The typical industrial worker, in so far as he existed, was a domestic worker. Under this system, the details of which varied widely in different parts of Europe, the workman worked up materials supplied to him by the manufacturer either directly or, more often, through an intermediary. His tools he might either own himself or hire from his employer. The goods he produced might then be finished in a factory of something like the modern type. An organization of this kind was almost universal in the textile industries, where the spinning of yarn and to a slightly less extent the weaving of cloth were normally done by domestic workers, the finishing processes then being often carried out under the employer's own supervision. Thus for example, the textile factory at Nova Kydne in Bohemia had 1,400 spinners and 100 weavers working for it in their own homes in the 1770s, as against a mere 297 people employed within its own walls. The domestic system was found, however, in varying degrees in practically every branch of European industry. Even of the workers engaged earlier in this period in the production of mirrors at Neuhaus in Austria, obviously not an industry which lent itself to this type of organization, about 15 per cent worked in their own homes.

Labour of this kind, which had gained ground rapidly in the previous century at the expense of traditional forms of handicraft production, was essential to the economic existence of very large areas of Europe. The domestic system usually required a higher degree of organization and larger capital investment, above all in stocks of materials, than had been needed in the relatively small-scale handicraft industries which had preceded it. Its spread thus marked an important step in the development of modern capitalism. Moreover guild hostility and privileges, and the difficulty of obtaining enough labour in towns, tended to drive industry to the countryside and to weaken the position of many of the old and guild-dominated cities. In rural Bohemia over 200,000 domestic workers, mainly women, were engaged in spinning flax during much of the century. They provided the basis of an important export industry whose products reached North and South America as well as almost every part of Europe. In the same way it was estimated in 1797 that in the Chemnitz area of Saxony a third of the whole population were employed in spinning at home, while a few years earlier in the canton of Glarus in Switzerland over 34,000 domestic spinners were to be found scattered over the countryside. In the middle of the century a sail-maker of Warrington claimed that he had formerly employed 5,000 people in this way, and a producer of silks that he gave employment to people in London, Gloucestershire, Dorset and Cheshire. Even in Russia, where the spread of serfdom and the unusual importance of the army and navy as consumers of standardized products made the creation of large factories easier than anywhere else in Europe, the domestic system was to be found as the basis of important industries. One of these was the manufacture of arms in the Tula area. Another was the sailcloth industry of Kaluga which by 1793 employed nearly 9,000 workers, mostly of this type.

The geographical distribution of industry in Europe underwent considerable changes during this period. When the eighteenth century opened the most highly industrialized areas of the continent were the United Provinces, some parts of France, and a few areas of Germany, notably Saxony. Several of the Italian States also retained some of their former significance in this respect. England was a very important exporter of woollen textiles, and to a lesser extent of tin and lead, but apart from these she produced few commodities which counted for much in the economic life of the continent. By the outbreak of the French Revolution the United Provinces had lost a good deal of their former importance. France had maintained and perhaps slightly improved her relative position; and the Italian States had declined into insignificance. Bohemia had become an important industrial area, especially from about 1770 onwards. England, equipped with new techniques and relatively plentiful supplies of capital, was preparing to acquire an industrial predominance which was absolute and above all qualitative, based not on superior physical resources but on superior technology and organization. Equally important, new industrial powers had emerged. Scotland in particular, backward and poverty-stricken at the beginning of the century, had become by its later decades in some ways the most industrially advanced country in Europe. As the possessor of an unusually well-educated population she was able to supply England and other parts of the continent with the skilled workers and managers who were now becoming more and more indispensable.

Most striking of all in some ways, Russia had established herself as one of the industrial powers of Europe. This position she achieved primarily because of her importance as a producer of metals—copper and above all iron. At the beginning of this period she already possessed a considerable iron industry in the Tula and Olonets areas. To this she added, during the reign of Peter I, a new and greater source of production in the southern Urals. Government encouragement, vast and accessible supplies of timber for fuel, the forced labour of peasants 'ascribed' to the foundries, a growing demand for arms while the war of 1700–21 with Sweden lasted—all contributed to a rapid growth of output. From the establishment of the first Ural foundry at Nevyansk in 1699 until Peter's death in 1725 expansion was almost unbroken. This expansion made the fortunes of a number of entrepreneurs, above all of Nikita Demidov, an illiterate artisan of Tula who founded the greatest industrial dynasty of the age. (By 1762 the family owned twenty-eight ironworks of various kinds.) The Tsar's death and the end of the war with Sweden were followed by a slackening of activity in the next two decades; but the number of metal works in the Urals doubled in the period 1745–62. The reign of Catherine II, though it was marked by the great peasant revolt of 1773–75 which completely disrupted the life of the area, saw the construction of thirty-two new ones. By 1800 the Ural deposits were producing 80 per cent of all Russia's iron and copper, and the majority of what they produced was exported. The ironmasters of Sweden, hitherto by far the greatest European exporter of iron, combined to restrict the production of their forges in order to maintain prices and conserve fuel supplies. Their attitude, backed by the Swedish government, culminated in the creation of perhaps the most successful cartel in European history and meant that from about 1730 onwards the level of exports from Sweden was remarkably stable. Russia was thus given the chance to become a great supplier of iron to the States of Western Europe, in some of which the shortage of timber for smelting purposes was now very serious. This chance she seized, so that Britain, where the fuel shortage had been most acute, was importing Russian iron even as late as the 1790s at an average rate of almost 26,000 metric tons a year.

Apart from the production of metals and a few other commodities such as sailcloth, industrial development in eighteenth-century Russia was disappointing. In spite of much government encouragement and the import of experts from abroad, it proved extremely difficult to stimulate the production of consumer goods such as silk, paper or glass on any substantial or permanent scale. (A similar position is seen in Sweden where in spite of subsidies and protective tariffs industry, apart from the metal industries, never employed much more than 1 per cent of the country's manpower.) Of the 300 most important industrial establishments of this type in Russia in 1780 only twenty-two had survived from the reign of Peter I. Foreign competition, lack of skilled labour, the limited market provided by a peasant country most of whose needs were still supplied by handicraft industries—all these factors ensured that Russia entered the nineteenth century still an exporter of raw materials and semi-finished goods and an importer of manufactures. The part she played in the economic life of Europe had, however, strikingly increased in this period.

Eighteenth-century industry was prevented from developing more rapidly not only by the slowness of technological advance and the shortage of capital, but also by the conservative and restrictive influence of the guilds. This influence was now in decline; but the decline was slow and uneven. Such unity and homogeneity as the craft guilds had possessed in medieval and early modern times had been undermined long before the beginning of this period by the action of new economic pressures and opportunities. In particular the rough equality which the medieval guilds had attempted to preserve between their members had been in most cases irreparably destroyed. Increasingly they were divided between a wealthy merchant group and a majority of small-scale producers whose products the former marketed and whom they increasingly relegated to a position of inferiority. One of the best documented examples of this process is that of the Lyons silk industry, where a distinction of this kind was well established by 1712. Moreover many of the guilds were now becoming increasingly exclusive, more and more unwilling to admit journeymen to the rank of master. In many cases they were now closed and largely hereditary groups whose main function was a jealous guardianship of their own privileges.

Their importance was being reduced during this period by the efforts of many governments to bring them under more complete State control, to make them docile instruments of State policy or even destroy them. Efforts of this kind, an example of the tendency of the age towards more effective political absolutism and greater concentration of power, were particularly marked in the German States, where the powers and independence of the guilds had hitherto been greater in many ways than in Britain, France or the Netherlands. Thus in 1731 an imperial decree gave the rulers of individual States the power to dissolve refractory guilds, while in Prussia in 1734–38 over seventy new codes of regulations (*Zunftordnungen*) governing their organization and conduct were laid down by the government. Their activities were regulated in the Habsburg Crown lands under Maria Theresa, and also in Baden and Württemburg. In the same way, in 1777 the Spanish government ordered those under its rule to be more liberal in the admission of new members, and even to accept suitable foreigners provided they were Catholics. In France the guilds continued to show some capacity for growth during the first decades of this period: paper-makers, for example, were formed into one in 1739. But they were now more and more controlled by the central government. There was a growing tendency to regard guild statutes as valid only if they had been confirmed by royal letters patent; permission to form new guilds was frequently refused by the government; and the activities of those which existed were increasingly hemmed in by royal officials, the inspectors of manufactures. By the 1750s and 1760s there were unmistakable signs that the whole structure of guild privileges was under official attack. This movement culminated in the abolition of most guilds in Paris by Turgot, the greatest reforming Controller-General of the century, in 1776. This measure was soon withdrawn, largely because of the weakness of Louis XVI; but it proved impossible in many cases to re-establish effectively what had been even very temporarily suppressed. It must be remembered also that almost everywhere in Europe during this period guild privileges were being circumvented by State grants of special rights to individual entrepreneurs, and by the setting up of important new industrial enterprises in the countryside, where the guilds had little or no jurisdiction. In 1762, for example, the French textile industries were given complete exemption from guild restrictions if they were located outside the towns.

Nevertheless the economic importance and political influence of the guilds remained very considerable to the end of this period in many parts of Europe. In France they were able to withstand at least to some extent attacks on their privileges until the Revolution. In Germany they retained very real economic importance until the middle of the nineteenth century. Over most of Europe their hostility to new productive processes, the demarcation disputes in which they frequently indulged and their tenacious insistence on their traditional rights, tended to restrain economic progress. Increasingly these defects outweighed the services they still performed in safeguarding standards of quality and training skilled workers.

A similar type of traditionalism and conservatism, on a smaller scale, can be seen in the associations of skilled workers of various kinds (stonemasons, locksmiths and cabinetmakers were the most important) which in France were known as the *compagnonnages*. These, it must be emphasized, were medieval fraternities far more than modern trade unions. They had originated from the need to provide lodging and other help for young journeymen who, as part of their traditional training in a skilled craft, were making their *tour de France*, or in Germany their *Wanderschaft*, gaining experience by working for a number of masters in different cities. They were pervaded by a strong religious atmosphere and sustained by an elaborate structure of mythology as to their origins. (The accepted belief was that the *compagnonnages* had been born in Jerusalem during the building of Solomon's temple under the inspiration of Hiram, his architect.) The reception of new members was a quasi-religious ceremony; and in German organizations of this kind the recruit often underwent even a kind of baptism which endowed him with a new name. None of this was in itself of great importance: in France at least the best days of this type of workers' organization were to come only in the first decades of the nineteenth century. But bodies of this kind, with their addiction to quasi-religious rituals and their largely illiterate membership, are yet another illustration of the extent to which the ordinary man almost everywhere in Europe still lived in a world which was medieval rather than modern.

The development of financial techniques during this period was seen most strikingly in Britain. There the archaic and inefficient organization of the Mint and the constant export of large quantities of silver, above all to the East, meant that the country (like many other parts of Europe) tended to be chronically short of coin, above all of coins of small denominations. Not until after 1821 was the Mint able to supply Britain with an adequate quantity of small change. The result was that throughout the eighteenth century private individuals, particularly industrial employers, frequently manufactured token coins of their own. By the beginning of this period these inadequate supplies of coined money were being supplemented by other forms of currency—the notes issued by the Bank of England (which had little circulation outside London), Exchequer bills, lottery tickets, and above all the notes of the private banks which were now beginning to multiply. In the years 1750–65 there were twenty to thirty private banks in London, while by 1800 this number had grown to seventy. Private banks in the provinces, though slower to develop, were also well established by the later years of this period. Indeed even before the end of the seventeenth century merchants, manufacturers and lawyers, both in London and the provinces, had been performing many of the functions of bankers. In Scotland also a national bank had been set up in 1695; and a number of joint-stock banks, more powerful and durable than most of the English private ones, came into existence there during the eighteenth century. By the middle of the century, moreover, London was the centre of a well-organized system of marine insurance. This did much business with foreign shipowners and hence tended to strengthen the country's balance of payments and increase her importance in international trade and finance.

This period thus saw the creation in Britain of a range of important new financial institutions. With them there grew up a new atmosphere of trust in the country's financial stability. The growth of this feeling was sometimes interrupted by severe financial crises. In particular the 'South Sea Bubble' of 1720 severely shook public confidence in the financial system as well as in the honesty of the ministers then in power. The crisis originated in an offer by the South Sea Company (a chartered company which controlled British trade with South America and the Pacific) to take over the existing national debt and accept from the government a rate of interest on it lower than was then being paid to its existing holders. The acceptance of this offer was followed by a rapid rise in the value of the Company's shares (which its directors had expected) and by an unforeseen and fantastic burst of speculation in hundreds of schemes put before the public by enterprising and some-times dishonest promoters. The collapse of this speculative mania in September 1720 ruined thousands of people and produced a wave of bitterness and cynicism for which there are few parallels in British history. Nevertheless the dominant feeling of this period in Britain where public finance was concerned was one of growing confidence. This confidence made it possible for the government to borrow success-fully both at home and abroad on a scale which impressed and some-times horrified contemporaries. It was thus one of the foundations of the political and military victories won by the country during the eighteenth century.

The evolution of new institutions and techniques in Britain did not rob the United Provinces of the dominant position they had enjoyed in the developing international finance of Europe during much of the seventeenth century. In many ways indeed they tended to strengthen it. Various forms of British government stock, and the shares of the East India and South Sea Companies, created new outlets for Dutch capital which from early in the century was invested in Britain in great and increasing quantities. It was estimated in 1737 that about £11 million of Dutch money was invested in Britain, while in 1776 the Prime Minister himself alleged that this sum had risen to £59 million—three-sevenths of the whole national debt. The second of these figures at least is now known to be much too high; but there is no doubt that Dutch investment of this kind was very considerable. The hostility and distrust with which many eighteenth-century English writers and statesmen regarded the growing national debt was undoubtedly stimulated in part by the heavy burden of interest payments to foreigners which it was believed, with much justification, to involve. Elsewhere in Europe moreover—in France, in Sweden, and in the later decades of the century in Russia—capital exported from the Netherlands was a factor of considerable importance in economic life and the calculations of governments. Amsterdam was thus able to consolidate and even extend the position it had established in the seventeenth century as the chief centre of the system of international finance which had now evolved in Europe. Challenged by London, especially as a centre of marine insurance, and to a lesser extent by Hamburg, it retained this position until the cataclysm which followed the French Revolution. 'The Bill on Amsterdam', it has been said, 'was to the eighteenth century what the Bill on London was to become to the nineteenth century.'[1] But there was another side to the picture. The Dutch were able to export capital on an unprecedented scale partly at least because there seemed little really profitable employment for it at home, because their trade was, during much of the century, growing more slowly than that of their main rivals, and because their industry was stagnant or even declining.

In France financial techniques developed more slowly than in the other leading States of Western Europe. A widespread and well-founded distrust of the financial stability and even honesty of the government, and the hopelessly inefficient and inequitable system of taxation, tended to discourage the growth of a national debt of the British type. The 'Mississippi Bubble' of 1719-20, when thousands of people suffered heavy losses in a burst of frenzied speculation provoked by currency inflation and the hope of vast profits to be made in colonial trade (a French equivalent of the 'South Sea Bubble') had psychological effects which persisted long after its collapse. It strengthened the already widespread distrust in France of paper money and large centralized financial institutions. The effect of this is seen in the slowness with which French public finance developed and in its failure to keep pace with the growth of the country's industry and trade. Thus although the Paris *Bourse* opened in 1724 it was until 1780 robbed of much of its usefulness by the prohibition of 'forward' transactions. One of the most obvious symptoms of French backwardness in this respect was the large and even dominant role played by foreigners (Swiss, Germans or Scots) in the belated growth of the country's financial system.

The years before 1789 saw a distinct quickening in the tempo of financial development in France. The *Caisse d'Escompte*, a bank of issue and discount, was founded in 1776 (significantly enough by a Scot and a Swiss and in face of opposition, based on traditional hostility to usury, from both the Sorbonne and the *Parlement* of Paris). The *Loterie Royale* established in the same year issued from 1783 onwards interest-bearing tickets repayable in eight years—in effect a kind of treasury bond. Joint-stock companies began to develop after the middle of the century; and this movement was greatly accelerated from about 1780 onwards. In 1788 a Swiss set up the first French company to offer insurance

[1] C. H. Wilson, in *The New Cambridge Modern History*, vol. VII (London, 1957) p. 44.

against fire. In spite of all this, however, France approached the Revolution with a financial organization decidedly inferior to that of her rival across the Channel. Its deficiencies, combined with those of her arbitrary and inefficient system of taxation, meant that her government was never able during this period to mobilize and use effectively her great economic resources.

Progress in this field elsewhere in Europe was still slower, and was concentrated largely in the later decades of the century. Genoa continued to be, as in the past, a financial centre of some importance: on a much smaller scale she acted as a kind of Mediterranean Amsterdam, a source of capital and a centre of dealings in bullion imported from Latin America. In the second half of the century both France and the Habsburgs borrowed fairly heavily on the Genoese money market. Hamburg, one of the most rapidly developing cities in Europe, consolidated her position as a centre of banking and international financial dealings. She also developed from the 1720s onwards a considerable business in marine insurance; and her economic growth was probably helped by the fact that her political structure, under the new constitution introduced in 1712, was less oligarchical than that of any other German city-state. The bankers of Geneva, another town whose economic importance was rapidly increasing, were already investing on a considerable scale in England, France and even the Netherlands during the War of the Spanish Succession (1702–13). Their close contacts with Cadiz gave them an important position in the European bullion market; and in the later decades of the century their influence on the financial life of France in particular became marked. On a much smaller scale both Berne and Zürich lent and invested abroad. All of these were city-states with favourable geographical positions, cosmopolitan outlooks, and governments which made comparatively slight demands on their subjects.

In other parts of Europe governments with very different outlooks and ambitions, inspired by the success of Britain and the Netherlands, attempted to stimulate the development of their relatively backward territories and gain greater control of their resources by the creation of central banks. Thus the *Bank der Stadt Wien* was set up in 1706; the *Courantbank* in Copenhagen in 1736; and the *Königliche Giro- und Lehnbank* in Berlin in 1765. In the same way and for the same reasons Berlin equipped itself with a *bourse* in 1737, and one was set up in Vienna in 1771. Few of these institutions proved very stable or permanent. Lacking skilled direction, established in States where there were few liquid resources available for investment, exposed to constant manipulation by impoverished governments, most of them disappeared or were drastically modified soon after their foundation. The failure of the German States in particular to develop an effective financial organization is seen in the continuing importance in their economic life of the Jewish bankers and moneylenders (*Hofjuden*) who had for so long acted as the financial agents of their rulers and earned so much popular hatred by doing so.

In Eastern Europe the position was different again. In Poland and the Ottoman Empire banking continued to be controlled by a small number of wealthy individuals, hardly any of whom were Poles or Turks, and was in general hardly more than old-fashioned money-lending. Neither country possessed much which could be dignified by the title of financial institutions. In Russia the real history of banking began only in 1754, when a Noble Bank and a Commercial Bank were established simultaneously. The latter had ceased to function by 1770 and was wound up in 1782; the fact that it was concerned only with trade passing through St. Petersburg had in any case limited its importance. The Noble Bank, which had a longer life and greater significance, was created not to develop Russian industry and trade but simply to safeguard by loans the economic and therefore social position of the Russian landowning class. This it did with some success; by the end of the century it and its successors had lent the *dvoryanstvo* from public funds a sum greater than the entire annual government revenue. Its very success, however, meant that scarce financial resources were being diverted from constructive purposes to consumption, often of a wasteful and unnecessary kind, and to propping up the position of an unbusinesslike and increasingly functionless class. The later decades of the century also saw in Russia the issue by the government of paper money on a scale and with a success unparalleled elsewhere in Europe. By 1796 over 156 million roubles worth had been printed; though by then, thanks to excessive issues in the 1790s, the paper rouble was already at a considerable discount against coin.

Most of the economic ideas of this period are usually lumped together by historians under the general heading of 'mercantilism'. It seems increasingly doubtful whether this term is a very useful one, or even whether it has any precise meaning at all. How far mercantilism was ever a unified body of doctrine, how far it envisaged economic progress merely as a means of increasing the political and military power of the State, the exact significance in mercantilist thought of the precious metals—these and other questions remain without generally-accepted answers. It seems clear, moreover, that such answers as have been provided to them have often been influenced by the nationality of the writer and his almost inevitable tendency to emphasize evidence drawn from the history of his own State or area. Thus German historians have tended to stress the political, 'State-building', character of mercantilism, while those of the Atlantic countries have tended to give greater weight to its more purely economic characteristics.

Nevertheless it is possible to formulate a considerable number of propositions which would have been accepted by all or most of the writers whom historians have conspired to bring under the mercantilist umbrella. They would have agreed that a State should attempt to acquire a large population concentrated in its metropolitan territory, and that emigration should be encouraged only when it was clearly to the advantage of the State. Few or none of them had any clear conception of the difficulties which could be created by pressure of population, or of the workings of the law of diminishing returns.[1] They would also have agreed that the economic interests of a State were not likely to be best served by the concession of unlimited freedom of action to individuals, that it was often necessary to sacrifice the immediate interests of the latter to the security and greatness of the former. Hume summed up a good deal of contemporary opinion in his remark that there 'seems to be a kind of opposition betwixt the greatness of the State and the happiness of the subjects'. They would have agreed that States were essentially competitive, and that their economic and other interests could never be completely reconciled. (Though perhaps only a minority would have gone as far as the German writer T. L. Lau, who in 1719 argued that plague, war, famine and other disasters in a neighbouring State were to be welcomed as increasing the relative strength of one's own.) They would have agreed that economic wealth and political and military strength were indissolubly interwoven. Large revenues and a high taxable capacity allowed a State to maintain armies and men-of-war, protect its trade and acquire colonies, while this very

[1] See for example Montesquieu's claim that 'the earth always gives a yield in proportion to what is demanded of it ... flocks grow in numbers with those who rear them' (*Oeuvres Complètes* (Paris, 1949–51), vol. II, p. 1093). He shows elsewhere, however, some vague realization of the fact that over-population is a possibility and that the numbers of a people must be proportioned to the resources of the territory it occupies.

trade and colonial expansion, by a circular process, paid for still more powerful fighting forces. They would have united, finally, in a common tendency to stress problems of production and consumption, and in a common indifference to those of distribution. This more than anything else differentiates them from the 'classical' economists of the early nineteenth century—Ricardo, McCulloch, Senior and others.

Mercantilism, even if it can be spoken of as a unity, was not an inquiry into the abstract principles of wealth in the sense that Adam Smith's *Wealth of Nations* was. Very few mercantilist writers made any effort to provide a comprehensive discussion of the workings of an entire economic system. Those who did, such as Sir James Steuart (if he can be described as a mercantilist at all), fell far short of Smith in width of views and depth of analysis. The vast majority of the mercantilist writings of the eighteenth century dealt with limited and concrete issues, immediate and practical problems. They were very often produced by or on behalf of men whose own material interests were involved in the questions which they discussed. Mercantilism was thus a collection of attitudes and assumptions, almost an administrative technology, rather than a science of economics.

Nor was it the only current of thought to influence economic ideas during this period. The rigidities, the harshness and austerity which had marked them in the seventeenth century were now being tempered by the development, at least in Western Europe, of a more generous and realistic, almost liberal, attitude. Thus in England it was possible to find even before the end of the seventeenth century a number of eminent publicists—Coke, Barbon, North, Petty—who dared to point out the advantages of increasing consumption and a high standard of living as against the frugality, abstinence and low wages still so desired by most of their contemporaries. This tendency was continued in the eighteenth century in the writings of Mandeville, Hume and Steuart; it was probably strengthened by observation of the futility of the sumptuary laws which had been enacted in past generations in almost every part of Europe. Simultaneously can be seen the beginnings of a rejection of the general mercantilist belief in the desirability of reducing imports from foreign States and replacing them at almost any cost in efficiency by domestically produced substitutes. As early as 1696 Davenant, in one of the most pregnant passages in the economic literature of the age, argued that 'Wisdom is most commonly in the Wrong, when it pretends to direct Nature . . . it can never be Wise, to endeavour the introducing into a Country, either the Growth of any

Commodity, or any Manufacture, for which, nor the Soil, nor the General Bent of the People, is proper . . . a Trade forc'd in this Manner, brings no National Profit, but is Prejudicial to the Publick.'[1]

The group of French writers usually known as the Physiocrats struck another severe blow at the declining prestige of mercantilist attitudes. Centred around Quesnay, Turgot, the elder Mirabeau and later Dupont de Nemours, their influence was at its height from the mid-1750s to the mid-1770s, above all in France. They equalled or surpassed the mercantilists in the stress they laid on the need to increase population. However their conception of an ultimate economic balance between different States and different types of activity in the same State; their view of land as the supreme, indeed in the last analysis the only, source of wealth; and the attitude of implicit hostility to industry and above all commerce which followed from this—these were quite impossible to reconcile with mercantilism. Above all their belief in a large degree of economic freedom, embodied in the phrase *laissez-faire, laissez-passer*, their stressing of the advantages to be obtained by allowing more play to the economic forces and ambitions naturally present in any society, had little in common with the mercantilist spirit.

Thus Adam Smith's *Wealth of Nations* was not given, in 1776, to a world altogether unprepared for it. The ideas he attacked, though still very widespread and influential, had already been under hostile scrutiny for several decades.

In spite of the developments which have been described above the predominant impression produced by a study of the economy of Europe in this period is one of stability. An agriculture based, except in a few areas, on independent small-holders or estates cultivated by depressed or unfree peasants; an industry dominated by domestic workers and craft guilds; a seaborne trade little less at the mercy of wind and weather than in the days of Columbus—these do not make up a picture of rapid progress. Productive processes were still based almost entirely on the use of the most obvious and naturally occurring sources of power—streams, the winds, the muscles of men and animals—and of organic materials, most of all timber. Nothing could be a greater mistake than to think of this period only or mainly in terms of its technological innovators or its great entrepreneurs, its Watts and Cokes, its Townshends and Wilkinsons, its Carron and Anzin companies.

[1] *An Essay upon the East India Trade*, p. 34.

This impression of backwardness is strengthened by the scarcity during the century of the commodity most essential for the formulation of effective economic policies—information (see pp. 7–8). Until well into this period few governments knew with any approach to accuracy even the number of their subjects. Efforts to improve their knowledge were likely to encounter opposition as impious, or as the likely forerunner of new taxation. Thus in Britain a Bill for the taking of an annual census of population, though passed by the Commons, was rejected by the House of Lords in 1753. Nevertheless in spite of often fierce objections and the considerable administrative difficulties involved some advances were made. In Sweden, where registration of births, deaths and marriages had been compulsory from the 1680s, a census was taken in 1749 and an embryonic statistical office set up in 1756. In Denmark-Norway censuses, though not completely reliable ones, were taken in 1769 and 1789. In Spain the first attempt at an accurate estimate of the population was made by Uztáriz in his *Theorica y Practica de Commercio y Marina* (Madrid, 1724), and censuses were taken in 1768 and 1787. In Russia Catherine II ordered provincial governors, in April 1764, to take a thorough census of the population under their jurisdiction, to have accurate maps of the provinces drawn and to collect information about trade and agriculture. Even in remote Iceland a remarkably complete and thorough census was carried out as early as 1703. France above all, in this as in so many other respects, acted as a model for the rest of Europe, at least in the second half of the century. Several remarkably good censuses of individual provinces were taken by energetic and reforming intendants, for example in Provence in 1765. From 1772 onwards annual reports from each province of population changes during the preceding year were sent to Paris and collated there by a *Bureau de Statistique*. The slowly increasing importance attached by the age to knowledge of this kind is also seen in the efforts of private individuals to compile great collections of statistical information, for example in the attempt of Alexander Webster to enumerate the population of Scotland in 1755 or the vast mass of material assembled by the Abbé d'Expilly in his *Dictionnaire Géographique, Historique, et Politique, des Gaules et de la France* (Paris, 1762–70).

Economic information of various kinds, particularly relating to trade, was also collected by some governments on a fairly considerable scale. Thus in England the office of Inspector-General of Imports and Exports was created in 1696. Though the figures assembled by its holder and his subordinates soon ceased to reflect the state of British trade with any accuracy (see p. 7) the desirability of collecting statistics of this kind was now more clearly recognized than ever before in the country's history. In France a *Bureau du Commerce* with somewhat similar functions was established in 1713. Moreover the later decades of the century saw in many countries efforts to carry out extensive surveys of landownership, very often with the intention of using them to reform or extend the system of taxation. Turgot, for example, attempted a survey of this kind in the French province of the Limousin when he was intendant there in 1761–64; and in 1763 a royal decree called for a similar effort on a national scale. Each French parish or commune, it was hoped, would henceforth be able to preserve in its archives a plan showing details of this kind for the area. Similar efforts, on a considerable scale, were made in Spain in the 1760s and in the Habsburg dominions from 1785 onwards. An earlier survey had been carried out in Savoy-Piedmont in 1728–38, and a very large one begun in Russia in 1750 had been extended to nearly half the country by the end of the century.

Even when allowance is made for all this, however, it is clear that essential economic information of many kinds was unobtainable in the eighteenth century.[1] It is equally clear that governments too often lacked the will as well as the ability to collect it. In Great Britain, so relatively advanced in other respects, no census was taken until 1801; and even then its results were not completely reliable. In Russia the Minister of Finance complained as late as 1808 that no effort had ever been made to calculate the country's balance of trade with any accuracy.

The still partially medieval character of eighteenth-century economic life can be illustrated in other ways. The idea of active competition between manufacturers or merchants as a normal and desirable thing was slow to develop; and governments often attempted to prevent price-cutting. Ideas which had taken root in a pre-capitalist and pre-industrial age, such as that of the 'just price', still retained much of their former vitality. Thus Savary des Bruslons, the author of the greatest commercial handbook of the age, *Le Parfait Négociant*, was still able in the 1724 edition to argue that the price of a commodity should be determined by what it was just that the vendor should gain. This idea

[1] A good example is the list of wildly conflicting estimates (or guesses) of the public revenue of Spain at different dates in the 1760s and 1770s which can be found in W. Coxe, *Memoirs of the Kings of Spain of the House of Bourbon* (London, 1815), vol. III, p. 384.

was repeated by a German writer as late as 1768. Nor were such feelings mere literary flourishes: they could inspire quite effective legal or administrative action. Thus in the summer of 1721 one of the greatest aristocrats in France, the Duc de la Force, was convicted of the traditional economic offence of 'engrossing' (the hoarding of goods in the expectation of a rise in their price) as the result of the discovery in a Paris monastery of a large stock of spices belonging to him. The *Parlement* of Paris sternly ordered him to be more careful in his future behaviour; and three of his collaborators were fairly severely punished.[1] A similar rejection of the capitalist spirit is seen in the almost universal tendency for resources to be squandered, as they had been for centuries, in conspicuous expenditure on buildings, plate, clothes, jewellery and paintings. This tendency was almost as marked in countries such as France, where opportunities for lucrative investment in trade and industry existed, as in those such as Poland where they were much more difficult to find. Comspicuous consumption of a traditional and economically irrational kind can be seen most strikingly of all, however, in the maintenance by wealthy men almost everywhere of huge households of servants and hangers-on, many or even most of whom had no real function. Inequality between rich and poor in eighteenth-century Europe showed itself even more in the consumption of services (or alleged services) than in that of material goods. These inflated and overgrown housholds (many of whose members received food and somewhere to sleep but little or no wages) were in the main the product of two factors. One was the feeling, impossible to justify in economic terms, that the great and wealthy man must show his importance in his style of life, that he must cut a public figure which reflected his status and importance. The other was a belief, surviving from the Middle Ages and still strong almost everywhere, that the rich had a moral obligation to provide subsistence in this way for the poor, by offering them employment, however fictitious, and maintenance, however scanty. The result could be seen at its most extreme in the troops of serfs to be found in the country houses of great Russian landowners and in the crowds of unemployed or underemployed servants who lounged around the palaces of Spanish and Neapolitan grandees. 'The profession of 15,000 people at Naples is to run ahead of a carriage', commented a foreign observer in 1786, 'and of 15,000 others to run behind.'[2] Nothing could be a more

[1] A. Jobez, *La France sous Louis XV* (Paris, 1864–73), vol. II, pp. 266–9.
[2] Quoted in M. Vaussard, *Daily Life in Eighteenth-century Italy* (London, 1962), p. 86.

flagrant infringement of the spirit of economic rationality, of measurement and calculation, which from its foothold in some parts of Western Europe was slowly in the next century to conquer the entire continent.

The same traditionalism is seen in the fact that a prejudice against life insurance, a feeling that the life of one of God's creatures should not be made the object of a wager, was still quite widespread in France (and no doubt in other countries) in the later years of the century. Some of the most important work of the period on population problems, moreover, was done by clergymen attracted by the fact that demography seemed to provide new arguments for religious belief. Thus William Derham wrote his *Physicotheology, or a Demonstration of the Being and Attributes of God from His Works of Creation* (London, 1713), the first important general study in English of population questions, as a statement of the 'argument from design' for the existence of God. The same is true to some extent of the more famous J. P. Süssmilch, whose *Die göttliche Ordnung in den Veränderungen des menschlichen Geschlechts* (Berlin, 1741) was used extensively half a century later by Malthus.

The most important of all these traditional prejudices in its economic effects was the continuing strong feeling against the lending of money at interest. In Catholic countries this often took the form of an outright prohibition of 'usury' which, though increasingly difficult to enforce effectively, was still far from meaningless. In France, for example, a group of bankers at Angoulême failed in 1745 to recover by legal process money owed them since, it was held, they had themselves by charging interest on the loan broken the law. It was only with the issue of the new Austrian law code of 1787 that the formal prohibition of interest ceased in the Habsburg dominions; and even then the maximum rate was limited to 6 per cent. In Britain throughout the century, although the charging of interest on loans was permitted, the rate was similarly limited—in this case to 5 per cent. The influence of this restriction on the industrial development of the country is still a controversial subject among historians[1]; but it may have been considerable.

The forces making for economic change and progress in the eighteenth century must not be undervalued: in England at least the national income may have trebled between the 1680s and the 1780s. Nevertheless it is easy to exaggerate their scope and immediate effect. If we attempt to see the period as it appeared to those who lived in it, particularly to

[1] The best discussion is L. S. Pressnell, 'The Rate of Interest in the Eighteenth Century', in *Studies in the Industrial Revolution Presented to T. S. Ashton* (London, 1960).

those who were not members of the educated or privileged classes, it is impossible to envisage it as one dominated by banks, stock exchanges, large factories or great trading companies. The horse-drawn wagons moving painfully over wretched roads, the sailing-ships sometimes delayed for weeks or months by contrary winds, the domestic workers at their bench or spinning-wheel, the unique social prestige still attached almost everywhere to the ownership of land—all these show us that we are still in many respects closer to the thirteenth century than to the nineteenth.

V

Government and Administration

During the eighteenth century few European States possessed efficient administrations. For this inefficiency there were several reasons. The governmental machines of the period were defective because nearly all of them were operated, to varying extents, by men who were not professional administrators; and because nearly all of them depended on the help of unofficial or semi-official bodies of various kinds. They were also weakened by the fact that the officials whom they employed, as well as being often few in numbers, were as a rule inadequately trained and poorly and irregularly paid.

The amateur and semi-official character of much eighteenth-century administration was bound up with the nature of society as an aggregate of traditional groupings and institutions (see pp. 28ff.). It seemed reasonable, and was often economical of money and administrative manpower, to allow groups and institutions of this kind not merely a high degree of autonomy in the regulation of their internal affairs but

BIBLIOGRAPHY. There are very few studies of the administration of the European States during this period on anything more than a national scale. The best-known is Sir Ernest Barker, *The Development of Public Services in Western Europe, 1660–1930* (Oxford, 1944), which is intelligent but in some ways superficial. It deals only with Britain, France and Prussia. On the Prussian administrative system a good deal is available: the student may consult R. A. Dorwart, *The Administrative Reforms of Frederick William I of Prussia* (Cambridge, Mass., 1953) or the less convincing H. Rosenberg, *Bureaucracy, Aristocracy and Autocracy: the Prussian experience, 1660–1815* (Cambridge, Mass., 1958). The latter does not supersede the important long article of W. L. Dorn, 'The Prussian bureaucracy in the eighteenth century', to be found in the *Political Science Quarterly* for 1931 and 1932. W. Mertineit, *Die Fridericianische Verwaltung in Ostpreussen* (Heidelberg, 1958) is an able treatment of a limited area; while the most recent studies of a more general kind are W. Hubatsch, *Frederick the Great: absolution and administration* (London, 1975) and H. C. Johnson, *Frederick the Great and his Officials* (New York and London, 1975). There is an excellent recent discussion of the government of one of the smaller German states in T. C. W. Blanning, *Reform and Revolution in Mainz, 1743–1803* also a large share in the execution of government policies which particularly concerned them. Where this was done such bodies might become for certain purposes virtually branches of the central administration, and their officers practically government officials.

Thus in France, where this process was carried to remarkable lengths, the University of Paris was entrusted by an *arrêt* of 1725 (which summarized much seventeenth-century legislation on the subject) with a large degree of control of the book trade. Similarly the weights and measures used by Paris shopkeepers were checked, not by government officials, but by the *corps des épiciers*, one of the most important guilds of the city. Corporate bodies, moreover, often became intermediaries between their members and the State in the allocation and collection of taxes. The University of Paris acted in this way after it was subjected to the *capitation* (a graduated poll-tax) in 1695 and the *dixième* (a tax on incomes) in 1710, deciding on its own initiative how much should be paid by different grades of teacher. In the city the collection of the *capitation* was supervised by municipal rather than royal officials. In a somewhat similar way most towns in Castile paid the government a fixed sum in respect of the *millones* (a kind of excise on meat, wine and other commodities) and collected the tax for themselves; while in 1703 Philip V of Spain ordered that all merchants and artisans in his dominions should become members of the appropriate guilds, since only through the latter could they be taxed with reasonable ease and efficiency.

In Britain there can be seen, in a rather different form, a tendency for functions of the greatest importance to the government to be entrusted,

(Cambridge, 1974). For France the classic work of Alexis de Tocqueville, *The Ancien Régime and the Revolution* (paperback ed., London, 1966) is still well worth reading: more specialized and recent studies are V. R. Gruder, *The Royal Provincial Intendants: a governing élite in eighteenth-century France* (Ithaca, 1968); J. D. Hardy, Jr., *Judicial Politics in the Old Regime: the Parlement of Paris during the Regency* (Baton Rouge, 1968); M. Antoine, *Le Conseil du Roi sous le règne de Louis XV* (Paris, 1970); Y. Durand, *Les Fermiers-Généraux au XVIIIe siècle* (Paris, 1971); and J. R. Bosher, *French Finances, 1770–1795* (Cambridge, 1970). For the Habsburg territories many of the books on Maria Theresa and Joseph II mentioned on pp. 131–2 are useful. An important specialized study is H. E. Strakosch, *State Absolutism and the Rule of Law: the struggle for the codification of civil law in Austria, 1753–1811* (Sydney, 1967). The best discussion of the administrative reforms of Catherine II is to be found in the articles assembled in a special issue of *Canadian Slavic Studies*, vol. IV, no. 3 (1970). On English administrative history during this period relatively little work has hitherto been done. However, W. R. Ward, *The English Land-Tax in the Eighteenth Century* (Oxford, 1953) and J. E. D. Binney, *British Public Finance and Administration, faute de mieux*, to amateur administrators. By 1698, for example, the Crown had lost control of the appointment of the commissioners set up a few years earlier for the collection in each borough and county of the land-tax, then by far the most important direct tax in the country. After that date the holders of these appointments were in effect nominated by the Members of Parliament for the area concerned. This undoubtedly contributed to the steadily declining efficiency with which the tax was collected in the eighteenth century and helped to impede the introduction of new forms of direct taxation.

The autonomy enjoyed by organizations of many kinds intermediate between the individual and the State could thus be of great administrative significance. It allowed the State to leave to such organizations functions which to modern eyes are essentially governmental, but which as yet they could perform with greater efficiency than the central government. All too often, however, guilds, chartered towns, universities, legal corporations, even village communes, opposed administrative progress. Too often they used their rights and privileges to place obstacles in the way of the levelling and centralizing efforts on which that progress clearly depended. The experience of Turgot in his efforts to abolish guild privileges in France in the 1770s, or of the Holy Roman Emperor Joseph II in his struggle with the privileged institutions of the Austrian Netherlands during the last years of his reign, were only the most important of many illustrations of this fact.

During this period a number of European States attempted with varying success to provide their bureaucrats with some systematic training and thus equip themselves with a *cadre* of competent officials. This policy was pursued most consistently in Prussia. There Frederick William I founded chairs of 'cameral studies' in two universities for the purpose; and from 1723 onwards young recruits (*Auskultatoren*) were admitted to various branches of the administration for practical training. This system was continued by his son Frederick II, who in 1770 set up a commission to examine such men at the end of their studies; while in 1792 his successor Frederick William II provided that they should also be examined before beginning their training. But neither these measures nor the repeated efforts of rulers such as Frederick William I and Joseph II to punish lazy or corrupt subordinates could guarantee an adequate supply of good and upright officials.

1774-1792 (Oxford, 1958) are detailed studies of importance, while M. A. Thomson, *The Secretaries of State, 1681-1782* (Oxford, 1932) is a very useful book of a wider-ranging kind.

Inadequate training and ineffective central control account therefore for some of the defects of eighteenth-century administration. Equally important was the fact that many officials purchased their posts, which were thus regarded by them, and by the State, as a kind of private property of which they could not be deprived without compensation. The sale of government offices was particularly widespread, and has been most intensively studied, in France. There the growth of a wealthy middle class eager for the security and social prestige which official rank could give created a large and profitable market. The last decades of the reign of Louis XIV saw the establishment on a hitherto unknown scale of the practice of creating new government posts, or even entire new classes of posts, merely for the sake of the money to be obtained by selling them. It continued to be indulged in, in spite of the damage it did to the administrative machine and in the long run to the government's financial position, until the end of this period. Sales of offices, though usually on a smaller scale than in France, could be found in many European States. Even in Prussia under the incorruptible and efficiency-minded Frederick William I every official newly appointed or promoted to a higher rank had to make a contribution to military funds. Some offices in Prussia were also sold outright, while officials who had been dismissed might be reinstated in return for a money payment.

The selling of government offices was justified by contemporaries on various grounds. In particular it was argued that it ensured that important (and thus expensive) appointments were held by men rich enough to be above ordinary financial temptations. The practice was also defended as a means by which the merchant class, still without real political power in most States, could play some part in the business of government. It was impossible, however, to reconcile with any modern system of administration, and in the last decades of this period was increasingly recognized as an abuse.

Eighteenth-century officials, in central and still more in local administration, also differed from their present-day counterparts in that many of them did not receive fixed and regular salaries. They were often paid instead, in whole or in part, by fees which they levied on private individuals for the performance of specific services. The fact that the amount of these fees often depended on the avarice or disinterestedness of the official concerned, who might himself be struggling to pay off liabilities he had contracted by buying or even accepting his office, created opportunities for oppression and over-charging which were not easy to eliminate. A good example of this is provided by the administration of the Tolbooth, the prison of Edinburgh, in the later eighteenth century. There a woman released in August 1787, after a short imprisonment for a debt of 6s. 6d., had to pay fees of £1 1s. 10½d. before she was allowed to leave. More striking still was the case of a debtor imprisoned six months earlier who, though he spent only two days in gaol, found himself confronted on his release with a demand for £17 6s. 5½d. in fees. The gaoler replied to complaints by pointing out that he had no salary and that his post was burdened with the payment of annuities and other unavoidable expenses to the value of about £70 a year.[1]

What functions were these eighteenth-century administrative systems intended to perform? In the first place they had to maintain so far as possible public order in the territories which they controlled or claimed to control. This was often far from easy; and the law in the eighteenth century was in general poorly observed by the standards of our own day. No government possessed any real equivalent of a modern police force. When riots or serious large-scale disorder of any kind threatened it was normally necessary to fall back on soldiers or some paramilitary force if they were not to get out of hand. This was a clumsy and inflexible method of control. Soldiers were not always easily available in sufficient numbers, and in the pre-railway age often could not be moved quickly from the area where they were stationed to that in which they were needed. It is true that discontent and disorder could to some extent be predicted. The classic type of eighteenth-century riot was sparked off by bad harvests and high food prices, the result of unfavourable weather, which generated mob attacks on mills and warehouses and the forcible seizure of the contents to be sold at a 'fair' price. The ability of governments and their officials to foresee trouble of this kind before it happened was often an important factor in preventing things getting out of hand. But in the larger cities in particular riot could be generated by many different causes. Even a spectacular execution might have this result. Thus when the celebrated forger (and Anglican clergyman) Dr. Dodd was hanged at Tyburn in 1777 the likelihood of disorder was considered so high that 2,000 soldiers were held in readiness in Hyde Park to deal with any emergency. No eighteenth-century government found any satisfactory answer to the problem of public order: that it was an endemic and serious one can be seen by a mere enumeration of the most important of the riots and similar outbreaks which occurred during a few years in the 1760s and

[1] J. Howard, *An Account of the Principal Lazarettos in Europe* (Warrington, 1789), p. 76, n.

early 1770s. In Madrid in 1766 popular demonstrations forced Charles III of Spain to dismiss his chief adviser, the Italian Squillace. In London there were serious riots in 1765 and 1768; those of the latter year, provoked by the political conflicts centring on John Wilkes and the refusal of the House of Commons to admit him to membership (see p. 143) were particularly dangerous. In Moscow in 1771 a devastating outbreak of plague led to widespread disorder and forced the government to take extraordinary measures to reassert its authority. In France in 1775 serious grain riots, the *guerres des farines*, spread to Paris from the surrounding area and had to be repressed by military measures. And throughout these years, of course, normal government and control by constituted and legal authority were breaking down over much of Britain's colonial empire in America. Nor was this decade, from the mid-1760s to the mid-1770s, abnormally lawless by comparison with the rest of the century.

The second great function of any eighteenth-century administration was to raise by taxation or other means enough revenue to allow the machinery of government, and above all its armed forces, to function with reasonable efficiency. This was also difficult to achieve; partly because the financial demands of governments were tending to increase in an age of large-scale warfare and increasingly expensive armies and navies, but above all because taxation systems, particularly in the first half of the century, were so irrational and inflexible. In general taxation was neither equitably assessed nor efficiently collected, with the result that governments found their revenues inadequate and that many of their subjects laboured under a strong and justified sense of grievance. Over much of Catholic Europe the Church paid less than its share, and continued to do so until the end of this period. In most countries the nobility and the landowners were favoured: in some, such as Hungary, Poland and to a lesser degree France, outrageously so. In many others, for example France and Lombardy, the towns tended to be favoured at the expense of the countryside. Moreover fiscal systems, even when good in theory, often had their effectiveness reduced by the existence of a complex structure of local rights and exemptions. The result was marked and even brutal inequity. Thus, for example, Necker, the Controller-General of Finance, estimated at the beginning of the 1780s that a Breton paid in all forms of taxation little more than 12 livres each year as against the 64 livres which had to be found by each inhabitant of the Île de France. Even if allowance is made for the greater wealth of the latter the disparity is still gross. Often differences of this kind can be explained in terms of difficulties of communication, especially in the larger States. There was a fairly general tendency (as in the example just quoted) for areas near the capital, where the government's hand lay relatively heavy, to pay considerably more than remote frontier ones where the effective authority of the central administration was reduced merely by the effects of distance. Sometimes, again, areas which could plead no legal privilege might be able to avoid paying their full share of taxation if they had some political leverage at their disposal. Thus the western counties of England were under-assessed for land-tax during this period mainly, it seems, because they were over-represented in the House of Commons.

The taxes themselves differed widely in different States. They might fall chiefly on land, as in the case of the *taille* in France or the land-tax in England; or on articles of general consumption, as with the Prussian and English excise duties and the French *gabelle* (a complicated and highly unfair tax on salt); or on individuals or households, as with the poll-tax in Russia and the *capitation* in France; or on imports from abroad, as with the customs duties of which every government made use. Whatever their nature, however, the burden which they imposed was almost everywhere more or less unfairly distributed. The one important exception, or partial exception, to this rule is to be found in Great Britain. She alone among the great powers of Europe possessed a politically privileged class which was willing, not merely to accept fairly heavy taxation (above all in the form of the land-tax) but even, through its dominance of Parliament, to impose such taxation on itself. This fact is not easy to explain; but it did much to make possible the strength of the country's fiscal system, and hence of her military and political position, during this period.

In methods of collection the most obvious defect was the common though by no means universal practice of tax-farming. Though it was unknown or unimportant in many of the great States of Europe—Britain, Russia or Prussia—it was practised during this period in some of the wealthiest parts of the continent, notably in France and until 1770 in Lombardy. Reduced to its essentials it meant that the State delegated to wealthy individuals or groups of individuals, in return for a lump-sum payment, the right to collect certain specified taxes. The greater the State's need of ready money, the less favourable the terms it could expect to make with the tax-farmers it employed. Not only did the practice enable a handful of wealthy men to make great profits and deprive the governments concerned of part of their revenues; it was also an implicit admission by these governments that they did not yet possess adequate administrative machines. Moreover even in States where the taxes were not farmed their collection was often in the hands of men who were not officials and who were under only a very moderate degree of control by the central government. Thus in Russia the effective raising of taxation depended on the co-operation with the government of the landowning class. Similarly in England the collection of the land-tax was in the hands of receivers-general for each county (or for groups or subdivisions of counties) who were usually country gentlemen and were paid for their services by being given a commission on the sums they collected.

Methods of this kind inevitably involved local variations in the efficiency of the machinery of collection, and thereby added a further element of unfairness to those which already afflicted most eighteenth-century fiscal systems. Nearly all such systems, moreover, suffered from two other important defects—the tendency of assessments, once made, to remain unchanged for decades, even generations; and the difficulty, often the impossibility, of collecting the arrears of payments which constantly tended to accumulate. The first of these is particularly striking to modern eyes. In Languedoc, to give only one of many possible illustrations, the distribution of the burden of taxation between the different dioceses which made up the province had been fixed in 1530 and was still essentially unchanged in 1789. Within dioceses the tax load was allocated between towns and villages on the basis of registers of landownership which were now hopelessly out of date: the diocese of Toulouse, for example, used throughout this period one compiled in 1551 and only one diocese, Narbonne, tried to modernize its arrangements in this respect during the eighteenth century.[1] When all these factors are considered it is not perhaps surprising that only two major States during this period could claim to be in a really strong financial position. One of these was Prussia, where for much of the century administrative efficiency and governmental economy were more marked than anywhere else in Europe. The other was Great Britain, where taxable capacity was increasing rapidly and where government borrowing was easier than in any other major country.

Another generally recognized function of eighteenth-century governments was that of increasing the wealth of their subjects. 'Prosperity by compulsion', as one historian has called it, was an objective all rulers

[1] G. Frêche, *Toulouse et la région Midi-Pyrénées au siècle des lumières (vers 1670–1789)* (n.p., ?1975), pp. 498–500.

of the period wished to attain, the 'empirical despots' of the first half of the century as much as the 'enlightened despots' who succeeded them. If achieved it meant an increase in the pool of wealth on which the government might draw by taxation or borrowing, and a consequent increase in the strength (which usually meant in practice the military strength) of the State concerned. Power, not welfare, was the guiding principle of eighteenth-century politics. The domestic policies of every country were influenced, often dominated, by the need to maintain and if possible strengthen its position in a system of ruthlessly competitive States.

The idea of State-induced prosperity as a necessary stepping-stone to power was most enthusiastically accepted in the poor and backward countries of East and Central Europe. It underlay the ambitious schemes of economic development which Peter I of Russia attempted to realize (see pp. 84–5). It can be seen in an almost equally pronounced form in the policies of the rulers of Austria and Prussia—in the grant to Trieste and Fiume of the status of free ports in 1719 and 1729; in the creation of the Ostend Company for trade with the East in 1722; in the considerable efforts made under Maria Theresa to improve the internal communications of the Habsburg territories; in the attempts of both Frederick William I and his son to develop the industries and increase the agricultural production of Prussia. In particular it was accepted by almost everyone that it was a duty of governments to increase if possible the populations of the countries they ruled; a growing population seemed the surest of all signs of a well-governed State. Thus it is not surprising to find Frederick William I and Frederick II doing their utmost to encourage the colonization by immigrants of uncultivated areas in Brandenburg and Pomerania; Catherine II of Russia striving, with some success, to attract German and Swiss settlers to the Volga basin and South Russia; Joseph II forbidding emigration from his dominions and encouraging immigration to them; and earlier in the century a Grand Duke of Tuscany bringing Greeks from the Peloponnese to populate the Maremma (a swampy coastal area of Tuscany). This emphasis on population as the greatest single foundation of a State's wealth had other effects. It underlay the stress laid by so much eighteenth-century economic theory on the preservation and development of labour-intensive industries, which would provide plentiful employment, on preventing as far as possible the export of food (since a cheap and plentiful food supply was correctly seen as the greatest single encouragement to population growth) and on encouraging the export of goods with a high labour content. It also meant that at least in the more developed parts of Europe governments made more or less systematic efforts to help their subjects avoid starvation in times of harvest failure and food shortage. In France particularly this type of paternalism worked with considerable effect. In Montauban, for example, there was from 1723 onwards an official *magasin du Roi* capable of storing 3,000 quintals of grain. This was intended primarly to supply seed to needy cultivators; but in times of shortage it also acted as a source of supply for the bakers of the city. When acute crisis threatened the area millers were compelled to surrender for public use stocks of imported grain held in the nearby port of Moissac; or if necessary the local intendants might import grain on government account for distribution to those in need. Thus in 1752 considerable quantities were obtained in this way for the *généralités* of Auch and Montauban. At Lyons, again, in the very bad winter of 1788–89, the lieutenant-general of police organized the public distribution of coal to the poor. He also kept four mills on the river Rhone at work to supply flour for the city by providing men who laboured day and night to break the ice which would have otherwise made it impossible for them to function. 'It can be said,' wrote a contemporary, 'that without his vigilance we should have lacked everything or could have obtained it only at high cost.' In essentially the same way the government of the electorate of Mainz during the severe shortage in 1771–72 bought grain in Poland and distributed it to the population of the city at moderate prices. When the Rhine burst its banks in 1784 and the Oder did the same in the following year, causing severe flooding in different parts of his territories, Frederick II provided from state resources substantial sums for the relief of distress.[1] These are merely isolated and almost random illustrations of an attitude shared to some degree by every eighteenth-century government. However limited and short-sighted their economic and political vision, however ineffective and rudimentary their administrative machines, all of them could see the advantages of ruling a wealthy and populous (and therefore contented and docile) State. In Great Britain and the Dutch Republic, where a high degree of government supervision and initiative in economic life was neither so necessary nor so practicable as further east, ideas of 'prosperity by compulsion' and official paternalism were less

[1] D. Ligou, *Montauban à la fin de l'ancien régime et aux débuts de la Révolution, 1787–1794* (Paris, 1958), pp. 176–7; Blanning (*see* Bibliography, p. 101), p. 113; L. Trenard, *Lyon de l'Encyclopédie au Préromantisme* (Paris, 1958), vol. I, p. 235. Hubatsch (*see* Bibliography, p. 101), p. 231.

wholeheartedly applied. There the assumption that the government had a duty to increase the wealth of the State by all means in its power was as fully accepted as in the Habsburg lands or Prussia; but by the middle of the century it was beginning to be widely felt that it could do this better by reducing than by increasing the scale of its interference with economic life. By then, moreover, the liberalizing ideas of the Physiocrats (see p. 95) were beginning to take shape in France. By the 1770s they were exerting, through important officials such as Freiherr von Gebler and Count Zinzendorf, some influence even on the economic policies of the Habsburg government.

Side by side with these fiscal and economic functions eighteenth-century governments had of course to maintain a judicial system, or at least a number of central law courts. The status and political importance of the judicial system varied widely in different States. In England it was independent of the administration (except that the Lord Chancellor and the other law officers of the Crown were appointed for political reasons and were normally displaced when a change of government occurred). Judges, from 1714 onwards, held office while they were of good behaviour, and could not be dismissed on political grounds. A whole series of leading cases in constitutional law during this period (the most important was that which established in 1763 the illegality of general warrants, i.e. warrants for the arrest of persons not individually named) showed that their independence was a reality.[1] The central courts of law in England indeed to a large extent controlled the actions of the administration, not because they were part of it but because, by the use of well-established *certiorari* and *quo warranto* procedures, they could compel officials to justify in terms of the existing law their actions or omissions to act. No other country possessed a judicial system so independent and so respected; and its existence is one of the keys to the divergence in constitutional development between England and almost all the other States of Europe during this period. In France also the *parlements* (see p. 46) enjoyed increasing prestige and popularity from the 1760s onward. They also acted as a check, though a much less efficient and reliable one than the English law courts, on the activities of the bureaucracy. In particular the *Parlement* of Paris, by using its right to issue 'remonstrances' against royal decrees, could hamper the execution of measures which it disliked or which were

[1] At least in England. It is difficult to make such a claim with equal confidence where the Scottish and Irish judges are concerned.

imcompatible with what it chose to regard as the French constitution. The French and English judicial systems differed enormously, not least in their size. The *Parlement* of Paris had 240 judges in 1715; and most of the provincial *parlements* had about 100. These, combined with the four royal courts of appeal which were not formally *parlements* but had some independence in fact, meant that at the highest level there were about 1,200 royal judges in eighteenth-century France. In England the number presiding in the central courts of common law and chancery (not allowing for the more specialized Admiralty and Church courts) seldom exceeded fifteen. Nevertheless there were some important underlying similarities. In both States the judicial system, at least in its higher ranks, was a conservative force. In both it restricted or attempted to restrict, for good or evil, the freedom of action of the administration.

In Eastern and Central Europe the position was quite different. In the great States of the West, England, France or Spain, it was possible to claim, with varying degrees of truth, that a constitution existed. In each there was, it could be argued, a structure of rights and established procedures which would be upheld at least to some extent by the law courts and which could not, in practice, be easily overridden by an autocrat or a great official. Even in France this claim was not altogether justified; in Eastern Europe it was even more difficult to make. In Russia, to a large extent in Prussia, and in the Habsburg hereditary lands if they are considered as a whole, the administrative system was the real constitution. In all these States the judiciary, at least in its higher ranks, was a department of the administration. In them it had evolved largely as part of the machinery of absolute government. It is true that the eighteenth century saw almost everywhere in Europe an increased emphasis on the idea of governments as applying and controlled by law (which was equated with reason). This idea enjoyed growing influence in Eastern Europe as elsewhere. It helped to popularize there the conception of the judicial system as a regulating element within the administrative machine and to stimulate attempts to give it greater independence. Thus in 1748 Frederick II forbade administrative bodies in Prussia to interfere in judicial proceedings. In the following year the judicial functions of the central government in the Habsburg hereditary provinces were for the first time clearly separated from its administrative ones when the *Directorium in publicis et cameralibus* was set up to supervise administration and finance while a quite distinct new organ, the *Oberste Justizstelle* (in effect a combined Ministry of Justice and Supreme Court), was established to oversee judical matters. Throughout this period, however, the administration of the law in Eastern and Central Europe continued to be essentially a branch of the administration in general. Administrative bodies tended to acquire judicial or semijudicial functions (the Senate in Russia under Peter I is a good example). In Prussia, and above all in the Habsburg territories, legal training continued to be required for appointment to the higher ranks of all branches of the administration to a degree unequalled anywhere in the West.

In all parts of Europe the law itself, as distinct from its administration, left much to be desired. Almost everywhere the need for codification, for the law to be expressed simply and comprehensively, for redundant and outdated legislation to be amended or repealed, was great and increasingly felt. This was especially the case in France. There a number of differing legal systems, based in the main on Roman law in the south and on customary or common law in the north and centre, provoked an understandable demand for a unified and simple code—a demand expressed in many of the *cahiers* of 1789. The position was even worse in Russia. There, until the end of this period, many decrees (*ukazy*) were issued without being printed or published, especially if they related to purely private or local issues. Moreover many government departments issued orders which had the force of law. Commissions to codify this chaotic system were set up by Peter I in 1700, 1714 and 1720, and another by the Empress Elizabeth thirty years later. Yet another, the most famous of all, which included elected representatives of the nobility, the towns, and the other strata of Russian society, was assembled by Catherine II in 1767. None of these had any practical result; and the chaos of Russian legislation was reduced to order only in the early nineteenth century in the great work of codification inspired by M. M. Speranskii. The eighteenth century saw several more successful efforts of this kind elsewhere in Europe. In the Habsburg hereditary lands the position was as complex as anywhere in Europe, since there prevailed in them a complex mixture of Roman and customary law with many regional variations, a chaotic situation which impeded economic development, led to endless jurisdictional disputes between competing courts and even made it difficult to transfer officials from one province to another. Here the ministers of Maria Theresa began the codification of civil law in 1753, though the process was not complete until 1811; and in 1766 an important effort to systematise criminal law, the *Codex Theresianus*, was produced. Most impressive of all in many ways was the great Prussian code, the *Preussisches Allgemeines Landrecht*, promulgated in 1794. Over much of the continent, however, the demand that the law be made more comprehensible and accessible to the ordinary man remained unsatisfied.

Nor was its administration appreciably improved. Slow-moving, expensive and tradition-bound, the law courts remained almost everywhere one of the aspects of government most frequently complained of and most resistant to change. The attempts of a number of autocratic rulers to improve their procedure and increase the speed with which cases were decided had little effect. This was largely because hardly any eighteenth-century government was willing to spend money on a considerable scale on improving the machinery of justice. The governmental reforms of the period were almost all aimed, directly or indirectly, at increasing the military and political power of the State, at developing its capacity to survive and to expand territorially. States, it was quite correctly believed, fell or were defeated because they were weak, not because they failed to achieve some ideal standard in the administration of justice. Judicial reform thus appeared something of a luxury, admirable in principle but with a less pressing claim on available resources than the improvement of the armed forces or the development of economic life.

Moreover it must be remembered that underlying the structure of royal and State justice which has been briefly discussed in the preceding paragraphs there existed an enormous network of seigneurial or, to use a somewhat meaningless word, 'feudal', justice. Over much of Europe landlords had the right to hold courts of their own, to compel their peasants to use these courts for certain purposes, and to profit from the process. In France, again the State in which this aspect of eighteenth-century life has been most intensively studied, such courts were still very numerous and often very burdensome. In Brittany (admittedly the most 'feudal' of French provinces, and hardly typical) about nine-tenths of all judicial business was still transacted in seigneurial courts, of which there were about 2,500 in existence as late as 1789—an average of two to each parish. There were at the outbreak of the Revolution about 70–80,000 full and part-time judges in courts of this kind in France as a whole. In Prussia the local judicial functions of the landowner were one of the foundations of his power, indeed of the entire structure of the Prussian State. Elsewhere in Germany the old assembly courts of the village communities (*Landgerichte*) had been largely taken over by nobles by the end of the sixteenth century; and the Thirty Years War had seen noble influence extended in many cases over the comparable courts of the towns. In Russia the land courts, the only significant judicial institutions at the village level and important instruments of social and political control, were completely controlled by the land-owning class.[1] In Scotland the heritable jurisdictions which had hitherto allowed their owners to control and punish their tenants and humbler neighbours were abolished only in 1747, when regality courts and heritable stewartries and sheriffdoms were swept away. The whole question of grassroots justice of this sort, traditional, class-dominated and intensely local in outlook and operation, is too complex and has been too little studied to be entered into here in any detail. It should never be forgotten, however, how many Europeans in this period had their only first-hand experience of law and legal processes in courts of this kind. Governments sometimes made efforts to ensure that minimum standards of competence and fairness were enforced in the administration of seigneurial justice. In 1680 Louis XIV, for example, demanded that judges in the 'high' seigneurial courts (those from which appeals were taken directly to the *parlements*) should have received at least two years of legal training. But there were many parts of Europe in which the justice which impinged directly on the ordinary man in the course of his daily life was controlled only very imperfectly or not at all by the ruler and the State. Moreover the noble landowner's position as a judge or a court-owner tended to endow him also with a wide variety of police powers with regard to public health, morals, fire precautions and economic life generally in the locality concerned.

A demand for better administration of the law can be seen developing during this period in several countries, especially from the 1760s onwards. The publication in 1764 of Cesare Beccaria's *Dei Delitti e delle Pene* was the first systematic attack on the unscientific penal systems of the age. Both directly and through its influence on other writers, above all on the English legal theorist Jeremy Bentham, it was to have great influence in the future. Almost simultaneously two great judicial scandals in France, the Calas and Sirven affairs,[2] advertised all over Europe by the interest taken in them by Voltaire, helped to shake still further

[1] For a good account of these courts see J. P. Le Donne, 'The provincial and local police under Catherine the Great, 1775–1796', *Canadian Slavic Studies*, vol. IV (1970), pp. 513–28.

[2] Calas, a Protestant whose son had died violently in mysterious circumstances, was executed in March, 1762, on a charge of having murdered him to prevent his conversion to Catholicism. Sirven, another Protestant, was accused of the murder of his daughter, who had been taken from him and sent to a convent to be brought up as a Catholic. In January, 1764, he escaped death by flight.

public faith in traditional procedures. Nor was this demand for a more enlightened judicial system altogether ineffective. In particular the use of judicial torture was abolished or discarded in many parts of Europe—in the Habsburg hereditary lands in 1774 and by stages in France in 1780 and 1788. Nevertheless the idea, universally accepted in past generations, that public order and the protection of the citizen demanded the severest punishment of wrongdoers, was still very widespread. A decade after the appearance of Beccaria's work it was still possible for a book published in England to advocate the vivisection of murderers.

Finally there must be mentioned one function of the administrative machinery of this period which is sometimes overlooked. This was the preservation and protection of the State religion. The importance attached to this in different countries and by different rulers varied greatly, from the passionate Catholicism of the kings of Spain to the indifference of Frederick II, from the intolerance of Portugal or Savoy to the relative freedom of the United Provinces. In very few cases however were governments prepared to dissociate themselves to any marked degree from religion, or to abandon their traditional role as the protectors of the faith of their subjects, or of the majority of them. The idea that religious belief was the most effective of all social cements, the ultimate and irreplaceable source of all morality, was still very much alive everywhere. As a result rulers and ministers themselves completely lacking in religious feeling were willing to foster religion, as Turgot admitted, not because it was true but because it was useful. Monarchs hostile to the power or envious of the wealth of their State Churches, or of particular religious groups such as the Jesuits, seldom allowed these feelings to lead them into opposition to religion as such. Thus Peter I, although he destroyed the political influence of the Orthodox Church in Russia (see p. 411), was a devout adherent of its doctrines. Catherine II, who secularized its lands two generations later, lost no opportunity of advertising to her subjects her personal piety. Joseph II, though he was anxious to reform, if necessary by force, the Catholic Church in his dominions, and to inculcate a greater degree of religious toleration there (see p. 409) nevertheless considered it his duty to persecute atheists and even deists.

If the essential functions of the administrative system were the same in all parts of eighteenth-century Europe the methods by which these functions were carried out varied widely in different areas.

Throughout much of the century Prussia seemed to many contemporaries the best administered of European States, the outstanding example of what good government could do to strengthen a country and increase its power and importance. The creation of an efficient bureaucracy, like that of a powerful army, was to some extent forced on her rulers by the complete lack of any geographical unity or common history to bind together the different provinces which they controlled. A group of disjointed and disparate territories strung out across the North German plain from Königsberg to Wesel could hardly have been maintained indefinitely as a political unit without a centralized and efficient governmental machine: it is worth remembering that though the ruler held the title of 'King in Prussia' from 1701 and 'King of Prussia' from 1772 it was only in 1807 that 'Prussia' became the official designation of the monarchy as a whole.

The creation of the army and bureaucracy which were to provide the backbone of the new State, the centralization of authority in Berlin and the reduction of the power of the provincial estates and the nobility which were the prerequisite of real administrative improvement, had all been begun in the previous century by the Great Elector Frederick William. They were carried further by King Frederick William I, especially in the first decade of his reign. These years (1713–23) saw the creation of a number of new government departments—the General Finance Directory, the General War Commissariat, the Audit Office and others. By the 1720s they had been combined in three great institutions; the General Directory, which supervised military, police, economic and financial affairs; the *Justizstaatsrat*, which supervised the judicial system, religion, and education; and the *Kabinetsministerium*, which was concerned primarily with foreign affairs. A systematic effort, which continued to the end of the reign, was made to fuse the component parts of the monarchy more completely together, notably by refusing to employ officials in the province of which they were natives. Repeated, and on the whole successful, attempts were also made by Frederick William to assert the principle that the members of the bureaucracy were his personal servants and owed him implicit obedience. 'One must serve the king', he wrote in 1714, 'with life and limb, with goods and chattels, with honour and conscience, and surrender everything except salvation. The latter is reserved for God. But everything else must be mine.'[1] This attitude expressed itself in

---

[1] R. A. Dorwart, *The Administrative Reforms of Frederick William I of Prussia* (Cambridge, Mass., 1953), p. 36.

royal efforts to control and supervise the day-to-day work of the whole governmental machine, notably by an order of November 1716 which regulated in great detail the work of the chanceries attached to various government departments. It can also be seen in the extension of the system of *Fiscals* (officials charged with watching the workings of the administration and denouncing inefficiency and corruption) which the king had inherited.

In the sphere of finance Frederick William's whole reign was dominated by the desire to exploit to the full every possible source of income. This was done by the creation of government monopolies of various products; by the imposition of heavy excise duties; and by the efficient administration of the royal domains, which as late as 1740 provided nearly half the public revenue. Simultaneously by the most rigid economy in civil expenditure he accumulated a large reserve of bullion for use in emergency. The diplomat and publicist Gentz, himself a Prussian official at one stage in his career, was justified in claiming that 'the first and principal part' of the Prussian administrative system was 'the amassing of treasure'.[1]

Many of these trends continued under Frederick William's more famous son. Frederick II like his father supervised personally the whole governmental machine. He did this mainly by means of written instructions and comments on reports submitted to him, partly by tours of inspection in the summer of each year during which he examined officials and heard the grievances of his subjects. The *Fiscals* continued to be extensively used. Government income and expenditure continued to be scrutinized with a care unknown in any other major State except Great Britain. The creation of specialized ministries, which had begun in the last years of Frederick William I, was continued by the establishment of new ones for commerce, Silesia, and army affairs—though the General Directory, the main central institution of the previous generation, continued to exist until 1806.

However, methods well adapted to the Prussia of 1713 were ceasing to be practicable in the much larger and appreciably wealthier State which was emerging in the two decades before 1789. In particular it was becoming steadily more difficult for Frederick II, in the second half of his reign, to exercise effective personal control of the administration, while the position was made still worse by the king's touchy vanity and resentment of criticism or even suggestions from inferiors.

[1] F. von Gentz, *On the State of Europe before and after the French Revolution* (London, 1802), p. 33.

The result was a tendency for the orders issued from Berlin to become increasingly confused and unrealistic and for Frederick's subordinates to conceal difficulties or unpleasant facts from him. Moreover as the bureaucracy grew in size (the General Directory was roughly three times as large at the end of Frederick's reign as at its beginning) the king's jealous desire to control the entire machine and to make all decisions, often hasty and badly thought-out ones, had serious results. It tended to throw real power increasingly into the hands of his ministers and still more into those of the heads of the provincial chambers, the men most responsible for the day-to-day administration of the different parts of the Prussian monarchy. Thus East Prussia, the most remote from Berlin of the major provinces, was visited by Frederick only three times (in 1740, 1750 and 1753); and though the president of the provincial chamber there reported to the king monthly and was summoned each year in June to the capital to see him personally, it is clear that Frederick was not really well informed about East Prussian affairs. All this amounted to the growth, in the later years of the reign, of a kind of unplanned, unconscious and *de facto* decentralization of effective control. The reputation of the Prussian administrative system thus reached its peak, after the Seven Years War, at a time when its real efficency was tending to decline.

In one important respect, moreover, Frederick II broke with the traditions bequeathed him by his father. Under Frederick William I men of non-noble birth had played an exceptionally important part in the administration, indeed a more important one than at any time before 1918. It seems clear that the king actively distrusted at least the greater and more ancient Junker families. In his *Political Testament* of 1722 he flatly described those of the Altmark and the Magdeburg area—the Alvenslebens, Schulenburgs and Bismarcks, names which resound through the whole of Prussian history—as the enemies of the monarchy. Of the eighteen privy councillors in office in 1740, when he died, only three were of noble birth. Under his son the administrative importance of noblemen increased sharply. Recruitment to the bureaucracy became more dependent than in the past on family connexions; and the higher ranks of the administration came in time to approximate to a hereditary caste. From this point of view, as from some others, the cultured Frederick II was really less in sympathy with the progressive tendencies of the age than his 'mad drill-sergeant' father had been.

The administrative history of eighteenth-century Russia is in some ways similar to that of Prussia, in others very different. There as in

Prussia the bureaucracy and army held the country together. The vigorous personal control by the ruler to which Prussian officials were subjected was paralleled to some extent in Russia, at least under Peter I, who borrowed from his Western neighbour the system of espionage and denunciation by *Fiscals*. Under him moreover, as under Frederick William I, there was a tendency to entrust high administrative posts to men of low birth or to foreigners, a tendency which was largely abandoned under his successors. It was impossible nevertheless to create in so huge and undeveloped a country as Russia a bureaucratic machine as efficient as that of Prussia. The distances involved, the weakness or indifference of many of the rulers concerned, above all the lack of educated and honest officials; all forbade it. The result was that throughout this period, as has already been pointed out (see p. 108) the central government was very dependent on the landowning class for the execution of its policies. It could never override its wishes or interests even to the limited extent to which the kings of Prussia could disregard those of the Prussian landlords.

The administrative system inherited by Peter I at the end of the seventeenth century was the product of generations of haphazard and unplanned growth. At the centre were the *Boyarskaya Duma* (a council dominated by members of the upper nobility) and over forty departments (*prikazy*) whose functions varied very widely in importance and geographical scope and whose spheres of activity overlapped and intersected in a highly irrational way. Control of local administration was largely in the hands of the provincial governors (*voevodas*) When Peter died in 1725 the picture was quite different. The *Boyarskaya Duma* had ceased to exist (its fall was one of many indications of the declining power of the old noble families) and had been replaced by a series of new institutions, notably the Senate founded in 1711. The *prikaz* system had been largely replaced, from 1718 onwards, by the creation of nine administrative colleges of the type now well-established in Prussia and Sweden, each with a well-defined sphere of activity. In the provinces a series of complicated changes in 1708, 1715 and 1719 made the control of the central government more effective by subjecting local officials to the Senate and later to the colleges. By the date of the great Tsar's death the country had been divided into fifty provinces, each headed by a *voevoda*, while a large number of new local officials with specialized functions (the *ober-kommandant*, the *ober-kommissar*, the *landrichter*, etc.) had been created.

Peter had thus endowed his country, mainly in an effort to mobilize and develop her resources for military purposes, with an administrative system more bureaucratic and more centralized than any she had hitherto known. Under his immediate successors the machine he had created remained intact in a number of essentials and continued to function, though with declining efficiency. A series of new central institutions for the formulation of policy was set up—the Supreme Privy Council in 1726, the *Kabinet* in 1731, the *Konferentsiya* in the 1750s—but these were all in effect the same body under differing names. The Senate lost some of its power, and was divided by Catherine II into six separate departments, but it continued to transact a vast amount of business. The colleges created by Peter remained in existence, though most of them became unimportant in the second half of the century. Local government as it existed at the end of his reign was drastically remodelled in 1728, however, mainly by increasing the importance of the *gubernii* (great territorial divisions each including a number of provinces) and their governors.

The reign of Catherine II is important in the administrative history of Russia above all because it witnessed a partly unconscious decision by the government to base the administration more than ever on the privileged landowning class. In a sense the government took this class into partnership, and thus tempered the autocracy of the ruler in practice if not in theory. The closeness of the *de facto* alliance which was growing up between the monarchy and the smaller and medium-sized landowners had already been seen in a very striking way in 1730. When in that year the young Tsar Peter II died, the Supreme Privy Council chose as his successor Anna, niece of Peter I and Duchess of Courland. Her acceptance as ruler was, however, made conditional on her agreement to a series of conditions drawn up by Prince D. M. Golitsyn, a member of the Council and also of one of the oldest noble families in Russia. These conditions provided that she should rule with the advice of the Council, and that she should not make war or peace, or grant military promotions to ranks above that of colonel, without its consent. Nor was she to marry or name a successor on her own initiative. If put into force, these proposals would have substituted for the autocratic rule traditional in Russia that of a noble oligarchy; and Golitsyn is known to have planned also the creation of representative bodies for the lower nobility and the towns. But such ideas were confined for the most part to a few great noble families. The lesser landowners were anxious to obtain some share in government, above all in local government. But they were quite unwilling to limit the power of the monarchy, which they saw as the defender of their interests against the encroachments of the old *boyar* families. The result was that the attempt of Golitsyn and his associates to create some limited form of constitutional government in Russia broke down almost immediately and that autocracy reasserted itself with undiminished powers. These powers it now held, in part at least, by the will of the landowning class.

The half-century which followed saw an almost unbroken series of concessions by the Crown to this class. The obligation to perform compulsory State service which Peter I had imposed on it was progressively reduced, and finally abolished in 1762 (see p. 45). In 1775 its administrative influence was greatly increased by a very important reform of provincial government. The details of this are complicated, but their effect was to transfer many of the functions of the colleges to new institutions, the provincial chambers, which were dominated by the landowners of the areas concerned. Ten years later the landowning class was granted a charter which conceded it a wide range of legal and economic privileges. This extended still further its control of provincial administration, a control which was intensified by the inability of the Russian towns to play an independent role of any importance. Thus by the end of this period Russia possessed an administrative system which was in some ways highly centralized and autocratic. In fact, however, her government was based on the predominance of a single class and involved in practice a considerable decentralization of authority in the interests of that class.

Nevertheless the purely administrative achievements of Catherine II were remarkable. She went far towards creating what eighteenth-century Russia had never previously possessed—a rationalized structure of civilian bureaucracy capable of administering this gigantic and thinly peopled empire at least in a rudimentary way. An important set of Staff Regulations for officials, enacted in December 1763 only a few months after her accession, standardized salaries and, largely by the creation of new posts, almost doubled the number of civil servants. In the following year civilian officials were ordered to assume responsibility for the collection of the poll-tax which since its introduction by Peter I from 1718 onwards had been collected by the army simply because there was no civilian machinery capable of doing the job. In 1773 a special Office of State Revenues was created as a subdivision of the Senate; the result was that in 1781 it was possible to submit to the empress 'the first meaningful budget in the history of Imperial Russia'.[1] Since at

[1] J. A. Duran, Jnr., 'The reform of financial administration in Russia during the reign of Catherine II', *Canadian Slavic Studies*, vol. IV (1970), p. 493.

Catherine's accession there had been about fifty distinct government agencies with the right to collect specified revenues and to spend the money thus raised (a typical pattern of medieval public finance) this must rank as an administrative triumph. Even in the very concrete and visible form of the creation of new provincial towns, built by government decree simply for administrative purposes, a vast amount was accomplished. The provincial reform of 1775 provided for the division of the empire into districts (*uezdy*) of 20,000 to 30,000 inhabitants, each of which was to have a town to act as a centre of administration. The result was the foundation in the following decade of well over 200 such new towns, an achievement which no other eighteenth-century government could approach and which was one of the most important practical legacies of the age of Catherine. The highly rationalistic character of this town-building and its marked emphasis on uniformity (the new towns were to be of a standard size of four versts (4 kilometres) in diameter and were not to spread beyond this except with official permission) give it a certain general resemblance to the rationalizing of local government in France by the revolutionaries from 1790 onwards. However the sheer lack of resources from which the Russian government still suffered in the later eighteenth century must never be underestimated. At Catherine's accession the entire empire, in all its vastness, had about 16,500 officials at work in the machinery of central and local administration combined. Frederick II, who ruled about one per cent of the land area of Russia, had at the same date about 14,000 under his control. Only if facts such as this are given their proper weight can the Empress's achievements be fairly judged and her reliance on the support of the landowning class be seen for the inescapable necessity it was.

The position in the Habsburg hereditary lands resembled that in Russia and Prussia in that there too the creation of a centralized and reasonably efficient administration seemed essential if the State were to develop or even survive. But in Central Europe the obstacles which impeded the growth of a strong central government and an elaborate bureaucracy were greater than anywhere else on the continent. The Habsburg territories were very extensive, their internal communications were poor, their economic life was generally backward. Also the Habsburgs had inherited a position of power, even leadership, in Europe which was becoming increasingly difficult to maintain: during this period they were more preoccupied than most European dynasties by the need to defend their existing possessions against encroachment and if possible to acquire others. This intensified the need for efficient administration of their territories but also helped in some respects to make efficiency harder to attain.

Moreover in Prussia noble families on the greatest scale, owning vast estates and great wealth, had never existed. In Russia they had been largely stripped of political power by Peter I. In the Habsburg lands, by contrast, they remained of very great importance throughout this period. In the reign of Charles VI, when their influence was at its height, the hereditary dominions of the Habsburgs were in some ways rather an aristocratic republic, a federation of great noble families, than a genuine monarchy. It is significant that the administrative reforms of his daughter Maria Theresa and her son Joseph II were carried out by ministers drawn largely from the nobility, even the high nobility—Haugwitz, Kolowrat, Chotek, Kaunitz and others.

Most important of all, almost every major subdivision of the Habsburg dominions—Bohemia, Milan, Upper and Lower Austria, the Netherlands—retained a distinctive character, a deep-rooted and strongly marked political tradition of its own. These were embodied in local institutions whose outlook was profoundly conservative and which often wielded considerable power. In particular Hungary continued to be in many ways a foreign country so far as the rest of the Habsburg monarchy was concerned. From 1687 onwards its kingship was hereditary in the Habsburg family and its privileged class lost the right of armed resistance to their ruler (*jus resistendi*) which they had hitherto possessed. This did not, however, prevent the outbreak of a serious nationalist revolt against Habsburg rule in 1703 which was ended by negotiation (Peace of Szatmár) only in 1711. Throughout the eighteenth century the country retained its own system of administration, dominated by the gentry and based on their county assemblies (*komitats*). Equally important, this class retained, in spite of the efforts of the government in Vienna, enormous privileges in respect of taxation. Moreover the bourgeoisie, in many other parts of Europe the most powerful supporter of the idea of centralized absolutism, was in many of the Habsburg territories, above all in Hungary, exceptionally weak. All these factors combined to make impossible centralization of authority on the scale achieved in Prussia or even in Russia.

Administrative improvement was inevitable none the less. The obsolete semi-feudal system of government which had been inadequate even in the reign of Charles VI was drastically modified, though never completely swept away, as a result of the struggles of 1740–63 with Prussia. Improved administration, and above all greater administrative unity and uniformity, was clearly a prerequisite of the recovery of

Silesia, perhaps even of the continued existence of the Habsburg monarchy. Prussia had shown what could be done to strengthen, by efficient administration, a state otherwise apparently doomed to poverty and weakness; and for the next half-century her example was to inspire in Vienna efforts at change in the administrative almost as much as in the military sphere. Thus a series of reforms in the 1740s began to break down the privileges which the nobility and Church had hitherto enjoyed with regard to taxation. Simultaneously new agencies of the central government (*Repräsentationen* and *Kammern*) were created in many of the provinces; and the control of the provincial estates over the taxation paid by the areas they represented was greatly weakened. In particular the financial reforms carried through by Haugwitz in 1748 provided for a large increase in government revenue. New central institutions were developed—a State Chancery for Foreign Affairs in 1742, the *Directorium in Publicis et Cameralibus* (a union of the hitherto separate chanceries of Bohemia and Austria under the presidency of Haugwitz) in 1749, and the Council of State in 1760. All this meant that by the 1760s, as a great Prussian historian has admitted, the Habsburg hereditary lands enjoyed a bureaucratic system more efficient and more modern than anything which Prussia herself could boast.[1] The decline in the power of the provincial estates continued after 1763, while the social dominance and hence political influence of the nobility began to be undermined, though slowly, by legislation limiting in various ways their hitherto almost absolute control of their serfs.

The effect of these changes was geographically uneven. In particular Hungary, entrenched behind her peculiar and remote relationship with the rest of the monarchy and the self-interest of her ruling class, was little affected by them. Even in 1764 the other Habsburg provinces, excluding Milan and the Netherlands, paid over four times as much towards the military expenses of the State as she did. Nevertheless the foundations of many of the radical and centralizing policies of Joseph II (see pp. 167ff.) had been laid long before his assumption of sole power in 1780, or even his promotion to co-ruler with his mother in 1765.

To the great States of Eastern and Central Europe reasonably efficient administration (which in practice meant centralized administration) was a necessity, almost a condition of existence. The position in Britain was completely different. To the exposed land frontiers and vulnerability to

[1] O. Hintze, 'Der österreichische und der preussische Beamtenstaat im 17. und 18. Jahrhundert', *Gesammelte Abhandlungen* (Gottingen, 1962), vol. I, p. 345. This famous article was first published in 1901.

foreign attack characteristic of all States east of the Rhine, she opposed a geographical position which gave her, while she controlled the seas, a very high degree of physical security. To their general poverty she opposed a wealth whose rapid growth was making her the envy of the rest of the continent. To the emphasis upon military needs which marked their administrative systems she opposed a distrust of and contempt for the army which made her unique in Europe. To the centralization which increasingly characterized their bureaucracies she opposed a system of government still in many ways highly decentralized. To an extent unparalleled elsewhere in Europe she was a State dominated by legislation, or by traditions having in effect the force of law. Her constitution was real, an amalgam of law and habit, not the system of bureaucratic practice which did duty for one in many continental States. Her government controlled its agents by legislation or, as has already been pointed out, by various legal procedures, as much as by purely administrative means. Administration in eighteenth-century Britain was the application and execution of common or statute law, and little more.[1]

Her central government was controlled and its policies formulated by a number of ministers and great officials: the councils and committees still so prominent in many continental States were in Britain of little importance. The Lord Chancellor, the First Lord of the Admiralty, the First Lord of the Treasury (an office which gave its holder control of many subordinate appointments and from the 1720s onwards was often held by the chief or Prime Minister) and the two Secretaries of State for the Northern and Southern Departments were among the more important of these ministers. Others—the Lord Privy Seal and the Lord President of the Council—had less executive power. All of these were normally members of the Cabinet, as that rather amorphous institution gradually evolved (see pp. 141–2). Most of them owed their position, at least until late in this period, largely to royal favour, and regarded the king as a master to whom they owed a personal loyalty. With few exceptions, however, they also owed something to their possession of electoral or parliamentary influence (since the government had to be able to retain the support of a majority in the House of Commons) and the importance of this factor tended to increase as poli-

---

[1] Exchequer procedure, for example, was still almost completely dominated by judicial methods and considerations until the end of this period. See Binney (see Bibliography, p. 102), chap. v, sect. 4.

tical parties of a loosely organized type slowly developed (see pp. 142ff.). The king's choice of ministers was thus not completely unfettered. To the end of this period it was rare for a minister to be forced by parliamentary or popular pressure on a ruler unwilling to accept him. (The clearest examples of this occurred in 1744, when George II was compelled to give office to Henry Pelham and his elder brother, the Duke of Newcastle; and in 1757, when he had to accept the elder William Pitt as Secretary of State.) Nevertheless the men who made up the government of Great Britain were much more than the courtiers and favourites who often bulked so large in the governments of continental States.

The departments over which these ministers presided varied greatly in size and structure. Many of them were inefficient by the best continental standards. In spite of the relatively advanced methods of public finance which had now been evolved in Great Britain, hardly any Treasury officials were paid regular salaries until after 1782. Even then they were not paid out of public funds, but from 'a domestic fund nourished by fees'. Military administration in particular remained for nearly a century after the end of this period an administrative jungle of divided responsibilities, overlapping jurisdictions and competing vested interests. Here the Secretary at War, the Master-General of the Ordnance, the Secretaries of State and the Commander-in-Chief (when he existed; the office was in abeyance during much of the century) all had fingers in the pie. Even more striking than this inefficiency to modern eyes is the narrowness of the outlook of the central administration in Britain during this period. Its utter indifference to education could be paralleled in other parts of Europe; but the extent to which it was willing to leave the development of the country's system of communications or the relief of distress to purely local initiative was unusual even in an age in which the effective powers of central governments were in general so limited.

The decentralized and amateur character of so much British administration is seen most clearly in the extraordinarily large part played in it by the Justices of the Peace. For the most part landowners or Anglican clergymen (the two categories to a large extent overlapped) they bore a very wide range of responsibilities and carried out, often in virtual independence of the central government, a great variety of functions. In Quarter Sessions they acted as a court of law for their localities and decided large numbers of serious and important cases. They bore the main responsibility for the maintenance of public order in the areas under their jurisdiction, helped in the recruiting of men for the armed forces, controlled the administration of the poor law and vagrancy law, and acted in many other ways as the virtual rulers of their own districts. The best-known example of their independence of central control is the introduction, by a group of Berkshire justices in 1795, of the 'Speenhamland System' of outdoor relief for heads of families who had appealed to the poor law authorities for support. The system, which was widely imitated in other parts of England, was not in fact a complete novelty. Nevertheless this episode was a striking illustration of the way in which a group of private individuals could in Britain create policy on its own initiative on a matter of great national importance, acting almost as though it enjoyed legislative power.

The French administrative system occupied a position midway between the centralization seen in Prussia under Frederick William I and Frederick II and the decentralized parliamentary system of Britain. In theory and to a large extent in practice it was highly centralized, at least in its upper ranks. At this level the power of the ruler was wielded partly through a number of councils. The most important of these were the *Conseil d'État*, in theory the main policy-making body, the *Conseil des Dépêches*, the *Conseil des Finances*, and the *Conseil Privé*, a kind of supreme legal tribunal. These had been very important during much of the seventeenth century but were now mere shadows of their former selves. Much more significant was a small group of ministers or great officials—the Chancellor, the *Garde des Sceaux*, the four Secretaries of State (for Foreign Affairs, War, the Navy, and the *Maison du Roi*) and the very powerful Controller-General of Finances who also supervised communications and many aspects of the nation's economic life . These ministers were the king's ministers: their power depended on their personal relationship to the monarch and the degree of attention he paid to their advice. By far the most important royal agents outside Paris were the intendants who had evolved in the seventeenth century as a means of extending the monarchy's control of the provinces. Under the ministers and intendants functioned a great bureaucracy, both central and local. This included many men of real ability and produced an immense volume of correspondence, reports and memoranda. It too, however, was complex and hierarchical, sometimes ridiculously so, and correspondingly slow-moving. The needs and wishes of provincial communities could easily be lost sight of in a morass of paper-work and official procedure. The intendants, it has been said, were 'committed to a perpetual drudgery in administrative bad habits, to a wearisome tidying of endless lumber'.[1] The administrative centralization which was so marked a feature of the revolutionary *régime* after 1789, and which was bequeathed with little fundamental alteration to the France of the nineteenth and twentieth centuries, was in many ways merely a streamlined and rationalized version of the bureaucracy of the *ancien régime*.

This bureaucracy, like those of Prussia and the Habsburg provinces, was essentially legal, even legalistic, in its outlook. It was an instrument of despotism, and designed as such, but of a despotism which could not in practice be unlimited or grossly irresponsible. More important, the degree of central control which could be achieved in pre-revolutionary France was limited by conditions and institutions inherited from the past. The fact that the country lacked any unified system of law, or even of weights and measures, and that its fiscal system was riddled with anomalies, hampered the efforts of the bureaucracy to increase the power of the central government. Above all institutions such as the *parlements*, the provincial estates (representative bodies of a medieval kind organized by classes), the guilds and above all the Church, still possessed real powers which could not be easily overridden. In France bodies of this kind retained an importance which they had lost during the reigns of the Great Elector and Frederick William I in Prussia: in Russia most of them had never even existed. By acting as a buffer between the central government and the ordinary man they helped to ensure that France, which during this period produced more great administrators than any other European State, remained in many ways a badly administered country.

[1] D. Dakin, *Turgot and the Ancien Régime in France* (London, 1939), p. 27.

VI

Monarchs and Despots:
Tensions within the State

Every State in eighteenth-century Europe, with a few relatively unimportant exceptions, was a monarchy. Almost everywhere the monarch
was, and was expected to be, the moving force behind the machinery
of government which has been briefly described in the preceding chapter. The importance of this fact can scarcely be exaggerated. At their
highest level the internal politics of the European States were the
politics of monarchy. This meant that political conflicts normally
took the form of struggles between parties or individuals for influence
over the ruler, struggles in which the victor secured the all-important
privilege of easy access to him and in which the vanquished were
dismissed, disgraced or exiled. The fate of a fallen minister or favourite
might be even harder if he had aroused real fear and hatred in his
opponents—the executions (or rather judicial murders) in 1719 of Baron
Goertz, the adviser of the dead Charles XII of Sweden, and in 1772 of
Count Struensee, the progressive-minded but tactless favourite who

BIBLIOGRAPHY. There is no satisfactory general study of monarchy in
eighteenth-century Europe. Perhaps the nearest approach to one is F. Bluche,
Le Despotisme éclairé (Paris, 1968); and there is a shorter attempt at an analytical
study of the same phenomenon in M. Lheritier, 'Le despotisme éclairé de
Frédéric II a la Révolution française', *Bulletin of the International Commission of
Historical Sciences*, vol. IX (1937). J. G. Gagliardo, *Enlightened Despotism*
(London, 1968); T. C. W. Blanning, *Joseph II and Enlightened Despotism*
(London, 1970); and F. Hartung, *Enlightened Despotism* (Historical Association
Pamphlet, London, 1957) are very summary but useful. C. Morazé, 'Finance et
despotisme: essai sur les despotes éclairés', *Annales*, vol. III (1948) is an article
of some originality; while R. R. Palmer, *The Age of the Democratic Revolution*,
vol. I, *The Challenge* (Princeton, 1959) is an interesting discussion of some of
the questions touched on in this chapter. The peculiar position in Great Britain
is well explained in R. Pares, *Limited Monarchy in Great Britain* (Historical
Association Pamphlet, London, 1957); in the same author's *King George III and
the Politicians* (Oxford, 1953), which is by far the best general study of the

had for several years dominated the court of Denmark, are good illustrations of this.

Few people seriously questioned the practical advantages and moral justification of hereditary monarchy as a system of government, above all in the larger and more powerful states. Its superiority to its rivals seemed proved not merely by argument but by experience. In Italy a few famous and ancient republics—Venice, Genoa, Lucca—continued to exist; and in some of them republican government, even in the highly oligarchical form which had prevailed in these small States for centuries, continued to arouse genuine loyalty. The successful revolt of 1746, for example, which expelled an Austrian garrison from Genoa, expressed a powerful urban patriotism which drew strength from the city's long republican tradition. But none of these states was strong enough to make much difference to the general picture of eighteenth-century Europe as overwhelmingly monarchical. In some others elective monarchy provided opportunities of limiting the powers of each ruler at his election. Each of the ecclesiastical electors in Germany (those of Mainz, Cologne and Trier), on being chosen as ruler by the cathedral chapter concerned, had to sign an agreement (*Wahlkapitulation*) in which he confirmed and promised to respect its ancient privileges. The *Pacta Conventa* which the nobility imposed on each newly elected king of Poland performed, on a much more important scale, a similar function. Each Holy Roman Emperor, the supreme example of an elected mon-

second half of the century; and in Sir L. B. Namier, 'Monarchy and the party system', an essay in his collection *Personalities and Powers* (London, 1955). J. Brooke, *King George III* (London, 1972) is a perceptive study of the king as a person, based on immense knowledge of the sources. Little of value has been written on either Louis XV or Louis XVI. On the former G. P. Gooch, *Louis XV, the Monarchy in Decline* (London, 1956) is an English work of some merit; and J. Egret, *Louis XV et l'opposition parlementaire* (Paris, 1970) is an important specialized study. Some of the more important German biographies of Frederick II are mentioned in the Bibliography on p. 241. The most perceptive one in English is G. Ritter, *Frederick the Great: an historical profile* (London, 1968), a translation of a German original: D. B. Horn, *Frederick the Great and the Rise of Prussia* (London, 1964) is a short but useful introduction. P. Paret (ed.), *Frederick the Great: a profile* (London, 1972) is a well-chosen collection of comments on the king by contemporaries and later historians. The best books on Maria Theresa are in German: E. Guglia, *Maria Theresia* (Munich–Berlin, 1917); and H. Kretschmayr, *Maria Theresia* (Gotha, 1925). E. Crankshaw, *Maria Theresa* (London, 1969) is popular in tone and concerned with the first half of the reign. On Joseph II the standard work is still P. von Mitrofanov, *Joseph II: seine politische und kulturelle Tätigkeit* (2 vols., Vienna–Leipzig, 1910):

arch, had to accept the same kind of limitations when he was chosen by the imperial electors. Even this does not seriously modify the picture. Every successful large State in eighteenth-century Europe, every one which made significant territorial gains or played a great independent role in international affairs, was ruled by a powerful hereditary monarchy. Those which lacked this essential source of strength were either impotent small ones on the fringes of the great political developments of the age, such as the Italian republics, or, in the case of some more important States, were notably less well governed and less effectively led than their neighbours and competitors. Of the latter group both the United Provinces throughout the century and Sweden during the period of weak and limited monarchy from 1718 to 1772 were examples; while the destruction of Poland was the supreme warning of the fate in store for any State whose rulers were too weak to repress internal dissension or ward off the attacks of external enemies.

The United Provinces, a cumbersome federation of seven units each with estates and administrative machinery of its own, was an uneasy compromise between the monarchical and republican forms of government. Each province had its own Stadtholder (the formal head of its administration, chosen by its estates). It was possible, however, for a member of the House of Orange (the descendants of William the Silent, the leader of the struggle for independence against Spain in the later sixteenth century) to be elected Stadtholder of all or most of the provinces and thus attain the position of General Stadtholder of the federation. He thus became in a sense a monarch, though one whose powers were strictly limited and often jealously scrutinized by the provincial governments and estates. The monarchical tendencies typified by the Orange family were stoutly opposed by the republican

the best general study in English is P. P. Bernard, *Joseph II* (New York, 1968), while F. Fejto, *Un Habsbourg révolutionnaire, Joseph II* (Paris, 1953) is a useful semi-popular but scholarly work. F. Valsecchi, *L'Assolutismo illuminato in Austria e in Lombardia* (2 vols., Bologna, 1931) remains important for many aspects of Joseph's activities. T. C. W. Blanning, *Reform and Revolution in Mainz, 1743–1803* (London, 1974) is an illuminating discussion of the problems of enlightened government in a small German state. Of Catherine II there is still no really good biography in any language. The best modern one is probably the essay by P. Milyukov in *Hommes d'État*, ed. A. B. Duff and F. Galy, vol. III (Paris, 1936); in English the extracts collected in M. Raeff (ed.) *Catherine the Great: a profile* (London, 1972) provide the most illuminating study available. P. Dukes, *Catherine the Great and the Russian Nobility* (Cambridge, 1967) is an important specialized work.

forces which were strong in Holland, by far the most powerful province of the federation, and notably among the great merchants of Amsterdam. The result throughout this period was a continuous struggle between republican and Orangist groups and an uneasy oscillation of power between them. The death in 1702 of the Stadtholder William III (King William III of England) who left no son to succeed him, was followed by over forty years of republican dominance. His heir, John-William Friso, was Stadtholder only of the province of Friesland, while the government of the United Provinces fell under the dominance of Anthony Heinsius, Grand Pensionary of Holland, who remained until his death in 1720 one of the leading figures in European politics. The power of the republicans suffered a serious setback in 1747, at a moment of crisis when French invasion seemed imminent, by the victory of the Orangists and the accession to power of William IV, the posthumous son of John-William Friso. In that year he received the title of Captain and Admiral-General and became Stadtholder of all the provinces. When he died in 1751 he was succeeded by his son William V, then a child of three. The republicanism of Holland, however, was far from dead. Encouraged by the long minority of the new Stadtholder it helped to influence Dutch policy in a pro-French and anti-British direction during the Seven Years War (the Orange family, now closely associated by marriage with that of Hanover, was generally pro-British in outlook). It did much to bring about the Anglo-Dutch conflict of 1780. In 1787 it led the country to the verge of civil war and provoked the intervention of the Prussian army in defence of William V and his wife (who was a Prussian princess).

What one British envoy called the 'crazy constitution' of the United Provinces thus appeared to contemporaries a poor advertisement for any form of government which attempted to escape from the conventional pattern of monarchy. This impression may have been strengthened by the slow decline in the country's commercial importance (see pp. 72-3), though this would have taken place whatever its political structure. Even the judicial system in the Dutch republic, in so many ways still among the most advanced parts of Europe, suffered from the lack of a powerful monarchy able to press effectively for the sort of reform which rulers in many less developed areas were now forcing upon their subjects. It is significant that judicial torture was abolished in the province of Holland only as late as 1798, while in the generally more backward Austrian Netherlands the Emperor Joseph II had ended it as early as 1784. Moreover the United Provinces showed themselves throughout the later decades of the century notably less welcoming than their southern neighbours to ideas of penal reform of the kind now being put forward by Beccaria and others.

In the same way the constitution of 1720, which drastically limited the powers of the Swedish monarchy, hitherto one of the most absolute in Europe, seemed to condemn the country to perpetual divisions and faction-fights and therefore to impotence in international affairs. It was for precisely this reason that Russia, which had far more than any other State to fear from strong government and an active foreign policy in Sweden, did everything in its power to uphold that constitution (see p. 228). Sweden continued to be in some ways deeply divided even after the *coup d'état* by which Gustavus III reasserted in 1772 the power of the monarchy; but his action restored to her policies an element of continuity and decision which had been lacking for many years.

Above all the fate of Poland illustrated the necessity of strong monarchy and the fatal disunity which usually followed when it was lacking. At the end of the sixteenth century the 'crowned republic' of Poland had been in some ways one of the great powers of Europe. Her decline to the position she now occupied, that of a helpless victim-State, was the product of many factors—economic and social backwardness, long frontiers unprotected by natural obstacles to invasion, religious divisions and the aggression of her neighbours. But underlying all these was the fact that the power of the Polish monarchy had evaporated since its elective character (which had existed in theory since the 1430s) had become finally established in practice from the 1570s onwards. Henceforth each successive royal election provoked party conflicts and personal intrigues which often led to civil war, as well as pressure and even forcible intervention from abroad on behalf of the competing candidates. The kings of Poland, often foreigners, their hands tied by promises made to the nobles at their accession, had to submit to continuous scrutiny and control by the same nobles. Any effort to increase their powers, above all any suggestion that the Crown might once more become hereditary, at once aroused the most violent opposition. At their disposal were a ludicrously inadequate army and an administrative machine so primitive that one observer in the early eighteenth century alleged that the tiny Italian city-state of Lucca possessed a larger civil service than they. A strong monarchy could have developed a powerful army and an effective bureaucracy. It could have defended the frontiers, repressed religious intolerance and done something to accelerate economic and intellectual progress. The rulers of

Russia, Prussia, and the Habsburg territories succeeded in varying degrees in achieving all these aims. Without such a monarchy progress in Poland, though not impossible, was very difficult. Only from the 1760s and 1770s onwards were there signs that it might be achieved. By then it was too late: the destruction of the country's independence was already under way. Only political units which were small and remote from the international conflicts which agitated the greater powers, as were the Swiss cantons and some of the city-states of Germany and Italy, could hope to dispense permanently with some more or less effective form of kingship.

Monarchy in eighteenth-century Europe was thus buttressed by powerful utilitarian arguments. It was also strengthened by the assumption, inherited from the Middle Ages and still very widely accepted, that the relationship between a ruler and his subjects was analogous to that of father and children. 'The true image of a free people, governed by a patriot king,' wrote Lord Bolingbroke, one of the most sophisticated intellects of the century, in 1738, 'is that of a patriarchal family.' Even some of the articles of the great *Encyclopédie*, the supreme general expression of a radically enlightened view of the world and society, as its successive volumes appeared in the 1750s and 1760s (see p. 365), contained distinct traces of the same pervasive traditional assumption. In small States it was often possible for the ruler to express very effectively by his own actions this paternalist view and to have some more or less personal contact with an appreciable fraction of his subjects. Thus John V of Portugal (1706–50) gave public audiences regularly twice a week at which he personally received petitions for the redress of grievances. At the same time he gave alms with his own hand to the poor from a basket of coins placed by his side. In Mainz an ordinance of 1788 announced that the elector would give general audiences every Monday at precisely 4 o'clock in the afternoon: at these every inhabitant of the electorate was entitled to attend and present in person any grievance he might have. In the larger States contacts of this direct and relatively informal kind between ruler and ruled were obviously impossible on a large scale. Even in them, however, the assumption that the monarch was in some sense a father of his people and that he should therefore be freely accessible to them died hard. In the 1760s Catherine II of Russia had in self-defence to issue decrees ordering her subjects to petition her only through the appropriate officials and not by the direct personal presentation to her of their grievances and requests. The extent of the childlike and almost filial loyalty felt by the ordinary man everywhere towards his ruler, the great fund of emotion of this sort upon which a monarch could still draw, are clearly seen in France in the great crisis of 1789. Many of the *cahiers* (the statements of grievances and proposals for their rectification drawn up for the guidance of the States-General when it met in May 1789) proposed the building of public monuments to Louis XVI in recognition of his action in calling the States-General and thus restoring the 'liberties' of his people. Some also suggested that a national holiday be established in his honour or that he be given some honorific title—*le Bienfaisant* or (significantly) *Le Père du Peuple*.

Paternalist assumptions were an aspect of the deeply entrenched feeling, which time and education were only slowly eroding, that legitimate rulers were in some sense the agents of God. From this it followed that kingship, like fatherhood, was a divine institution to which resistance was not merely impolitic but sinful. Ideas of Divine Right were, it is true, becoming increasingly difficult to justify in intellectual terms. In the later decades of this period particularly, they could seldom be openly asserted with the degree of conviction which had been possible in the sixteenth century and much of the seventeenth. Indeed the years immediately before 1789 saw in some of the greatest European monarchies (most notably in Prussia) a growing demand for the drawing up of fundamental laws which would prevent the ruler from behaving in an arbitrary manner, particularly by increasing the importance of legal insititutions. Among ordinary people almost everywhere, however the idea of monarchy continued to possess great emotive power. The ruler continued to enjoy, unless he were unusually vicious or unlucky, a respect which sometimes verged on worship. One of the Russian admirers of Peter I actually hung the Tsar's picture among the holy ikons in his house and burnt candles before it. Few things in the history of the eighteenth century, indeed, are more significant than the unquestioning support which the Russian monarchy continued to receive from its subjects in spite of the wild vicissitudes of intrigue and revolution through which it passed.[1] Even the wars and internal reforms of Peter I, bitterly unpopular as they were with great masses of his people, could not eradicate the feeling that the Tsar was, in some ultimate sense, the father and protector of the ordinary Russian.

[1] These involved, apart from palace revolutions and conspiracies, the murder of two rulers: Ivan VI (1740–41) and Peter III (1762), assassinated in 1764 and 1762 respectively; and of one heir to the throne (Alexis, son of Peter I, put to death on his father's orders in 1718).

The institution of monarchy thus dominated the political horizon, whether it was thought of in terms of Divine Right or merely as a secular institution guaranteeing civil peace and security. Republican theories were never a serious factor in the politics of any major European State during this period. The 'republicanism' of the great merchants of Amsterdam or the nobles and gentry of Poland (unlike that of Venice and some of the Swiss cantons) was in no sense a system of ideas. It was rather a façade behind which classes and individuals with a vested interest in weak and decentralized government could entrench themselves, and also a mere mechanical adherence to established practices and institutions. The ideology of republicanism aroused some interest; but it was thought of in terms of ancient history rather than contemporary politics, in terms of the world of Lycurgus, Solon and Pericles rather than that of Louis XV, Frederick II or Catherine II. Genuine republican feeling, in so far as it existed at all in the major States, was a nostalgia or very occasionally an aspiration, never a programme.

The great monarchies of eighteenth-century Europe, like its administrative systems, can be roughly classified into groups. Russia and Prussia are at one extreme, Great Britain at the other. France, Spain and the Habsburg dominions occupy intermediate positions. Of Russia and Prussia little need be said, for there, as has been seen (see p. 112) the administrative system was the real constitution. In autocratic States such as these limits to the authority of the monarch were imposed by the efficiency of the bureaucracy and the strength of the army rather than by political institutions capable of opposing him. But without political institutions enjoying some real power it is difficult to have political conflict or political life in any but a very narrow sense of the term. It can thus be argued that Russia and Prussia have in the eighteenth century a very important and interesting administrative history but little real political, still less constitutional, history. In both, though much more in the former, can be seen struggles between competing ministers for royal favour and support. In both a change of ruler or minister often had drastic repercussions, particularly on the conduct of foreign policy. Thus the death of Catherine I of Russia in 1727 and the changes it produced in Russian policy in the Baltic brought about a reconciliation with Britain after a long period of antagonism; the rise to power in the 1740s of Count Bestuzhev-Ryumin gave a strong anti-Prussian tinge to Russian policy; and above all the accession to the throne of Frederick II was an essential preliminary to the Prussian attack on Silesia in 1740. In both Russia and Prussia the dependence of the government on a single class, a landowning service nobility, was very great. In both public opinion of a modern kind scarcely existed during this period (see p. 18). In both therefore it is difficult to speak of political life or political problems except in a rather limited and rudimentary sense.

At the other extreme stood Great Britain. Here too the monarchy was central to the political life of the country; but it was a monarchy to which the rest of Europe offered no parallel and which therefore calls for description in some detail. Its powers were wide. The government was still the king's government: the monarch retained great influence over the administration and to the end of the century expected to have a say, even a dominant say, in the making of policy. In particular the degree of negative control he could exert over the actions of the government, his ability to obstruct change, remained important until well after the end of this period. In 1801 and 1807 ministries fell from power because of the obstinate resistance of George III to the grant of equal political rights to Catholics. Moreover there were certain branches of the governmental machine and certain aspects of policy on which the king was considered to have a special right to make his views heard. Such were the army, in which both George I and George II took a strong personal interest, and foreign policy, about which as a rule few ministers knew or cared very much. The king also retained a considerable range of prerogative powers (i.e. powers inherent in the office of king and not conferred on him by legislation or the common law). Of these some, such as those of creating peers and making promotions in the armed forces, could have very real political importance. Parliament, moreover, was normally under considerable royal influence, since a large proportion of its members, both in the House of Lords and the House of Commons held offices, pensions or contracts awarded by the Crown. An effort to exclude office-holders of this type from the House of Commons was made, with no great success, by the Act of Settlement of 1701. A more thoroughgoing attempt to reduce the parliamentary influence of the Crown by the 'Economical Reform' legislation of 1782 was little more effective. Also throughout this period some members of the House of Commons, though their numbers steadily decreased, owed their election to the influence which the Treasury and Admiralty were able to exert over certain constituencies. The exercise of electoral influence of this kind, by individuals as well as by the government, was made possible by the fact that most of the members representing boroughs, who made up over four-fifths of the membership of the House of Commons, were elected by very small numbers of voters. The county members and those who sat for the few boroughs in which the franchise was reasonably wide were normally the most independent of eighteenth-century M.P.s; but they were in a minority. The extent to which the Crown could control the composition of Parliament was, however, habitually exaggerated by contemporaries, at least from the 1760s onwards. The House of Commons was far from being a genuinely representative body, but it was not the mere tool of the king. It was rather a kind of oligarchy, with a strong hereditary element in its composition. It is important also to remember that a post or pension given to a member could be a reward for past services as well as a bribe to secure future ones.

The Hanoverian monarchy could also draw on a more profound and lasting source of strength than any of these. This was the very widespread feeling (at least in Parliament: public opinion normally tended to be suspicious of ministerial projects) that the king and his ministers had a right to the support of all loyal and patriotic subjects. In particular it was almost universally agreed, at least until near the end of this period, that it was wrong for any group of politicians to unite to offer systematic and continuous opposition to the government. A 'formed opposition' of this kind was frowned on even by professional politicians; and opponents of the ministers in power usually attempted, if they could, to group themselves round some discontented member of the royal family and thus acquire a kind of respectability. Thus, for example, the death in 1751 of the Prince of Wales, who had long been on bad terms with his father, led to a virtual collapse for the time being of all political opposition. In other words monarchy was, in Britain as almost everywhere else in Europe, a genuinely popular institution. It retained its popularity even though none of the Hanoverian kings was an inspiring personality and none, with the possible exception of George I, a man of much intelligence. In any political conflict the king always tended, so far as the ordinary man was concerned, to be given the benefit of the doubt. No government which was known to enjoy the support of the Crown was defeated in a general election until well into the nineteenth century.

Nevertheless the real power of the monarchy in Great Britain certainly declined during the three generations which followed the revolution of 1688–89. In the first place its prerogatives were considerably reduced by legislation. The Declaration of Right of 1689 abolished the power claimed by James II to suspend the operation of any law, and to some extent the power which he had also claimed to exempt individuals or groups from the operation of certain laws. Five years later the Triennial Act imposed a limit of three years on the life of any Parliament (it was raised to seven years by the Septennial Act of 1716). It thus became impossible for any king in future to prolong indefinitely the life of a compláisant House of Commons, as Charles II had done with the 'Cavalier Parliament' of 1661–79. More fundamentally, the Act of Settlement of 1701, by asserting the right of Parliament to decide the succession to the throne, struck a decisive blow at the mystique of absolute hereditary monarchy still so widely accepted in many parts of the continent.

Moreover under William III, who was a foreigner, and Anne, who was a woman and a stupid one, the influence of Parliament over foreign policy grew rapidly. The long struggle with France in 1689–1713 meant an unprecedented raising of money for government purposes by methods such as the levying of a land-tax and the creation of a funded debt. This could be achieved only through Parliament. As a result, from the end of the seventeenth century onwards both Houses increasingly demanded to be informed about the negotiations with foreign States which made necessary the taxation and borrowing to which they were being asked to agree. The position in this respect remained more or less the same in the eighteenth century. To speak of Parliamentary control of foreign policy would be quite misleading. Nevertheless the influence of Parliament in this respect could be considerable and the need to give it at least a certain amount of information about foreign affairs could hardly be avoided.

Thus the generation 1690–1720 saw a considerable transference of real power from the king to Parliament, partly as a result of specific acts of legislation and partly because of the enormous changes in the country's fiscal system and relationship to Europe which occurred in these years.

The next four decades saw a slow but fairly steady erosion of royal power. This was produced not so much by Parliamentary aggression as by the personal characters of George I and George II. The former, a middle-aged German prince at his accession, was always more interested in Hanover, and more at home there, than in England. George II was essentially a weak and second-rate man. The result was a slow leakage of power, to individual ministers and the new and still half-formed institution of the Cabinet rather than to Parliament itself. Under George III there was, in a sense, an effort to restore and increase the authority of the Crown. The king did not attempt to achieve this by overthrowing or even modifying the constitution, for which he had a sincere and perhaps exaggerated respect. Rather he asserted and tried to use to the full in the 1760s and 1770s powers which he undoubtedly possessed in theory but which under his predecessors had begun to be whittled away in practice. Above all he demanded the right to choose his own ministers, who were to be responsible to him alone, and to exercise an effective supervision over the workings of the machinery of government. During the long ministry of Lord North (1770–82) he seemed for a time to have achieved this objective. But his efforts to regain the ground which the monarchy had lost were stultified by Britain's defeat in the War of American Independence. They also aroused much antagonism; and the last years of the war saw a determined effort by the king's opponents to reduce his influence over Parliament and the political life of the country. Public discontent at the defeats Britain had suffered, coupled with resentment of the unrepresentative character of the House of Commons, helped to produce in 1779–80 a movement of almost revolutionary character. The County Associations which were then formed to demand a widening of the suffrage and a redistribution of Parliamentary seats, and the General Association, a substitute Parliament, or anti-Parliament, in which some of them proposed to combine, seemed for a time to threaten drastic and violent constitutional changes. In the event the movement collapsed quite quickly in the summer of 1780, largely because there was no sustained demand for such changes in the country as a whole. Nevertheless the monarchy did not escape the crisis unscathed. The 'Economical Reform' programme of 1782 was the most determined attack on the power of the Crown since 1641, though its practical effect was not very great.

Englishmen thought of the internal politics of their country in the eighteenth century largely in what had now become the traditional terms of a dialogue, usually though not always amicable, between king and Parliament. Almost imperceptibly, however, the dialogue was now being transformed into a general conversation by the emergence of new and immensely important institutions—the Cabinet and the political parties.

The development of the Cabinet is one of the most obscure and difficult aspects of British history in this period. By about 1740 and probably earlier a definite distinction had emerged between the 'formal Cabinet', a relatively large body which included a number of holders of great court and ceremonial offices, and the 'effective Cabinet', a much smaller and more compact group of ministers. The former met rarely and for purely formal purposes. The latter, an active body including the heads of all the great departments of State, was in fact the 'government'. However even the 'effective Cabinet' was not during this period a real political organism. Some of its members were leaders or representatives of the small and competing groups into which Parliament was normally divided. Others were essentially experienced professional administrators. Their allegiance was thus to the king, who had appointed them and was the source of their power, and to their followers, for whom they sought offices, titles and pensions, rather than to their colleagues or to any leader amongst them. The result was that Cabinets were often divided by personal rivalries—the schisms in those led by Sir Robert Walpole (First Lord of the Treasury and Chancellor of the Exchequer, 1721-42) are a good example—and this lack of unity tended to increase the influence the king could exert over individual ministers and the Cabinet as a whole. In particular the whole idea of a Prime Minister was looked on with the gravest suspicion. Walpole, who has been traditionally and wrongly regarded as the first British Prime Minister, always took pains to deny that he occupied such a position. As late as the 1760s the ideal government, in the eyes not merely of George III but of the great majority of his subjects, was one consisting of a number of heads of departments, each performing his task efficiently and responsible only to the king and Parliament. Both the unity of the Cabinet and its independence of the king began to be unmistakably and effectively asserted only after the end of this period, during the long premiership of the younger William Pitt (1783-1801).

In the long run the most fundamental check to the power of the British monarchy was that imposed by the growth of more or less organized and coherent political parties. It was these which, by limiting the king's freedom of manœuvre, in the end destroyed his ability to play a great role in politics. At the end of this period matters had by no means gone as far as this, for the growth of political parties in eighteenth-century England was curiously erratic. Under Queen Anne parties of a modern kind did not exist; but it is possible to speak without gross inaccuracy of Parliament and the politically active part of the nation as being divided for the most part into Whigs and Tories. Between these two groups, each including within itself many sub-groups, there was on most of the great issues of the day a fairly clear division. The Whigs favoured the accession to the throne, on the queen's death, of the

Elector of Hanover, the later George I. They demanded that England should give effective support on the continent to the Dutch and the Emperor against Louis XIV during the War of the Spanish Succession (1702–13). They were in general tolerant in their attitude to the Protestant Dissenters. Some of the more extreme Tories, by contrast, flirted with the idea of restoring the son of James II, the Catholic Stuart king deposed in 1688, while most of them demanded that the British war effort be concentrated on a mainly naval and colonial struggle against France. Above all they were much more aggressively Anglican than the Whigs.

Peace with France in 1713, the accession of George I in the following year, and the easy suppression of a revolt of the Jacobites (the partisans of the exiled Stuarts) in 1715, changed this position completely. Excluded from power by the new king who understandably distrusted them, discredited by their connexion with the defeated Jacobites, the Tories as a significant Parliamentary group soon ceased to exist. In the middle decades of the century every leading figure in British politics would, if pressed, have described himself as a Whig. Parliament by then had become atomized, divided into small and continually fluctuating groups or 'connexions', which were usually formed around some leader or based on family or regional relationships. This lack of real parties during the period of Whig supremacy in 1714–60 was made possible by the lack during these years of real issues of principle around which opinion could crystallize and in terms of which politicians could arrange themselves. With the Hanoverians secure on the throne (especially after the defeat of a second and more serious Jacobite revolt in Scotland in 1745–46), with the grant of a considerable degree of *de facto* toleration to the Dissenters, the questions which had dominated internal politics in the reign of Anne appeared to have been settled. Nothing now remained to contend for but the possession of office: politics were reduced to a struggle between 'ins' and 'outs'.

In the 1760s the position began to change again. Once more genuine issues of principle arose. The career of the demagogue John Wilkes aroused political passions fiercer than any seen for half a century, passions which were often rooted in real political idealism. It was his publication in 1763 of what the courts decided to be a seditious libel on George III which led to the judicial decision that general warrants were illegal (see p. 111). His election on three separate occasions as M.P. for Middlesex in 1768–69, and the repeated refusals of the House of Commons to admit him as a member, did much to stimulate in London the current of political radicalism which was later to run so strongly there. Simultaneously the far more important question of relations with the American colonies, and of the moral justification of the demands which the mother-country was now making on them (see pp. 302–03), roused intense feeling and stimulated widespread political discussion, much of it at a relatively high level of sophistication. This injection of principles and ideas into British politics made impossible a continuation of the easygoing cynicism which had been the keynote of the generation before 1760. Political groupings now began to emerge which more closely resembled modern parties than anything hitherto known. The Whig group led by the Marquis of Rockingham provided, in the 1760s and 1770s, the first example of this; while many of the ideas for which it stood inspired the somewhat similar group led by Charles James Fox in the 1780s and 1790s. Above all the younger Pitt, during his long tenure of office, laid the foundations of the nineteenth-century Tory party. By the end of this period the political parties which were to carry out the great changes of the next century in Britain, though very far from having assumed their late-Victorian form, were slowly evolving.

It is easy for us, with the advantages of hindsight, to think of the political structure of eighteenth-century England, with all its defects, as the best in Europe. It is all the more necessary, therefore, to remember that for most of the century this admiration was not felt by the majority of continental observers. Not until the 1760s did Britain begin to live down her reputation (based on the violence of the period 1640–1714) as an inveterately turbulent and factious country where almost anything could happen. 'The people are really richer here than anywhere else,' wrote a French observer in 1747, 'and they partly at least owe this advantage to the wisdom of their laws. But amidst all this abundance, the nation is so disunited and rent by continual factions, that it seems at every moment to be threatened with the horrors of civil wars. . . . A man tortured by a continual fever with exacerbations, to me appears the image of the English government, constantly disturbed by parties, and frequently altered by revolutions.'[1] It was the victories won during the Seven Years War of 1756–63 much more than any intrinsic merits of the British constitution which led foreigners to revise disparaging estimates of this kind.

The French monarchy, like the French administrative system,

---

[1] Abbé le Blanc, *Letters on the English and French Nations* (London, 1747), vol. I, pp. 106–7.

occupied during this period a position intermediate between the extremes to be found in Russia and Prussia on the one hand and in Great Britain on the other. The kings of France possessed in theory great personal power. They were the supreme embodiment of sovereignty; the army owed obedience to them personally; the debts of the State were their personal debts; they could override or anticipate the decisions of any court of law. Louis XV was stating what had, at least until very recently, been a commonplace, when he claimed in 1766 that 'in my person alone resides sovereign power . . . I alone possess complete and untrammelled legislative authority.' Even the most extreme partisans of absolute monarchy were prepared to admit that there were theoretical limits to the power of the king. He could not change the monarchical nature of the government or the hereditary nature of the monarchy. Nor could he disregard the Salic Law which forbade the accession to the throne of a woman. Most theorists, moreover, would have agreed that he must obey divine law by doing justice and showing mercy and that, at least beyond a certain point, he had no right to infringe his subjects' property rights or their personal liberty. These restrictions, however, were vague and impossible to define accurately; and the plenitude of royal power was thus little affected by them. Above all there was no individual or institution in France with any right to override or control the actions of the king.

Such was the position in theory. In practice it was strikingly different. At certain points in the machine of government the power of the king was still great. His ministers depended on his favour for their continuance in office. They were thus subject to effective control if the king chose to exercise it. The sudden fall of an able and apparently powerful minister such as the Duc de Choiseul in 1770 showed that even in the last years of the lethargic and indifferent Louis XV this control was real. But it was a negative control. 'Each (minister) is absolute master in his department', wrote the Emperor Joseph II to his mother after a visit to Paris in 1777, 'but fears to be, not controlled, but displaced, by the sovereign. . . . The king is absolute only in his power to pass from one slavery to another. He can change his ministers; but unless he is a transcendent genius he can never be master of the conduct of affairs.'[1] Lower down the administrative hierarchy royal influence was much less effective. In particular the fact that so many

---

[1] A. von Arneth (ed.), *Maria Theresia und Joseph II. Ihr Correspondenz* (Vienna, 1867–68), vol. I, p. 133.

officials had bought their offices and thus made them their personal
property (see p. 104) made it very hard to dismiss them, since the
government could seldom afford to refund the purchase price. The
lower and even the middle ranks of the bureaucracy were to a considerable extent decentralized and independent of royal power. As
time went on their responsiveness to local pressures and needs, as
opposed to those of the central government, tended if anything to
increase. Even the intendants, who had been under Colbert and
his successors the greatest of all agencies of administrative centralization, showed tendencies of this kind in the last decades of the period.
'For long [before the revolution of 1789]', wrote a contemporary, 'the
intendants, directed by public opinion, sought rather to distinguish
themselves by their care for the people and by works of public utility,
than by their obedience to ministerial wishes.'[1] Some, such as Turgot in
the *généralité* of Limoges and Orceau de Fontette in that of Caen, were
much in advance of the central government in their attitude to the
areas they administered. An able and strong minded intendant could
enjoy during the last decade of the *ancien régime* a remarkable degree of
autonomy and independent initiative.

Moreover the French monarchy found itself, in the generation before
1789, faced by increasing opposition from the *parlements* and to a lesser
extent from the estates, normally dominated by the nobility, which still
existed in one or two provinces. In September 1715, immediately after
the death of Louis XIV, the *Parlement* of Paris had restored to it by the
Regent, the Duc d'Orléans, the right of remonstrance which allowed
it to impede royal legislation. This it at once began to use to hamper the
government's efforts to cope with the desperate financial situation.
Proposals to suppress unnecessary offices, to fund part of the state debt
and to debase the currency, all had to face stubborn resistance. This
increasingly impossible situation was brought to a head when the
Parlement was temporarily exiled to Pontoise in 1720 and threatened
with the creation of new judicial institutions which would take over
much of its work. Such measures brought it to heel for the time being;
but this was to be the last occasion before the end of the old monarchy
when the government won a real victory over this increasingly dangerous
opponent. On a number of later occasions—in 1749, 1753, 1771-74 and

[1] G. Sénac de Meilhan, *Du Gouvernement, des Moeurs, et des Conditions en
France avant la Révolution* (Hamburg, 1795), p. 91. This view, which has been
generally accepted by historians, has been challenged by a leading authority on
the subject. See M. Bordes, 'Les intendants de Louis XV', *Revue Historique*,
vol. CCXXIII (1960), pp. 52–61.

1788—the device of exiling the *Parlement* to a provincial town was resorted to; but every one of these struggles was ended by concessions made solely or mainly by the king and his ministers. From the moment its powers were revived in 1715 the *Parlement* had been a strong supporter of the Jansenist minority in the French Church (see pp. 402–03). From the 1730s onwards, therefore, it was involved in intermittent but sometimes very bitter disputes with the government, which was notably more orthodox in its attitude to religious matters. In 1749–51, with the support of the Church and much of the nobility,the *Parlement* was able to defeat a series of efforts by Machault d'Arnouville, the Controller-General of Finance, to impose a tax of one-twentieth on all incomes. This victory of the privileged was one of the decisive events of the century in France. The struggle over Machault's proposals was fought with a bitterness which for several years partially paralysed the workings of government and led to widespread speculations of imminent revolution. Above all the defeat of the government in this conflict condemned it, irretrievably as events were to show, to extreme financial weakness and vulnerability. This, made worse by the wars of 1756–63 and 1778–83, was to destroy it in 1787–89.

Moreover by the 1750s the provincial *parlements*, hitherto relatively inactive, were increasingly following the lead of that of Paris. The *Parlement* of Bordeaux, for example, gave forcible expression in a remonstrance of May 1757 to the idea that it was the guardian of the 'ancient and fundamental laws' of France and could and should not register any legislation which infringed these. In 1763 that of Toulouse went so far as to place the Governor of Languedoc under arrest merely because he had done his duty by attempting to collect new taxation ordered by the government; while for several years in the 1760s Brittany was convulsed by a violent conflict between the Governor, the Duc d'Aiguillon, and the *Parlement* of Rennes, over the same issue. In 1783–84 the *Parlement* of Bordeaux was able, after a struggle, to force the removal from office of an intendant who had tried to reform the system of *corvées* (forced labour, mainly on road-building) in the area of its jurisdiction. All this to modern eyes looks like, and indeed very often was, mere selfish defence of local and sectional interests. Yet it is important to realise that in the last decades of the old régime in France the *parlements* were often expressing more or less accurately what public opinion there was on the issues at stake, and that they had frequently widespread popular support for their attitudes. They were, after all, the only secular institutions which could claim some formal independence of the Crown and the nearest approach to a constitutional opposition which France could muster. This meant that in spite of their class selfishness and narrow legalistic pedantry they were widely regarded as the defenders of liberty and established rights (the two were still largely synonymous) against royal autocracy and 'ministerial despotism'. This function they performed only in a limited and highly conservative way; but there was hardly any other institution in France which could perform it at all. Their power, at least in a negative sense, increased in the last years of the monarchy. In 1771 the Chancellor, Maupeou, exiled the *Parlement* of Paris once more and abolished the offices held by its members. He thus, in the face of furious opposition, cleared the ground for the drastic overhaul of the fiscal system which was now more essential than ever. Three years later, however, he was dismissed on the accession of Louis XVI and the powers of the *parlements* restored. Henceforth they were consistently to impede necessary reforms and thus help to destroy the monarchy they claimed to serve.

The generation before the Revolution saw not only the self-interested opposition to royal power offered by the *parlements* and their allies but a growth in criticism of the monarchical régime of a more fundamental and ultimately more dangerous kind. Demands were now being made that the people, or at least the educated and property-owning classes, be given more effective means of making their wishes felt. Suggestions that some representative element be added to the government, an idea which very few people would have taken seriously before the third quarter of the century, were now being put forward. In 1763 the *Cours des Aides*, one of the chief legal and financial institutions of the monarchy, asked for the convocation of the States-General (a primitive representative body, organized by classes, which had originated in the later Middle Ages and had not met since 1614). In 1775 the Physiocrat Dupont de Nemours drew up an elaborate scheme for a hierarchy of local and provincial representative bodies with a national one as its culminating point. Three years later the Controller-General Necker created an assembly, one-third of whose members were to be nominated by the king and the rest elected, for the province of Berry. A similar one was set up in 1779 in Haute Guienne; and in 1787, in the last desperate efforts to save the old régime in its death agony, no fewer than nineteen similar assemblies were established in *géneralités* throughout the country.

Underlying and largely explaining the ambivalent position of the French monarchy during this period were the personal characters of the monarchs concerned. Louis XV became king of France in 1715 as a child of five. His reign thus began at a moment when, as a result of defeat and financial stress, the difficulties which now faced the monarchy were beginning to become all too visible. The Regency period (1715–23), during which the government was controlled by the able if dissolute Duc d'Orléans, saw a violent reaction against the rigidity and authoritarianism of the régime of Louis XIV. The most striking political expression of this reaction was the establishment of the system known as *polysynodie* (government through councils or committees in place of Secretaries of State) in 1716–18. The experiment was short-lived and a failure; but it suggested that the young king might not be able to reckon as a matter of course on wielding all the powers of his great predecessor. It was, however, his own personality at least as much as the difficulties of the position he had inherited which prevented his following in the footsteps of Louis XIV. Served by an able chief minister, Cardinal Fleury (1726–43), and Controller-General, Orry (1730–45), he remained personally popular until the middle of the century; but the limitations of his character had already begun to show themselves. The sexual irregularities of which biographers have made so much were not in themselves important or unusual for a ruler of that age. What gave some of his mistresses, above all Madame de Pompadour, political significance was Louis's own weakness. The charge which the historian must bring against him is not that he was vicious but that he was timid, selfish and above all lazy. Apart from the system of secret diplomacy under his personal control which he developed after 1745 (see p. 206), and which served merely to complicate and frustrate the foreign policies carried on by his ministers through regular channels, he took little interest in the machinery of government. He exercised no effective supervision of the great departments of State. His unwillingness to face serious opposition, his tendency to seek an easy solution for every difficulty at the expense of the real interests of the monarchy, are well illustrated by his abandonment of Machault's taxation proposals of 1749; in the last years of his reign, embittered by the consciousness of external defeat and domestic unpopularity, he sank into a kind of sullen apathy. 'His lamentable reputation in history,' it has been said, 'derives less from what he did than from what he never tried to do. For him all evils were incurable.'[1] His last years saw in Maupeou's attack on the *parlements* a real effort to give the monarchy more freedom of action, and in the fiscal expedients of the Abbé Terray (Controller-

[1] G. P. Gooch, *Louis XV: the monarchy in decline* (London, 1956), p. 77.

General, 1770–74) a partially successful attempt to ease its financial position. Nevertheless as his reign drew to a close Louis was perhaps more hated and certainly more despised than any king of France for generations. He was, wrote a contemporary critic, 'A king whose death was . . . the triumph of the nation'.[1]

His grandson and successor Louis XVI was not the man to regain either the power or the popularity of the monarchy. Well-meaning and pious, morally much superior to his predecessor, he was of mediocre intelligence and inherited the timidity which had been one of Louis XV's greatest weaknesses. His recall of the *Parlement* of Paris within a few months of his accession, his failure to support his greatest minister, the radically reforming Controller-General Turgot (1774-76), showed that he was no more able than his grandfather to withstand the opposition of the privileged classes. More serious still, during his reign the lack of contact and sympathy between ruler and people, already growing during the last two decades of the life of Louis XV, became still more marked. Apart from a visit to Cherbourg in the 1780s to see the new harbour works there his movements were confined entirely to a group of royal châteaux in the neighbourhood of Paris. To the day of his death on the guillotine in January 1793 France remained to him an unknown land.

Like France, Spain and the Habsburg territories can be regarded as occupying an intermediate position in the spectrum of European monarchy in the eighteenth century. In each rulers were faced, in their efforts to create an efficient administrative machine, by stubborn opposition from privileged groups and institutions. In each they struggled with considerable success to overcome that opposition. In the explicit limits to their power which they had to accept in some of the areas they ruled (especially in Hungary and the Basque provinces) the Habsburgs and the Spanish Bourbons had something in common with the Hanoverians. On the other hand in the fact that they were not limited by any central representative institutions, and that they based their power largely on their armies and bureaucracies, they were in the main stream of continental absolutism.

It is above all in the general success of their rulers in improving the position of the monarchy that the history of Spain and the Habsburg lands differs during this period from that of France. In both the challenge offered to the central government by provincial particularism was far greater than in France. The importance of this factor in the Habs-

---

[1] *Les Fastes de Louis XV* (n.p., 1782), vol. I, preface, p. i.

burg territories has already been mentioned (see p. 124). In Spain the struggle over the succession in 1702–13 had seen a prolonged effort by Catalonia and much of Aragon to throw off Castilian rule, an effort which drove them to support the Habsburg Archduke Charles against the eventually victorious Bourbon claimant to the throne, Philip V, grandson of Louis XIV. Throughout the century, moreover, the Basque provinces retained a remarkable degree of autonomy (notably the right not to be taxed without their consent) while the *cortes* (provincial estates) of Castile and Navarre continued to meet, though infrequently and ineffectively.

There were thus substantial obstacles in Spain and the Habsburg lands to the creation of an effective centralized absolutism, obstacles more substantial than those which existed in France. Yet the Habsburgs and Spanish Bourbons attacked and partially overcame them. They did not surrender to them as Louis XV and Louis XVI did to the opponents of monarchical power. It was only in October 1714 that Barcelona at last surrendered to Philip V after a long siege. Not until the following year, when Majorca was forced to submit, did armed resistance to him in Spain come to an end. As late as 1719 there was a plot to hand over the island of Ibiza in the Balearics to the British; but by then Catalan resentment of rule from Madrid, though still a factor of importance, was ceasing to be an immediate danger to the unity of Spain. The Basque provinces, though they could not be taxed at will, were persuaded by Philip and his successors to provide the monarchy with considerable sums in the form of free gifts (*servicios*). If the *cortes* of Navarre and Castile prolonged a phantom existence that of Aragon vanished for ever. Moreover a new drive towards administrative efficiency was seen in the reorganization by 1714 of the higher ranges of the bureaucracy on the French model. This involved the creation of an Intendant-General of Finance and a number of Secretaries of State: the cumbersome system of councils on which the Spanish Habsburgs had relied so heavily in the previous century began to fall into disuse, the Council of Castile alone remaining important. The new machinery, though it had considerable defects, proved more efficient and much more flexible than the old.

In the Habsburg territories also, as has been seen, a series of able ministers backed by Maria Theresa, the greatest ruler of the dynasty, created from the 1740s onwards a whole range of important new organs of administration (see p. 125). They broke down to some extent, particularly in Bohemia, the former administrative separatism of the provinces, and provided the monarchy with an income far greater and an army far stronger than it had ever possessed before.

Thus in Spain and the Habsburg provinces progress was made in the creation of powerful monarchies and centralized administrations. In France this process was halted and even reversed. The contrast cannot be explained entirely in terms of personalities; nevertheless the characters of the rulers concerned were of the greatest importance in this connexion. In Spain the feebleness of the melancholic Philip V was partially redeemed by the energy of his masterful second wife, Elizabeth Farnese. Charles III was hardworking, patriotic and conscientious, though intellectually unremarkable. In the Habsburg States Maria Theresa displayed a courage and tenacity equalled by very few eighteenth-century rulers, while her son Joseph II, whatever his faults, had no lack of energy and public spirit. The strength of their personalities partially explains the fact that Charles III was able to exert more effective authority than any ruler of Spain for generations, and that the powers of Maria Theresa were greater than those wielded by any of her predecessors. The French monarchy under Louis XVI was by contrast in many ways a shadow of what it had been under Louis XIV. In an age of monarchy there was no substitute for an able and energetic ruler.

It is often claimed that the government of many European States in the generation or more before the French Revolution is distinguished from the practice of the first half of the century by the existence of something called 'Enlightened Despotism'. How far is this claim justified? Clearly some rulers and ministers were being affected in the second half of the century by the complex and often conflicting currents which made up the great intellectual movement of the Enlightenment (see Chap. XV *passim*). In the 1760s the Physiocrats in France laid much of the ideological foundation for a new form of monarchy by popularizing ideas of a natural social order which could be easily discovered by the use of the human intelligence and which all unbiased men of goodwill must support. This natural harmony of interests, it seemed, could be most easily given political expression by an enlightened government, which in eighteenth-century conditions must be the work in the main of an enlightened monarch. In 1767 one of these thinkers, Lemercier de la Rivière, in his *L'Ordre naturel et essentiel des sociétés politiques* (1767), presented such a ruler as not legislating in any positive sense but merely declaring and applying fundamental laws which were immanent in the nature of things, in the structure of the world as it is and must be. In this capacity he was entitled to obedience from the subjects whose welfare he served. This concept of 'legal despotism' had for a time considerable importance, at least in intellectual circles. The belief, universal in the political thinking of the Enlightenment, that the best form of government is one in which the individual is subject to known and clearly expressed laws did not at all rule out the possibility of these laws being enunciated by a monarch. Such attitudes were an expression of the tendency of the age to produce simple, general answers to what in modern eyes seem highly complex and intractable problems. Underlying them was a widespread assumption that the principles of good government were clear, absolute and unchanging, that they could therefore be applied anywhere with relatively little modification. Even a Tatar Khan in the Crimea in the years before the Russian annexation of 1783–84 is said to have wished to rule in terms of 'enlightened' ideas.

The ideology of Enlightened Despotism, however, as it existed in the three or four decades before the French Revolution, was not the expression merely of intellectual forces. Underlying it was also a vein of genuine practicality. Despotism seemed, to the French writers who were much the most important source of this type of thinking, to promise more rapid progress than was possible under balanced and 'mixed' régimes in which power was widely distributed, such as that in Britain. What mattered, after all, was the use made of power, rather than its formal institutional aspects. The enlightened ruler must first of all laicize monarchy. He must free himself from the control of any established church and its priests and instead subordinate them to the State. As his ministers he must take men of true enlightenment; great nobles with an interest in maintaining a feudal past and its practices should be kept at arms length. A monarch who behaved in this way could rely on the applause of many of the leading intellectuals of the age, however despotic his power. Though there were important figures of the Enlightenment (Helvétius, Holbach, above all Diderot) who distrusted any kind of despotic rule, few consistently opposed all forms of despotism on principle. Even Rousseau was opposed only to the despotism of individuals.

The difficulty is to relate this body of theory to what rulers, ministers and officials in fact did in specific situations. Clearly it was possible to have great administrative, fiscal and even social progress under a ruler who was not personally at all in sympathy with the Enlightenment. The

Empress Maria Theresa presided over a transformation of the Habsburg hereditary territories which was the greatest achievement of its kind anywhere in Europe during this period. Without her work the power of the Habsburgs could hardly have survived in so predatory a state system as that of eighteenth-century Europe. Yet in intellectual and to some extent in practical terms her attitudes were overwhelmingly conservative. She was opposed to toleration of Protestants and Jews in her dominions; she wished for good relations with the Papacy, which was the target for the scorn and hostility of almost every leading figure of the Enlightenment from Voltaire downwards; she regretted the dissolution in 1773 of the Society of Jesus; she wished so far as possible to respect in her dominions the rights of the provincial estates, the greatest bastions of resistance to change. Yet the permanent achievements of her reign were not surpassed by any other ruler of the age. In many States, moreover, efforts at more or less enlightened reform were inspired by history and tradition rather than by abstract ideas. They were rooted in the necessities of the countries concerned and in earlier efforts to meet these necessities, not in the mere words of intellectuals, however plausible. Thus in Spain the reforming work of Charles III and his ministers was a reflection of well-marked national traditions. The idea of radical change in terms of a few basic ideas runs through many of the proposals for reform of Spanish government and society made in the seventeenth and early eighteenth centuries as well as those produced by the age of the Enlightenment. In particular the regalism, the desire to assert royal rights over the Church and notably over Church property, which was a notable feature of this movement of reform in Spain, had deep roots in the earlier history of the country. It is note-worthy that of all Charles's ministers the one who most forcibly asserted rights of this kind, Pedro Rodriquez Campomanes, was also the one least influenced by 'enlightened' ideas, which in Spain were very much a foreign, overwhelmingly French, import. For all his regalist attitudes Campomanes showed the sincerity of his Catholicism by dying a member of the third order of the Franciscans.

None of this means that the element of intellectual conviction was negligible in the policies of many of the rulers of Europe in the generation before the French Revolution. It is clear that the greatest of them had beliefs about their relationship to and responsibility for their subjects different from those of their seventeenth- or early eighteenth-century predecessors. The welfare of those they ruled and still more the greatness of the State (now clearly separated from the ruler and the ruling dynasty) dominated their calculations as never before; indeed an ideal of State service was the one thing which they had in common. This ideal was sometimes expressed by partisans of Enlightened Despotism with almost religious fervour. 'The State', wrote one, 'is a lifeless mass, to which the monarch first gives life; a machine without motion, which the monarch first sets moving and to whose mechanism he gives reality . . . the monarch lives for the State and the State lives through him.'[1] Attitudes of this kind meant that purely dynastic considerations played strikingly little part in the thinking of most of these rulers. Family feelings and any sense of monarchs as a divinely blessed group had in general little hold on them. In Prussia Frederick II was often on bad terms with his younger brothers, whom he treated with great severity; and he disliked and neglected his nephew and heir. His lack of family feeling and unquestioning assumption that it must always be sacrificed to necessities of State emerge clearly from his *Political Testaments* of 1752 and 1768, the most revealing of all statements of his basic ideas. In Russia Catherine II, after conniving at the overthrow and murder of her husband in 1762, was on continuously bad terms with her son and heir, Paul, who feared and hated her and whom in the last two decades of her reign she scarcely ever saw. In the Habsburg territories Joseph II treated other members of the ruling family with a studied rudeness which shocked contemporaries: in the 1780s he deeply antagonized his younger brother Leopold, Grand Duke of Tuscany, by pressing for the merging of the Grand Duchy with the hereditary lands of the monarchy. The history of every European dynasty is full of rivalries and antagonisms; such things could flourish very well without ideas of enlightened government to give impetus to them. Nevertheless there is little doubt that in the cases of Frederick and Joseph at least a feeling that an enlightened ruler ought to be above merely personal and family considerations, that it was his duty to sacrifice them ruthlessly on the altar of the State, was a factor in their behaviour to their own blood relations. The contrast with the unbridled dynasticism of the age of Louis XIV is a striking and significant one.

No ruler of a large State, however, could afford the luxury of uncritical adherence to an ideology, even one so loosely defined as that of enlightened government. All of them, to only slightly varying extents, were inevitably the prisoners of history. For all of them limits to possible action were set by economic, social, political or military

[1] A. L. von Schlözer, *Neuverändertes Russland, oder Leben Catherina der Zweyten, Kaiserinn von Russland* (Riga–Mittau–Leipzig, 1771–72), vol. 1, Vorrede.

considerations which were in the main the legacy of the past. Completely 'enlightened' government was a goal which, even had they wished to attain it, the internal complexities of their own countries and the external pressure of others placed beyond their reach. Only small States, freed from the burden of playing a leading role in international affairs and often more homogeneous economically and socially than their more powerful neighbours, could afford to apply the political panaceas of the Enlightenment with some approach to thoroughness. Thus the only European ruler to introduce, even on a restricted scale, the *impôt unique* (a single tax on land) which was perhaps the most important practical innovation advocated by the Physiocrats, was the Margrave Charles Frederick of Baden. (The experiment was a failure.) With the great exception of Joseph II the rulers of the major States in the later eighteenth century were not prepared to face the problems involved in really radical changes of this kind. Louis XV and his successor clearly had neither the desire nor the ability to become enlightened despots. In Britain government of this type was always out of the question.

Frederick II of Prussia is of all the major rulers of the century the one about whose stature historians have disagreed most violently. There is no doubt that to his contemporaries he seemed, for much of his reign, the outstanding example of a modern and enlightened ruler. By raising Prussia from the position of a second-rate State to that of at least a kind of great power, and by achieving this with very limited physical resources, he provided the supreme illustration of what might be accomplished by an intelligent and dedicated ruler inspired by enlightened ideas. The decade after 1745, when the successful struggle for Silesia, which had transformed Prussia's international standing, was followed by internal consolidation and some limited domestic reform, saw his reputation at its height. In these years Frederick gave Europe its first real example of enlightened despotism in action. Moreover throughout his life he continued to pay at least formal allegiance to a system of ideas which stressed very heavily the moral obligation of the ruler to use his powers selflessly, unsparing of his own peace and comfort, for the good of the State. From his *Anti-Machiavel* (1741) to his *Essai sur les formes de gouvernement* (1781) he expressed a view of monarchy which was utilitarian, secular, antidynastic and untraditional. The people, by a tacit and irrevocable act of delegation, had handed over their powers to the monarch. This surrender was legitimized only if the monarch devoted himself unsparingly to the good of the state and his subjects.

Indeed he alone could see clearly what that good was; for in virtue of his position he was impartial and disinterested as no mere section of society, no corporate body or representative assembly, ever could be. This austere doctrine meant for Frederick a lifetime of toil and effort: no monarch in the history of Europe has worked so hard over so long a period to meet obligations which were essentially self-imposed. It was also a view of monarchy quite compatible with a deep contempt for the subjects whom the ruler served from above and whose interests he safeguarded with such jealous care, often against their own misguided inclinations. Frederick himself showed this contempt, in writing and conversation, with an often brutal lack of restraint, especially as he became soured by decades of effort and struggle. The humanitarian side of the Enlightenment, the emphasis it laid on making the ordinary man happier through religious toleration, economic progress and education, certainly made a genuine appeal to him throughout his reign. But the necessities of the State, its imperative demands for physical security and therefore for military strength and administrative efficiency, for him took precedence over everything else. To these the happiness of individuals (not least of Frederick himself) were always sacrificed without hesitation. The idea of the humane, creatively enlightened State, which cared for ordinary men and their development, was in his thinking always overshadowed by that of the power-State, austere, demanding and careless of the feelings or immediate interests of the individual. Duty and service, not freedom or happiness, are the notes which reverberate through the history of eighteenth-century Prussia. Yet it must be stressed that in the eyes of Frederick, and in those of most of his contemporaries, his rule was never a crude despotism. On the contrary, the Prussian State was seen as having been turned consciously, by a great act of will on the part of its ruler, on to paths which were constructive and enlightened. Justice, religious toleration and codification of the laws; economic progress, through internal colonization and a great variety of government measures; intellectual life, above all through Frederick's own example as a writer and the symbol of the Enlightenment enthroned—all these seemed to be served by his rule.

Yet it is when we turn to Frederick in action, to the administration of Prussia during his forty-six years on its throne, that the ambiguity of his position becomes fully clear. Throughout his reign he trod, where day-to-day rule was concerned, in paths already marked out for him by his father, to whom the Enlightenment had meant nothing. In spite of the profound dissimilarities between father and son, and the bitter personal conflicts between them, Frederick II remained always the executor of Frederick William I. 'Only his care', he wrote of his father, 'his untiring work, his scrupulously just policies, his great and admirable thriftiness and the strict discipline he introduced into the army which he himself had created, made possible the achievements I have so far accomplished.'[1] Frederick was fully conscious, as perhaps his father had never been, of the State as an entity completely distinct from the person of the ruler, its greatest servant. Nevertheless his only important addition to the system of administration which he inherited was a series of judicial reforms which were in the main the work not of the king himself but of one of his ministers, Samuel von Cocceji. In one important respect, his active and explicit preference for aristocratic ministers and officials as against commoners, Frederick's reign sees a definite regression from what had preceded it (see above p. 119). In economic life, in spite of a long series of efforts, little was achieved. Canal-building, monopolistic trading companies, a state bank, an elaborate new excise scheme of 1766: none of these had much success. Prussia remained, in spite of all Frederick could do, what the most severe of his modern critics has quite fairly called 'a backward, retarded, autocratic and sergeant-like (*feldwebelhaft*) economy'.[2] In cultural terms, again, it is very easy to overrate what Frederick achieved. His flute-playing, the vast quantity of bad French poetry he wrote, his friendship with Voltaire (carefully advertised but when put to the test no more than skin deep) impressed many contemporaries and have impressed some historians. Yet they count for little when balanced against his blindness to the cultural ferment which was agitating educated Germany by the later decades of his reign, and his ignorant contempt for most of the greatest German writers and scholars of the age. It is no accident that so many of the latter—Wieland, Winckelmann, Lessing, Gottsched —disliked both him and Prussia.

Frederick thus presents the paradox of a ruler who was sincerely attracted by at least some of the ideas of the Enlightenment, who voiced these ideas and advertised his adherence to them throughout his life, and yet whose policies in practice were hardly affected at all by the new intellectual currents of the age. He was, to be fair, in a position which left him little real freedom of action. Prussia, even after the

---

[1] Quoted in Hubatsch, p. 125 (*see* Bibliography, p. 101).
[2] Augstein, p. 264 (*see* Bibliography, p. 241). Chapter 7 of this book is the most scathing of all attacks on the king's economic policies.

territorial gains of his reign, was a relatively small and weak state surrounded by more powerful neighbours. The imperative needs of self-
defence meant the fullest possible mobilization of all available resources.
The king had, therefore, to command and manipulate his subjects with
much of the harshness of a Prussian sergeant drilling new recruits. A
more liberal regime, a greater degree of freedom, serious political
experiment of any kind, even had Frederick ever desired such things,
were luxuries too dangerous to be indulged in under these conditions.
Moreover under his rule the extent to which Prussia was committed to
Eastern Europe and had her centre of gravity east of the Elbe was
markedly accentuated. The alliance of 1764 with Russia was a politic,
even necessary, move after the frightening demonstration of Russian
military power during the Seven Years War (see p. 261 below).
Yet coupled with the seizure of Polish territory in 1772 it helped to
emphasize Prussia's affinities with her eastern rather than her western
neighbours. The deep ambiguities of the Prussian State as it existed in
the nineteenth century, intellectually a part of Western Europe yet with
a social and military structure much of which continually tended to
align it with Russia, trace largely from Frederick's reign. He himself did
not much value the small detached territories—Cleves, Mark, Ravens-
berg—which he ruled in the Rhineland. He discriminated against them
in his tariff policies and would have been willing to exchange them for
land in Pomerania, Saxony or Mecklenburg. In terms of his own
situations and interests this attitude is perfectly understandable. Yet it
illustrates once more how throughout his reign, in spite of his personal
adherence to so many of the attitudes and ideas of the Enlightenment,
he was turning Prussia's energies and attentions to the East, with all that
this implied for the future.

Catherine II of Russia is almost as controversial a figure as Frederick.
Throughout most of her reign, and particularly in its early years, she
made strenuous efforts to show herself an adherent of advanced ideas
of government, indeed of the ideas of the French Enlightenment in
general. On a superficial level this can be seen in her long and mutually
admiring correspondence with Voltaire, and in her financial help to
Diderot and the unsuccessful visit to Russia which he paid at her
invitation. On a more serious one the same efforts underlay the calling
in 1767 of the Legislative Commission, the most ambitious effort made
in eighteenth-century Russia to provide the country with a rationalized
and workable legal code. The Instruction (*Nakaz*) which Catherine
personally drew up for the guidance of the deputies who made up this

Commission was a conflation of ideas drawn, with little alteration, from West European writers, above all Montesquieu and Beccaria. Though it was completely lacking in originality its publication in Western Europe drew the admiration of many of the leading figures of the Enlightenment. The Legislative Commission produced no results. The outbreak of war with the Ottoman Empire in October 1768 led to the suspension of its work; and the explosion of the great peasant and Cossack revolt led by Pugachov in June 1773 ensured that it was not reconvened. But though Catherine was clearly disappointed by its failure to produce a new code of laws as quickly and easily as she had hoped, and perhaps not very reluctant to end its activities, there is no doubt of the sincerity of her motives in calling it. Nor is there any question of the reality of the belief in the principles of enlightened government which underlay the *Nakaz*. Moreover, as has been seen (p. 122), the 1760s witnessed in Russia the beginnings of a remarkable process of administrative reform which culminated in the great overhaul of provincial government in 1775.

All this gives Catherine II apparently formidable claims to be re-garded as a genuinely enlightened ruler. Yet many historians would argue that these claims were fraudulent, or at least contained a large element of the unreal and the unjustified. Criticism of the empress has developed along at least three different lines. In the first place it is argued that the real motive which underlay her ostentatious partisanship of enlightenment, especially in the 1760s, was not a concern for the well-being of her subjects or even a strong belief in the intellectual justification of ideas of enlightened government, but mere vanity. She was inspired, it is argued, by nothing higher than a desire for self-advertisement and for the applause of Voltaire and his fellow-writers in Western Europe. Doubts of the sincerity of her much advertised desire for reform were already being voiced in the early years of her reign. A British commentator, for example, writing in 1768 when her reputation as an enlightened ruler was at its height, thought that 'there is a sort of whim or affection of singularity, in the manner of conferring her favours, that looks as if the desire of being spoken of, fully as much as the desire of doing good, was the fountain from which they flow'.[1] Certainly there is no doubt of the strength of Catherine's desire for a good press in Western Europe and of her sensitivity to criticism of any kind: vanity and *amour propre* played a greater role in her policies than in those of any other ruler of the period.

[1] W. Richardson, *Anecdotes of the Russian Empire* (London, 1784), p. 26.

A second and more serious line of criticism is that the empress's claims to real enlightment and concern for the welfare of her subjects are shown to be a hollow pretence by the intensification and geographical extension of serfdom in Russia during her reign. That these developments took place, in spite of much fruitless discussion in St. Petersburg of the possibility of abolishing serfdom, is beyond doubt. The marked deterioration in the position of the Russian peasant under Catherine's rule has allowed historians to point the contrast between the enlightened ideals which she proclaimed and the oppressive despotism which she allegedly practised. In particular the decree of May 1783, which in effect established serfdom definitively in the Ukraine, has attracted much criticism. Yet the question is not a simple one. The most recent work on the subject stresses the complexity and ambiguity of much of the legislation of this period regarding the serf population of Russia: it also suggests that after 1775 repression of peasant disorder may have been less arbitrary than before and that it was sometimes accompanied by efforts by provincial governors to persuade landowners to treat their peasants with greater humanity. It has also been argued that the halting of peasant movement in the Ukraine and the extension there in 1783 of the poll-tax, which doomed the Ukrainian peasant to serf status, were inspired by a desire to end the privileged position enjoyed by many border area of the empire, and to some extent by the need to increase revenue, rather than by the extension of serfdom as a matter of policy.[1] Moreover it is true that in one or two specific minor ways the empress tried positively to limit serfdom—by ordering in 1781 that war prisoners were in future to become free men if they were converted to Orthodoxy; and by reducing the possibilities which had hitherto existed of enserfment by marriage. But none of this modifies significantly the fact that when she died there were more serfs in Russia than ever before and that they were worse treated than under any of her predecessors.

Finally Catherine's claims to be a genuine enlightened despot can be impugned, like those of Frederick II, on the grounds that she was merely carrying on policies inherited from her predecessors. In many essentials this charge is undeniable. The reform of provincial government in 1775 had been anticipated by proposals made in the 1750s under the Empress Elizabeth. So had the great survey of landownership in

---

[1] Isabel de Madariaga, 'Catherine II and the serfs: a reconsideration of some problems', *Slavonic and East European Review*, vol. LII (1974), especially pp. 39–54; D. M. Griffiths, 'Catherine II: the republican empress', *Jahrbücher für Geschichte Osteuropas*, neue Folge, Band XXI (1973), pp. 329–30.

Russia which Catherine set in motion in 1765 and even the Legislative Commission of two years later. The secularization of Church lands in 1764 was the completion of a process begun early in the century by Peter I. The system of government which Catherine perfected, an autocracy based on the support of the landowning class, was entirely Russian. Only in a few cosmetic details did it owe anything to French or other West European influences. Like every other ruler of a great state, the empress was the captive of the historical situation in which she found herself, a situation which in her case forbade any radical change in the social structure of Russia or any far-reaching amelioration from above of the position of the peasant. It is unfair to see her, as Soviet historians have done, as the mere representative of the Russian nobility, trampling underfoot the interests of the great mass of the population to serve those of a small ruling class. It is significant that the huge grants of land and serfs to noble favourites and officials, for which she has been so much blamed, followed the first partition of Poland in 1772. After the original grants to her supporters in the *coup d'état* of 1762 which placed her on the throne, Catherine made very few presents of this kind during the decade 1762–72, when her dependence on noble support is usually supposed to have been at its height. Nevertheless as a woman, a foreigner and a usurper, Catherine was never in a position to dispense with the backing of the landowning class in Russia, even had she ever dreamed of doing so. This, coupled with the insuperable physical difficulties of governing a huge, thinly populated empire, set inescapable limits to what she could hope to achieve. 'How', asked a French observer at the end of her reign, 'was a woman to effect that which the active discipline of the cane, and the sanguinary axe of Peter I, were inadequate to accomplish?' After all, he went on, 'it was solely by suffering her power to be abused that she succeeded in preserving it'.[1]

It would be a mistake to end this discussion of Catherine's work on a merely negative note. Apart from the very real administrative achievements of her reign she had some grasp of the advantages of giving the nobility, the townsfolk and even the state peasants an improved status as efficient and creative autonomous groups within Russian society (see p. 46). Moreover her rule saw in Russia an unprecedented growth of intellectual life and a flow and expression of ideas more free than ever before in the country's history. The members of the Legislative Commission of 1767 received from the areas which elected them both

[1] *Secret Memoirs of the Court of St. Petersburg* (2nd ed., London, 1801), p. 61.

instructions and statements of grievances: digests of these were studied by the empress and had considerable influence on her later activities, notably on the reform of provincial administration in 1775. This upward flow of information and suggestions for change was something new in Russian history. A different expression of a roughly similar tendency can be seen in the fact that the total production of books in Russia during the years 1762–1800 was about three and a half times that in the entire period from the introduction of printing down to 1761.[1] Catherine is best seen, in the last analysis, in essentially the same terms as Frederick II. She was, in other words, a genuine believer in the ideals of enlightened government (perhaps a more sincere one than the king of Prussia); but her application of these ideals was limited to some extent by her personal weaknesses and far more by the demands and pressures of the situation in which history had placed her.

There were none the less in the later eighteenth century a number of rulers and ministers in Europe who were prepared to break radically with the past, to override vested interests and disregard deep-rooted traditions in the interests of the States they ruled. Yet in almost every case of this kind the difficulty of relating theory to practice, of showing that radically reforming policies were inspired or even strongly influenced by theories of enlightened government, is marked. Most of them are to be found in southern and Mediterranean Europe, an area in terms of its society and institutions closer to France than to Prussia or Russia. In many of the States concerned, Portugal or the Kingdom of the Two Sicilies for example, the machinery of administration was poor, very much poorer than in Prussia. Few of the rulers or ministers who attempted far-reaching reform in these areas were much influenced by the Enlightenment and none advertised his adherence to its ideas as Frederick II and Catherine II did. (This explains the small amount of attention given them by contemporary theorists of enlightenment in contrast to the adulation lavished on the Prussian and Russian rulers.)

In the kingdom of Savoy-Piedmont a series of remarkable reforms throughout the century went far, at least in theory, towards creating a modern State and society. A unified legal code was established there in 1725–29. The completion of a great survey of landownership in 1725–38 paved the way for a high degree of equality in respect of taxation: the nobility and clergy retained tax privileges only in respect of properties

---

[1] K. A. Papmehl, *Freedom of Expression in Eighteenth Century Russia* (The Hague, 1971), p. 133.

which they could prove they had held before 1584. In January 1762 King Charles-Emmanuel III freed all serfs on the royal estates and encouraged those of the nobility to negotiate their own freedom. Another decree of December 1771 began the abolition of feudal rights, which were to be redeemed by money payments to their owners. In Savoy as elsewhere, it was one thing to issue a decree and another to make it effective. Not all this legislation was quickly or completely put into force. The poverty of the peasants and the village communes meant that in 1792 less than half the redemptions of feudal rights envisaged two decades earlier had been completed. Nevertheless in theory and to some extent in practice a programme of very far-reaching change was carried out; and this was achieved in one of the most intellectually backward and undeveloped areas in Western Europe. None of the men who introduced these reforms felt much sympathy with the Enlightenment, or even perhaps knew much about it. Change had been forced on them, as earlier on such 'empirical' despots as Peter I in Russia and Frederick William I in Prussia, by the imperative need for greater practical efficiency, and to some extent perhaps by an instinctive feeling for rationality, not by theories propounded in Paris.

The same is true of the Marques de Pombal, who for over a quarter of a century (1750–77) was virtual ruler of Portugal as all-powerful chief minister of King Joseph I. His efforts to revive the country's economic life and challenge the dominance which British merchants had for decades wielded over its foreign trade, his ferocious repression of noble opposition, his brutal expulsion of the Jesuits in 1767, show a far more truly radical attitude to tradition and established interests than Frederick II displayed. Yet his claims to be considered an 'enlightened' minister are very doubtful. His policies were empirical, dictated by what he saw as the necessities of the immediate situation. Though he destroyed the power of the Jesuits in Portugal he left untouched the politically less threatening one of the Inquisition. Though he had served as a diplomat in both London and Vienna he seems to have owed little to the ideas of the Enlightenment: his favourite author was Molière, not any eighteenth-century writer.

Rather similar arguments apply to Bernardo Tanucci, the most important single reformer in the Kingdom of the Two Sicilies. Tanucci was an innovator only to a very limited extent. An edict of 1738 against abuses of the judicial system, for the promulgation of which he was responsible, led to no real change. A commission for legislative reform set up in 1742 produced a decade later not a legal code but a mere collection of edicts and regulations, neither amended nor unified. In one area Tanucci did aim at far-reaching change. He was bitterly hostile to the enormous powers and privileges of the church in southern Italy and thus abolished the Holy Office in the Two Sicilies and attacked the right of mortmain which had over generations accumulated vast amounts of property in clerical hands. In 1762 he even secured a royal edict which compelled the clergy to contribute a fifth of their income to charitable purposes, though this soon had to be withdrawn. Yet in spite of this he remained a convinced Catholic, regarding Voltaire and the *Encyclopedia* as profoundly dangerous.

Charles-Emmanuel III, Pombal, Tanucci: all these were severely practical and utilitarian in their attitude to the problems of government. To them enlightened rule, in so far as they thought in terms of it at all, meant simply effective solutions to immediate problems. Of the Enlightenment as Kant or Voltaire saw it (see pp. 364, 366 below), as the human mind liberating itself from the self-imposed tutelage of centuries, a new birth of intellectual adventure, they had no inkling. The same is true of Charles III of Spain (1759–88) and his most important reforming ministers, Campomanes and Jovellanos. It is important to remember that the Enlightenment as a set of economic, administrative, or even penological or hygienic reforms, could be conscientiously and effectively applied by men indifferent or hostile to it in its higher sense as a movement transforming the human consciousness.

The Grand Duke Leopold of Tuscany (1766–90) presents a more difficult problem. He was in many ways the most remarkable and most interesting of all the 'enlightened despots'. Tuscany at the beginning of his reign was still what it had been since the formation of the Grand Duchy in the sixteenth century, a personal union of a number of medieval city-states, of which the most important were Florence and Siena. These for generations had remained distinct in their administration, their laws and their economic institutions. From this unpromising inheritance Leopold had created by the end of his reign, at least on paper, one of the best-governed states in Europe. Aided by some of the ablest ministers possessed by any eighteenth-century ruler (Pompeo Neri until his death in 1776; Francesco-Maria Gianni after the date) he changed every aspect of the life of his dominions. Here as elsewhere in Catholic Europe reform meant a reduction in the stifling power of the Church. The right of mortmain was limited in 1769, the Holy Office abolished in the Grand Duchy in 1782 and in 1785 the powers of religious tribunals limited to spiritual affairs. Reform in Tuscany also had important economic aspects. In 1767 the import and movement of grain was freed from restriction; while the craft guilds were suppressed in 1770 and a great survey of landownership begun in 1781. Municipal government throughout the Grand Duchy was overhauled in the 1770s. Most striking of all was the constitution which Leopold presented to his subjects in September 1782. This provided for the sending by the communal assemblies already existing in the Tuscan towns of representatives to provincial ones. These in turn were to be represented in a central assembly for the entire State. Without the consent of the latter neither the succession to the throne nor the territorial limits of the Grand Duchy were to be changed; nor was war to be declared or existing legislation altered. These proposals remained only a paper scheme; but they constitute the most remarkable constitutional document to take shape in any European State during the generation before the French Revolution. If we interpret Europe as excluding Great Britain there is a good deal of force in the claim of one historian that Leopold was 'the first constitutionally-minded monarch known to European history'.

There is no doubt, moreover, of the sincerity of the Grand Duke's belief that he was merely a trustee acting on behalf of his subjects, whose interests must to him always be paramount. In one of the most striking of his letters to his brother, the Emperor Joseph II, he stresses the need for a ruler always to be willing to give his subjects a complete account of the finances of the state and of their administration; such action, he writes, is 'glorious, useful and just'. The State finances are 'entirely a public matter' and the ruler merely their administrator. He is entitled to spend money only 'in accordance with the intentions of his principal' (i.e. the people), for the advantage of the State and the individuals who compose it.[1] Such attitudes are a striking reflection of the idealistic and libertarian aspects of the Enlightenment. Since Leopold ruled a small State and had neither fears nor ambitions so far as territorial changes were concerned (he wished to establish the perpetual neutrality of the Grand Duchy as a tradition of European diplomacy, to give it more or less the status which Switzerland was to enjoy in the following century) he was able to accept radical ideas and even attempt to realize them in practice in a way quite impossible to Frederick II or Catherine II. There is no doubt moreover that, unlike Charles-Emmanuel III in Savoy or Charles III in Spain, he was in close

---

[1] A. von Arneth (ed.), *Joseph II und Leopold von Toscana, ihr Briefwechsel von 1781 bis 1790* (Vienna, 1872), p. 23.

personal contact with the most progressive thought of the age on political and social problems. His tutor, Anton von Martini, was one of the foremost representatives of the Enlightenment in the Habsburg territories. He read extensively many leading political writers of the age, notably Turgot. He was deeply interested in the progress of the American Revolution, and possessed and studied in some detail a copy of the constitution of Pennsylvania. Yet not even Leopold was merely the Enlightenment enthroned. Another force underlying his policies, one which helps to explain his ready acceptance of ideas of limited monarchy and some degree of representative government, was aristo-cratic conservative influences, derived particularly from the Habsburg province of Carinthia and the traditions of its estates, which were strongly represented in his entourage.

The only great late-eighteenth-century example (though it was a very great one) of the ruler-ideologue, the monarch who attempted as an act of faith to impose enlightened rule upon his subjects, was the Emperor Joseph II, the elder brother of the Grand Duke Leopold. In outlook and temperament the brothers differed sharply. Where Leopold was uninterested in territorial gains Joseph spent much of his life in often fruitless efforts to add to the Habsburg power in Germany, Italy, Poland or the Balkans. It was his strongly expressed desire to annex the Grand Duchy of Tuscany to the hereditary provinces of the monarchy which at least in part prevented the putting into force there of the constitution of 1782. Where Leopold was cautious and realistic, Joseph was rash, obstinate and inflexible. Where the younger brother was moderate and willing to compromise, aware of the rights and claims of his subjects and of the impossibility of ruling despotically, the elder was conscious of no such limitation and, with the highest inten-tions, was deeply intolerant of all opposition. The contrast is well illustrated by some of the entries in Leopold's diary during a visit to Vienna in 1778–79. In these he criticizes severely his brother's régime as 'arbitrary despotism' and accuses Joseph of wishing to 'dispose despotically and capriciously of the lands, persons and goods of his subjects'.[1]

Joseph's view of kingship had no particular originality; it was essen-tially the same as that of Frederick II, whom he greatly admired and took in many respects as a model. He thought of his authority as dele-

---

[1] A. Wandruszka, 'Joseph II und der Verfassungsprojekt Leopolds II', *Historische Zeitschrift*, vol. CXC (1960), p. 21.

gated to him by his subjects and thus contractual in origin. He was the mandatory of his people, the trustee of the general good. The power delegated to him must never be misused for merely personal or even dynastic ends. It was, however, absolute. The people, having once surrendered it, could not revoke their delegation; and no subordinate authority in his dominions, whether of a guild, a religious order or the estates of a province, could be valid unless it emanated from or was confirmed by him. He thought always much too easily, in highly unrealistic terms, of the peoples he ruled as a mere aggregate of individuals face to face with an absolute State. The real and continuing importance in many parts of his dominions of institutions intermediate between ruler and subject he underestimated grossly almost to the end of his reign.

His objectives were no more original than his political ideas. As with Frederick and Catherine, his overriding consideration was the power and well-being of the State. It was his ability to achieve that power and well-being which alone justified his despotism. In practical terms this meant curbing the powers and reducing the property rights of the Catholic Church; hence the 'Josephinism' which was one of his most important legacies to his successors (see pp. 409–10 below). It also meant centralized and rationalized administration; hence efforts were made to extend to Hungary, so jealous of its autonomy, the administrative system of the hereditary provinces. Joseph's attempts to end the dominance of the Hungarian county assemblies by the local gentry, and to substitute German for Latin as the language of administration, provoked deep and passionate national resentment. State power and the public good also demanded efforts to improve the position of the peasant: free peasants would be more productive than unfree ones. Hence the *Unterthanspatent* of 1781, which abolished personal servitude, though not labour services, in the hereditary provinces; the *Strafpatent* of the same year, which limited the lord's right to punish his peasants; and the introduction in 1789 of a very ambitious though shortlived scheme of tax reform which provided that in future the peasant should pay to State and lord combined only 30 per cent of his gross income. Some limited degree of universal education was another obvious step towards the strengthening of the State and the fostering of general well-being. Basic literacy, which was all that was aimed at, would allow the people to grasp more easily the intentions of the ruler and thus ensure their more effective cooperation in his policies. Hence the creation in the Austrian provinces and Bohemia, beginning with the *Allgemeine Schulordnung* of 1774 (though this was the work of an official, J. I. Felbiger, not of Joseph himself) of the first truly universal system of education in European history.

None of these policies had any essential novelty. The greatest period of administrative reform in the history of the Habsburg territories had come in the two decades after 1749 (see p. 125); here Joseph achieved much less than his mother. Official efforts to protect the cultivator against an oppressive lord went back at least as far as 1680; and in many ways Maria Theresa showed a truer concern for her peasant subjects than her son was ever to do. In the 1770s, for example, she had envisaged the abolition of serfdom in Bohemia, Joseph merely its amelioration: his attitude probably contributed to the outbreak in the province of the peasant revolt of 1775. 'Josephinism' in religious matters, it is now clear, had behind it a long tradition extending back to the first years of the century. In one significant way, it is true, the reign of Joseph marked a distinct break with the past. It saw, especially in its early years, a great advance in freedom of expression on political and other questions in the Austrian provinces and the emergence of an embryonic public opinion there. The relaxation of the censorship which was one of his first actions after the death of his mother meant that in 1780–81 an extraordinary flood of pamphlets (many of them admittedly on very trivial subjects) engulfed Vienna. In March 1782 the British ambassador there spoke of a freedom of political debate 'almost as extensive as in England'. But for the great bulk of Joseph's subjects this was a meaningless luxury; and in any case the later years of the reign, as opposition mounted, saw the government's control of publication and the press partially reasserted. In the main, Joseph's work was a logical continuation of that of his mother and her ministers.

What was novel about his reforms was not so much their content as the spirit in which they were carried out. A dogmatic intolerance which refused to recognize that he might sometimes be mistaken, a haste which incessantly demanded immediate and clearly identifiable results, undermined policies always well meant and sometimes even well conceived. About many of the emperor's actions there hangs an atmosphere of niggling dogmatism, of intolerant high-mindedness, which makes him, for all his good intentions, personally one of the least attractive of eighteenth-century rulers. Thus Joseph realized one of the objectives of radical idealists throughout Europe by virtually abolishing the death penalty in the Austrian provinces: only one execution took place there during the whole of his reign. But the hard labour for criminals which replaced judicial execution took place in conditions so appalling that it was in effect a living death. The genuine and constructive concern for elementary education which the emperor showed was combined with a marked dislike of scholars, whom he regarded as useless parasites. The result was that though his reign saw a growth in popular literacy, the setting up of Jewish and Protestant schools and the supply by the government of free textbooks for elementary teaching, it also witnessed a serious attack on secondary education and the universities. When he died there were only about half as many pupils in secondary schools as at his accession to the throne. Moreover the number of universities in Joseph's dominions had by 1790 been reduced to a mere three (Vienna, Louvain and Pest) and these had been forced to concentrate on such useful subjects as medicine and law and virtually to end the teaching of luxury ones such as foreign languages. The fostering of economic growth was a constructive objective, at bottom perhaps the most important of all. But it was not helped by such petty interferences with ordinary life as a decree of 1781 which forbade young men under the age of twenty-eight to travel abroad, or another of 1789 which forbade the granting of a marriage licence to peasant couples unless they could prove that they had already enriched the state by planting a number of fruit trees. The mental atmosphere of Joseph's reforms—idealism, effort and self-sacrifice combined with dogmatism, intolerance and a humourless lack of any sense of proportion—is very reminiscent of many aspects of the French Revolution. The emperor himself, indeed, was well aware of this similarity. Shortly before his death he complained with much justification that his Belgian subjects were refusing to receive from him as a gift benefits which the French were at the same moment extorting from Louis XVI by a great upheaval.

A man of this stamp, ruling what was still in essentials, in spite of the reforms of Maria Theresa, a mere group of provinces, a random aggregation of territories, was certain to encounter opposition. Of the great established interests in his dominions—Church, nobility, provincial estates, privileged towns—none was on his side. Active and intelligent support Joseph could expect only from a small number of officials. Moreover his domestic position was seriously weakened by his obvious lack of success as a diplomat and a military commander. His failure to gain much of Bavaria in 1778–79, or to exchange the whole electorate for the Austrian Netherlands some years later (see pp. 264–6 below), or to achieve real military success against the Turks in the war of 1788–90, undoubtedly did a good deal to increase the difficulties he faced within his own dominions. To these difficulties he himself added immensely by his insistence on extending his reforms to Hungary and the Austrian Netherlands. Had he confined his attentions to the Austrian provinces and Bohemia the story might have been very different; but the nationalism of the Hungarians (or at least their ruling class) and the ingrained particularist conservatism of the Netherlands provinces, above all Brabant, proved too much for him. Yet far from leading him to abandon or modify his policies, opposition incited him to more drastic methods. If his subjects were unwilling to accept the progress and enlightenment he offered, so much the worse for them. If they could not be enlightened by persuasion it must be done by force. We are thus faced in his later years by the paradox of a ruler who had spent his life in efforts to make his subjects prosperous and happy compelled to create a system of secret police (the ancestor of that of the Metternich era) and to hold down considerable parts of his territories by armed force. A Lombard observer, commenting on his methods, remarked that 'the time seems to have returned in which Mahomet, sabre in hand, was the most eloquent teacher in the world'.[1] Events were to show that the persuasive power of force was not lasting and that some parts of the Habsburg lands were still able to defend their privileges effectively against the pressure of the central government. The emperor's reforming policies in the Austrian Netherlands, in particular his efforts to reduce the power of the Catholic Church there and to override provincial traditions and institutions, meant that from 1787 onwards much of the area was in open opposition to him. This, coupled with the almost equally difficult situation in Hungary, seemed about to disrupt the fragile unity of the Habsburg dominions. Even before his death in February 1790 Joseph, ill and discouraged, had been driven to revoke some of his most unpopular measures. His brother, who succeeded him as the Emperor Leopold II, was able to restore peace in the disturbed areas by a skilful mixture of force and concessions.

Enlightened Despotism is not a mere figment of the historian's imagination. It had a real existence, in the sense that a number of rulers in the period 1750–90 attempted, to differing extents and in differing ways, to shape their policies in terms of a body of current theories about the duties of monarchs and the nature of good government. They were more influenced than their predecessors by consciously held and relatively sophisticated beliefs and less by unthinking traditional assump-

[1] Fejto (*see* Bibliography, p. 132), p. 215.

tions. Yet if we look at what they in fact did, it is striking how little practical differences these beliefs really made. In almost every case (Leopold in Tuscany is perhaps the one real exception) the new façade of fashionable ideology clothed policies which followed smoothly and without any break in continuity from what had been attempted by relatively unenlightened predecessors. No ruler of the later eighteenth century except Joseph II was willing to press home 'enlightened' policies in the face of really formidable opposition; and his fate showed the near-impossibility of doing this successfully. All eighteenth-century governments existed, in the last analysis, by the consent or at least the acquiescence of the governed. No ruler, therefore, could force his subjects for very long to accept innovations, however enlightened, which they really disliked. In every State the mass of the uneducated and a large fraction of the educated were deeply hostile to change, quite untouched by the intellectual currents of the Enlightenment and intensely suspicious of any government-inspired innovation. In particular any tampering with traditional religious institutions or observances, of the kind so common among enlightened rulers and ministers, was likely to generate deep resentment. In Bohemia under Joseph II opposition to the burial of Protestants in cemeteries hitherto reserved for Catholics was so great that it required the presence of a considerable force of cavalry to ensure that one such burial took place; while the disastrous flooding of 1785, when the Danube broke its banks, was widely regarded as a divine punishment for the emperor's impious attacks on the Church. Attempts to interfere with the liturgy; the abolition, for economic reasons, of some of the very numerous religious holidays; the dissolution of the Jesuits, still deeply respected over much of Catholic Europe—all these manifestations of enlightenment could easily arouse widespread and sincere opposition. The experience of the Electorate of Mainz, hardly one of the most backward parts of Europe, is illuminating in this respect. When the Jeruits were expelled from the city in September 1773 public resentment was so real that the entire garrison had to occupy key points and patrol the streets to maintain order. When in 1787 a new hymn book in German was introduced by a reforming elector this aroused bitter popular hostility. The peasants tore up and burned the copies they received; and often it was simply ignored and the singing of hymns in Latin continued.[1] It is important to remember that however misguided, selfish or shortsighted this opposition to reform may seem, it was none the less sincere. Almost always

[1] Blanning (*see* Bibliography, p. 132), pp. 123, 207–9.

it was underlain by a passionate feeling that genuine rights were being trodden underfoot, that the structure of custom and tradition by which all but a small minority of Europeans lived was being wantonly shaken, that any increase in government activity must bode ill for the subject. What the ordinary man demanded of the State above all was that it should so far as possible leave him alone. His attitude was well illustrated during the Hungarian revolt of 1789 against the innovations of Joseph II, when the new registers of land titles (an essential tool of modern government which it had taken years of labour to compile) were ceremonially burnt to the accompaniment of music, drinking, feasting and general rejoicing. Members of the estates then took a public oath that no trace of these hated documents should be preserved. The more enlightened and reforming a government the more obviously it must flout feelings of this kind; and sometimes the price to be paid for flouting them was high.

However limited its immediate effects, the ideology of Enlightened Despotism had great importance in the long term. Its central idea, that the ruler, however absolute, was ultimately no more than the supreme representative and first servant of his people, helped to lay the foundations of the epoch of revolutions which opened in the 1780s. A heavier emphasis than ever before was being laid in the later eighteenth century, notably by monarchs themselves, on a ruler's duties to his subjects. These duties were now increasingly defined in terms of progress towards a better, or even an ideal, form of society and government. The frequent acceptance of ideas of this kind by monarchs helps to explain the lack of hostility, sometimes even enthusiasm, with which the French Revolution in its early stages was received by many of them. In St. Petersburg in 1789 the French ambassador was publicly congratulated by the Grand Duke Alexander (later Alexander I) on the fall of the Bastille, while Alexander's younger brother the Grand Duke Constantine, who was later to become an extreme reactionary, was also at first an enthusiastic partisan of the Revolution. In the same way the Emperor Leopold II approved of much of the work of the Constituent Assembly. Even when the more violent and disruptive aspects of events in France had become clearly visible, it was often the methods as much as the objectives of the revolutionaries which aroused opposition. Increasingly in the later eighteenth century it was felt, at least in intellectual and opinion-forming circles, that monarchy was on trial, that kings must now provide not merely good government but progressive government. By the 1770s or 1780s there were few European rulers who could feel quite the same unquestioning self-assurance as Louis XIV a century earlier.

VII

Armies and Navies

In 1764 James Boswell's friend Rose claimed, in a conversation which the two men had at Leyden, that 'wars were going out nowadays, from their mildness'.[1] Nearly three decades later a British publicist had no doubt that 'the refinement of modern ages has stripped war of half its horrors'.[2] They were expressing a point of view widespread among their contemporaries, at least in Western Europe, a feeling that for several generations warfare had been becoming steadily milder and its influence on the ordinary man more limited. Many historians have shared this view.

Are such judgements justified? Certainly as far as Western Europe is concerned there is a good deal of evidence to support them. For nearly a century and a half after the end of the Thirty Years War in 1648 there was a tendency for the ratio of casualties to total numbers engaged in West European wars to fall and for that of prisoners to other casualties to rise. There are clear signs that warfare was tending to become less

[1] *Boswell in Holland, 1763–1764*, ed. F. A. Pottle (London, 1952), p. 164.
[2] D. Ramsay, *The History of the American Revolution* (London, 1793), vol. II, p. 281.

BIBLIOGRAPHY. Some of the social and economic implications of eighteenth-century warfare are discussed in the relevant parts of J. U. Nef, *War and Human Progress* (London, 1950) and A. Vagts, *A History of Militarism* (London, 1938). Both are written from definite points of view with which not all readers will agree. E. Silberner, *La Guerre dans la pensée économique du XVIᵉ au XVIIIᵉ siècle* (Paris, 1939) gives many references to writers of the period. The chapters on 'Armies and navies' and 'Armed forces and the art of war' in the *New Cambridge Modern History*, vols. VI–VIII (Cambridge, 1957–70) are the best general account of the subject and a mine of useful information. The relevant sections of E. M. Earle (ed.), *Makers of Modern Strategy* (Princeton, 1944) are useful on the evolution of tactical and strategic ideas, as is E. Carrias, *La Pensée militaire française* (Paris, 1960). O. L. Spalding and others, *Warfare: a study of military methods from the earliest times* (New York, 1925) is a good introduction to the more technical side of the subject. Much has been written on the French armed forces: A. Corvisier, *L'Armée française de la fin du XVIIᵉ siècle au*

bloody. By the end of the seventeenth century a pamphleteer commenting on this tendency could write that now, in contrast to the attitude of
former times, '20,000 Men are accounted great Slaughter'.[1] Widespread
looting of the kind which had disfigured almost every war of the sixteenth and early seventeenth centuries was very largely brought under
control in this period (in the interests of discipline rather than humanity)
and replaced by the more or less orderly exaction of fixed contributions
from the population of the areas in which fighting took place. Adam
Smith even argued in 1763 that 'war is so far from being a disadvantage
in a well-cultivated country, that many get rich by it. When the Netherlands is the seat of war, all the peasants grow rich, for they pay no rent
when the enemy is in the country, and provisions sell at a high rate.'[2] It
is true also that warfare had little influence on the arts, the most obvious
indicator of the 'climate of opinion', during the eighteenth century. The
best example of this is the fact that none of the greatest music of the
period was inspired by the idea of military conflict (as some of that
written by Beethoven in the following generation clearly was). Its
'military' music is that of courts and *Te Deums*, or at most of parade
grounds, not that of battlefields.

Moreover the element of ritual, of formality, of traditional ceremony,
bulked large in much eighteenth-century warfare in Western Europe.
This was particularly marked in attacks on fortresses and fortified
towns; while the armies of all West European States tended to be slow-
moving, tied to elaborate fixed magazines and supply depots and further
restricted by the ever-present fear of desertion. These limitations did
not make rapid movement impossible, as Marlborough showed in 1704
and Frederick II in 1757; but they ensured that it should be the

[1] N. Barbon, *A Discourse of Trade* (London, 1690), p. 43.
[2] *Lectures on Justice, Police, Revenue and Arms* (London, 1896), p. 273.

ministère de Choiseul: le soldat (Paris, 1964) is a splendid work based upon enor-
mous research; and E.-G. Leonard, 'La question sociale dans l'armée française au
XVIII*ᵉ* siècle', *Annales*, vol. III (1948) is a useful article. For Russia the only
comprehensive and up-to-date work is L. G. Beskrovnyi, *Russkaya armiya i flot
v XVIII veke* (Moscow, 1958), which is packed with detailed information. In
German there is an extensive discussion of the military history of the period in
H. Delbrück, *Geschichte der Kriegskunst im Rahmen der politischen Geschichte*
(Berlin, 1900–36), vols. IV–V, though this is written from a rather narrowly
technical standpoint. For Britain the standard work, though now in various
respects outdated, is J. W. Fortescue, *History of the British Army* (2nd ed., London, 1910), vol. II. Some books on naval history are mentioned in the bibliography to Chapter XII (p. 289).

exception rather than the rule. Also commanders were not as a rule eager to fight decisive battles; and victories were seldom followed up with real energy. (The obvious if partial exception here is again Frederick II; but he never controlled the material resources needed for a truly Napoleonic strategy and became steadily more cautious and conservative in his later years.) A good many observers even doubted whether wars between States at approximately the same level of civilization could have any decisive result. The growth in Europe's population and the increased number of fortified towns to be found on every frontier, wrote a pamphleteer at the end of the seventeenth century, made it more difficult than ever before to conquer great areas of territory. The diffusion of military techniques, he went on, had the same effect, for 'now both Parties are Equally Disciplin'd and Arm'd; and the Successes of War are not so great; Victory is seldome gained without some Considerable Loss to the Conquerour'.[1] A hundred years later the same ideas were still widespread. 'Conquests are never very extensive or rapid,' wrote the historian Robertson, 'but among nations, whose progress in improvement is extremely unequal.'[2] Moreover many of the leading thinkers and writers of the period—Hume, Pope, Herder, Helvétius—tended to be contemptuous of traditional ideas of heroism, honour and even physical courage. The mental climate of the eighteenth century lacked the violence, the hatred, religious or national, which had generated the struggles of the Counter-Reformation and was to produce those of the nineteenth and twentieth centuries.

None of this meant that war was a rare or unimportant phenomenon in the eighteenth century or that the demands which it made on the peoples of Europe were negligible. The political and diplomatic history of the period was dominated by warfare (as will be seen in the chapters which follow) and its economic history profoundly influenced by it. With the partial exception of the two decades which followed the Treaty of Utrecht (and even then there were probably never less than half a million men under arms in Europe) there was scarcely a year in the century during which a large-scale struggle was not either raging or about to break out in some part of the continent. Europeans, almost as much as in preceding generations, took war for granted as a normal part of their lives. These struggles, moreover, could still inflict intense and widespread suffering on non-combatants, as the Russian

[1] Barbon, *op. cit.*, pp. 41, 49.
[2] *The History of the Reign of the Emperor Charles V* (London, 1769), vol. III, pp. 430-1.

sack of Memel in 1757 or the French devastation of Westphalia two years later were to show. It is true that among intellectuals, influenced by the cosmopolitanism of the Enlightenment, there was a fairly general feeling that war was unworthy of an age in which reason was slowly gaining control of human affairs. 'Nothing is so evident,' wrote Sir James Steuart, one of the most important economists of the period, 'as that war is inconsistent with the prosperity of a modern State.'[1] By the last years of the period there were indications that antimilitarist ideas were beginning to influence even the policies of a few important statesmen—Turgot, Vergennes, possibly the younger Pitt. They had little importance, however, outside a small minority of the educated classes.

A tendency towards a general, though slow, increase in the size of most European armies is visible during this period. There was a widespread feeling that very large armies were undesirable because they were difficult to supply and manœuvre. The Maréchal de Saxe, one of the best-known military theorists of the century and himself a highly successful commander, thought the 'acting body' of an army should not exceed 46,000 men, 'for multitudes serve only to perplex and embarrass'.[2] It was also possible to argue that the size of armies must be drastically limited by the capacity of society to maintain them: Montesquieu believed that a ruler could never afford to have more than one per cent of his subjects under arms simultaneously, and other writers put the proportion still lower. But such ideas were unduly cautious. Half a century before Saxe wrote, the forces engaged in the great battles of the War of the Spanish Succession had sometimes amounted on each side to 60–90,000 men: he himself is said to have commanded 130,000 at Raucoux in 1746 and 98,000 at Lawfeldt in the following year. This numerical growth is seen strikingly in the extraordinary development of the Prussian army. At the most critical moment of the Seven Years War it amounted to 4·4 per cent of the total population of the country, the highest proportion of this kind reached in any State during the century. Even more remarkable in some ways was the emergence of the Russian army. Still an inefficient, partly feudal and not particularly large force at the end of the seventeenth century, it had become by the last years of Peter I one of the most powerful in Europe. In 1731 its strength was fixed at over 132,000 men: by 1796 (i.e. before Russia had

---

[1] *An Inquiry into the Principles of Political Economy* (London, 1767), vol. I, p. 448.
[2] *Reveries, or Memoirs concerning the Art of War* (Edinburgh, 1759), p. 76.

begun to play an active part in the struggle against the French Revolution) it numbered 458,000. The same tendency to growth is seen, less strikingly, in Spain and some of the smaller States, notably the Kingdom of Sardinia.

Also if the destructiveness of warfare was declining, militarism was increasing, and was indeed largely a creation of this period. Louis XIV, during much of his reign an aggressive ruler, was not a soldier by taste, outlook or training. He would have regarded it as a breach of etiquette for a French nobleman to present himself at court in uniform. All his war ministers were civilians; and the commanders of his armies tended to be aristocrats first and professional soldiers second. It is true that the Marquis de Chamlay, his most important military adviser in his later years, had the title of *Maréchal-Général des Logis*; but he had little real experience of active service and was often employed on non-military tasks. There were some seventeenth-century rulers of importance whose interest in military affairs was both profound and active—Gustavus Adolphus and Charles X of Sweden, and the Stadtholders Maurice and William III of the United Provinces are the most obvious examples. They were, however, relatively few in number.

From the beginning of the eighteenth century this position changed rapidly. There was a striking increase in the attention paid by most European rulers to military details of all kinds. A number of monarchs —Charles XII of Sweden, Frederick William I of Prussia, Paul of Russia, to some extent Peter I and Frederick II—began to regard uniform as their normal dress. In England George I and George II devoted their energies to the organization and discipline of their army in a way that no Stuart king had ever done. Even in Spain, none of whose rulers had the slightest pretensions to military ability, royal interest of this kind can be seen in the frequency with which military uniforms were remodelled under Charles III and Charles IV. More important, as armies became more highly organized, more permanent and more self-conscious, the temptation to use them as moulds in which civilian societies might be recast became stronger. A tendency thus developed to militarize society in general in the quest for greater political and economic efficiency. It was in the relatively poor and backward States of Eastern and Northern Europe that this trend was most marked. There it bore fruit in Peter I's Table of Ranks of 1722 (see p. 44), itself based largely on Swedish precedents, and in the subjection in Prussia of the administration and much of the economic life of the country to the needs of the army.

Finally it must be remembered that many of the checks on the ferocity of West European warfare did not exist, or were less effective, farther east. In the West most eighteenth-century campaigns were fought in densely populated and wealthy areas. In the East Russian, Turkish, Swedish and Polish armies struggled with one another in country which was usually poor and sometimes almost uninhabited. There rapid movement tended to be easier, sieges less frequent and pitched battles more important. In the West armies were cosmopolitan and religious animosities relatively insignificant. In the East the Russian and Swedish forces were remarkable for their national character and resulting homogeneity; and every Russo-Turkish war was a religious, at least as much as a political, struggle to the ordinary soldier on both sides. The result was that in the long Russo-Swedish conflict of 1700–21 both combatant States endured sacrifices surpassing those of any Western country in the War of the Spanish Succession, while Russia's wars with the Ottoman Empire were fought almost in the spirit of a crusade. In the West, again, warfare was largely, though by no means completely, dominated by a defensive spirit. There tactics were strongly influenced by reliance on line formation and fire-power, as against attack at close quarters. In Russia at least, on the other hand, commanders such as Rumyantsev and Suvorov had developed to a high pitch of effectiveness by the end of this period the more aggressive method of attack in column with the bayonet (though the contrast between Russian and West European tactics has been greatly exaggerated by some Soviet historians). Above all, in the West warfare was increasingly governed by rules which gave some degree of protection to prisoners and civilians. In the East these restrictions were either almost unknown, as in the Ottoman Empire, or were only slowly winning acceptance, as in Russia. Thus the early years of the century, when war was taking on 'so decorous an aspect' in Western Europe, saw the conquered provinces of Livonia ravaged by the armies of Peter I with a ferocity which shocked Western observers. Later events, such as the devastation of East Prussia by Russian troops in 1758 or the terrible slaughter which followed the storming of the Turkish fortress of Ismail in 1790, underlined to con-temporaries the freedom from conventional restraints which charac-terized warfare in Eastern Europe.

The nature and value of every European army was inevitably deter-mined largely by its recruiting system. Most States developed during the century some system of compulsory service; but all of these were in varying degrees haphazard and inequitable. In many countries militias of widely differing efficiency existed. In some they played a role of significance as sources of recruits for the regular army in time of war—for example in France, where a system of militia service was established by Louvois in 1691 and revived in 1726, and in Piedmont. In others forces of this kind were unimportant or non-existent: in these the defence of the State rested as a rule upon armies raised largely by conscription. Such was Prussia, where a new system of recruiting, based on the allocation to each regiment of a defined area upon which it could draw for its manpower, was introduced in the 1730s. Such again was Russia. There Peter I had developed at the beginning of the century a system by which a specified number of peasant households had to provide, on the demand of the State, a recruit to serve for no less than twenty-five years. In Spain also a system of choosing men for military service by lot, the *quinta*, was in operation during most of the century.

Thus many though by no means all European States had at their disposal means of recruiting by compulsion considerable numbers of men for military service. With the exception of Russia, however, no major European power attempted to raise the bulk of its forces, at least in peacetime, by this means. In most States the army was still dependent largely on voluntary enlistment, though this process was almost invariably accompanied by fraud, bribery and even threats. This was the position in France, Piedmont and above all Great Britain. The size of the forces which might be raised by these primitive and inequitable means, especially at moments of real crisis, should not be underestimated. In France, for example, during the most critical years of the Spanish Succession war in 1704–8 and 1712, one in six of the male population was serving in the army or the militia; and in the period 1700–63 about two million men were enrolled for military service there (though some 300,000 of these were foreigners).

The idea that the army should be a microcosm of the nation, or representative of it in any true sense, would have seemed to most contemporaries ridiculous or even shocking. It was generally agreed that it should be raised as far as possible from the social groups of least economic value. 'It would undoubtedly be desirable,' wrote the Comte de Saint-Germain, perhaps the greatest French war minister of the century, 'if we could create an army of dependable and specially-selected men of the best type. But in order to make up an army we must not destroy the nation; it would be destruction to a nation if it were deprived of its best elements. As things are, the army must inevitably consist of the scum of the people and of all those for whom society has no use.'[1] Frederick II himself had argued a few years earlier that 'useful hard-working people should be guarded as the apple of one's eye, and in wartime recruits should be levied in one's own country only when the bitterest necessity compels'.[2] This assumption that the productive and educated parts of society were too valuable to be squandered in battle, that their function was to pay for wars not to fight them, was almost universally accepted. A few theorists—Saxe in his *Rêveries* (1757), Justus Möser in his *Patriotische Phantasien* (1775–1804), Guibert in his *Essai générale de tactique* (1772)—as well as purely political writers such as Montesquieu, Morellet and Mably, might advocate some form of extensive or even universal military service; but there was no serious possibility of their ideas being adopted by any government. One result of this attitude was that the strain placed by warfare on the economies of most European States was less than the mere number of men engaged in fighting might seem to indicate, since these were drawn so largely from the least productive elements of society. Another was greatly to minimize the impact on the educated and property-owning classes (and hence on the towns) of the rudimentary conscription systems of the period. It was calculated that in Prussia at the end of the century 1,700,000 men in a total population of 8,700,000 were completely exempt from military service (1,170,000 because of privileges possessed by most of the Prussian towns, 530,000 because of their social status or occupation). In 1745 the municipality of Seville, one of the largest cities in Spain, claimed that only 201 of its inhabitants were liable for military service, all the others being covered by exemptions of some kind. In France the more well-to-do cultivators (those who paid 50 livres or more in *taille*) were exempt from militia service, as were the servants of nobles or clerics, though exemptions of this kind were increasingly cut down as the century went on. It was only in 1742, moreover, that the militia there began to recruit from the urban as well as the rural population. Even in Russia the years after the death of Peter I saw the exemption from service of considerable social groups hitherto liable—the merchants of Astrakhan in return for a money payment, the arms-makers of Tula, Church servants, some groups of the better-off peasantry.

In these circumstances almost every eighteenth-century army was likely to contain an element of ne'er-do-wells, social misfits and even

[1] Nef (*see* Bibliography, p. 174), p. 306.
[2] Earle (*see* Bibliography, p. 174), p. 54.

criminals. In Britain, where suspicion of the amy as a possible instrument of tyranny together with a generally rising level of prosperity made recruits unusually hard to obtain, this element was prominent. In the War of American Independence three British regiments were composed entirely of reprieved criminals, while vagrants and other undesirables were often forced into the army in wartime. Such elements could be found in varying degrees in the fighting forces of most European States. The desire to shelter large sections of the population from military service also contributed to the willingness of most governments to employ foreign mercenaries, who retained throughout this period much of the importance they had possessed since the Renaissance. The French army included in the middle of the century over 50,000 foreigners, and still had over 40,000 serving in it on the eve of the Revolution. Foreign units in French service were commanded in their own language and had their own disciplinary arrangements: those who served in them also received higher pay than French soldiers. Of 133 battalions of infantry in the Spanish army in 1751 twenty-eight were composed of foreigners; and it was seriously proposed in that year to raise twenty more abroad. The United Provinces had a Scottish brigade in their service until the last years of the century, while there were 80,000 foreigners (mainly Germans) in the Prussian army as late as the disastrous battle of Jena in 1806. The Swiss cantons and Ireland continued, as in the previous century, to provide considerable numbers of recruits for the armies of foreign States (Spain had six Swiss regiments in her service as late as 1808). They were now surpassed as exporters of military manpower, however, by some of the smaller German States, above all by Hesse-Cassel. Between 1677 and 1815 the rulers of this poor but relatively populous State concluded thirty-seven treaties (seventeen of them with Great Britain) by which they agreed to provide, for a money payment, specified numbers of their subjects for service in foreign armies. The hiring-out of auxiliary forces of this kind was normally held not to involve a State in the war in which they were employed. It thus remained throughout the century an accepted means by which impecunious governments could share some of the wealth of their neighbours. Nor were mercenaries of this type supplied only by very small or weak States. Denmark and Saxony hired out considerable forces to the anti-French coalition during the War of the Spanish Succession, while Britain employed Russian auxiliaries in 1747-48 and confidently expected to obtain others for use against the American colonists in 1775.

Armies so non-national and drawn so largely from the lowest strata of the social pyramid were prone to lose men by desertion. This was so serious a threat to their efficiency, especially in wartime, that officers and N.C.O.s were compelled to spend much of their energies in check-ing and forestalling possible efforts by their men to desert. Thus in the army of Frederick II it was a rule that when passing through wooded country in which escape would be relatively easy infantry units must always be surrounded by cavalry patrols; and that when detached to fetch wood or water ordinary soldiers must always be accompanied by an officer. The need to guard against desertion had considerable influ-ence even on the development of tactics. Governments naturally made efforts to repress a practice which so obviously threatened the strength and morale of their armies. In 1711 Frederick I of Prussia ordered that in future deserters should have their nose and one of their ears cut off and be sent to hard labour for life, while after the Seven Years War a chain of military posts was set up on France's frontiers to prevent the escape abroad of soldiers fleeing from their units. That eighteenth-century generals and governments were justified in the attention they gave to this problem is beyond doubt. In 1713–40, a period during which it did hardly any fighting, the Prussian army lost over 30,000 men by desertion. During the Seven Years War the Austrian army is said to have lost over 62,000 men in this way, that of France about 70,000, and that of Prussia about 80,000. In the 1780s it was estimated that of the troops raised in Great Britain on the Irish establishment one-sixth deserted every year. Most striking of all perhaps are the figures for the militarily futile War of the Bavarian Succession in 1778–79, in which the Prussian army lost only 3,400 men in battle but over 16,000 by desertion. Even in Russia, which was to some extent spared these difficulties by the rela-tively high morale and national feeling of her soldiers, 20,000 deserters were counted in 1732. It should be remembered, of course, that quite often a man who deserted would rejoin the same army a short time later in a different unit, perhaps under another name; the fecklessness of the ordinary soldier means that the figures quoted in this paragraph have to be taken with a small pinch of salt. Nevertheless there is no doubt of the reality and size of the problem which desertion presented to every eighteenth-century army.

These armies of peasant conscripts, mercenaries and ne'er-do-wells were officered predominantly and in many cases overwhelmingly by nobles. In the seventeenth century army service had sometimes offered to ambitious men of low birth the prospect of raising themselves in the social scale, and perhaps of acquiring nobility for themselves and their descendants. Even then, however, the great majority of successful commanders were of noble origin; and by the early eighteenth century it was becoming increasingly difficult in many countries for a commoner to acquire commissioned rank in any but the more technical branches of the service. This tendency was not universal. In Spain for example, where the social importance of a commission was comparatively slight, would-be officers were required to prove noble descent only in a few cavalry regiments. Nevertheless in some of the most important European States social status became increasingly the passport to military rank as the century progressed. For this growing noble monopoly of commissions there were a number of reasons. Rulers in many cases felt that a hereditary privileged class alone possessed the sense of personal honour which was regarded as an essential ingredient in the make-up of a successful officer. The middle classes, it was argued, more attached to their own comfort and more influenced by rational calculations of private profit, could never make good officers. To allow them to attain commissioned rank, wrote Frederick II in 1775, would be 'the first step toward the decline and fall of the army'. Even a relatively liberal and progressive administrator like Saint-Germain was extremely unwilling to grant commissions to *parvenus* at the expense of poor but military-minded nobles. Again in poor or backward countries the landowning class might well be the only social group possessing the qualities of leadership and the minimum of education without which an officer was useless. This was the case in Russia, where Peter I, in the face of great hostility and obstruction, succeeded in forcing the privileged landowning class to become in effect a group of hereditary State servants (see p. 45). It also applied, to a lesser extent, in Prussia. There Frederick William I, again in spite of much opposition, achieved a similar success and became the real creator of the Junker officer. Both he and his son regarded the Prussian middle classes and peasantry, in Srbik's phrase, as 'filling material of the State [*füllende Materie des Staates*] without independent existence'.[1] In many countries, especially in the later decades of the century, the privileged classes came to regard a monopoly of commissions (except perhaps in the artillery and engineers) as a right to be jealously defended against bourgeois encroachments. This attitude can be seen in Prussia, and perhaps even more strikingly in France. There the officer class, which consisted at the regimental level largely of provincial nobles with a well-developed

[1] H. Ritter von Srbik, *Deutsche Einheit*, vol. I (Munich, 1935), p. 106.

military tradition, showed itself increasingly hostile to the purchase of commissions by rich bourgeois, even if recently ennobled, and to the invasion of the army by the power of money. The dependence of many French nobles on army pay or pensions for their livelihood added point and bitterness to the social struggle involved. It also led to a fantastic inflation of the number of commissions. 'I have officers whom I do not need,' said Louis XV, 'but I am sure that they need me.'[1]

The eighteenth century was not an age of rapid development in military techniques. It saw no change comparable to those wrought by the large-scale use of artillery in the sixteenth century or the growth of standing armies in the seventeenth. Nevertheless it was not a period of stagnation in this respect. It witnessed the introduction of new arms, tactics and methods of organization, which made the armies of the 1780s appreciably different from those of the 1700s.

It was in the first place a great age in the growth of military education. The *Accademia Reale* set up in Turin in 1677, the Noble Cadet Corps established in Saint Petersburg in 1731, the *Ecole Royale Militaire* which came into existence in Paris in 1751, the military academies established at Wiener-Neustadt in 1752 and Zamora in 1790, were all essentially schools intended to prepare young nobles for a military career. On a different level the academy established at Woolwich in 1741, the great engineering school set up at Mézières in 1748, the combined artillery and engineer school created in Russia in 1756, and a number of similar establishments, provided the armies of Europe with a greater fund of technical knowledge than they had hitherto possessed. From such new creations, notably in France, came a high proportion of the most important writing on military problems produced during the century.

The technical improvements of this period centred around the problem of increasing the fire-power of armies; and towards this end a good deal of progress was made. At the beginning of the century the average well-trained soldier could fire about one round per minute. By its middle years the introduction of a number of relatively minor improvements, such as cartridges and iron ramrods, had allowed this rate of fire to be trebled in the most efficient European armies. A general tendency towards making artillery lighter and more mobile can also be seen in the later decades of the century. It is visible especially in France, where the changes introduced by Gribeauval in the 1770s were of revolutionary importance. After his reforms a French 12-pounder gun

[1] M. Loir, *La Marine royale en 1789* (Paris, 1894), p. 98.

could be drawn by only six horses and an 8-pounder by only four (in each case about one-third of the number needed two centuries earlier) while the interchangeability of wheels and other parts which he introduced made it possible to carry out repairs and replacements with hitherto unheard-of speed. From the 1760s onwards both the British and French armies made intermittent and rather unsuccessful experiments with explosive shells, while shrapnel was first demonstrated publicly at Gibraltar in 1787. The bayonet, perhaps the greatest contribution to warfare made by the seventeenth century, was well established almost everywhere in Europe by the beginning of this period.

Nevertheless the scope and importance of these technical changes should not be exaggerated. Compared to those of the century which followed they were slight. The smooth-bore muskets which British soldiers used against Napoleon did not differ very substantially from those which their ancestors carried against Louis XIV in the War of the Grand Alliance; Marlborough, if brought back to life, would have found on the field of Waterloo comparatively little with which he was not already familiar.

In the field of tactics the main interest of the eighteenth century lies in the slow modification of the traditional line formation of troops on the field of battle by the new or rediscovered idea of attack in column. In Western Europe the idea of attack by columns in close formation seems to have been put forward for the first time by the Chevalier de Folard in his *Nouvelles Découvertes sur la Guerre* (1724). It was soon taken up by other French writers, many of whom were attracted by its reminiscences of the classical phalanx, and a prolonged controversy between the advocates of the new system and those of the traditional line formation developed. The supporters of the new school of thought were not completely victorious. Columns of men in close order moved slowly and were very exposed to enemy fire. Moreover to change quickly from column to line formation and vice versa was a complicated business, though methods of doing this were evolved, notably by Guibert, the greatest military theorist of the century. Nevertheless the rigidity of the traditional and somewhat mechanical line tactics which dominated most European battlefields in the eighteenth century had been shaken, with important results for the future. In Russia too, where ideas of linear formation had never taken such deep root as in the West, attack in column became, in the hands of generals such as Suvorov, a weapon capable of achieving great results. Moreover all tactical systems were, in the eighteenth century, becoming more effective simply because of the improvement in discipline which the period witnessed and the increasingly effective training to which the ordinary soldier was now subjected. More and more armies were becoming reliable though still very cumbersome machines, mechanisms which could be relied on to perform competently on the battlefield the evolutions in which they had been trained, and to stand enemy fire without flinching. This development is usually associated particularly with the Prussian and Russian forces. But the same trend is clearly visible in Western Europe also. From the Spanish Succession war onwards, for example, there is an increasing tendency for French soldiers to receive wounds in the left side—that which in line formation was exposed to the enemy's fire.[1] This is one of the most convincing of all proofs of increasingly rigid discipline on the battlefield.

This period also saw the introduction into every major European army of various forms of mobile and lightly-armed troops to supplement the slow-moving line regiments. Units of this kind were first used on a considerable scale by the Austrian army in the 1740s; and the Croat sharpshooters who composed them were considered by Frederick II the most dangerous opponents he had to face. They were soon copied by the French, who developed formations of this kind on a large scale from the 1760s onwards, while light infantry were used for the first time in Europe by the Russians at the siege of Kolberg in 1761. The British army had created a regiment of light infantry in 1757 for scouting duties in North America; and in the war of the American Revolution troops of this kind were perhaps the most effective part of Britain's forces in the colonies.

Finally, important changes took place in the eighteenth century in the means by which armies were controlled and maintained by the governments for which they fought. Even before it opened they had become emanations of the State, a branch of the machinery of government. There was little scope left for the *condottiere*, no possibility of the rise of a new crop of Wallensteins or Mansfelds, the warlords and military entrepreneurs who had played so great a part in the struggles of the 1620s and 1630s. The last great assertion by the government of a major European State of its monopoly of military power in its own territory can be seen in the whittling away by Peter I of the autonomy of the Zaporozhian Cossacks on the Dnieper from 1709 onwards, and in its final destruction by Catherine II in 1775–83. Many aspects of military life,

[1] Corvisier (*see* Bibliography, p. 174), p. 978.

however, were still only indirectly controlled by the State, at least in Western Europe, at the beginning of the eighteenth century. Many armies still relied on civilians to drive their artillery train and baggage-wagons, and on draught animals commandeered from civilians to pull them. Civilian contractors were normally responsible for provisioning these armies, and often for supplying them with arms, ammunition and uniforms. Military hospitals also were left in many cases in civilian hands, usually with unhappy results.

The period saw in most Western countries a series of intermittent and disjointed efforts to remedy this state of affairs. Thus the British government acquired a powder-mill of its own in 1759, though it seems to have made little use of it, and another in 1787. In 1793 two companies of horse artillery were formed, the first British artillery units to have their own drivers; and this reform was later extended to the whole of this branch of the army. The same increasing central control and rationalization can be seen also in the introduction in 1720 of a regular tariff for the purchase of commissions; in the 1750s of the custom of numbering regiments rather than referring to them by their colonel's name; and in 1792 of a common system of drill, based on that of Prussia, for the whole army. In France State-owned arms factories were set up at Maubeuge and Charleville in 1718; the government made itself responsible for the supply of uniforms in 1747; and the old system of military hospitals, which had left them largely in private hands, was abolished in 1788. More important, an *ordonnance* of December 1762 made recruitment for the first time a direct concern of the government, taking it out of the hands of the regimental officers who had hitherto controlled it. Countries such as Prussia, Russia, and to some extent Sweden, in which economic life was less developed and the individual entrepreneur less important, had for these very reasons been able to avoid many of the difficulties inherent in this extensive civilian influence in army matters.

The eighteenth century is thus a period of slow evolution rather than radical change in military affairs. It sees the continuation of a number of tendencies already visible in the reign of Louis XIV—a growth in the size of armies, a formalization of tactics, an increase in the importance of the technical branches of the service, an increase in the effectiveness of State control. It was by no means a period of stagnation. It was an age of militarism, though not yet of popular militarism; its wars and battles were a good deal more than the courtly and rather ineffective rituals which some historians have tended to imagine.

Eighteenth-century navies fluctuated in size and efficiency far more, and far more rapidly, than armies. For almost all European States with vulnerable land frontiers it was easier and safer to neglect the navy than the army. Moreover navies were, in proportion to the manpower they employed, far more expensive than armies. The temptation to economize on them in times of financial stringency was thus correspondingly more acute. Exact comparisons of the naval strength of different States at any particular time are also complicated by the difficulty of deciding how many of the ships which these States possessed on paper were really fit for service, and sometimes by differences in the methods by which vessels were classified.

Throughout this period Britain had the largest fleet in the world. She emerged from the War of the Grand Alliance in 1697 as the greatest of European naval powers; and this position she never lost. In 1721 she had 124 ships of the line and 105 smaller vessels, of which roughly a quarter had been built since 1714. These figures were virtually unchanged when war broke out with Spain in 1739; but lack of maintenance under the Walpole régime meant that she had only 35 of the line fit for immediate use. By 1762, however, she had 141 of the line and 224 smaller vessels; while by 1783 these figures had risen to 174 and 294, by far the most powerful fleet hitherto possessed by any State. The development of the French navy was a good deal more erratic. The War of the Spanish Succession and the financial strain it involved had reduced France's strength at sea to a very low ebb, so that in 1719 she possessed only 49 ships of all rates. Yet twenty years later, largely as a result of the work of Maurepas, an energetic Secretary of State, she had nearly 50 ships of the line and was once more clearly the second greatest European naval power. The war of 1744–48 with Great Britain involved her in fairly heavy losses; but by 1754 she possessed 57 ships of the line and 24 frigates. Even during the much more disastrous Seven Years War she made strenuous efforts under the Duc de Choiseul to recover her lost seapower, and these were continued in the 1760s and 1770s. In 1773 she had 66 ships of the line: by 1780, when she had 81, she was stronger at sea than ever before in her history. The development of Spanish naval strength was in step to some extent with that of France. Her fleet, which had almost ceased to exist by the end of the War of the Spanish Succession, was rapidly revived in the two decades which followed by able ministers such as Alberoni and Patino. By 1737 it included 33 ships of the line. Her losses in the great wars of the mid-century were smaller than those of France; and after 1748 the attention given to the navy by another Spanish statesman, Ensenada (which included the recruitment of a considerable body of shipbuilders and technicians in Britain) led to a fairly rapid increase in its strength. By 1774 she had 58 ships of the line: she is said to have possessed 72 in 1789.

More dramatic still was the growth of the Russian fleet. Its Baltic squadron, always the most important part of it, began to take shape only after Russia had acquired a foothold on that sea in 1703. Yet in the face of almost every conceivable difficulty—widespread and bitter popular hostility to the whole idea of naval development, the need to import from abroad officers and technicians of all kinds, the surrender of Azov and consequent loss of the Black Sea fleet in 1711 (see p. 233)— Peter I had by his death in 1725 made Russia one of the great naval powers of Europe. His successors did not share his passion for maritime affairs; and in the 1730s and 1740s the fleet he had created was allowed to decline sharply in numbers and efficiency. Under Catherine II it was rapidly revived; and by 1788 the Baltic fleet numbered 37 ships of the line. Moreover the later 1770s and 1780s saw the re-creation of a powerful Russian squadron in the Black Sea, a squadron which by 1791 possessed 22 ships of the line. Russia had thus become a naval power equal or almost equal to Spain and little inferior to France.

The minor European naval powers can be briefly dismissed. Neither the Swedish nor the Danish navies were able to recover after the Great Northern War (1700–21) the importance they had enjoyed before its outbreak. Both were now overshadowed by the superior power of Russia, a fact which was driven home by the general lack of success of the Swedish fleet in the war of 1788–90 with her great eastern neighbour. The United Provinces, still a great naval power at the end of the seventeenth century, sank rapidly to a second-rate position in the early years of this period. In the War of the Spanish Succession they were seldom able to keep more than fifty warships of all sizes at sea simultaneously; and declining economic strength and the complications of their federal constitution made a recovery of their former status impossible. Neither the decaying seapower of Venice, which after the Treaty of Passarowitz in 1718 was used only in unsuccessful punitive expeditions against the Barbary States; nor the insignificant squadrons of Tuscany and Naples; nor the small and inefficient navy of Portugal, were factors of much significance in the balance of European naval power. The Ottoman Empire possessed a substantial fleet; but its ships were poorly designed (Turkey was the last important Mediterranean State to use galleys on a large scale), often inadequately armed and until fairly late in the century execrably manned. Its efficiency was still further reduced by the fact that, almost alone among European navies of any size, it saw no active service between 1718 and 1769. It is not surprising therefore that in 1770 at Chesmé, off the coast of Asia Minor, it suffered at the hands of the Russians perhaps the most complete defeat in all naval history (see p. 235). Efforts to strengthen and improve it in the last decades of the century had only moderate success.

Most eighteenth-century navies, like the armies of the period, were recruited by a mixture of inducements and compulsion. In Russia the latter element was uppermost, and peasants were conscripted as sailors in very much the same way as for the army. In France a more elaborate and complex coercive apparatus existed than anywhere else in Western Europe—the system of *classement* set up by Colbert in 1663. It involved the registration of the seafaring inhabitants of the coastal areas of France (and later also of the population on the banks of navigable rivers) and the creation in this way of a pool of experienced sailors who could be used in manning the fleet. Like the system of militia service it pressed heavily upon the poorer sections of the groups it affected and fell comparatively lightly on the middle classes of the French seaports. This, coupled with the corruption and favouritism of many of the officials who administered it, made it widely unpopular and led to much evasion of the obligations it imposed. As a result the French navy was normally short of seamen throughout the century. In Spain, where a somewhat similar system was introduced in 1737, the same difficulties were encountered and the same disappointing results achieved.

The very moderate success of these methods elsewhere did not prevent suggestions that they be copied in Britain. Throughout the century proposals for the creation of some form of reserve of seamen were put forward, all of them without success. Fear of encroachments by the government or the forces on the liberty of the subject, coupled with a feeling that it was unjust that one particular class should be singled out for treatment in this way, combined to defeat all such suggestions. The British navy continued to depend on what men could be allured by bounties, snapped up by the press-gang, or recruited more or less forcibly from convicts and debtors. The results were what might have been expected. 'In a man-of-war,' wrote an officer in 1756, 'you have the collected filths of jails. . . . There's not a vice committed on shore but is practised here. The scenes of horror and infamy on board of a man-of-war are so many and so great that I think they must rather disgust a mind than allure it.'[1] As in eighteenth-century armies, moreover, the defects of naval recruiting-systems were reflected in a crippling rate of desertion. In less than four years, in 1776–80, over 42,000 men deserted from the British navy; and there is no reason to suppose that this was an unusual number by contemporary standards.

Both Britain and France found difficulty in obtaining sufficient volunteers for their fleets, partly because the wages they offered their sailors compared very poorly with what could be obtained by service on a merchantman, and still more so with what might be made on a successful privateer. The pay of a sailor in the French navy in 1789 was practically the same as it had been a century before, though during that period prices had almost doubled. In Britain the wages of an ordinary seaman remained unchanged (at 19s. per month) during the whole of the period 1651–1797. Moreover these inadequate wages were often months in arrears, and were paid, at least in the earlier years of the century, not in cash but in tickets which could be cashed only at the Navy Office in London. The complaint of Admiral Vernon, in a parliamentary speech of 1749, that 'our fleets, which are defrauded by injustice, are first manned by violence and maintained by cruelty',[2] was substantially justified. In spite of efforts to give some semblance of fair treatment to the ordinary sailor (the most notable was the passage of Grenville's Navy Act in 1758) no radical improvement in the methods or rate of payment was made until after the mutinies of 1797.

Like eighteenth-century armies the navies of the period benefited from a certain amount of technical progress, but progress of a limited and evolutionary kind. One obvious aspect of this was the elimination from naval warfare of the galley. Its importance even in the Mediterranean, the sea which had given it birth, was rapidly declining by the later seventeenth century. Galleys took some small part in the indecisive battle of Cape Matapan between the Turkish and Venetian fleets in 1717; but apart from the large fleets of them maintained in the Baltic by Russia and Sweden they had become obsolete long before the end of this period. The French Corps des Galères was suppressed in 1748; and by the time of the French Revolution, except for the few maintained

[1] Sir W. L. Clowes, The Royal Navy. a history from the earliest times to the present (London, 1897–1903), vol. III, p. 21.

[2] Sir H. W. Richmond, The Navy in the War of 1739–48 (Cambridge, 1920), vol. I, p. 274.

by the Spanish fleet and one or two in the navies of the small Italian States, galleys had disappeared from the sea which they had so long dominated. Much was done, again, by the work of mathematicians such as Euler, Bernouilli and Borda on fluid resistance and floating bodies, to make possible an improvement in the lines of sailing-ships. Books such as the *Architectura Navalis Mercatoria* of the Swede Chapman (1768) and the *Examen Maritimo Teorico Practico* of the Spaniard Jorge Juan (1771) show that this was beginning to have some influence on shipbuilders. In France, where a new class of naval engineers concerned with the building and repair of ships was created in 1765, shipbuilding was perhaps carried to a higher pitch of perfection than anywhere else in Europe. To French builders, admitted a British historian of the early nineteenth century, 'is primarily owing the energetical improvement made in modern times in the form, dimensions, and general contour of vessels'.[1] The *États de Bourgogne* of 118 guns, designed by J.-N. Sané and launched in 1782, was technically the most successful ship of the age. She was used as a model until far into the nineteenth century and was still carrying an admiral's flag in 1848. In Britain by contrast the gap between theory and practice, between the discoveries of mathematicians and the rule-of-thumb traditionalism of shipbuilders, remained very wide. Apart from the *Treatise on Shipbuilding and Navigation* of Mungo Murray (1754) no book of a scientific kind on shipbuilding or ship design was written in English during this period. The Society for the Improvement of Naval Architecture, formed in 1791, was essentially a body of theorists and amateurs with little or no practical influence. The result was a general and generally admitted inferiority of British men-of-war to those of France. 'I have never seen or heard since my knowledge of things,' wrote a British admiral in 1745, 'that one of our ships alone, singly opposed to one of the enemy's of equal force, has taken her, and I have been in almost every action and skirmish since the year 1718, and yet we are daily boasting of the prowess of our Fleet.'[2] Complaints that British ships by comparison with those of France were too small, sailed badly and were encumbered by too many guns, continued to be heard to the end of the century and afterwards; while French prizes were frequently used as models for the design of new British men-of-war.

[1] J. Charnock, *A History of Marine Architecture* (London, 1800–02), vol. III, p. 172.
[2] H. W. Hodges and E. A. Hughes (eds.), *Select Naval Documents* (Cambridge, 1936), p. 121.

Nevertheless it was the British navy which pioneered the two inventions which did most to increase the efficiency of eighteenth-century men-of-war. These were the copper sheathing which greatly reduced the fouling of their bottoms by weeds and the loss of speed this entailed; and the carronade which so greatly increased their destructive power. The use of copper as a protection for the underwater parts of ships' hulls had been suggested in England as early as 1708. The idea was applied in practice for the first time fifty years later on an experimental basis. It proved so successful in preventing the growth of weeds and the ravages of the teredo worm that by the 1770s it had been generally adopted throughout the navy. In France the new technique was first used, by copying from a captured British vessel, in 1778. In the decades which followed it was generally diffused throughout the navies of Europe. The carronade, a short-barrelled large-calibre gun with a low muzzle velocity, easily handled and very effective at close quarters, was first developed by a soldier, General Melville, in 1774. It was manufactured in Britain on a large scale from 1778 onwards and by the end of the American War was mounted on several hundred British men-of-war of all sizes. It too was copied, first of all by France and later by other continental naval powers.

Eighteenth-century observers often tended to believe that naval battles between opponents of more or less equal strength were almost certain to be indecisive, that naval warfare was by its nature unlikely to produce victories of the kind which might be expected on land. 'Do you know what a naval battle is?' asked the French minister, Maurepas. 'I will tell you: the fleets manœuvre, come to grips, fire a few shots, and then each retreats ... and the sea remains as salt as it was before.'[1] Experience seemed to justify this view, for the period saw a considerable number of indecisive encounters of this kind; while the naval battles which produced some decisive result—Cape Passaro (1718); Hawke's victory over the French Admiral Du Bois de la Motte (1744); Lagos and Quiberon Bay (1759); Rodney's 'midnight chase' of the Spanish Admiral Langara in 1780—were nearly all marked by a preponderance of strength on one side. Not until the battle of The Saints in 1782 did a struggle between two fleets of approximately equal size produce a clear-cut victory for one of them.

The rigidity of eighteenth-century naval tactics, embodied in

---

[1] J. Tramond, *Manuel d'histoire maritime de la France* (2nd ed., Paris, 1927), p. 459.

detailed and restrictive fighting instructions and imbued with the idea of the importance of the line of battle and its preservation, undoubtedly discouraged initiative on the part of commanders. It thus contributed to the ineffectiveness of much of the warfare of the period. The very primitive signalling systems available and the extreme difficulty of ensuring that any order was understood and obeyed were equally important obstacles in the way of an original or aggressive admiral. The improvement in signalling methods which Kempenfelt and others brought about in the British navy in the last decades of the century was a greater contribution than the idea of 'breaking the enemy's line' to the defeat of Napoleon.

Decisive naval battles were also made less likely by ideas which persisted throughout the century as to the way in which wars at sea should be fought. In France and Spain, and to a lesser extent in Britain, it was widely believed that the most important function of a fleet was not to seek out and destroy that of the enemy but to protect the colonies and seaborne trade of the State to which it belonged and capture or harass those of its opponents. The restrictions which ideas of this kind imposed on the French navy were particularly serious, and can be seen influencing France's strategy at sea throughout the century. They underlay the division in 1744–48 of the ships at her disposal into small squadrons for commerce protection, which made impossible their use in any true strategic way. They inspired the efforts of Admirals D'Estaing and De Grasse in the War of the American Revolution to seize British West Indian islands and evade rather than destroy the fleets to which they were opposed. They can also be seen in the popularity in France of the idea of attacks on British commerce as a means of forcing the traditional enemy to her knees, the belief that a *guerre de course* of this kind, avoiding large-scale engagements and making extensive use of privateers, would be more effective than a strategy which aimed at securing effective control of the seas. Alone among French sailors the Bailli de Suffren showed himself willing, in his campaigns of 1781–83 in the Indian Ocean, to challenge this fundamentally defensive attitude and the emphasis it laid on minor tactical and territorial advantages.

Nor was a similar outlook unknown on the other side of the Channel. In 1695 and 1708 Parliament, stung to action by the clamours of the London merchants, passed legislation which compelled the Admiralty to allocate specified numbers of ships to the task of protecting commerce; a Bill for the same purpose was introduced, though it failed to secure a majority, in 1742. Only with the emergence in 1747, in an embryonic form, of a Western Squadron dedicated to cruising off the main French Atlantic bases of Brest and Rochefort, did strategic considerations overcome purely commercial and tactical ones in British thinking on the functions of the navy. With its establishment in the Seven Years War as an integral part of the war effort at sea their victory may be regarded as decisive.

The increase of State control which has already been seen as a feature of military organization in this period is also visible where navies are concerned. It involved the disappearance from the line of battle of every European fleet of the converted merchantmen which had remained so important in wars at sea until the second half of the seventeenth century. It involved an increasing tendency for all men-of-war, at least of the larger types, to be built in government dockyards rather than by private contractors. It involved an increasingly rational and symmetrical organization of navies, the division of their ships into well-defined classes, each with relatively specialized functions and a fixed quota of men and guns. Most important of all, it involved a decline in the relative importance of privateers and even, at least in Britain, a tendency to regard them as a hindrance to the work of the navy proper. Throughout the century intensive official encouragement of privateering by any State was usually a result of inferiority at sea, an implied admission that the enemy's fleet could not be defeated in open combat.

War was the greatest single factor in the international history of eighteenth-century Europe. It established Russia and Prussia as great powers. It greatly reduced the influence of Sweden and accelerated the decline of the Ottoman Empire. It substituted Spanish for Austrian influence in southern Italy. It made Lorraine a French province. Though it probably did not benefit her economically as much as has sometimes been thought, it endowed Britain with a great colonial empire and virtually unlimited opportunities of further expansion. On the economic and social history of the period its influence was also enormous. The need to create powerful fighting forces had repercussions on Russian society which were almost revolutionary, and underlay almost every aspect of the development of Prussia. The history of the generations which preceded the French Revolution almost as much as of that which followed it must be written in terms of warfare.

VIII

Diplomacy and International Relations

By the beginning of the eighteenth century the framework of European diplomacy was well established. From the fifteenth century onwards, first in Italy and then in Western Europe generally, States had begun to maintain representatives more or less permanently in each other's capitals. These representatives corresponded regularly and sometimes very frequently with the governments for which they acted; from the early sixteenth century onwards their despatches and reports, preserved in the organized official archives which were now beginning to be formed, are one of the most important sources of information available to the historian. More slowly, ministers and departments of State charged more or less specifically with the conduct of foreign affairs emerged in most West European countries, though it was not until late in the eighteenth century that this process began to reach completion. The conception of a balance of power, again originating in Italy, spread rapidly to the other States of Western and Central

BIBLIOGRAPHY. Of general histories of international relations during this period the most useful are M. Immich, *Geschichte des europäischen Staatensystems von 1660 bis 1789* (Berlin-Munich, 1905) and G. Zeller, *De Louis XIV à 1789* (Paris, 1955), a volume in the series *Histoire des Relations Internationales* edited by P. Renouvin. Vols. VII and VIII of the *New Cambridge Modern History* (Cambridge, 1957, 1965) contain useful chapters of an essentially narrative kind. The most complete account of the workings of any foreign office is the official *Histoire de l'administration des Affaires Étrangères de Suède* (Upsala, 1940); it is not easy reading. For France two well-known works, C. Picavet, *La Diplomatie française au temps de Louis XIV* (Paris, 1930) and F. Masson, *Le Département des Affaires Étrangères pendant la Révolution, 1787–1804* (Paris, 1897) are of value for this period. For Russia the earlier pages of another official history, *Ocherk Istorii Ministerstva Inostrannykh Del', 1802–1902* (St. Petersburg, 1902) are useful, and D. B. Horn, *The British Diplomatic Service, 1689–1789* (Oxford, 1961) is a detailed and comprehensive study. P. R. Rohden, *Die klassische Diplomatie von Kaunitz bis Metternich* (Leipzig, 1939) appears to be the only modern attempt at a substantial general discussion of eighteenth-century diplomacy. The best discussion of the balance of power in this period is M. S.

Europe. From the time of the Emperor Charles V (1519–56) onwards the idea, if not the phrase itself, was part of the common currency of European political life.

In this network of institutions and ideas the eighteenth century saw no fundamental change. It was not essentially different on the eve of the French Revolution from what it had been during the reign of Louis XIV. From the beginning of the century, however, it was being extended to include large areas hitherto oniy on the fringes of the European system of international relations. The greatest of these was Russia. Until the end of the seventeenth century the diplomatic contacts of this vast country with the States of Western Europe had been intermittent and usually unimportant (see p. 218). In 1695, when the great Tsar Peter I first acquired effective control of the government, Russia had no permanent diplomatic representatives in foreign capitals. The officials chosen to represent her on intermittent and short-lived embassies were usually ignorant of the languages of the countries to which they were sent and often 'Moscow Germans' (descendants of foreigners who had settled in Russia) rather than Russians by birth. The *Posolskii Prikaz* (Department of Embassies) had for several generations been a part of the central administration, but it was far from being a genuine foreign ministry. Under Peter this position changed completely. From 1699 onwards, when the very able A. A. Matveev was sent as minister to the United Provinces, a network of diplomatic representatives abroad comparable in its extent and efficiency to that of any European State was rapidly created. By 1721 Russia had

Anderson, 'Eighteenth-century theories of the balance of power', in Ragnhild Hatton and M. S. Anderson (eds.), *Studies in Diplomatic History* (London, 1970); both G. Zeller, 'Le principe d'équilibre dans la politique internationale avant 1789', *Revue Historique*, vol. CCV (1956) and C. Morandi, 'Il concetto della politica d'equilibrio nell' Europa moderna', *Archivo Storico Italiano*, vol. LXXVII (1940) are thin. F. Gilbert, *To the Farewell Address: ideas of early American foreign policy* (Princeton, 1961) has a good deal of relevance to European thinking; and the same author's 'The new diplomacy of the eighteenth century', *World Politics*, IV (1951–2) is useful. A. Rein, 'Uber die Bedeutung der überseeischen Ausdehnung für das europäische Staatensystem', *Historische Zeitschrift*, vol. CXXXVI (1928), is an interesting attempt to illustrate the way in which events overseas influenced European politics. The most recent discussion of the main eighteenth-century peace projects is K. von Raumer, *Ewiger Friede* (Freiburg-Munich, 1953). The best-known eighteenth-century proposal for the systematic training of diplomats is discussed in H. M. A. Keens-Soper, 'The French Political Academy, 1712: a school for ambassadors', *European Studies Review*, vol. II (1972).

twenty-one permanent diplomatic missions in foreign countries (including one in Pekin and another in Bokhara) a number which was not to be exceeded during the remainder of the century. Simultaneously the number of foreign diplomats more or less permanently resident in Russia also increased. In 1702 there were only four of these (apart from unofficial agents of the Hospodar of Wallachia and of some dissident Serbian groups). By 1719 there were eleven, a figure which would have been higher but for the continuance of the war with Sweden and the very strained relations with Great Britain which then existed.

This expansion of diplomatic contacts between Russia and the other States of Europe did not take place in a political vacuum. It was merely one aspect of the Tsar's efforts to strengthen and develop his country by every means available. Nevertheless it did not end with his reign. Though the number of Russian diplomatic missions abroad tended to fall somewhat in the decades which followed Peter's death—there were nineteen in 1779 and (largely for reasons of economy) only fourteen in 1800—the country did not relapse into the isolation of the seventeenth century, attractive though such an idea was to the more conservative elements in Russian society. European diplomacy had thus extended its frontiers far to the East; a new, large, and in some ways awkwardly shaped piece had now to be fitted into the jigsaw of international relations. A new and heavy weight was now available to be thrown on one side or the other of the balance of power. In 1716 the French *Almanach Royal* for the first time listed the Romanovs as one of the reigning families of Europe, an important recognition of Russia's new status: by the 1750s the completeness and irrevocability of her emergence as a great power had been brought home to most observers. 'The influence of the northern Princes on the general affairs of Europe', wrote a publicist three years before the outbreak of the Seven Years War, 'is now greater than it has ever been.'[1]

At the beginning of this period the Ottoman Empire occupied a position akin to that of Russia. From the end of the fifteenth century she had been a factor in European diplomacy. She had played an important part in the long series of struggles between France and the Habsburgs which dominated the age of Charles V. By the early seventeenth century France, England, Venice and the United Provinces were all maintaining permanent representatives in Constantinople (though the English and Dutch ones were commercial rather than diplomatic agents). Yet she

---

[1] J. H. Maubert de Gouvest, *Testament politique du Cardinal Jules Alberoni* (Lausanne, 1753), p. 427.

was clearly not a European State, and she never became during the eighteenth century completely incorporated in the European diplomatic system. Until far into this period there were many important States which were not represented at Constantinople (Sweden had no resident minister there until 1734, Prussia none till 1758). More important, it was not until after it ended that she began to possess permanent representatives of her own in the major capitals of Europe. Nevertheless the political and diplomatic links which bound her to the rest of the continent were slowly multiplying and becoming stronger. The importance of the role she was now, willy-nilly, being forced to play in European affairs, in spite (or perhaps because) of her increasing weakness and inefficiency, is shown by the great though unsought significance of her part in the first partition of Poland (see p. 236). In the Balkans and the Levant, as in Russia, the European diplomatic system was extending its scope.

This increasingly complex and extensive diplomatic network was given a rather specious unity by the increasingly general use of French as the language of international relations. Its establishment as the diplomatic language *par excellence*, supplanting the Latin and Italian which had been widely used in previous generations, was the result (though a largely unplanned one) of the victories of Louis XIV and the cultural prestige acquired by France during his reign. By his death it was firmly established as the normal language of international intercourse in Western Europe. Nearly all the great treaties of the century after that of Utrecht were drawn up in French, though in each case with a saving clause providing that this was not to be taken as a precedent. Such was its prestige and attractive power that by the second half of this period it was being used on a considerable scale in many countries for correspondence between diplomats and their governments. Frederick II normally wrote in French to his agents in foreign capitals. Austrian diplomats quite often used French in preference to German. In 1787 Catherine II found it necessary, as a result of the growing use of the language by her representatives abroad, to order them to use Russian when writing to her or her ministers. It is true that French never completely superseded all its competitors. German and Latin continued to be used in treaties between the States of the Holy Roman Empire. In the Near East Italian remained the normal language of diplomacy until the end of this period; and in treaties with the Ottoman Empire Turkish, Russian, French, Latin and Italian were all used at various times. Nevertheless the international status of French was throughout this period beyond challenge. It was an unmistakable expression of the prestige which France continued to enjoy in spite of serious military and political defeats.

The increasing importance of the diplomatic network which bound together the States of Europe was reflected in the eighteenth century in the development in most countries of central institutions for the direction of foreign policy. Foreign Offices of a modern kind, specialized in their functions, subdivided into departments with still more specialized duties and employing considerable numbers of experts of all kinds, now appear for the first time in the major European capitals.

In this development France led the way. Her Foreign Office remained throughout this period the object of admiration and envy on the part of many other countries. By the end of the seventeenth century she already possessed the most efficient diplomatic organization in Europe, one which had at its disposal able negotiators, plentiful funds, expert knowledge and the prestige of past success. In the two generations which followed the death of Louis XIV it was further extended and elaborated. In the last years of his reign a tendency towards the creation of specialized departments within the ministry had become visible. A *dépot des archives* was set up in 1688; while the Marquis de Torcy (Louis's last Foreign Minister) had begun about the same time the creation of a rudimentary Press bureau. Departments for the handling of current diplomatic business also began to develop, each under a high official, the *premier commis*, of whom there were usually two or three. The number of departments in the ministry and the function of each changed frequently during the century; but there was a general tendency for them to become more numerous. Thus a *bureau topographique* was set up in 1775 and soon accumulated the finest collection of maps in Europe; while a *bureau géographique* (formed largely to look after these maps) came into existence five years later. A department concerned with the cyphering and decyphering of despatches seems to have been set up in 1767. By 1784 the ministry had four main divisions: two *bureaux pour l'expédition des dépêches* which handled between them the correspondence with all French representatives abroad; a *bureau des fonds* which controlled its finances; and a *bureau du dépot* which supervised its archives, then lodged in a specially constructed fireproof building at Versailles. However each of the four Secretaries of State, of whom the Secretary for Foreign Affairs was one, continued until the Revolution, in addition to their other responsibilities, to supervise the administration of a group of French provinces. In spite of the excellent organization of the Foreign Ministry there was thus no minister in France during this period whose duties were confined solely to the supervision of foreign policy.

Nor was this organization as invariably efficient in fact as it should have been in theory. The accumulation and arrangement of its archives, for example, was not always thorough or complete. Thus in 1779, when it was desired to refer to Choiseul's despatches relating to the Family Compact of 1761, they could not be found and copies had to be obtained from Madrid. Nevertheless the ministry was the best and most complete of its kind in Europe; and in the second half of this period, under Secretaries of State such as the Duc de Choiseul (1758–70) and the Comte de Vergennes (1774–87) was becoming steadily a more and more effective machine. By 1789 it had assumed in most respects its nineteenth-century form.

Even more striking than this picture of developing efficiency in France was the growth in Russia of the *Posolskii Prikaz* and its successor the College of Foreign Affairs. The great expansion of diplomatic contact between Russia and the rest of Europe brought about by Peter I inevitably led to an increase in the size and activity of the *Posolskii Prikaz*. As early as 1705 it was one of the largest Foreign Offices in Europe, with over forty translators at its disposal. Moreover it was becoming for the first time, as a result of Peter's administrative reforms, an institution concerned solely with diplomacy. It no longer supervised, as in the seventeenth century, the administration of certain Russian provinces, or acted as a tax-collecting body. This process of stripping away extraneous duties continued under its successor, the College of Foreign Affairs, which began to function in 1719. In 1724 relations with the leading figures of the Orthodox Church (mainly in Palestine) which had hitherto been handled by the college, were transferred to the Synod, the new directing organ of the Church in Russia. Relations with the Ukraine, which in the early eighteenth century was in many respects a foreign State, were placed under the control of the Senate in 1756. Those with the Kalmuks and other nomadic peoples of Central Asia were taken over by the governors of the provinces concerned in the 1770s. Finally in 1782 the postal department of the college was transferred to the Senate. Thus well before the end of the century this process of specialization had been completed. The college had become a body concerned with the formulation and execution of foreign policy and nothing else.

Like the French Foreign Ministry, again, the *Posolskii Prikaz* and College of Foreign Affairs showed during the eighteenth century an increasing tendency to divide into specialized departments. As early as 1705 the former was split into five of these with well-defined functions, each handling relations with a specific group of countries. A similar division continued after the creation of the College of Foreign Affairs; and new departments were added as time went on (notably a Ceremonial Department which evolved in the reign of Catherine II). The growth in the complexity of Russian diplomatic machinery can be seen in the rapidly increasing number of people employed in its control and direction, especially under Catherine II, and its still more rapidly increasing cost.

No other Foreign Office grew with the speed of those of France and Russia; but in almost every European State existing arrangements for the central control of foreign policy became more complex and efficient. In the Habsburg territories Joseph I set up in 1709 a new permanent committee of nine officials to control foreign affairs. This, reorganized by Charles VI in 1721, continued to be one of the most important organs of government until the rise of the dominating figure of Kaunitz just after the middle of the century. Almost equally important was the ending, by a series of agreements in 1745, 1773 and 1790, of a struggle for influence which had been going on for generations between the *Reichskanzlei* (Imperial Chancery) under its hereditary head, the Elector of Mainz, and the *Hofkanzlei* (the Chancery of the Habsburg hereditary lands). In Sweden arrangements for the control of foreign affairs were complex and unstable during the period 1720-72; but strenuous efforts were made to improve them and Gustavus III's *coup d'état* in the latter year increased their efficiency. Britain, sheltered by the sea and the strength of her navy from the necessity of having a good diplomatic organization, never attempted to compete with the great continental States in this respect. Even in the 1780s the Foreign Office had probably fewer than twenty employees in all; and throughout the century the efficiency of British foreign policy was hampered by the lack of effective arrangements for preserving diplomatic correspondence and by a shortage of translators. Nevertheless an important step forward was taken in 1782 by the creation of the office of Secretary of State for Foreign Affairs. This concentrated in the hands of one individual, normally controlled by the Prime Minister and the Cabinet, the supervision of foreign policy which had hitherto been entrusted, together with a vast range of other business, to the Secretaries of State for the

Northern and Southern Departments. Even in Poland some attempt to improve existing arrangements for the control of what foreign policy the country had becomes visible after 1775.

The diplomats whom these increasingly efficient Foreign Offices supervised were now as a rule natives of the country which they represented. Eighteenth-century diplomatic services were never as cosmopolitan as eighteenth-century armies. Many countries continued to make use of foreigners to fill such subordinate posts as those of resident, consul or secretary; and some might appoint foreigners to positions of importance if no suitable native were available. Such appointments, however, were exceptional. Long before the end of the century the diplomatic services of all the major European States had become overwhelmingly national.

It had also become an accepted rule that diplomats were to be paid by the State which they represented and not by that to which they were sent. In the later seventeenth century the older practice by which States were expected to maintain, at least for a certain period, foreign ambassadors accredited to them, had still been adhered to by a few countries on the fringes of the European State-system, notably by Russia. By the eighteenth century this custom had fallen into complete disuse except in a few States, nearly all of which were insignificant. (The only one of importance was the Ottoman Empire, which continued on occasion to pay allowances to foreign diplomats.) Traces of it could still be found, for example in Venice and Genoa, but these were of little more than historical interest.

This period therefore saw the culmination of tendencies already visible in previous generations, tendencies which made the diplomatic services of Europe more or less efficient and homogeneous institutions effectively controlled by the governments of the various States. It also saw frequent proposals that diplomats should be given some systematic training to fit them for the posts they were to occupy. The best-known effort of this kind was that made by Torcy in 1712 to prepare young men for the French diplomatic service. Six of them were to classify and arrange the archives of the Foreign Ministry, and thus acquire by studying the records of past negotiations a knowledge of the principles of diplomacy. They were to be joined by six *attachés libres* who were also to receive special diplomatic training. This system, however, lasted only until 1720. A generation later, in 1747, Frederick II set up a training school for the Prussian diplomatic service, again on a small scale. This came to an end during the Seven Years War; and although it was refounded in 1775 it seems to have been designed merely to produce men capable of filling such relatively minor posts as those at Warsaw and The Hague, where it was not necessary for the Prussian representative to be of high social rank. Ideas similar to those of Torcy and Frederick II can be seen in the *ukaz* of 1797 by which the Tsar Paul ordered the admission to the College of Foreign Affairs of thirty young men who were to be trained there for diplomatic careers. None of these schemes had much practical importance. In every European State the majority of the more important diplomatic posts were filled by aristocrats, sometimes very great aristocrats, who were unwilling to submit to the drudgery of specialized training and often unable to acquire large amounts of specialized knowledge. Moreover it was widely and probably correctly felt that good diplomats were formed by experience rather than by study, by mixing in good society and watching negotiations in progress rather than by poring over documents in archives. Would-be ambassadors thus continued to be trained, in so far as they were trained at all, by the time-honoured method of acting as secretaries to older and more experienced diplomats, or by being attached in some subordinate capacity to one of their country's embassies abroad.

The diplomacy of the eighteenth century has frequently been accused of immorality and lack of scruple, of being contaminated by the doctrine of *raison d'état*. Sometimes these accusations are carried to excessive, almost ridiculous, lengths, as in the assertion that during this period 'international law was a mockery and public ethics practically non-existent'.[1] It is none the less true that the international morality of the age, though probably more elevated than that of most of the seventeenth century, was far from high. The opening of hostilities without any formal declaration of war, for example, remained a commonplace of international relations. 'The Declaration of War', wrote an English pamphleteer in 1740, 'is generally now accompanied by an Army, and often first published by an Army's entering the Territories of the Enemy.'[2] Fifteen years later the British government provided a striking illustration of the truth of this dictum by seizing several hundred French ships before declaring war on France.

Secret diplomacy, though in itself perfectly legitimate and indeed

[1] J. W. Thompson and S. K. Padover, *Secret Diplomacy: a record of Espionage and double-dealing, 1500–1815* (London, 1937), p. 112.
[2] *Britain's Mistakes in the Commencement and Conduct of the Present War* (London, 1740), p. 21.

essential to the functioning of the European diplomatic system, on various occasions during the century complicated and stultified the policies of a number of European States. This was particularly marked in France, where from 1745 onwards Louis XV created a complex mechanism of secret diplomacy, the *Secret du Roi*, designed to give effect to his personal policies. This organization functioned side by side with the official diplomacy controlled by the king's ministers. Though completely ineffective in obtaining the results at which Louis feebly aimed, above all the strengthening and safeguarding of Poland, it did much, until his death, to confuse and weaken French policy, particularly in Eastern Europe. Moreover diplomats, as in the seventeenth century, were frequently corrupt; and the attitude of contemporaries to short-comings of this kind remained remarkably casual by modern standards. Perhaps the most striking case of this is J. A. F. de P. Thugut, Austrian representative at Constantinople in 1769–75, who was throughout these years an agent in French pay regularly transmitting confidential information to his French colleague, the Comte de Saint-Priest (though it is true that France and Austria were at that time allies, at least in theory). This fact, which was well known in his own lifetime, did not prevent his becoming Foreign Minister of the Habsburg monarchy in 1793. Espionage continued to be an essential and sometimes very important ingredient in the conduct of international relations. The most obvious example of the significance it could have is Frederick II's invasion of Saxony in August 1756. This attack, which made inevitable the out-break of a great European war (see p. 259) was in part provoked by the contents of documents which a Saxon government clerk had been bribed to betray to the Prussians. On a lower level of importance there are numerous examples of the prevalence and occasional success of political espionage. For five years (1770–75) the entire correspondence of John Murray, British Ambassador to the Porte, was copied by one of his servants and the copies sent to his French colleague and rival; simultaneously the Cardinal-Prince de Rohan, French Ambassador at Vienna in 1772–74, obtained through an anonymous intermediary a great amount of confidential correspondence relating to the policies of Austria and many other States.

The interception and copying of the despatches of foreign diplomats by official organizations created for the purpose (*cabinets noirs*) was also a regular practice in many States. The Austrian government in particular had a great reputation for its skill in this respect and maintained offices for the purpose in Liège, Brussels, Frankfurt and Ratisbon, as well as in

Vienna. The Thurn und Taxis family, which had since the sixteenth century controlled the postal services of the smaller German States, maintained on behalf of the Emperor similar establishments in many cities of the Holy Roman Empire. France too possessed a very efficient *cabinet noir*; and down to the fall of the Duc de Choiseul in 1770 most of her Foreign Ministers held the post of *Surintendant-Général des Postes*, thus maintaining effective control over so valuable an auxiliary. By the 1780s it had twelve employees; and complaints against its interference with the correspondence of private citizens figured in a number of the *cahiers* presented to the States-General in 1789. In Britain the position was somewhat similar. It had been established by the Post Office Act of 1711 that private letters could be opened on the warrant of a Secretary of State; and in 1730 the Duke of Newcastle ordered the Postmaster-General to make copies of correspondence passing through his hands addressed to any of a list of 112 people, including the sovereigns and leading statesmen of Europe. After 1765 lists of this kind were replaced by general warrants ordering the copying of all diplomatic correspondence passing through London. By 1741 the British version of the *cabinet noir*, the 'Secret Office', was employing nine people; and its cost tended to increase in the second half of the century. It was at least as successful as its French equivalent in intercepting the correspondence of foreign diplomats, and far more so in keeping its activities secret. It has been suggested that its efficiency contributed to the diplomatic victories won by Lord Palmerston in the 1830s and that its decline and eventual abolition in the middle of the nineteenth century helps to explain the relative failure in this respect of his later years.

The commencement of wars without formal declaration, secret diplomacy, bribery, the interception of correspondence—none of these were in any way peculiar to the eighteenth century. They had existed long before it: they were to exist long after it. They were the result, not of some unique wickedness of the age, but of the natural exigencies of a system of competitive States. It could indeed be argued with some force that international morality was tending to improve slightly during this period. There was at least no example in Western Europe in the eighteenth century of the premeditated murder by secret agents of one country of a diplomat belonging to another, a thing which had been seen under the rule of Louis XIV.[1]

[1] In 1739 the Swedish representative at Constantinople, while returning home, was murdered in Silesia by Russian agents; but such an outrage would hardly have been committed by those of Britain, France or the Netherlands.

The traditions and attitudes of the seventeenth century were continued in the importance attached, particularly in the first half of this period, to questions of diplomatic precedence. To ensure that his sovereign's dignity was not slighted by any infringement of the precedence claimed by his representatives continued to be one of the major tasks of the European diplomat; and the continuing importance of questions of precedence is shown by the continuing production of books which claimed to elucidate them. 'Points of honour, rank, precedence, are the most delicate aspects of political life,' wrote the author of one of these. 'Princes will cede towns, even provinces, but all the ability of the most adroit negotiators cannot persuade them to give up a rank to which they believe themselves entitled.'[1] The great peace congresses which punctuated the history of the period gave particular scope, by bringing together in one place the representatives of a large number of different States, for disputes of this kind: it is a sign of the slowly increasing political maturity of the age that serious negotiations were less frequently impeded by such quibbles than in the previous century. Even so, the attention devoted to questions of precedence, though declining, remained disproportionately high until late in this period. In particular the assumption of the title of Emperor by Peter I of Russia in 1721 set off a series of complicated controversies which dragged on intermittently for decades.

The interrelations of the European States continued to be dominated in the eighteenth century, almost as much as in the age of Louis XIV, by the idea of the balance of power. Theoretical justifications of such a balance were frequent; and by the middle decades of the century it was being discussed in terms of hitherto unknown confidence and precision. By then Europe was clearly becoming a single State-system. The localized 'inferior balances'—between Sweden and Denmark in the Baltic, between France and the Habsburgs in Germany and among the Italian States—in terms of which many writers and politicians had hitherto thought, were becoming merged in a general balance which covered the whole continent.

In the first half of the century this continental balance was envisaged as essentially one of France, supported at times by Spain and some of the German States (above all Bavaria), against the Austrian Habsburgs, supported in general by Great Britain and the United

[1] J. Rousset de Missy, *Mémoires sur le Rang et la Préséance entre les Souverains de l'Europe* (Amsterdam, 1746), Introduction.

Provinces. The apparent symmetry of this arrangement was rapidly shown to be superficial and delusive. A number of diplomatic episodes (notably the Anglo-French alliance of 1716 and the Austro-Spanish combination of 1725: see pp. 274–6) showed that in this respect the presumptions of the previous century were no longer valid. Moreover the fact that after 1713 no State in Western Europe was in a position to dominate the area, as France had done during much of the reign of Louis XIV, introduced into the politics of the period an element of flexibility which had previously been lacking. Above all traditional conceptions of the balance of power were now being undermined by the rapid emergence of great new political forces in East and East Central Europe, those of Russia and Prussia. However the full significance of this went unperceived until the 1740s; and even then habit and intellectual inertia were sufficient to keep the minds of most observers running in the old channels of Bourbon-Habsburg rivalry till the Diplomatic Revolution of 1756. (Louis XIV had seen in the last days of his reign the growing pointlessness of the traditional Franco-Austrian antagonism, but his efforts to achieve some agreement with the Habsburgs were not followed up by his successors.) It was the Seven Years War which broke up completely and decisively the old system of balance and inaugurated a generation of diplomatic confusion.

With France and the Habsburgs now allies the pivot on which the old system turned had disappeared. The tradition of Anglo-Austrian co-operation against France, wearing somewhat thin in the time of Walpole and strained unbearably by the peace settlement of 1748, was also submerged by the events of the 1750s. Prussia had established, at least for the time being, her position as one of the great European powers; and the personal prestige of her ruler stood higher by far than that of any other European monarch. The Habsburgs had been stung by the loss of Silesia into a series of far-reaching administrative reforms, while Russia had once more displayed her military strength and had consolidated her dominant position in Poland. The result of these changes was to move the centre of gravity of European diplomacy considerably to the east after 1763. The growth in the importance of Prussia and Russia, the renaissance of Habsburg power, now contrasted sharply with the isolation and internal divisions of Britain and the financial weakness and diminished military prestige of France. The main problems of European politics after the Seven Years War were Eastern ones, those of Poland and European Turkey, not, as a generation earlier, those of the Netherlands, the Rhineland or Italy. The inability of the States of Western Europe to play a decisive role in the solution of these new questions was shown clearly by the impotent resentment with which the French government had to watch the first partition of Poland in 1772 and the Russian annexation of the Crimea in 1783–84. The European balance of power was thus after the Seven Years War a more subtle problem in many ways than in the first half of the century. It now covered a greater geographical area and involved a greater number of powerful States than ever before.

Side by side with this European aspect of the balance of power went another and increasingly important one—that constituted by events on the oceans and in Europe's colonies overseas. Most contemporaries realized that the two aspects were intimately connected. In particular they believed that a State which could dominate the sea and Europe's trade with the outside world would have gone far towards making herself mistress of the continent. Defoe proclaimed that 'to be Masters of the Marine Power is to be Masters of all the Power and all the Commerce in Europe'.[1] Similarly a French pamphleteer in the middle of the century argued that 'the power which is strongest at sea must necessarily be the strongest commercially and thus the most formidable . . . dominance of the sea would give a nation universal monarchy'.[2] From these assumptions there naturally followed the idea that the existing balance between the maritime strengths of the European States must be perpetuated in the same way as that between their territories in Europe. Such an idea was beginning to be enunciated at least as early as the 1720s.

In this maritime and colonial struggle the main protagonists were Great Britain and, in opposition to her, France normally supported by Spain. In most of the continental States this aspect of the balance of power aroused anti-British feelings. To them it was essentially an effort, on the whole an unsuccessful one, to restrict and if possible reverse the enormous growth of Britain's maritime strength and overseas possessions. The vigour, sometimes amounting to brutality, with which she utilized her seapower in time of war by wholesale interference with neutral shipping carrying contraband or trading with her enemies, did much to increase the hostility with which she was now widely regarded. It meant that merchants and public opinion in the United Provinces, Sweden or the Hanse towns, were easy targets for French propaganda stressing the dangers of her dominance at sea and the need for Europe to combine to restrain her use of it. Propaganda of this kind was

[1] *A Plan of the English Commerce* (London, 1737), p. 147.
[2] Rein (*see* Bibliography, p. 198), p. 63.

particularly copious and violent during the Seven Years War, and spread the idea of a *balance du commerce* which must be defended against the excessive strength of Britain just as the territorial balance in Europe must be safeguarded from the overgrown influence of any of the continental States. The English, alleged the Duc de Choiseul, 'while pretending to protect the balance on land which no one threatens . . . are entirely destroying the balance at sea which no one defends'. Nor were these arguments without practical effect. The approaches made in 1759 by the Danish government to the United Provinces for the creation of a maritime union to defend neutral rights were only one of a series of proposals for some anti-British combination of this kind which culminated in the Armed Neutrality of 1780.

Analyses of the working of the balance of power, whether continental or colonial, became increasingly numerous and elaborate in the eighteenth century. It was now no longer sufficient to accept it as the more or less automatic result of the existence of a number of completely sovereign States bound together by geographical contiguity. More and more it tended to be regarded not merely as a useful political device but as something with a moral value and justification of its own. Arguments of this kind normally started from the assumption that the powers of Europe were still in a 'state of nature' with respect to each other and that each of them was engaged, consciously or not, in a ceaseless struggle to increase its influence at the expense of its neighbours. 'Each nation in its natural state,' wrote a widely read commentator in the 1740s, 'must be considered as the enemy of all others; or as disposed to be such.'[1] 'We cannot rely on virtue; it is weak and equivocal, or hidden and unknown; . . . we must thus take as our starting-point only the possible and even probable abuse of power,' wrote another two generations later.[2] If these pessimistic assumptions were justified, how could the smaller States protect their interests or even their existence? Only by a tacit but real agreement to combine against any power which seemed to menace them, in other words by the creation of a balance of power. A balance of this kind, it was contended, was an essential condition of the continued existence of the European State-system. It was even argued that a State could justifiably be compelled, by the other members of that system, to sacrifice for the common good territory to which it

[1] L. M. Kahle, *La Balance de l'Europe considérée comme la règle de la paix et de la guerre* (Berlin-Gottingen, 1744), p. 33. Cf. *ibid.*, pp. 53–5.
[2] J. P. F. Ancillon, *Tableau des révolutions du système politique de l'Europe* (Berlin, 1803–05), vol. I, Introduction, p. 32.

had every legal right, just as it in its turn could compel one of its subjects if necessary to sacrifice some of his wealth to its needs; for 'the most legitimate rulers must sometimes renounce their rights in order to maintain the balance'.[1]

Such theories were exposed to obvious practical objections. In particular they assumed that it was possible, at any given moment, to make reasonably precise comparisons of the real strength of the States concerned, to estimate accurately the advantages of Britain's wealth as against Russia's population or Prussia's efficient bureaucracy. The power of the various European States was in practice estimated by commentators largely in the somewhat crude terms of the extent of territory each possessed. This, however, was seen by some of them to be an unreliable criterion. Spain under her last Habsburg kings, it was pointed out, had controlled incomparably more territory than any other European country and had none the less been a victim-State on the point of internal collapse. It was also possible to classify the States of Europe according to their ability to wage war, whether on their own or with the help of subsidies and other encouragements from their more powerful neighbours. This, though a more realistic standard of judgement, was also not entirely satisfactory. Discussions of how the relative strength of States should be evaluated were common, but none of their authors succeeded in finding a clear or universally applicable solution to the problem. The most original and noteworthy was perhaps that put forward by the first serious critic of the balance of power idea, J. H. G. von Justi, in his *Die Chimäre des Gleichgewichts von Europa* (Altona, 1758). He argued that the real criterion of a country's strength was the efficiency of its government. From this premise he went on to claim, logically and damagingly, that if the balance of power were to prevent excessive growth of the relative strength of any State it implied a right of intervention to limit constructive internal changes or reforms in the country concerned.

It would of course be easy to find in the political writing of the eighteenth century, and especially in its vast pamphlet literature, frequent rejection of the idea of the balance of power. On closer examination, however, much the greater part of this turns out to be the product, not of reasoned consideration and reflection, but merely of some political manœuvre or party attitude. Fundamental criticism of the idea of safeguarding the rights and interests of individual States by

[1] Kahle, *op. cit.*, pp. 143–4, 147.

means of some form of balance came only from the authors of the various peace projects produced during this period.

These writers, like the theorists whom they criticized, started from the assumption that the governments of Europe were still in a 'state of nature' and that some means must be found of restraining their innate propensity to attack and injure one another. They agreed in rejecting the balance of power as a hopelessly inefficient mechanism for this purpose. It was, wrote the best-known and most influential of them, the Abbé de Saint-Pierre, 'that vain Idol to which the Nations have Sacrificed so blindly, so fruitlessly, and for so long a Time, so much Blood and Treasure'.[1] Peace and security, they argued, could be achieved only by the creation of some effective international authority able to override the selfish or aggressive impulses of any individual ruler and to persuade him, if necessary by force, to respect the rights of his neighbours. In other words what was wanted was something equivalent, on the international level, to the 'social contract' from which the States themselves were thought to have originated. Just as men had at some remote date in the past surrendered some of their individual rights to a sovereign and thus created civil society, so now each State must surrender some of its sovereignty to a supranational authority. The suggestion of a 'social contract' between States had already been made in the first half of the seventeenth century by Grotius. It had been repeated at the end of that century by Leibniz, who attempted in the collections of treaties and other documents which he published, the *Codex Juris Gentium Diplomaticus* (1693) and *Mantissa Codicis* (1700), to provide a basis for it. The form which this idea normally took, that of a federation of States ruled by some central body which included representatives of all of them, was probably encouraged by the great political and economic success achieved in the seventeenth century by the new federation of the United Provinces. Its practicability was also sometimes alleged to be proved by the existence of the Holy Roman Empire or the Swiss cantons, both of which could be considered as types of loose federation.

Various more or less precise suggestions as to the structure of the ruling body of such a federation were put forward by different writers in the earlier years of this period—by the Quaker William Penn in his *Essay towards the Present and Future Peace of Europe* (1693), by another

---

[1] C. I. Castel de Saint-Pierre, *A Project for Settling an Everlasting Peace in Europe* (London, 1739), p. 20. The first edition was published in French at Cologne in 1712, and four (with slightly differing titles) had appeared by 1729.

Quaker, John Bellers, in his *Some Reasons for an European State* (London, 1710), by the author of *Cardinal Alberoni's Scheme for reducing the Turkish Empire to the Obedience of Christian Princes* (London, 1736) and by Saint-Pierre himself. Similar proposals continued to be made in various forms in the second half of the century, though none of them were elaborated in as much detail as those of Saint-Pierre or attracted as much attention. Thus Richard Price, the English radical, suggested in very general terms in 1776 the creation of a senate in which all the States of Europe would be represented and which would have power to intervene in disputes between them. A decade later Jeremy Bentham, with the pseudo-logic and disregard of realities characteristic of much of his work, suggested that the armed forces of all the European States should be reduced to low fixed levels, that all colonies should be 'freed' (one of the first recognitions in schemes of this kind of the importance which overseas possessions were now assuming in European politics) and that a 'common court of judicature' should be set up to settle international disputes. More original, though hardly more practical, was the proposal of Thomas Pownall, a former Governor of Massachusetts, for the creation of 'a Council of Commerce, for all Europe and North America (absolutely exclusive of all and every point of politics)'.[1] This he hoped would enforce freedom of the seas and promote freedom of international trade. It might also, he modestly suggested, tend to prevent wars, and would at least help to codify and enforce maritime law in time of war.

Pownall's suggestion is of interest as an important example of an approach to the problem of international peace which, from the 1770s onwards, increasingly supplanted schemes of the essentially traditional sort typified by that of St. Pierre. This involved most notably a stress on the power of economic forces to overcome existing divisions between States. Free trade, it was argued, would at last give free play to the natural harmony which should exist between peoples and end the artificial and destructive tradition of political and dynastic division which had hitherto kept them, at such economic and human cost, apart. Hopes of this kind owed much to the influence and example of the Physiocrats in France (see p. 95); but their power in the English-speaking world on both sides of the Atlantic, and indeed amongst European intellectuals generally, was considerable. Associated with them was the potentially much more radical assumption that the foreign

[1] *A Memorial most humbly addressed to the Sovereigns of Europe, on the present State of Affairs between the Old and New World* (London, 1780), pp. 120-2.

relations of States were indissolubly bound up with the structure of their internal politics. It followed from this that real international peace could be attained only through far-reaching political reform within the European States and the weakening or destruction of the monarchical, aristocratic and military influences which had hitherto dominated them. If this could be achieved, wrote the English radical Tom Paine in the early 1790s, 'the intrigue of courts, by which the system of war is kept up, may provoke a confederation of peoples to abolish it'. But ideas so uncompromising as this could hardly be voiced, at least on the eastern shores of the Atlantic, until after the French Revolution had broken out.

No eighteenth-century peace plan had the slightest chance of being put into practice. Not only the statesmen of the age but also public opinion, partly sheltered from the realities of war by the employment of mainly professional armies, were untouched by the enthusiasm for peace which usually prompted such schemes and indifferent to the dreams which they embodied. The only political figures of importance to be seriously influenced by ideas of this kind were the Marquis d'Argenson, who controlled French foreign policy, with small practical success, in the years 1744–47, and perhaps the Comte de Vergennes, who occupied a similar position in 1774–87.

Eighteenth-century plans for universal peace were also weakened by the fact that, in an age in which the relative strengths of the European States were rapidly altering, they shared the conservative bias, the desire to maintain the *status quo*, which seems inherent in any scheme of this kind. All of them tended to assume that the territorial division of Europe existing at the moment of their publication was, or could in some way be made, permanent and sacrosanct. In some cases their authors avowed openly their desire to perpetuate the distribution of territory which existed when they wrote. Thus Saint-Pierre specified that existing frontiers were not to be changed in any way, and that no exchanges of territory were to take place or treaties between States to be made except with the consent of the federation which he wished to create. Eighty years later Immanuel Kant, in his *Zum Ewigen Frieden, ein philosophisches Entwurf* (1795) proposed as one of the preliminary conditions of a lasting peace that no State should ever pass under the control of another by any means—inheritance, exchange, purchase or donation. To generations which had seen Russia's conquest of a Baltic coastline and later acquisition of a foothold on the Black Sea, Frederick II's attacks on Silesia and Saxony, and the partitions of Poland, such ideas appeared utterly unrealistic.

IX

The Expansion of Russia:
Poland, the Baltic and the Near East

We have seen in Chapter VI that the internal politics of most European States were powerfully influenced by the personalities of their rulers. This was equally true of their foreign policies. Dynastic considerations, though slowly becoming less important, still bulked very large in international relations. Except in States such as Great Britain, the United Provinces or Sweden, where the monarchy was in some way limited, it was still easy for kings and ministers to assume that the interests of a people were identical with those of its ruling family. Sometimes this assumption was justified. Territorial or strategic advantages which increased the personal or family prestige of the ruler might also give his subjects greater security from invasion, or better access to the sea or to important routes of communication. The expansion of Russia to be described in this chapter, and the wars by which it was accomplished, were in the long run desirable from the point of view of the ordinary Russian. Moreover kings realized, as has been pointed out in Chapter V, that the prosperity of their peoples contributed to their

BIBLIOGRAPHY. The relevant chapters of R. Wittram, *Peter I, Czar und Kaiser* (2 vols., Gottingen, 1964) contain an excellent account of the Tsar's foreign policy in general. Russia's relations with the German states down to 1756 can be followed in detail in W. Mediger, *Russlands Weg nach Europa* (Brunswick, 1952); while on Russo-Swedish relations the best book is E. Amburger, *Russland und Schweden, 1762-72* (Berlin, 1934), which contains a long introductory chapter dealing with the subject in the period 1721-62. G. von Rauch, 'Zur Baltischen Frage im 18 Jahrundert', in *Jahrbücher für Geschichte Osteuropas*, neue Folge, vol. V (1957) is an important article. On the partitions of Poland much has been written. They can be followed in vol. II of the *Cambridge History of Poland* (Cambridge, 1941); and H. H. Kaplan, *The First Partition of Poland* (New York-London, 1962) is the best English account of its subject, particularly good on the internal politics of Poland in the years 1764-73. A. Sorel, *The Eastern Question in the Eighteenth Century* (London, 1898) is still useful for its linking of own power. Nevertheless dynastic and national interests could conflict; and when they did the former usually prevailed. The purely dynastic policy pursued so tenaciously by Philip V of Spain and his wife in Italy (see Chapter XI), a policy of no benefit whatever to the country they ruled, is a good example of this.

The increasing efficiency of governments and diplomatic services and the growing size of armies, which have been described above, meant that foreign policies could be carried out with increasing vigour and continuity. In a world in which monarchies were powerful and the existence of social problems largely ignored, foreign policy bulked larger in the calculations of most governments than in the century which followed. In the great States of Europe the Foreign Minister was usually the most important of all ministers. The greatest legacy of the eighteenth century to modern times is the changes in inter-State relationships which it saw. The emergence as major powers of Russia and Prussia, the expansion of the first British Empire, the achievement of American independence, are relevant to the present day in a way in which much of the art, literature and intellectual life of the period are not.

In the later seventeenth century Russia was still, for most purposes, outside Europe. For well over two hundred years European experts of various types—architects, cannon-founders, doctors and soldiers—had been filtering into the country, bringing with them techniques and to a lesser extent ideas. In the second half of the sixteenth century first the English and then the Dutch had established direct commercial relations

events in Poland with those in the Balkans during the crucial years 1768–74. On Russo-Turkish relations H. Ubersnerger, *Russlands Orientpolitik in den letzten zwei Jahrhunderten*, vol. I (Stuttgart, 1913) is fundamental. B. H. Sumner, *Peter the Great and the Ottoman Empire* (Oxford, 1949) is a brilliant work of compressed learning; while the first chapter of M. S. Anderson, *The Eastern Question, 1774–1923* (London, 1966) gives a short introductory account of the subject in the later eighteenth century. E. I. Druzhinina, *Kyuchuk-Kainardzhiiskii Mir 1774 goda* (Moscow, 1955) is the only substantial study of this very important treaty and contains much information on the diplomacy of the Russo-Turkish war of 1768–74. One of the great steps in Russian expansion is ably discussed in A. W. Fisher, *The Russian Annexation of the Crimea, 1772–1783* (Cambridge, 1970), and from a diplomatic point of view in M. S. Anderson, 'The great powers and the Russian annexation of the Crimea, 1783–4', *Slavonic and East European Review*, vol. XXXVII (1958–9). Some interesting general points about events in the Balkans and the Black Sea area are made in Chapters iv and v of W. H. McNeill's *Europe's Steppe Frontier, 1500–1800* (Chicago, 1964).

with her by way of the White Sea. During the generations which followed, especially after about 1630, the influx of foreigners and foreign ideas notably increased. In the 1680s, under the Tsarevna Sophia (who acted in 1682–89 as Regent for her brother and half-brother, the Tsars Ivan V and Peter I) considerable schemes of westernization were proposed, above all by her favourite and chief minister, Prince V. V. Golitsyn.

At the end of the century, nevertheless, Russia was still far from being really a part of Europe. As yet she possessed no coastline except in the north, on the White Sea which was frozen for a large part of the year. In the west she was cut off from the Baltic by Sweden's possession of Livonia, Ingria and Finland. In the south the Ottoman Empire and its Tatar vassal-State in the Crimea divided her from the Black Sea. To European economic life she contributed nothing except a few raw materials and a limited market for manufactured goods. Russian embassies began to be sent to the States of Western Europe in increasing numbers in the later seventeenth century, above all in the 1680s, but the country still played a very modest part in European diplomacy. So little was known in Western capitals about even the most obvious aspects of her political life that in 1657 Louis XIV addressed an official letter to the Tsar Michael, who had then been dead for twelve years. The greatest of all obstacles to the westernization of the country, however, was the influence of the Orthodox Church, ruled by its Patriarch, which was extremely conservative and hostile to foreigners. The breaking of its political power by Peter I, which began at the end of the century (see p. 411), was thus an essential step towards the emergence of a modern State in Russia. To foreigners in the seventeenth century the Russians and most aspects of their life seemed Asiatic rather than European. Their drunkenness and cruelty, which surpassed even those common in the West, appeared proofs of their barbarism.

Peter I, who had become Tsar jointly with his imbecile half-brother Ivan V in 1682, was established as more or less effective ruler of the country by a revolution which overthrew Sophia in 1689. He dominated every aspect of its life with increasing completeness from about 1695 onwards. Even as a youth he gave evidence of a desire to break with the past—in his friendships with foreigners and interest in foreign techniques, in his efforts to improve the mechanism of government and above all in his desire to create a fleet. Largely as a result of his attitude, intellectual contacts between Russia and Western Europe expanded very rapidly for a number of years from the 1690s onwards. He found

that to raise his army to European standards of efficiency and to con-
struct a navy (the most cherished of all his projects) he had to import
large numbers of soldiers, sailors, engineers and shipbuilders from the
West. His first military success, the capture from the Turks in 1696
of the port of Azov at the mouth of the Don, was made possible partly
by Austrian engineers provided by the Emperor Leopold I. The construction of the first Russian fleet, the flotilla of light craft built on the
Don in 1695–96 for the successful campaign against Azov, was carried
out largely by foreign experts, above all Italians and Dutchmen. Peter's
great journey to the West in 1697–98, during which he visited Prussia,
the Netherlands, England and the Habsburg territories, an event quite
unprecedented in Russian history, was inspired in part by the desire
to recruit foreign technicians of all kinds for his service. It led to the
engagement of several hundred of them. Simultaneously numbers of
young Russians began to be sent to Western Europe to study. The
majority went to the Netherlands, Italy and England to learn the arts
of shipbuilding and navigation, while others in Germany studied
languages, fortification and even medicine.

Peter's attitude to the West and its culture was, at least until near
the end of his reign, entirely utilitarian and pragmatic. He was interested
in its techniques rather than its ideas. He admired its power and wealth
rather than its philosophy or political thought. Nevertheless Western
influences of a non-material as well as a material kind were now steadily
increasing in Russia, a tendency illustrated by the foundation in 1699
of the first Russian order of knighthood, that of St. Andrew.

These developments had for some time little influence on Russia's
political relationships with the rest of Europe. In 1676–81 she had
fought a costly and indecisive war against the Turks; and since 1686 she
had been the ally of Poland, and *de facto* also of the Emperor Leopold I
and of Venice, in another long struggle against the Ottoman Empire.
The campaigns against Azov in 1695–96 had been the main Russian
contribution to this conflict; and she had played an extremely subordinate
rôle in the anti-Turkish coalition. She had won no victories comparable to those gained by the Habsburg armies on the Danube from
1683 onwards and had never been able to influence the policies of her
allies. When in 1699 the Emperor, Poland and Venice made peace with
the Turks at Carlowitz, after a war which had lasted for nearly two
decades, Russia played no part in the negotiation of the treaty and her
interests were completely ignored in the drawing-up of its terms.
Abandoned by his allies, Peter made peace with the Porte at Con-

stantinople in 1700; but he failed to secure possession of Kerch, at the entrance to the Sea of Azov, and thus the secure outlet to the Black Sea for which he had hoped. He never forgot the way in which he had been left in the lurch, and drew from it the obvious conclusion that Russia was still too weak and remote to be able to force the powers of Europe to pay attention to her wishes.

Only a few weeks after peace had been made with Turkey Peter joined in the attack which Denmark and Saxony had already launched, in the first months of 1700, against the Swedish Empire. The Great Northern War, thus begun, was to last for over two decades (1700-21). The Tsar's motives in entering it were mixed, but the main one was his desire to acquire an outlet to the Baltic, a recurring dream of Russian monarchs and statesmen for the last century and a half. By his action he brought his country into closer political contact than ever before with Western Europe. The war in the Baltic was, from the moment of its outbreak, closely linked with the simultaneous conflict over the Spanish Succession between Louis XIV and a hostile coalition which began in 1702 and lasted till 1713. In particular both France and her opponents hoped to end the Great Northern War by political action and then hire Swedish troops for use in their own quarrels. These hopes led to a series of efforts in the first decade of the eighteenth century by Louis XIV and his English and Dutch adversaries to mediate in the Russo-Swedish struggle. None of these came to anything. This was partly because of the obstinacy of Charles XII, the young king of Sweden, and to a lesser extent because of the refusal of Peter to surrender the territory at the mouth of the river Neva which he overran in 1703 and on which he at once began to build his new capital of St. Petersburg.

Both sides in the West also made efforts to use Russia more directly for their own purposes in the Spanish Succession struggle. In 1701 and 1707 there were proposals that she should intervene actively in the war on the French side, while in 1707-8 there were protracted discussions in London on her possible adherence to the anti-French coalition. These negotiations, however, were always very tentative and were not taken very seriously by the British and French statesmen engaged in them. Russia was still a remote and apparently weak country on the fringes of the European State-system. Moreover Charles XII seemed for some years to be invincible. He drove Denmark out of the war in 1700, after a landing on the island of Zeeland which seemed to threaten Copenhagen itself. In the same year he inflicted a humiliating defeat on

Peter outside Narva, an important fortress in Esthonia to which the Tsar had laid siege. In 1707, after a series of brilliant successes in Poland (of which the Elector Augustus of Saxony was King), he forced the latter to make peace at Altranstädt. His victories made it appear very doubtful whether Russia could long withstand a Swedish onslaught. They thus greatly reduced her value as an ally in the eyes of contemporaries.

In July 1709 a Swedish army which had invaded the Ukraine, commanded by the king in person, was totally defeated by the Russians at the battle of Poltava. This defeat led a few days later to its complete destruction as a fighting force: Charles himself took refuge in Turkey with a handful of followers. The battle revolutionized the whole position in Northern and Eastern Europe. It at once revived the coalition of Russia, Denmark and Saxony which had been destroyed by the victories of Sweden in previous years, and by so doing threatened the complete destruction of the Swedish Empire. Nor was the threat an empty one. Sweden's territories in Livonia and Esthonia were already in Russian hands before Poltava (though Peter temporarily withdrew his army of occupation from them after 1707, to meet the onslaught of Charles XII on Russia itself) and by 1716 she had lost her last German possessions. When Charles XII was killed in Norway in 1718, and Sweden thus plunged into a series of bitter dynastic and constitutional struggles, all hope of recovering the Baltic Empire built up in the seventeenth century vanished. Poltava also made Russia's influence dominant in Poland and opened up prospects of her control of much of the Baltic coastline and even of parts of North Germany. Moreover it enormously raised her standing, and that of her ruler, in Western Europe. It endowed them with the prestige which military victory alone could give. After 1709 fear of Russia, an emotion hitherto suppressed though of considerable importance, became much more visible and active among her neighbours. Now far more than ever before she began to appear a source of danger to them. Almost as soon as news of the battle had been received in Vienna Baron Urbich, the Russian minister there, told Leibniz that 'people begin to fear the Tsar as formerly they feared Sweden', while the philosopher agreed that 'it is commonly said that the Tsar will be formidable to all Europe, that he will be a kind of northern Turk'. Feelings of this sort began to show themselves in proposals for an alliance of the States of Northern Europe to resist further expansion by Russia. In 1711 a Prussian diplomat, himself a former minister to Moscow, proposed an alliance of Denmark, Prussia, and Saxony-Poland to resist her, and other suggestions of the kind were made.

Until 1713 the Western States were fully occupied by the War of the Spanish Succession: they could not effectively resist the growth of Russian power even had they desired to do so. Moreover in 1714 George I, already as Elector of Hanover a member of the anti-Swedish coalition, became king of England and gave that country's policy, for the time being, an anti-Swedish direction. The United Provinces, for their part, were too closely bound to Russia by the lucrative trade they carried on with her to be willing openly to oppose her. Not until 1716 did any of the West European States come into open conflict with her.

In the summer of that year it seemed that a Russo-Danish army, supported by British and Dutch squadrons under the command of Peter himself, was about to land in southern Sweden. At the last moment the Tsar, impressed by the strength of the Swedish defence and distrustful of the loyalty of his allies, very sensibly abandoned the enterprise. Many of the Russian troops assembled for the projected campaign were quartered in the Duchy of Mecklenburg during the winter of 1716–17; and this apparent occupation of German territory aroused violent suspicions of Peter's intentions in Denmark and Hanover, and to some extent in England. Anglo-Russian relations, exacerbated by other factors—by English fears of Russian help for the Jacobites, or of a Russian monopoly of the supply of naval stores from the Baltic—remained extremely strained for the next decade. In 1719 and 1720, when British squadrons were sent to the Baltic in an effort to bolster up Swedish resistance to Russia, the two countries came close to open war. Nevertheless the very violence of the emotions aroused by the events of 1716 showed how completely Russia was now becoming a part of the European political system. She might be feared or hated but could no longer be ignored. The Treaty of Nystadt, which ended the long struggle with Sweden in 1721 and gave Russia Esthonia, Livonia and part of Karelia, established her finally as a Baltic power: Peter's almost simultaneous assumption of the title of Emperor (*Imperator*) seemed to symbolize the astonishing rise in her international standing under his rule.

Side by side with this increase in the country's political importance after 1709 went a growth in her cultural and intellectual contacts with Europe. European influences were now stronger than ever before in her history. The great reforms of 1718–19, in particular the creation in these years of administrative colleges as important organs of central government (see p. 120), were powerfully influenced by European, above all German and Swedish, models. Peter's financial policies and methods of taxation were also based to a considerable extent on foreign examples. Moreover it can be argued that the Tsar's attitude to Western culture and intellectual life changed in his later years. His outlook after about 1714, when the war with Sweden had clearly been won, became more liberal and less narrow and utilitarian. He now began, for the first time in his life, to show some interest in cultural matters in the wider sense of the term. In the last years of his reign he bought pictures and statues abroad and began to build palaces in the Western style, though as yet on a relatively modest scale. Simultaneously young Russians were sent to study painting at the *Accademia di Disegno* in Florence, while artists and architects were imported on a hitherto unprecedented scale from France, Germany, Switzerland and Italy. In particular St. Petersburg, the new capital, owed much to foreign architects such as

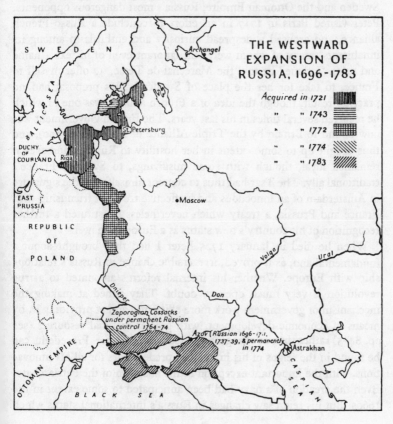

THE WESTWARD
EXPANSION OF
RUSSIA, 1696-1783

Acquired in 1721
"   " 1743
"   " 1772
"   " 1774
"   " 1783

Härbel, Schlüter and Trezzini. The new width of Peter's outlook and interests is also visible in his efforts to develop education in Russia, and particularly in the foundation of the Academy of Sciences in 1725 (this took place just after his death, but the plans for the new institution had been drawn up under his inspiration).

These foreign cultural influences came for the most part from Germany, Scandinavia and the United Provinces. In Russian life Britain and France, now the intellectual leaders of Europe and indeed of the world, as yet counted for relatively little in this respect. British cultural and technical influences were never of great importance at any time during Peter's reign, except where the navy was concerned, and were further restricted by the decade of hostility between the two governments which followed the crisis of 1716. French ones were also relatively slight, largely because of France's traditional friendship with Sweden and the Ottoman Empire, Russia's most dangerous opponents. Peter visited Paris in 1717 in an effort to conclude a Russo-French alliance, and aroused widespread curiosity and enthusiasm among its inhabitants (many of whom were still ignorant even of his exact name and title). 'I come,' he told the Maréchal de Tessé, 'to offer myself to France, to take for her the place of Sweden.' This proposal had no practical result, though the idea of a French alliance was one to which he recurred several times in his last years. The French Government was now bound to Britain by the Triple Alliance of 1717 (see p. 290), and thus caught up to some extent in her hostility to Russia. Moreover it remained loyal, though with some misgivings, to Sweden, France's traditional ally. The Tsar had thus to content himself with the signature in Amsterdam of an innocuous and ineffective treaty of friendship with France and Prussia, a treaty which nevertheless constituted a further recognition of his country's new status as a European power.

When he died in January 1725 Peter I had thus brought about a fundamental and, as it proved, irreversible change in Russia's relationship with Europe. Whether his internal reforms amounted to a true revolution is very much open to doubt. They aimed at making the mechanism of government work more efficiently and at providing it, by means of economic development, with greater material resources (see pp. 84–5) rather than at changing its essential character. Precedents can be found in the reigns of his immediate predecessors for all his innovations, with the important exception of the abolition of the Patriarchate. Even the creation of a navy had been anticipated to some extent in the 1660s. But his reign saw changes in Russia's international status which can fairly be called revolutionary. Neglected and despised at the end of the seventeenth century, she found herself when he died feared by her neighbours and courted as a political and military, if not yet a cultural and economic, equal by the greatest powers of Europe.

Her position as a leading European State was not, however, completely secure by 1725. The suffering and sacrifice which Peter's wars involved had provoked widespread discontent, above all among the peasants: his reforms were generally unpopular. Foreign cultural and intellectual influences were still relatively limited in scope, and conservative forces in Russia remained very powerful. In 1718 the heir to the throne, Peter's son Alexis, had been put to death because of his opposition to his father's policy of internal westernization and external expansion. The attitude which he typified was still very widespread even among the landowning class and was almost universal among the peasantry. The position which the Tsar bequeathed to his successors was thus, though brilliant, unstable. Many contemporaries expected the country to relapse after his death into the weakness and relative unimportance of the seventeenth century.

These expectations were partially realized. Peter was followed by a series of weak and incompetent monarchs—his wife Catherine I (1725–27), his grandson Peter II (1727–30) and his niece Anna (1730–40). Then after a period of great confusion in 1740–41, marked by factional struggles and palace revolutions, relative stability was restored during the reign of his daughter Elizabeth (1741–62). Her successor, Peter III, reigned only a few months before being deposed and murdered in a *coup d'état* led by his wife, who succeeded him as Catherine II. None of the rulers of Russia in 1725–62 possessed much strength of character or intellect; and the fact that most of them were women further weakened their position. Throughout this confused period of over a generation much real political power was therefore in the hands of the guards regiments in St. Petersburg and of court favourites—Prince A. D. Menshikov under Catherine I, the Dolgoruky family under Peter II, Johann Biren, Duke of Courland, under Anna, to a lesser extent Count K. G. Razumovskii under Elizabeth. In 1730 there was even an unsuccessful attempt by a group of great nobles to impose on Anna what amounted to a written constitution drastically limiting her powers (see p. 121), an attempt whose failure has sometimes been regarded (quite wrongly) as a turning-point in Russian history. This internal instability naturally made an unfavourable impression on Western observers. 'The Crown of Russia,' wrote one English periodical in 1759, 'may now be deemed elective, and of the worst kind of elective monarchies.'[1]

Nevertheless the country continued, in spite of many internal weaknesses, to play a great part in European affairs. In 1726 an alliance was signed with Austria. It was renewed several times, notably in 1746, and remained the pivot of Russian foreign policy until the end of the Seven Years War. It was based partly on the mutual interest of the two States in maintaining their influence in Poland and the *status quo* there, and above all on their mutual hostility to the Ottoman Empire. It was replaced in 1764 by a Russo-Prussian alliance, which was also founded on a desire to co-operate in Poland as well as on the eagerness of Frederick II, after the lessons of the Seven Years War, to keep on good terms with his great Eastern neighbour. This was succeeded in its turn, in 1781, by an *entente* between Catherine II and the Emperor Joseph II again directed against the Turks. In other words Russian foreign policy during this period can be envisaged as dominated alternately by pro-Austrian and pro-Prussian influences. The former, typified by statesmen such as Count A. I. Ostermann and Count M. P. Bestuzhev-Ryumin, were in the ascendant in the generation from the 1720s to the 1750s; the latter, represented above all by Count N. I. Panin, were dominant in the 1760s and 1770s.

With France Russia's diplomatic relations were throughout this period generally bad: no real friendship between the two States was possible. This was above all because France was the traditional friend and protector of Sweden, Poland and the Ottoman Empire, the weak and in the last two cases decaying States against which Russia's expansion was directed. As has been seen, this factor had nullified the efforts of Peter I to secure a French alliance; and for half a century after his death France clung to her traditional policy of supporting these States and thus made really good relations with Russia impossible. The *de facto* alliance which united Louis XV and Elizabeth against Prussia in 1757–62 (see pp. 260–2) was never secure and involved no lasting change in the relationship between the two countries. 'Everything that may plunge Russia into chaos and make her return to obscurity', wrote Louis XV in September 1763, 'is favourable to our interests.'[2] The 1760s and 1770s saw, however, the beginning of an alteration in France's atti-

---

[1] *Universal Magazine*, vol. XXV, p. 35.

[2] Quoted in P. Rain, *La Diplomatie française d'Henri IV à Vergennes* (Paris, 1945), p. 265.

tude. Her government in the last years of the *ancien régime* became increasingly willing to abandon the Ottoman Empire to its enemies, and perhaps even share in the spoils if it were partitioned. This made possible a slow improvement in relations with Russia, so that a commercial agreement with her was signed in 1787 and active negotiations for a quadruple alliance of France, Spain, Russia and Austria were under way when the revolution broke out in Paris. At no time during the eighteenth century, however, were the two States able or willing to co-operate effectively on any major international issue.

With Britain on the other hand Russia's relations, at least from the 1730s onwards, were always relatively amicable. The antagonism between them which had emerged in 1716 evaporated rapidly after the death of Catherine I in 1727. For the next two generations they were on good though sometimes rather distant terms and tended to regard each other as traditional friends. For this there were obvious reasons. Britain had few territorial interests or commitments in Europe, and none in Eastern Europe: Russia had none overseas. Territorial rivalry between them was impossible. Britain with her wealth and naval power, Russia with her great armies, seemed to complement rather than compete with each other. The fact that Russia could be regarded as the enemy of France and that her victories tended to reduce French influence in Eastern Europe recommended her strongly to British opinion. Above all the two States were now bound together by a growing and lucrative trade on which the finances of many Russian nobles, whose estates produced timber, hemp and other raw materials for export, largely depended. It is noteworthy that even when Anglo-Russian relations were at their worst, in the last years of his reign, Peter I made no effort to interfere with British merchants in Russia. These factors aided the conclusion of somewhat ineffective Anglo-Russian treaties of alliance in 1742 and 1746, while serious though eventually unsuccessful negotiations for another alliance were carried on for many years in the 1760s and 1770s.

The importance of the part Russia was able to play in international relations during the eighteenth century was increased by the very high reputation for courage and tenacity, if not for skill, enjoyed by her army. Its prestige had been raised to a high pitch by the defeat of Sweden in the Great Northern War. It was raised still further by Russia's victories over the Turks in the wars of 1736–39 and 1768–74, and above all by her participation in the Seven Years War (see p. 261). The extraordinary courage and endurance shown by the ordinary Russian soldier when faced by the troops of Frederick II at Zorndorf and Kunersdorf aroused widespread admiration. 'Experience has proved,' wrote one observer a year or two later, 'that the Russian infantry is by far superior to any in Europe, in so much that I question whether it can be defeated by any other infantry whatever.'[1]

Russia's military strength had indirect as well as direct importance in international affairs. It not only increased her own influence but also allowed her to supply the other States of Europe with large contingents of mercenary troops for use in their struggles with each other. In 1735 a force of this kind was hired by the Emperor Charles VI for use on the Rhine against the French army in the War of the Polish Succession, while in 1747–48 a large contingent of Russian troops was engaged by the British and Dutch governments for the defence of the Netherlands against France. In 1775 Lord North's Cabinet confidently though mistakenly expected to be able to hire 20,000 Russians for use against the American colonists; and in 1799 that of the younger Pitt discussed the possibility of garrisoning Ireland with Russian troops.

From the Russian point of view, however, the country's relations with her immediate neighbours—the Baltic States (above all Sweden), Poland and the Ottoman Empire—were more important than those with the greater but more remote powers of Western or Central Europe. This was reflected in the fact that during most of the century the Russian ministers in Stockholm, and still more those in Warsaw, were paid considerably higher salaries than those in London, Paris or Vienna. Events near the country's frontiers were normally of greater significance to Russia than those in the Netherlands, Italy or even Germany; and her relations with the greater European powers were often profoundly influenced by happenings in these border areas.

Russian policy in Sweden was dominated, after the peace of 1721, by the desire to preserve peace and the *status quo*. Any danger of a Swedish attempt to recover the lost Baltic provinces by a war of revenge must be warded off. This meant that Russia consistently supported the Swedish constitution of 1720 (which she had guaranteed by Article VII of the Treaty of Nystadt). This constitution, drawn up during a violent reaction against the despotism of Charles XII and its disastrous results, severely limited the power of the monarchy and placed control of the country in the hands of the Council and the Estates. The latter were normally divided by party strife which was often bitter. They were thus

[1] H. Lloyd, *The History of the late War in Germany* (London, 1766), vol. I, p. 145.

very vulnerable to Russian influence, which was exerted usually by bribery and occasionally by threats. By these means it was hoped to maintain in power at Stockholm a moderate and hence by implication pro-Russian régime. This was achieved for two decades after the Treaty of Nystadt; partly because in 1723–27 Russia and Sweden were acting together to support the claims of the Duke of Holstein-Gottorp to parts of Schleswig and Holstein; and partly because Count Arvid Horn, the most important Swedish politician of the 1730s, was anxious to avoid a war with Russia which he realized his country was unlikely to win.

Anti-Russian feeling nevertheless remained very powerful in Sweden, stimulated by the great influence which France continued to enjoy in Stockholm and by the judicious distribution of French money to the members of the noble oligarchy which ruled the country. In 1733, when Russia became involved in the War of the Polish Succession, and again two years later when she began hostilities against Turkey, there was a strong demand from the opposition in Sweden for intervention against her. In July 1741, after Horn had fallen from power, these feelings led to a Swedish declaration of war. This attempt at revenge ended disastrously two years later with the signature of the Treaty of Åbo, by which still more of Finland was surrendered to Russia. Though French influences remained very strong at Stockholm, it was now clear that a successful attack by Sweden on her great Eastern neighbour was out of the question.

From the early 1750s onwards a court party grouped around the Queen, Louisa Ulrica, began to emerge in the Swedish capital. Though for many years it had little influence over the country's policies it showed that there were now influential people in Sweden who were prepared to envisage a drastic revision of the constitution of 1720. From the 1760s onwards the French government, instead of trying to maintain a pro-French majority in the Council and the Estates, began to use its money and influence to overthrow the constitutional régime and restore the power of the monarchy. The feeble King, Adolphus Frederick, was hardly the man to carry through so drastic and indeed revolutionary a change. After his death in February 1771, however, his abler son and successor, Gustavus III, was able in August 1772 to destroy the constitution and set up a more or less absolute régime by a brilliantly successful *coup d'état*. This revolution made impossible Russian dominance of Swedish policy of the kind so frequently seen in the previous half-century. It thus naturally aroused great anger and alarm in St. Petersburg and can be regarded as the most serious, indeed the only serious, political defeat suffered by Russia during the reign of Catherine II. Nevertheless it did not lead to the immediate Russo–Swedish conflict which was widely expected. Though hopes of a recovery of Livonia and Esthonia were still far from dead in Swedish ruling circles it was not till 1788 that the ambitions of Gustavus III impelled him to try conclusions once more with Russia.

Relations with Poland were more important in the development of Russian policy, and of greater significance for the country's future, than those with Sweden. Hardly anyone in Russia wished or expected to make territorial gains at the expense of Sweden proper. Even Finland, parts of which were acquired in 1721 and 1743, was desired, in so far as it was desired at all, for essentially defensive purposes—to protect St. Petersburg and act as a buffer between the two States. By contrast Poland was the essential land link between Russia and the West. It was, as one historian has said, 'the threshold over which Russia stepped into Europe'. Any challenge to her leading position there, whether by the Poles themselves or by some third party, therefore raised issues of fundamental importance for Russia.

Her influence, as has already been seen, had become predominant in Poland after the battle of Poltava. It tended to become even more complete as time went on. Its extent was shown by the action of the Russian minister in bringing about in 1717 the signature of the so-called Treaty of Warsaw, an agreement between Augustus II and the Polish nobility which, among other things, drastically limited the size of the army. Its growth was still more clearly illustrated by the War of the Polish Succession (1733–35). In these years Russia, supported by Austria, imposed on the Polish nobility a king (Augustus III, Elector of Saxony) whom most of them obviously did not want, at the expense of another claimant (Stanislas Leszczynski, father-in-law of Louis XV of France) whom most of them were prepared to accept. Russian dominance was demonstrated most conclusively of all when in 1764 Catherine II, supported by her new ally Frederick II, established as the last king of an independent Poland one of her former lovers, Stanislas Poniatowski. Moreover the Duchy of Courland, still theoretically a fief of the Polish Crown, was virtually annexed by Russia in 1718. Henceforth the appointment and maintenance in power of its rulers depended entirely on Russian goodwill, though it did not formally become Russian territory till 1795.

Under the last of her Saxon rulers, Augustus III (1733–63), Poland's internal weakness and political incoherence became, if anything, worse than before. Her kings were now merely the puppets of foreign powers and domestic factions. Her political life was little more than a series of struggles between a few great noble families; above all between the Potockis, who were pro-French, and the Czartoryskis, who looked for support, at least after 1756, to Russia. Her army, ridiculously small in proportion to the size of the country and the length of its exposed land frontiers, was poorly equipped and trained. Her public revenue, it has been estimated, amounted in the middle of the century to about one-thirteenth of that of Russia and one-seventy-fifth of that of France. In 1757–62 much of the country was occupied and plundered by Russian troops *en route* to the battlefields of Brandenburg and Pomerania, and thus exposed to retaliatory raids by the forces of Frederick II. In the 1760s the helplessness of her government was underlined once more by the emergence of the powerful Confederation of Bar, which united a large part of the privileged classes in hostility to Russia. (Confederations —semi-legal associations of the nobility and gentry whose formation was usually the prelude to civil war—had for long been a feature of Polish political life and proliferated in the 1760s.) All things considered, it is surprising that the country survived for so long as an independent or pseudo-independent State.

Nevertheless until the end of the Seven Years War the idea of a partition played little part in the development of Russian policy in Poland. It was by no means a new idea. It had been originally put forward in the 1650s; and a number of plans for a division of the country had been proposed during and after the Great Northern War. Russian statesmen, however, had seldom shown much interest in such schemes. Poland seemed to them most useful if kept intact as a buffer-State under the domination of her Eastern neighbour, while a partition would bring Russia into direct contact with such dangerous potential rivals as Austria and Prussia. During and after the struggle of 1757–62 with Frederick II, nevertheless, there were signs that a new attitude was beginning to develop in St. Petersburg. In 1759 and 1761 revision of Poland's eastern frontier in favour of Russia was proposed by different Russian statesmen. In the autumn of 1763 Count Zakhar Chernyshev, one of the Empress's main advisers on military affairs, urged that large annexations in eastern Poland should be made when the imminent death of Augustus III took place. In November 1768 the State Council (*Gosudarstvenny Soviet*) stressed the need for a revision of Poland's eastern boundaries in the interests of Russian security. Thus the idea of a seizure of Polish territory was beginning to attract attention in Russia well before 1772, while the intolerance with which the Roman Catholic Poles treated not only the Orthodox population of White Russia and Ruthenia but also the Uniates (Catholics of the Greek rite) who inhabited these areas provided obvious pretexts for Russian intervention.

There were still, however, many influential people in Russia who wished to avoid a partition of Poland. In particular Count N. I. Panin, who had great influence on Russian foreign policy for nearly two decades after the accession of Catherine II, hoped in the 1760s to make the country part of the 'Northern System' which he was trying to create in order to reduce French influence in Eastern and Northern Europe. The conception of an alliance of this kind, a combination of Russia, Prussia, Britain, Denmark-Norway, Sweden and Poland, dominated Russian policy for a number of years. Panin placed high hopes on it, believing that it would 'draw Russia away from her continual dependence on others and place her . . . in such a position that she will be able to play an important role in the affairs of Europe, and also to preserve quiet and stability in the North'.[1] But the Northern System, like so many proposals for new combinations of States put forward during the eighteenth century, was impossibly grandiose and unwieldy. The British government was unwilling to give Catherine II, as the price of an Anglo- Russian alliance, the support she demanded in Sweden and the Ottoman Empire. Frederick II wished to remain the only important ally of Russia and threw his weight at St. Petersburg against any treaty arrangement with Britain. The formal results of the whole Northern System idea were therefore confined to a Russo-Danish treaty of mutual aid and guarantee signed in March 1765. Nevertheless it had some influence on Russo-Polish relations. Panin, its main supporter, believed that if the political structure of Poland were modernized and overhauled she might become once again an effective State. She would then be able to act as Russia's main ally against the Ottoman Empire, assuming the place hitherto held by Austria in Russian policy. Not until early in 1771 did the idea of a partition of Poland become dominant in St. Petersburg. To see why it did it is necessary to look at the course of events in the Near East.

Peter I was much less successful in his relations with the Turks than in his long struggle with the Swedes. The capture of Azov in 1696

---

[1] *Sbornik Imperatorskogo Russkogo Istoricheskogo Obshchestva*, vol. LXVII (St. Petersburg, 1889), p. 25.

failed, as has been seen, to secure for Russia an outlet to the Black Sea or permission for her ships to trade there. More serious, the Tsar suffered in 1711 at the hands of the Turks the greatest defeat of his reign, a defeat which, for the time being at least, put a total stop to any hope of Russian expansion southwards. In November 1710 the Porte, under the influence of Charles XII and above all of Devlet-Girei, the very anti-Russian Khan of the Crimea, declared war on Russia. Peter was at first reluctant to accept the challenge while his hands were so full in Poland and the Baltic provinces. Nevertheless he carried on the struggle with his usual energy in the spring and summer of 1711. An appeal was issued to the Balkan Christians, urging them to rise against their Turkish overlords. For the first time since the tenth century a Russian army entered Moldavia and Russian cavalry watered their horses in the Danube. However numerical inferiority, shortage of supplies and the failure of the Hospodar of Moldavia to provide the help which had been expected of him, led almost at once to a catastrophic defeat. In July, with his army surrounded on the river Pruth, Peter was forced to make peace on humiliating terms. Azov, Taganrog and the squadron based on them were to be given up: Russian interference in Poland was to cease, as was Russian diplomatic representation at the Porte.

The setback on the Pruth, though severe, was not final. In 1720 Peter forced the Turks to agree to the re-establishment of a Russian representative in Constantinople; and his successful efforts to conquer the southern shores of the Caspian from 1723 onwards led to acute Russo-Turkish rivalry for influence in Persia. Russia's relations with the Ottoman Empire continued, in other words, after the Pruth campaign as before, to be those of explicit or implicit hostility. The points on which the two Powers differed were numerous and important. Apart from their inter-mittent rivalries in Persia they were divided by the plundering raids of the Crim Tatars (still under Turkish suzerainty) in the Ukraine and South Russia and the complaints they evoked from St. Petersburg; by Turkish dislike of Russian dominance in Poland; and above all by the persisting and inevitable desire of Russia, for both strategic and economic reasons, to secure an outlet to the Black Sea. Also there was by now a long tradition of enmity between the two States, which was given emotional weight on both sides by religious prejudice.

For nearly two generations after the campaign of 1711 the Turks held their own fairly successfully against pressure from the north. Russia was hampered in any struggle with them by the great difficulty of main-

taining an army across the still largely uninhabited steppe lands which
bordered the Black Sea, by the fact that maritime power on that sea was
a Turkish monopoly and by the constant possibility of a Swedish attack
in the Baltic. Supply difficulties had been the main reason for Peter's
defeat in 1711; and they bulked very large in the Russo-Turkish war of
1735–39. This struggle, in which Russia was rather ineffectively supported by Austria from the beginning of 1737 onwards, seemed at one
time to promise great results. The Russian delegates to a peace conference which opened at Nemirov in the Ukraine in August 1737 were
ordered to press for the cession by the Turks of all territory between the
rivers Kuban and Dniester: in case of further Russian victories the
independence of the Danubian principalities, which were under Turkish
suzerainty, might be demanded. Even Peter I had seldom contemplated
success on this scale. However, the military weakness of the Austrians and
the mutual distrust which reigned between Russia and her ally forced a
drastic modification of this ambitious programme even before the conference broke up in October. When peace was made at Belgrade in
September 1739 the Russians retained none of their conquests except
Azov, which they had taken in 1737. They were forced, moreover, to
promise to dismantle its fortifications. The effects of the disastrous
campaign of 1711 had thus been only very partially nullified.

The generation which followed saw intermittent Russo-Turkish
tension—over the activities of the Crim Tatars, over rivalries in the
Caucasus, over the building by the Russians of fortifications in the
Ukraine—but no serious conflict broke out until 1768. The war which
began in October of that year was largely a result of the growth of
Russian power in Poland. The resentment which this aroused in Constantinople was skilfully stimulated by the Comte de Vergennes, the
able French ambassador. It was fanned to white heat when Ukrainian
partisans in Russian service, in pursuit of members of the Confederation
of Bar, crossed the Turkish frontier and burnt the little town of Balta
in Moldavia. The ensuing explosion of rage at Constantinople led, in
spite of the efforts of the Russian minister there to preserve peace by
bribery, to an immediate declaration of war.

The struggle which followed was the most disastrous in Turkish
history. Thirty years of peace had destroyed most of what little efficiency
remained in the Ottoman army, while the fleet was in even worse
condition. The result was that though Russia had neither desired nor
expected the war she began almost at once to win spectacular victories.
In 1769–70 most of Moldavia and Wallachia was occupied. In 1771 the

Crimea was overrun. Most remarkable of all, in 1769–70 three squadrons of Russian men-of-war were sent from Kronstadt through the English Channel and the Bay of Biscay to the eastern Mediterranean. There they helped to stimulate a serious though unsuccessful revolt in the Morea, and in July 1770 annihilated the Turkish fleet at Chesmé on the coast of Asia Minor. This remarkable naval campaign, though made possible only by British help, was a startling reminder to Western Europe of Russia's potentialities and the first really effective sign of Russian interest in the Mediterranean. Inevitably, such victories encouraged Catherine II and her ministers to think in terms of sweeping territorial and other gains. As early as November 1768 it had been agreed in St. Petersburg that when peace was made Russia must obtain a port on the Black Sea and freedom of navigation for her ships there. By the end of 1770 there had been added a whole series of much more sweeping demands—for Russian control of the Straits of Kerch, leading from the Sea of Azov to the Black Sea proper; for the placing of Moldavia and Wallachia under Russian control for twenty-five years after the end of the war as an indemnity for Catherine's war expenses; most important of all, for the erecting of the Crimean Khanate into an independent State free from Turkish control (and therefore exposed, more than in the past, to Russian influence).

These extraordinary successes, equally inevitably, aroused opposition. France was irritated by the spectacle of a Russian fleet circumnavigating Europe and, but for the attitude of the British government, might have taken active steps to exclude it from the Levant. More serious, Austria, faced by the possibility of Russian domination of the Lower Danube, was deeply alarmed. In July 1771 she signed a convention with the Porte by which, in return for Turkish subsidies and the promise of part of Wallachia, she agreed to aid the Turks against Catherine II. By the summer of that year a full-scale Austro-Russian war seemed imminent, although Russia, faced by French and Austrian opposition, had already dropped two of her most objectionable demands—those for the independence of the Principalities and the cession to her of one of the Greek islands. Such a war was desired neither in Vienna nor St. Petersburg, and the prospect of its outbreak could not fail to alarm Frederick II. Already obliged by the treaty of 1764 to give Russia financial support in her struggle with the Turks, he now saw himself on the verge of being drawn into a new European conflict over issues in which he had no direct interest whatever. It had already become obvious some months earlier, however, that an alternative to the Austro-Russian war which no one wanted could be found in the partition of Poland which hardly anyone was willing to oppose.

Frederick II had realized on the outbreak of war in 1768 that he might be able to obtain part of Prussian Poland as the price of his support for Catherine II. In the following year he unsuccessfully put forward indirect proposals for a partition, using the Danish diplomat Count Lynar as a stalking-horse. The action of Austria was more important. By occupying in February 1769 the two Polish counties of Zips, an en-clave within the Hungarian frontier to which she had a somewhat remote historical claim, she took a step which paved the way for further and more important seizures of territory. As early as May 1770 the Austrian government suggested to Frederick II the possibility of his acquiring West Prussia and Ermeland if there were a partition (though Kaunitz, the Austrian Chancellor, hoped to recover Silesia in compensation, and also perhaps to break up the Russo-Prussian alliance by encouraging Prussian aggression in Poland). Responsibility for the partition must therefore be shared among the participating powers, with Russia, at least from some points of view, shouldering less of the blame than the other two.

Events were precipitated by the visit to St. Petersburg at the end of 1770 of Prince Henry of Prussia, brother of Frederick II. For over a year he, much more than the king, had been envisaging a possible annexation of West Prussia in the immediate future: in October he had drafted a plan for joint supervision of Polish affairs by Austria, Prussia and Russia. He made a good impression at the Russian court; and on 8 January 1771 Catherine II, seeking in Poland an escape from the danger of war with Austria, suddenly suggested to him a partition of the country. The Prince leapt at the idea. On his return to Berlin six weeks later he overcame his brother's fears that its application might unduly strengthen Russia and won his consent to the proposal. In May Count Panin, hitherto the leading Russian opponent of partition, proposed that Austria be allowed to retain the territory she had seized and that Prussia be given some Polish provinces. By October Catherine II had agreed to surrender her claims on the Danube in return for com-pensation in Poland. The country's fate was sealed. The moral scruples of Maria Theresa, undoubtedly sincere and deeply felt, were overcome by the urgings of Joseph II and Kaunitz: in August 1772, after much heart-searching, she reluctantly accepted the treaty of partition which had been drawn up in February-March. Its detailed application was settled in a series of conventions in 1775–76.

Poland thus lost nearly a third of her territory and over a third of her population, though in White Russia and Galicia, the areas annexed by Russia and Austria, a high proportion of that population was not Polish. Frederick II failed to secure Danzig, for which he and his brother had hoped, and obtained less territory than the other partitioning powers. But he was able, by the annexation of West Prussia, to achieve his great object of linking up East (or Ducal) Prussia with the core of his dominions in Brandenburg. The partition undoubtedly strengthened Prussia more than Russia or Austria. Russia in many ways gained least, for in agreeing to a partition she sacrificed a very promising prospect of maintaining Poland undivided as her satellite and brought closer the day when she would have a common frontier with such formidable neighbours as Prussia and Austria.

The partition of Poland, though it deprived the Turks of any hope of effective outside help against Russia, did little to hasten the end of the Russo-Turkish war. Indeed by freeing Catherine II from the fear of a conflict with Austria it did something to stiffen her attitude towards the Porte. Simultaneously, however, the *coup d'état* of August 1772 in Stockholm caused acute though short-lived alarm in St. Petersburg, while in the following year the outbreak in East and South-East Russia of the great peasant and Cossack revolt led by Pugachev added very heavily to the empress's existing preoccupations. There were nevertheless certain demands, above all the insistence that the Crimea should become an independent State, which she was not prepared to abandon. Two prolonged peace congresses—at Foksiany, a small town in Moldavia, in August 1772, and at Bucharest in November 1772–March 1773 —broke down on this point. Finally in July 1774, after two years of mediocre achievement, the Russian army forced the issue. Advancing across the Danube, Field-Marshal P. A. Rumyantsev compelled the Grand Vizier to agree to peace terms at the Bulgarian village of Kutchuk-Kainardji. This treaty, one of the most important of the century, gave Russia the Kuban and Terek areas, the Black Sea steppe between the Bug and the Dnieper together with the mouth of the latter, a war indemnity and freedom of navigation on the Black Sea. Equally important in some ways, she obtained the right to make representations on behalf of 'the church to be built in Constantinople and those who serve it'. Upon this vague and therefore dangerous phrase was to be raised in the following century a structure of far-reaching claims. The Crimea became independent, except that the Sultan retained the formal right of investing its Khans with their office.

The Russian victory was exploited to the full. The appointment of consuls in the Principalities, in several of the Greek islands, even in Egypt, provided Catherine II with a fresh means of undermining the shaky structure of the Ottoman Empire. A new agreement, the Convention of Ainali-Kavak, reiterated in 1779 a number of the terms imposed on the Porte in 1774. Most important of all, a long series of conflicts in the Crimea between the Tatars, still loyal to Constantinople, and the puppet-Khans established by Catherine II, culminated in the summer of 1783 in the annexation by Russia of the peninsula. She thus immensely extended her coastline on the Black Sea and secured new bases for the powerful naval squadron she was now constructing there.

The decade which followed the peace of 1774 therefore saw Russia make a new and very important territorial gain. It also saw the rise of her international importance and prestige to a level higher than any hitherto reached, one which was not to be attained again until after 1812. In 1779 the short and ineffective war which Austria and Prussia had been waging over the Bavarian Succession was ended, in the Treaty of Teschen, by Russo-French mediation (see p. 266). As a guarantor of the settlement Russia could claim to have achieved for the first time a formal *locus standi* in German affairs, and to have placed the influence she had exercised there since the reign of Peter I on a secure legal footing. In December 1778 the French representative to the Imperial Diet complained, with perfect truth, that Russia was now the leading foreign influence in the politics of Germany, not, as for the last century and a half, France.

Only a few months separated the Treaty of Teschen from the formation, under Russian leadership, of the Armed Neutrality of 1780. This heterogeneous combination of States (Sweden, Prussia, Denmark, Portugal and others), united only by their common hostility to the way in which Britain defined and enforced her 'maritime rights', had limited practical effect. Its main result was to weaken the good Anglo-Russian relations which had prevailed for the last half-century. Nevertheless it helped to consolidate in Western Europe the impression of Russia's power which had been developing, though with occasional setbacks, ever since Poltava. After brilliant military victories and impressive territorial gains she seemed to have become the arbiter of Europe, courted and sometimes feared by Prussia and Austria in their German rivalries, by Britain and France in their maritime struggles, 'dictating a new code of maritime laws to mankind'.[1]

[1] *Annual Register*, 1780, p. 205.

The two generations which followed the death of Peter I saw, especially from the 1750s onwards, an accelerated growth of Western cultural influences in Russia. By the second quarter of the century the court and the higher nobility had become completely westernized, at least in externals. Foreign amusements such as dinner-parties, balls and card-playing, foreign drinks such as champagne and tokay, were rapidly adopted by the upper ranks of society. A whole series of guides to good (i.e. Western) manners and social accomplishments was published for the instruction of the landowning class and eagerly read by it. Foreign influences, as well as growing in scope, were also changing somewhat in character. Peter's visit to Paris in 1717 led to an increase in intellectual and cultural contacts with France; but until the 1740s Italian models were at least as eagerly imitated at the Russian court and among the higher nobility as French ones. From the 1750s onwards, however, French culture came to dominate almost every aspect of the lives of the Russian ruling class. The School of Fine Arts founded by Elizabeth in 1755 was staffed largely by French painters and sculptors. French books were translated in large numbers. French tutors were *de rigueur* for the children of Russian nobles. French reigned undisputed as the language of St. Petersburg society. Simultaneously Britain and Germany made less spectacular but still appreciable contributions to this westernizing process; the former through her literature and through the considerable role played by English and Scottish officers in the development of the Russian navy; the latter through the training received by many young Russians at her universities.

The reign of Catherine II thus witnessed not merely the import into Russia of European techniques, as under Peter I, but also the establishment there, more securely than ever before, of European ideas—the ideas of Locke, of Voltaire, even of Rousseau. By the second half of the century an educated Russian shared with his British or French counterparts a culture which was cosmopolitan and a system of ideas which transcended national groups or State boundaries. It is true that in Russia more than anywhere else in Europe this brilliant culture was in many ways very superficial. There it percolated only a very short distance down the social hierarchy, widening the gap between the privileged and westernized few and the ignorant and conservative many. Nevertheless Russia's military and territorial advances westward into Europe were paralleled by a simultaneous intellectual conquest of the country by the West, and above all by France. Russia was now a European State. Her newly established relationship with Western

Europe might on occasion be distorted by mutual hostility. It could never relapse into the indifference which had reigned on both sides during the seventeenth century.

X

The German States and the Rise of Prussia

Germany in the eighteenth century was more divided politically than at any time before or since. The decline in the effective authority of the Holy Roman Emperor (still its nominal ruler) which had been going on since at least the thirteenth century, and his descent to the position of an elective monarch (he was now chosen by a group of nine princes—the king of Bohemia, the archbishops of Trier, Mainz and Cologne, and the rulers of Saxony, Brandenburg, the Palatinate, Bavaria and Hanover) had set this process in motion. The religious divisions introduced by the Reformation, the repercussions of the Thirty Years War, the influence of foreign States, had reduced Germany by the beginning of this period to a state of political atomization which, at least in the west and south-west, could hardly have been more complete.

It is true that some institutions with jurisdiction over all the German States, at least on paper, continued to exist. The Emperor continued to command in theory the allegiance of the German rulers, who in 1648,

BIBLIOGRAPHY. There are two useful recent short discussions in English of the Holy Roman Empire in its last years: the Prologue, 'The "German Problem" in the eighteenth century', of T. C. W. Blanning, *Reform and Revolution in Mainz, 1743–1803* (Cambridge, 1974); and Carol M. Rose,'Empire and territories at the end of the old Reich', in *The Old Reich: essays on German political institutions, 1495–1806*, ed. J. A. Vann and S. W. Brown (Brussels, 1974). A. Himly, *Histoire de la formation territoriale des états de l'Europe centrale* (Paris, 1876), contains a good older account. Any discussion of the history of Germany in the eighteenth century must centre largely on the personality of Frederick II. In addition to the books noted above in the Bibliography to Chapter VI there may be mentioned R. Koser, *Geschichte Friedrichs des Grossen* (7th ed.; Berlin, 1921–25) which is the standard large-scale biography in three volumes; A. Berney, *Friedrich der Grosse* (Tübingen, 1934), which takes the story only to 1756; and R. Augstein, *Preussens Friedrich und die Deutschen* (Frankfurt-on-Main, 1968) which presents an unflinchingly hostile but well-informed view. The basic large-scale work on the Diplomatic Revolution of 1756 is still R. Waddington, *Louis XV et le renversement des alliances, 1754–1756* (Paris, 1896): there is an excellent short account by D. B. Horn in *New Cambridge Modern* at the end of the Thirty Years War, had been recognized as possessing not complete sovereignty but merely 'territorial supremacy' (*Landeshoheit*). A Diet consisting of representatives of the States continued to meet and deliberate at Ratisbon. An Aulic Council continued to function at Vienna for the conduct of German affairs, and a *Reichskammergericht*, a supreme law court for the whole empire, to sit at Wetzlar. These institutions were not complete nullities; and the Empire continued, until its fall in 1806, to be widely regarded in Germany as a guarantee of existing rights of all kinds and to enjoy genuine popular support. But their powers were essentially negative. They could, within fairly narrow limits, inhibit change. But their ability to do anything new or constructive was non-existent.

The Emperor, as Emperor, still possessed great prestige and considerable influence over the German princes; but he had no real authority. For close on four centuries (1439–1806), with one short but important gap in 1740–45, every holder of the imperial title was a member of the Habsburg family. Long before the eighteenth century it had become virtually hereditary. The real powers of its holders were derived almost entirely from their own hereditary lands, from the fact that they were Habsburgs, not from the fact that they were Holy Roman Emperors. The German States provided them neither with an army nor with any significant amount of money. It is true that the Diet and the administrative Circles into which the Empire was divided could, if the rulers concerned agreed, raise a composite force to defend imperial territory against outside attack or to repel agression by any of the German States against its neighbours; but a force of this kind was never effective or lasting. The Emperor's revenues amounted to the derisory

History, vol. VII. Some of the origins of this famous change in the European diplomatic position can be followed in W. J. McGill, 'The roots of policy; Kaunitz in Vienna and Versailles, 1749–1753', *Journal of Modern History*, vol. XLIII (1971). The controversies among historians to which Frederick's attack on Saxony in 1756 has given rise are interestingly summarized in H. Butterfield, *The Reconstruction of an Historical Episode* (Glasgow, 1951); while one aspect of the disunity of his enemies is discussed in L. Jay Oliva, *Misalliance: a study of French policy in Russia during the Seven Years' War* (New York, 1964). There are useful accounts of the War of the Bavarian Succession in H. W. V. Temperley, *Frederick the Great and Kaiser Joseph* (London, 1915) and the more recent P. P. Bernard, *Joseph II and Bavaria* (The Hague, 1965), while the struggle is placed in its historical context by E. F. S. Hanfstaengl, *Amerika und Europa von Marlborough bis Mirabeau; die weltpolitische Bedeutung des belgisch-bairischen Tauschprojekts* (Munich, 1930).

sum of less than 14,000 florins (derived from a tax on the Jews of Frankfurt and Worms and from small annual payments by the imperial free cities). Strictly speaking the rulers of the German States could impose tolls or strike coins only with his permission. Also he alone could give universities the right to confer degrees, or could grant titles of nobility (though his monopoly of this privilege was disputed). But these theoretical powers meant little in practice. The German princes were by now in fact independent, complete sovereigns in their own States. The Diet, which consisted of three *curiae*, those of the electors, the princes and the towns, met regularly throughout this period; indeed in theory it had been in permanent session since 1663, and the capitulations agreed to by various Emperors on their accession, in 1711, 1742 and 1745, provided that it must be summoned at least once in every ten years. Nevertheless it was almost completely ineffective. It was hampered by incessant disputes between and within the *curiae* (notably between the electors, anxious to maintain their privileges and superior status, and the other ruling princes). It was also weakened by religious differences. Article V of the Treaty of Osnabrück in 1648 had provided for its division into Catholic and Protestant groups whenever religious questions were to be discussed, and for the settlement of such questions, not by majority vote, but by amicable agreement between the two parties. It was normal, moreover, for a number of States to be represented in it by proxy and to share a single representative, a practice which had the advantage of making it a small and manageable body but which also showed how little importance many of its members attached to it. All these factors combined to make it almost impossible for the Diet to take decisions on matters of general importance to the Empire; and any decision it did reach could usually be safely ignored by the more powerful German princes.

Nor had the Aulic Council and the *Reichskammergericht* any real authority. The former occasionally issued decrees, even in the later eighteenth century, against rulers who abused their powers; but never against the more important ones. Its greatest achievement was perhaps to help in forcing the Duke of Württemberg, in 1770, to make an agreement with his Estates by which he confirmed their powers and restored the constitution: but Württemberg, though not negligible, was not a State of the importance of Prussia, Saxony or Bavaria. The *Reichskammergericht* was weakened by the hostility of the German princes, who regarded its existence as a threat to their authority and in many cases denied their subjects the right to appeal to it. The slowness with which it worked, which had been notorious for generations, was such that by 1772 there were over 61,000 cases awaiting trial. Moreover a ruler condemned at Vienna or Wetzlar would often appeal to the Diet and thus evade compliance with the decisions of the Aulic Council or the *Reichskammergericht*. In other words, eighteenth-century Germany was, as a contemporary put it, 'a Knot of independent States leagu'd together, with a Prince or Staadtholder at their Head, cloath'd with the Ornaments of Royalty, but without that Power which ought to be deem'd essential to it'.[1] It is not surprising that by the later 1770s Joseph II had decided that the imperial title was a liability rather than an asset to him and was thinking in terms of its abdication and the severing of all ties between the Empire and the Habsburg territories— the cleavage finally forced on his successors in 1866.

The States into which Germany was divided varied enormously in size, in wealth, in military strength and in their systems of government. They can be divided into four groups. The first two—nobles who held their land immediately from the emperor, and free cities— were politically unimportant. The territories of the former, nearly all in south-west Germany, had at the end of the century less than 500,000 inhabitants out of the empire's total population of 28–30 million. The free cities had in all 6–700,000 inhabitants: of them only Nuremberg and Ulm possessed much territory beyond their walls. Some of those in Swabia were mere villages with populations of a few hundreds. The towns which increased in size, and importance in the German world in the later seventeenth and the eighteenth century were, very significantly, not the old imperial cities but the capitals of the more important territorial princes, *Residenzstädte* such as Munich, Berlin, Stuttgart and of course, Vienna. A third group, the ecclesiastical principalities, included some States of political significance—the Electorates of Cologne, Mainz and Trier, the Archbishopric of Salzburg, the Bishoprics of Bamberg and Münster—but the areas which comprised it were inhabited by only three million people in all. Moreover the ecclesiastical States more than ever in the past were now anachronisms exposed to the greed and expansionism of their greater secular neighbours. Plans for their secularization were drawn up during the short-lived reign of the Wittelsbach Emperor Charles VII (1742–45) and also during the Seven Years War; though these had no result they were clear anticipations of the events of the Revolutionary and Napoleonic epoch. Finally came a

---

[1] *The Present State of Germany* (London, 1738), vol. II, p. 312.

group of secular States—Brandenburg-Prussia, Saxony, Hanover, the Palatinate, Bavaria and a few others—which wielded varying degrees of real power and could play roles of varing importance not merely in German but in European politics. Out of the 360 or so 'States' into which the country was divided (the number rises to about 1,800 if all the imperial knights of the south-west are included) there were perhaps ten or twelve ecclesiastical principalities and twice as many secular ones which really deserved the title.

'It is scarcely possible', wrote an eighteenth-century expert, 'to conceive a greater difference in the internal constitutions of any countries whatever than there actually is between the various States of Germany.'[1] Certainly their political and administrative structures varied very widely. With the exception of the free cities, which were normally controlled by oligarchies (see p. 57) nearly all the German States were under some form of absolute rule which was usually the result of the weakening or destruction of the estates of the principality concerned. Even this generalization did not hold good everywhere. In Mecklenburg-Schwerin the estates persuaded the Emperor to depose an unpopular duke in 1728 and extracted important concessions from another in 1755. In Württemberg also they were able to establish a strong position in a long struggle with Duke Karl-Eugen (1737–93). With few exceptions, however, the German States were absolutisms, and often absolutisms of a peculiarly oppressive kind. Brandenburg-Prussia, endowed with large territories and favoured with a series of able rulers, was able to develop a fine army and a still more remarkable system of administration. The other principalities of Germany, lacking both such resources and such leadership, remained throughout the century, with few exceptions, sunk in tradition and narrow in political outlook. The greater States of Europe, in return for the sacrifices they demanded of their citizens, had something at least to offer—military glory, the real if irrational satisfaction to be derived from membership of a powerful political unit, in some cases the economic opportunities which a large politically unified area alone could provide. Hardly any of the German ones could offer compensations of this kind to offset the burdens imposed by their very existence.

In almost all of them the demands of the ruler and his court were a heavy drain on the State's finances. Saxony in the first half of the

[1] J. S. Pütter, *An historical development of the present political constitution of the Germanic Empire* (London, 1790), vol. III, p. 270.

century, under the Electors Augustus I and Augustus II, was particularly famous for the lavishness of its court and for the ostentatious luxury in which ministers such as Count Flemming and Count Brühl lived. Conspicuous consumption of this kind was normal, however, in most of the smaller German States. It explains the tendency of so many of their rulers to run heavily, sometimes hopelessly, into debt, and thus helps to account for the undignified greed which many of them displayed for foreign subsidies and pensions. In many States, again, the rulers tended to emphasize their importance, sometimes to a ludicrous degree, by the assumption of long and complicated titles. A French observer claimed that 'there is no small sovereign in the Empire with less than three times as many titles as the King of France'.[1] More serious, the German princes often gratified their *amour-propre* and provided appointments for their courtiers by maintaining oppressively large armies and grossly inflated bureaucracies. Thus the Elector Palatine at one time possessed thirty regiments (about a quarter of whose strength consisted of officers) and a Grand Admiral to command the few small craft he maintained on the Rhine; while it has been estimated that during the eighteenth century Germany had twice as many officials, in proportion to its population, as after the unification of 1866–71. The weakness of the imperial cities, the importance in every sizeable state of military and bureaucratic influences and psychology, the fact that in the developing territorial capitals economic life revolved very largely around the court and its demands; all this meant a society in which an independent middle class of merchants, manufacturers or professional men was exceptionally weak by the standards of England, the Netherlands or even France.

Equally important was the constricting effect which the political division of Germany had on her intellectual life. The despotisms which ruled nearly the whole of the country were, with few exceptions, hostile to intellectual novelties or even modified freedom of thought. Newspapers and the publishing trade developed slowly. In the 1760s the total number of titles published annually in Germany—about 1,500—was no greater than it had been in 1610; and it was only at the end of the seventeenth century that Latin was replaced by German as the country's main literary language. In these circumstances it is not surprising that German intellectual life was in many ways at a low ebb in the first half of this period. Its growth was further retarded by the immense cultural

[1] A. Fauchier-Magnan, *The Smaller German Courts in the Eighteenth Century* (London, 1958), p. 21.

prestige of France (see pp. 359–60), which made German art and literature appear backward and provincial (as indeed they were until the
1750s or 1760s). The contempt for their subjects' intellectual attainments
which was widespread among the country's rulers until late in the century is epitomized by Frederick II's refusal to appoint the classical
scholar Winckelmann as his librarian at a salary of 2,000 thalers on the
grounds that 'a thousand thalers is enough for a German'.

The political divisions of Germany and the military weakness of most
of the German States made it inevitable that the political as well as the
cultural life of the country should be greatly influenced by foreign
pressures. These were already well-established at the beginning of the
eighteenth century. France, most notably, had been influencing the
policies and playing upon the ambitions of the German rulers for
centuries, and had thus acquired important territorial gains at the expense
of the Holy Roman Empire. In 1648 most of Alsace had fallen under
her control. In 1681, by one of the most naked of all Louis XIV's
aggressions, she had seized the city of Strasbourg. It is true that these
aggressions aroused a good deal of hostility. The French minister to the
Diet reported in 1723 that 'the Germans in general see with bitterness
the King in possession of Alsace', while the recovery of the province
had been one of the Habsburg war aims in the Spanish Succession
struggle. Nevertheless throughout the century her military power, her
money and her cultural prestige made France an important factor in
German politics. Moreover she was slowly and almost imperceptibly
'rectifying' her eastern frontier and establishing for the first time in
history a relatively clear-cut geographical boundary between French and
German territory. Thus part of the *baillage* of Gemmersheim, which
surrounded the French fortress of Landau and which Louis had tried
to seize through his *Chambres de Réunion* in the 1680s, became French
by agreement with the Duke of Zweibrücken and the Elector Palatine
in 1766 and 1768. By 1786 the Comte de Vergennes, the French Foreign
Minister, could claim that the enclaves of non-French territory left in
Alsace by the Treaty of Ryswick ninety years earlier had been eliminated.

Sweden, which like France had gained important German territories
in 1648, lost most of them in the first two decades of the eighteenth
century. Simultaneously, however, new foreign influences were brought
to play upon German politics by the choice of the Elector of Saxony as
King of Poland in 1697 and by the accession of the Elector of Hanover
to the British throne in 1714. In the latter year the Elector of Bavaria
proposed that he should become King of Sardinia as part of the settle-

ment at the end of the War of the Spanish Succession. Above all the power of Russia to influence events in Germany, first seen clearly in her occupation of Mecklenburg in 1716 (see p. 222), increased throughout the century. Inevitably, moreover, the German policy of the Habsburgs was continually influenced by their territories and interests outside the boundaries of the Holy Roman Empire. Thus in the eighteenth century, as in preceding generations, the German States, with few exceptions, were the impotent spectators and victims of the struggles of the greater powers of Europe.

It was against this depressing background that the political history of eighteenth-century Germany unfolded. That history was dominated by one overriding fact—the success of Brandenburg-Prussia in raising herself to the status of a great power and the profound and lasting enmity of the Habsburgs which resulted from that success.

She had already, in the later seventeenth century, shown signs of her ability to lift herself out of the ruck of the other German States. Larger than Saxony, Bavaria or the Palatinate, her possession of considerable areas of uncultivated land gave her greater opportunities than they of increasing her population by immigration and internal colonization. The 'Great Elector' Frederick William (1640–88) had begun to create the army and administrative machine which were to dominate her future evolution. The significance of these factors, however, took two generations or more to become obvious. In the War of the Spanish Succession Prussia, whose ruler acquired the title of king in 1701, played a respectable but unimpressive role on the anti-French side. Her gains at the end of the struggle—the principality of Neuchâtel and Spanish Gelderland—did little to increase her real power. Under Frederick William I the bureaucracy was remodelled and made the most efficient in Europe (see pp. 117–18); simultaneously the army became in some ways the best in the world. The king was, in fact, providing the weapons with which his son was to transform Prussia's international position.[1] But he was too cautious, too little skilled in diplomacy, too loyal to the emperor and perhaps in his own way too moral, to use these weapons himself. During his reign Prussia's only territorial gain was part of West Pomerania, acquired with comparatively little effort in 1719 in the dismemberment of the Swedish Empire. The fact that for all his

[1] As Frederick II himself pointed out more than once in later years. See for example his letter to his brother, Prince Henry, of 5 August 1774, in *Politische Correspondenz Friedrichs des Grossen* (Berlin, 1879–1939), vol. XXXV, p. 473.

obsessive interest in military affairs Frederick William fought no war of any significance obscured, for most contemporaries, the real importance of his reign, in some ways the most crucial in the history of Prussia. The secondary role played by the country in the tortuous diplomacy of 1713–40 concealed from them his success in raising a very impressive structure of State power on narrow economic and demographic foundations.

The will to expand was active in Berlin throughout his reign. Indeed it could hardly be otherwise in such a State, spread discontinuously from East Prussia to the Lower Rhine, with her main territories separated by the lands of her neighbours (notably Poland and Hanover) and still partially cut off from the Baltic by Sweden's retention of West Pomerania. By the end of the seventeenth century Brandenburg-Prussia had reached a position in which it was impossible for her to remain indefinitely. She must expand or resign herself to stagnation and perhaps to eventual dismemberment. Dreams of annexing Polish Prussia and the remainder of Swedish Pomerania passed through Frederick William I's mind; but in general he regarded such gains as lying in a more or less remote future. Throughout his reign, and especially in its second half, much of his foreign policy was dominated by the desire to acquire for Prussia, on the death of their ruler the Elector Palatine, the small but strategically placed West German duchies of Jülich and Berg to which he had a dynastic claim. This claim he wished to have recognized by the powers of Europe, and above all by the Emperor, whose support in a matter of this kind was still extremely valuable. In 1723, by the Treaty of Charlottenburg, he secured British and Hanoverian support for his acquisition of the duchies. In December 1728 he made an agreement with Charles VI by which he was guaranteed the succession to Berg (Jülich was to go to the rival claimants, the Pfalz-Sulzbach family) in return for a Prussian guarantee of the Pragmatic Sanction.

The latter, one of the central facts of the European diplomacy of the period, was a formal act promulgated by the Emperor in April 1713. By it he attempted to ensure that his territories (which it is convenient to lump together under the shorthand term 'Austria') should pass undivided to his children in the male or female line or, on their failure, to the two daughters of his elder brother Joseph I. Dynastic provisions of this type had long been common in the German States; and the extent of the Habsburg territories, their geographical dispersion (which was accentuated by the acquisition of the Netherlands and the new Italian possessions in 1713), and the virtual autonomy of many of them

in the regulation of their internal affairs, seemed to make such an arrangement almost indispensable. In 1720–23 Charles secured the acceptance
of the Pragmatic Sanction by the Diets of all his Central European
provinces: henceforth, as his hopes of a son vanished and it became
clear that he must be succeeded by his eldest daughter, the Archduchess
Maria Theresa, Austrian diplomacy centred on a series of efforts to
have it guaranteed by the major powers of Europe. Spain promised to
uphold it by the Treaty of Vienna of 1725 and Russia by her alliance
with the Emperor in the following year. Britain added her guarantee in
1731 and France hers in 1735. The worthlessness of many of these
paper promises was soon to be shown by events.

Austro-Prussian relations remained good for some time after the treaty
of 1728, but by the end of the War of the Polish Succession in 1735 (see
p. 230) they had become very strained. By 1738 it was clear that Charles,
in spite of his undertakings, would oppose the inheritance of Berg by
the Hohenzollerns. The result was a secret Franco-Prussian agreement
of May 1739 by which Cardinal Fleury, who then controlled French
policy, promised his support for the acquisition by Prussia of most of
the duchy. Thus when Frederick William I died in May 1740 he
bequeathed to his son Frederick II a grievance against the Habsburgs
and a relatively close relationship with France. Within a few months of
his death German politics suffered a revolutionary change.

Charles VI died on 19 October. Two months later Prussian troops
invaded the Habsburg province of Silesia and thus began a struggle for
mastery in Germany which was to last for a century and a quarter.
The reasons for Frederick's dramatic and unscrupulous action seem
clear. He had always been conscious of Prussia's exposed position and
of the way in which her political geography forced expansion upon her.
As early as 1731, in one of his earliest surviving comments on international affairs, he had visualized increasing her geographical unity by
the acquisition of Polish Prussia and Swedish Pomerania. It was true
that the conquest of Silesia (to which he had legal claims, though very
weak ones) would considerably lengthen the already very long frontiers
which the Prussian army had to defend. At the same time, however, it would place at Frederick's disposal a province much wealthier
than any he already possessed, and would weaken the Elector of Saxony
by interposing a solid wedge of Prussian territory between his German
lands and his Polish kingdom. Nor had Frederick any illusions about the
morality of international relations or any scruples about the use of force
to uphold his claims. Already in 1737 and 1738 he had proposed the

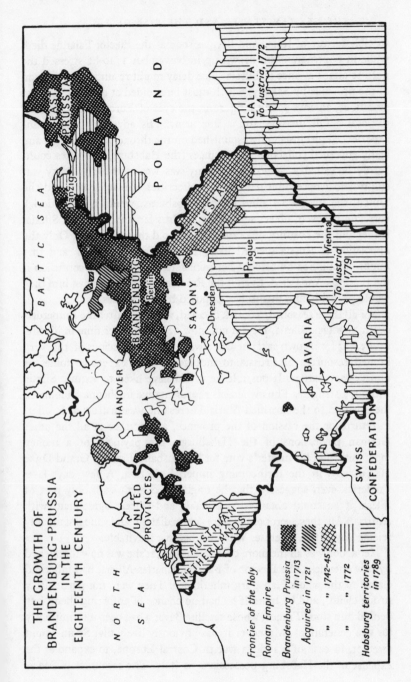

THE GROWTH OF
BRANDENBURG-PRUSSIA
IN THE
EIGHTEENTH CENTURY

NORTH
SEA

BALTIC SEA

POLAND

EAST PRUSSIA

Danzig

BRANDENBURG

Berlin

SAXONY

Dresden

SILESIA

Prague

GALICIA
To Austria, 1772

Vienna
To Austria
1779

BAVARIA

HANOVER

UNITED
PROVINCES

AUSTRIAN
NETHERLANDS

SWISS
CONFEDERATION

Frontier of the Holy
Roman Empire

Brandenburg Prussia
in 1713
Acquired in 1721

"   "   1742-45

"   "   1772

Habsburg territories
in 1789

forcible seizure of Jülich and Berg as soon as the Elector Palatine died; while in a memorandum drawn up in November 1740 he stressed the need to attack at once in Silesia since delay might result in the invasion of the province by Saxony, which must be avoided at all costs. Young, ambitious, anxious to cut a figure in the eyes of Europe, he had at his disposal a full treasury and a fine army. His adversary was an inexperienced girl insecurely established on the throne of a disunited and badly governed collection of provinces (the Habsburg territories could hardly be called a State) whose army was weak, whose treasury was empty and whose ministers were mediocrities. Great Britain and the Dutch, the traditional allies of the Habsburgs, would not, Frederick correctly believed, object seriously to a Prussian annexation of Silesia: if they did the hostility of France would hold them in check. Only the opposition of Russia seemed likely to disconcert his plans, and that might be nullified by bribing her ministers, or by internal confusion if the Empress Anna died. Even if the Russians did move against him they would probably find themselves opposed by the Swedes.

For all these reasons Frederick decided, very soon after the Emperor's death, to attack Silesia. He did not, now or at any other time in his life, desire war for its own sake; he was always far too conscious of the very limited resources of Prussia to indulge in such expensive follies as unnecessary battles. If possible he would have liked to acquire Silesia without a struggle. Thus when his representative in Vienna announced the invasion to the horrified Maria Theresa he was instructed to offer, in return for the cession of the province, a guarantee of all the other German possessions of the Habsburgs, the payment of a money indemnity, and his master's vote for her husband Francis, Grand Duke of Tuscany, in the forthcoming imperial election. A few days later Frederick even suggested that he might be content with only part of Silesia if he could obtain a 'reasonable and sincere agreement' with Austria. All these proposals were immediately and understandably rejected by Maria Theresa. War thus became inevitable.

Her action was all the more courageous in that she was now threatened by new enemies. The Elector of Bavaria, Charles Albert, had inherited claims to the whole Habsburg inheritance. They were not particularly strong claims, and by himself he had no chance of enforcing them; but behind him stood France, whose satellite Bavaria had been intermittently for two generations. Moreover it was obviously likely that Spain would attempt, in case of a serious war in Central Europe, to expand at the expense of the Habsburg possessions in Italy. The resources of Maria

Theresa's dominions, at least her financial resources, were inadequate to maintain a war of any length against so powerful an array of foes and very hard to mobilize effectively. The result was that almost from the moment Prussian troops crossed the Silesian border she was heavily dependent on outside help, above all from Great Britain. A British subsidy was granted her at the end of April 1741 and continued to be paid, though with growing reluctance, until the end of the war. It was provided not because any British statesman cared much about the fate of Silesia but because the strengthening of the Habsburgs seemed the best way of checking the growth of French power in Europe.

The development of French policy was the key to events in the spring of 1741. Cardinal Fleury, who had controlled the country's diplomacy since 1726, was now an old man of almost ninety. He had no desire for a new struggle against the Habsburgs and saw that France was unlikely to gain much from one. Ranged against him, however, were the weight of a long anti-Habsburg tradition, and also powerful military and aristocratic groups which had forgotten the defeats of Louis XIV's last years and hoped to win glory in a new struggle on the old battlefields of the Rhineland and the Netherlands. This resistance to Fleury's cautious policy was led by the Maréchal de Belleisle, who as early as January 1741 had drawn up plans for French intervention on a large scale in the affairs of Germany. In March he was sent as the envoy of Louis XV to those German States which seemed likely to support Charles Albert of Bavaria, who had now put himself forward as a candidate for the vacant imperial title. In the next few months Belleisle constructed an extensive though insecure anti-Habsburg coalition in Germany. In May Bavaria and Spain united against Maria Theresa by the Treaty of Nymphenburg; and in June France, by an agreement with Frederick II, committed herself to military intervention. Fleury had thus been overruled; but his struggle with Belleisle had virtually paralysed French policy for several months. It had thus given Maria Theresa at least a chance of survival. Nevertheless her position was extremely serious. Already in April the Prussian infantry had shown their quality by defeating the Austrians at Mollwitz in Silesia, the first battle of the war. In July George II, alarmed for the safety of his German Electorate of Hanover which seemed exposed to French or Prussian attack, signed without consulting his ministers in London a convention guaranteeing its neutrality. This made it almost impossible for Britain to give any direct help to her ally. In October French and Bavarian troops invaded Bohemia.

From this dangerous position Maria Theresa escaped mainly because of the disunity of her opponents. Frederick II was quite prepared to throw over the French whenever it suited him to do so, and early in October agreed to the Convention of Klein-Schnellendorf. By this he was allowed to occupy the whole of Silesia, in return for which he suspended operations against Maria Theresa. This allowed her to drive the French and Bavarians from Upper Austria and later Bohemia, to invade Bavaria and even to capture Munich. Charles Albert, with French backing, was elected Emperor in January 1742, but found himself almost at once driven from his own capital. In June of that year, by an agreement signed at Breslau, Frederick II obtained the cession of almost the whole of Silesia. Maria Theresa agreed to this only under heavy pressure from the British government, which demanded that her resources be concentrated on the struggle with France. Her need for British subsidies and her hope that a combined British, Dutch and Austrian force was about to launch a large-scale attack on France from the Austrian Netherlands led her to accept the surrender of Silesia— a surrender which she hoped and expected would be only temporary.

By the summer of 1742 the real decisions of the War of the Austrian Succession, as far as Germany was concerned, had thus all been taken. Frederick's aggression had been successful: Silesia was now Prussian territory. It was clear, on the other hand, that the structure of Habsburg power in Central Europe was still too solid to be pulled down by the apparently overwhelming but in fact rather ineffective enemies who attacked it in the later months of 1741. Though the struggle dragged on for another six years the ebb and flow of war could not affect these essential facts.

Maria Theresa's position continued on the whole to improve in 1743. The 'Pragmatic Army' of British, Hanoverian and Austrian troops which had now been formed in the Austrian Netherlands won an important victory over the French at Dettingen in June. A new invasion of Bavaria by the Austrians seemed for a time to threaten France herself with attack. These appearances, however, were misleading. In particular the wavering and lukewarm attitude of the Dutch made the British government unwilling to launch a direct attack on France (with whom Britain was not formally at war; she was still fighting merely as the ally of Maria Theresa). Moreover Anglo-Austrian relations were very seriously strained by the insistence of Lord Carteret, now the dominant figure in British foreign policy, that the Austrians should make substantial concessions to Charles Emmanuel of Sardinia in order to secure his support in Italy. These concessions were made by the Treaty of Worms, signed in September, but were deeply resented in Vienna.

Austria's successes in 1742-43 were nevertheless striking enough to alarm Frederick II, who quite rightly suspected Maria Theresa of wishing to annex part of Bavaria. Already can be seen in Berlin that determination to prevent any strengthening of Habsburg power in Germany which was to remain the most permanent element in Frederick's foreign policy until his death, and which he bequeathed to his successors. His fears and suspicions drove him to sign a new alliance with France in June 1744 and to invade Bohemia immediately afterwards. Maria Theresa was, however, far better placed to meet this onslaught than she had been to face that of December 1740. In January 1745 Charles Albert of Bavaria died, and she was able to make peace with his successor in April. In September she secured the election of her husband as Emperor, and thus re-established Habsburg control of what was still, at least in theory, the highest position of secular authority in Europe. Moreover she now enjoyed the support of Saxony. The result was that in spite of defeats at Hohenfriedberg and Soor she stubbornly refused for many months to agree once more to recognize Silesia as Prussian territory. She was forced to do so at last in December 1745, by the Treaty of Dresden; partly because of a threat that British subsidies would be cut off if she did not; partly by a brilliantly successful Prussian invasion of Saxony; and above all perhaps by the failure of a series of efforts to make a separate peace with France.

With this treaty the war, as far as Germany was concerned, virtually ended. The next three years saw much fighting in Italy and the Netherlands (see pp. 278-9, 294), but the repercussions of this on German affairs were of secondary importance. French efforts to persuade Frederick II to launch yet a third attack on Austria were unsuccessful. Thus when peace was made at Aix-la-Chapelle by Britain, France, Austria and the United Provinces in October 1748, Prussia, who was no longer a belligerent, took no part in the negotiations. The treaty which the British and French representatives drew up was accepted by Maria Theresa only with the greatest reluctance. This was because one of its clauses guaranteed, though in rather vague terms, Frederick II's possession of Silesia, the one really important result for Germany and indeed for Europe of the complicated struggles of 1740-48. The Empress, however, was far from having abandoned hope of regaining the lost province. The administration of her great possessions in Central Europe, though still full of faults, was improving rapidly. Her army, though still inferior to that of Prussia, had performed during the war as well as that of France and probably better than that of Britain. Her resources, at least on paper, were still much greater than those of Frederick II. A reconquest of Silesia was by no means beyond her powers.

But it was clear that such a reconquest could not be achieved with the help of Austria's traditional allies, Great Britain and the Dutch. Britain had, throughout the war, shown herself indifferent to the interests of the Habsburg monarchy. In 1742 and 1745 she had forced Maria Theresa to accept the Prussian seizure of Silesia. In 1743 Carteret had browbeaten her into promising large concessions to Sardinia. At Aix-la-Chapelle the British government seemed to have conspired with that of France against the Empress. Plainly Britain was interested in the Habsburg territories as an auxiliary against France and nothing more. Preoccupied above all with colonial and commercial problems, she had little in common with Austria, whose outlook was increasingly dominated by events in Central and Eastern Europe, above all by the question of Silesia. The Duke of Newcastle, who in the main controlled British foreign policy in the years after 1748, tried to consolidate the Austrian alliance by securing the election of the Empress's eldest son, the Archduke Joseph, as King of the Romans (i.e. heir to the imperial title). These efforts, however, cut little ice in Vienna. As for the Dutch the events of 1745–48 had shown up clearly their military weakness, their internal divisions and the almost catastrophic fall in their international importance.

The result was that from 1749 onwards, under the influence of Count Wenzel von Kaunitz-Rietberg who became Chancellor in 1753, the Austrian government played intermittently with the idea of breaking the Franco-Prussian alliance, isolating Frederick II, and then crushing him with the help of Russia and perhaps France. The idea was slow to bear fruit. An embassy to Paris by Kaunitz himself in 1750–53 failed to make much impression at the French court. However in the summer of 1755, when fighting between Britain and France had already broken out in America and at sea and when the divergence between British and Austrian interests had become unmistakable, a new approach to France was made, with very different results. The Abbé de Bernis, who had just returned to Paris after several years as French ambassador at Venice, was appointed by Louis XV to receive the proposals made by the Austrian ambassador Starhemberg and showed himself much more sympathetic than the ministers with whom Kaunitz had had to deal. Nevertheless it is very doubtful whether any important change in French policy would have been made, at least for the time being, but for the action of Frederick II.

By the end of 1755 the King of Prussia was seriously alarmed by the position in which he found himself. He knew that he must, in all probability, face the irreconcilable hostility of the Habsburgs for the rest of his life. He also realized that Russia, whose foreign policy was now controlled by the bitterly anti-Prussian Count Bestuzhev-Ryumin, was likely to aid Maria Theresa against him when a favourable opportunity arose. Moreover the weakness and disunity of the French government and its feeble reaction to British aggression on the high seas indicated that it was unlikely to give him much effective support. His uneasiness was brought to a head when in September 1755 Britain signed a convention with Russia. By this the Empress Elizabeth, in return for a subsidy, promised to maintain a force of 55,000 men in her Baltic provinces and to support them if necessary with a galley-fleet. This army was intended by the British government to protect Hanover against Prussian attack by threatening Frederick II from the rear, and the convention at once aroused in his mind fears of a concerted onslaught on him by Britain, Austria and Russia. From this dangerous position he decided to escape by an agreement with Britain for the neutralization of Germany and its exclusion from the Anglo-French war which was now raging: such an agreement was achieved in January 1756 by the so-called Convention of Westminster.

This limited and *ad hoc* Anglo-Prussian co-operation had disproportionately severe repercussions in France and Russia. At Versailles Frederick's secret negotiations with France's enemy, his tacit assumption that he was the equal of Louis XV, his barely concealed contempt for the weakness of French policy, aroused a wave of bitter and somewhat irrational hostility. It was irrational because the neutralization of Germany, by forcing the French government to concentrate its energies on the colonial struggle with Britain, served France's real interests. Moreover Frederick had been careful to exclude the Netherlands from the scope of the convention and thus leave the way open for French military action there. Nevertheless the Anglo-Prussian agreement made Louis XV and his advisers far more ready than ever before to listen to proposals from Vienna. They were still unwilling to contemplate offensive action against Prussia but, anxious to punish Frederick II for his independence, they concluded on 1 May 1756 with Starhemberg the defensive alliance usually known as the First Treaty of Versailles.

This bound each of the contracting parties to supply the other, if it were attacked, with a force of 24,000 men or a money equivalent.

The treaty was not a complete victory for Kaunitz and Maria Theresa, since the French government was almost as far as ever from being willing to join in the destruction of Prussia. Nevertheless it was regarded by contemporaries as marking a revolutionary change in the structure of international relations, and had widespread repercussions, above all in Russia. Frederick, with good reason, was more worried about the position in St. Petersburg than even about that in Vienna; and the spring and summer of 1756 saw the desire for war with Prussia become constantly more active and menacing in Russian ruling circles. At the end of March a scheme for an immediate attack on Frederick, which involved offering the Austrian government the backing of 80,000 Russian soldiers, was being actively discussed; later this offer was increased to that of Russia acting 'with her full strength'. It was also agreed that efforts be made to strengthen the Russian position in Poland by bribery and other means to prepare for a military advance westwards and that attention be given to improving relations with France to pave the way for possible co-operation against the hated King of Prussia. It was even decided to suspend work on a Russian fortress in the Ukraine to avoid annoying the Turks and minimize any risk of their being used by Frederick to divert Russia's attention and resources to her southern frontier. By June Russian war preparations were far advanced: it was by then the Austrians who, more hesitant, were asking that any attack on Prussia should be postponed until the following year. Frederick, though he was not fully informed about the position in St. Petersburg, was well aware of the danger looming up from that quarter. To avert it he relied mainly on British influence at the Russian court; and in the first seven months of 1756 he stressed repeatedly to the British government the need for it to do everything possible to restrain the belligerence of the Russian military and political leaders. But Britain's ability to achieve this was rapidly declining. The Empress Elizabeth had agreed to the subsidy treaty of September 1755 only since it appeared to her a weapon for possible and probably imminent use against Prussia. The Convention of Westminster made it clear that it would not be used in this way. It therefore caused deep disappointment in St. Petersburg and sharply reduced what influence the British government had hitherto possessed there. Frederick's hopes of avoiding a conflict with his great eastern neighbour were thus very insecurely based. By the early summer of 1756, if not before, Russia had become the key to the entire situation, though it was not until the very last day of that year that she acceded to the Austro-French treaty of 1 May.

That treaty, the kernel of what is usually called the 'Diplomatic Revolution' of 1756, was very quickly followed by a new Austro-Prussian struggle in Germany. This war was not the result of the treaty, which was defensive in form and, as far as France was concerned, in fact. It was, like those of 1740–42 and 1744–45, the result of a Prussian aggression; in this case of the attack which Frederick II launched on Saxony at the end of August. He took this desperate step because he had now come to realize that there was no real chance of separating Russia from the rest of his enemies. If he did not act, he believed, he would be attacked in the following year by a great alliance of Austria, Russia and Saxony, supported by France; and this belief was almost certainly justified. Inaction would thus be fatal. His only chance of survival seemed to lie in a sudden onslaught on Austria through Saxony, before Maria Theresa and her ministers were fully ready for the fray. It was even possible for Frederick to persuade himself that such an attack was not as dangerous as it seemed. He had ready for immediate action, after all, a fine army of 154,000 men, not counting various second-line formations. He hoped, quite wrongly as events were to show, that the Russians would not commit more than 45,000 men to a war against him; and in that case he might hope to be a match for both them and Austria. Moreover although the attack on Saxony was in essentials a defensive reaction to a very real threat it was also inspired to some extent by hopes of territorial gain if all went well. In the first days of the war which followed Frederick certainly played with ideas of annexing West Prussia from Poland or even retaining Saxony (whose elector might be compensated with conquered Habsburg territory in Bohemia). Ambitions of this kind, indeed, had figured prominently in the *Political Testament* which he had drawn up some years earlier, in 1752. Whatever the exact balance of motives behind it, however, the attack on Saxony unleashed one of the most desperate and dramatic struggles in European history.

The European phases of the Seven Years War are memorable above all for the extraordinary fluctuations of fortune which they witnessed. By the summer of 1757, after a year's fighting, Frederick's position was desperate. He had forced the Saxon army to capitulate at Pirna (October 1756), but a Prussian attack on Bohemia had failed, with heavy loss (June 1757). More important, the French government signed with Austria on 1 May 1757 the Second Treaty of Versailles. By this France bound herself to maintain a force of 105,000 men in Germany, as well as 10,000 German mercenaries, and to pay Austria an annual subsidy of 12 million florins. She was to receive in return four cities in the Austrian Netherlands, the rest of which was to go to Don Philip, Louis XV's favourite son-in-law; but these cessions of territory were conditional on the reconquest by Maria Theresa of the whole of Silesia. France thus committed herself to large-scale intervention in a war from which, unless it were completely successful, she was unlikely to gain anything. This commitment was to cost her dear and many Frenchmen were later to regret it bitterly. An offensive alliance of Austria and Russia was concluded a few days later; while the Circles of the Empire had already decided in January to supply contingents for use against Prussia, and Sweden had joined the anti-Prussian coalition in March. Moreover it was clear that Frederick could expect no active help from Hanover, which was overrun by the French during the summer. The Duke of Cumberland, commanding a considerable army of German troops there, signed at Klosterzeven in September 1757 an armistice which was virtually a capitulation. A Russian army invaded East Prussia in August. In October an Austrian force occupied Berlin itself, though for only a few days. It is not surprising, therefore, to find Frederick making efforts during these disastrous summer and autumn months to come to terms with France and offering to renew his old alliance with her.

Nevertheless by the end of the year a brilliant victory over the Franco-Imperial army at Rossbach in November, and a more fiercely contested one over the Austrians at Leuthen a few weeks later, had done much to restore his position. They had also raised his personal reputation higher than ever before. But the odds against Prussia were tremendous. The war had become what one German historian has called 'a struggle of five million against ninety million', and the country's long and exposed frontiers intensified her difficulties. Growing financial strain was reflected in a cabinet order of October 1757 which suspended payment of all salaries and pensions to Prussian civil servants and judges, with the one exception of diplomats serving abroad. Eventually partial payment was resumed so far as the lower ranks of the bureaucracy were concerned; but their superiors had to be content merely with promissory notes. The discontent and bribery which this produced, coupled with the disruption of communications because of the war, the long absences of the king on campaign and enemy occupations of Berlin, meant that the work of administering most of the Prussian provinces was carried on for several years with sharply reduced efficiency.

It is true that Frederick received, after April 1758, a British subsidy of £670,000 a year. Moreover from then onwards his western flank was protected against French attack by an Anglo-German army in West-phalia paid by Britain and commanded by the very able Prince Ferdinand of Brunswick. On the other hand the heavy losses suffered by the Prussian army in the first eighteen months of the war did much to reduce its quality: recruits could still be obtained, but the spendid fighting machine of 1756–57 could not be resurrected. Thus in the years 1758–61 Prussia's position became steadily worse.

In August 1758 Frederick defeated the Russians at Zorndorf in the most bloody battle of the century; but the same year saw a Swedish invasion of Prussian Pomerania and an Austrian victory in October at Hochkirch in Saxony. By 1759 it was clear that Prussia could not long continue the struggle on this scale. Frederick's army now numbered little more than 100,000 men (as against about 150,000 in the previous year) while his enemies could muster twice as many. His financial position was made tolerable only by the British subsidies, debasement of the coinage, and ruthless exploitation of the areas in Prussian occupation, above all Saxony. He was now willing to accept a peace settlement which gave East Prussia to Russia and left France in control of much of West Germany, provided he were compensated with Saxony; a change in the geographical structure of the Prussian monarchy which, if carried out, would have had very large repercussions on its future. Finally in August the Russians inflicted on him at Kunersdorf the most disastrous defeat of his career, reducing him temporarily to despair. 'I have no resources left,' he wrote to his minister Finckenstein, 'and to tell the truth I believe all is lost. I will not survive the ruin of my country.'[1]

In spite of appearances, all was not lost. The Russian commander, Saltykov, suspicious of the Austrians and perhaps influenced by expectations of the death of Elizabeth and her replacement on the throne by the pro-Prussian Grand Duke Peter, did not follow up his victory. Notwithstanding serious setbacks, therefore, Frederick managed, when the campaigning season ended, to retain control of most of Saxony. Moreover the French government had now decided, rather belatedly, to reduce its commitments in Germany. By the Third Treaty of Versailles, signed in March, its subsidies to Maria Theresa were cut by half and its military support of the Empress was reduced to 100,000 soldiers for use in Germany.

[1] *Politische Correspondenz*, vol. XVIII, p. 481.

In spite of all this Frederick's position was becoming more and more critical. In 1760 he put about 90,000 men in the field in face of the 232,000 maintained by his enemies, and admitted that it would probably be impossible to do as much in the following year. Debasement of the currency now meant that thirty talers were being struck from a single fine mark of silver, whereas before the war the accepted standard had been eighteen. Most serious of all, there were unmistakable signs that reluctance to shoulder the burdens of an unprecedented war effort was now rapidly growing in the Prussian provinces. In 1760 the landowners of the Electoral Mark of Brandenburg refused to contribute further; and in the following year the Estates of Pomerania protested that the province could give no more. It was the resources drawn from Silesia and Saxony, the most efficiently administered of the areas under Frederick's control, which alone permitted the war to continue: according to one calculation Saxony yielded during the entire struggle 48 million talers to her Prussian masters, and Silesia 18 million, whereas all the other Prussian provinces combined provided only 25 million. Frederick was still able, none the less, to win victories at Leignitz and Torgau, while the struggle was clearly beginning to tell on his opponents. Kaunitz warned Maria Theresa in December that it would be possible to finance only one more campaign; and in the spring of 1761 lack of money forced a reduction of 20,000 men in the strength of the Austrian army. That year, though no great battles were fought, saw the fortunes of Prussia reach their lowest ebb. By the end of the campaigning season Silesia and much of Saxony were held by the Austrians, Prussian Pomerania by the Russians. A little more initiative on the part of Frederick's enemies, particularly Russia, would have destroyed the Prussian monarchy. Efforts to persuade the Turks to attack Austria or Russia in the rear had no success. 'If fortune continues to treat me so pitilessly,' the king told his friend the Marquis d'Argens in January 1762, 'no doubt I shall succumb; she alone can deliver me from my present position.'[1]

He had already been delivered, though he did not know it when he wrote these words. On 5 January 1762 Elizabeth of Russia, in some ways a more inveterate enemy even than Maria Theresa, died at last. Her successor, the unstable Peter III, was a fanatical admirer of Frederick, and German far more than Russian in outlook and temperament. He ordered an immediate armistice, and early in May made peace

---

[1] *Oeuvres de Frédéric le Grand* (Berlin, 1846–56), vol. XIX, p. 283.

with Prussia and withdrew his troops from her territory. His murder in July and the accession of his German wife as Catherine II destroyed the Russo-Prussian alliance against Austria and Denmark which now seemed to be in the making, but did not upset the peace signed two months earlier. Maria Theresa, now virtually isolated (Sweden, which had never played a great part in the war, also made peace with Prussia in May 1762), could not hope to recover Silesia and was forced to abandon the struggle. At Hubertusburg on 15 February 1763 the German part of the Seven Years War ended on the basis of the *status quo ante bellum.* Saxony, part of which Frederick had hoped to retain, was restored in full to its ruler; though no compensation was paid for the immense losses it had suffered during the war. Silesia remained part of the Prussian monarchy which was now, at least during Frederick's lifetime, established as one of the great powers of Europe.

The *de facto* Anglo-Prussian alliance which had existed throughout the war ended in 1762 amid mutual recriminations. For its dissolution the British government, and above all the Earl of Bute, whose influence over the young George III was virtually unbounded, have usually been blamed by German historians. The charge has some foundation. Bute was undoubtedly anxious to withdraw from the struggle in Germany, especially after the declaration of war by Britain on Spain in January 1762 (see p. 300). Moreover both he and the Duke of Newcastle, who as First Lord of the Treasury still retained great influence on foreign policy, were conspicuously clumsy and tactless in their diplomacy. They alarmed Frederick by making advances to Maria Theresa for a renewal of the old Austro-British alliance. They angered him by giving the impression that they meant to force him to make territorial concessions to his enemies as the price of peace. Also opposition in Britain to the payment of subsidies to Prussia was steadily mounting now that the war with France was clearly won. On the other hand Frederick himself had never hesitated to sacrifice the interests of his ally to his own, or to make advances to his opponents for a separate peace when it seemed advisable to do so, notably in 1757. His relations with Peter III from March 1762 onwards, and in particular the way in which he encouraged the Tsar to assert against Denmark his dynastic claims in Schleswig-Holstein, were certainly contrary to the spirit of his connexion with Britain. What finally decided the British government in 1762 to refuse further subsidy payments was not mere stinginess, but much more fear that the money would be used by Frederick to finance a new war against Denmark or a continuation of the old one against Austria. Whatever the rights and wrongs of the quarrel the alliance, once broken, could not be reconstructed. In 1764 Frederick turned to Russia for support; Britain remained for the next two decades ingloriously and at length disastrously isolated.

The war of 1756–63 had left its mark upon both Prussia and her ruler. The country had felt the effects of the struggle very severely; some parts of it had been devastated in a way which recalled the Thirty Years War. Henceforth Frederick, though he never abandoned the idea of making new territorial gains, and in fact made very important ones in Poland in the first partition (see p. 237), feared nothing so much as another great war. From the 1760s to the 1780s it was Austria which was the revolutionary and dynamic force in German affairs while Prussia, quiescent though by no means satiated, stood on the whole for conservatism and the existing balance of forces. The rivalry with the Habsburgs to which the aggression of 1740 had given rise thus continued to dominate all Frederick's calculations. It was intensified by the growing influence at Vienna of the ambitious young Archduke Joseph, who in 1765 succeeded his father as Emperor with the title of Joseph II. A visit by him to Frederick at Neisse in Silesia in August 1769, and a return visit by the king at Neustadt in Moravia a year later, produced many protestations of goodwill on both sides but did nothing to bridge the gulf which separated the two rulers. Their mutual dislike and suspicion was brought to a head by the question of the Bavarian Succession in 1778–79.

When the Elector Maximilian Joseph of Bavaria died at the end of 1777 he was succeeded by a distant relative, the Elector Palatine. The latter, like his predecessor, had no legitimate children, but a number of illegitimate ones for whom it was his main ambition to secure an adequate provision. To obtain the support of the Emperor in this he agreed in January 1778 to surrender more than a third of Bavaria to him, an arrangement which has been justifiably described as 'the *reductio ad absurdum* of the principle of personal rule in the eighteenth century'.[1] Behind this partition treaty lurked the idea, which had attracted statesmen in Vienna for almost a century, of acquiring the whole of the Electorate in exchange for the Austrian Netherlands and thus creating a more powerful and compact block of Habsburg territories centred on the Danube valley. Quite apart from this, however, even such a limited accession of strength to the Habsburgs as that

[1] H. W. V. Temperley, *Frederick the Great and Kaiser Joseph* (London, 1915), p. 85.

provided for by the agreement with the new Elector, unbalanced by any compensation for Prussia, was certain to be opposed by Frederick II. He had already undertaken, in secret negotiations with France in the summer of 1777, to prevent Austrian expansion in Bavaria or the Balkans; and he was provided with a plausible pretext for opposing Joseph II by the fact that the Duke of Zweibrücken, the heir to the Electorate, formally protested to the Diet against its dismemberment. Moreover the Elector of Saxony had claims of his own to part of the Bavarian inheritance.

The result was a struggle of Prussia and Saxony against what appeared to be the dangerous ambitions of the Emperor. In this Frederick and his ally had the sympathy of most of the German States; and understandably so. Joseph's appetite for territorial gain and the lack of scruple he showed in his efforts to satisfy it had already antagonized much German opinion. His handling of the Bavarian situation did nothing to still these fears. Maria Theresa herself, now near the end of her life and anxious for peace, admitted that the Austrian claims in Bavaria were 'outdated and poorly based'[1] (the territory ceded in January 1778 was alleged in Vienna to consist of lapsed Austrian, Bohemian and imperial fiefs). Yet Joseph and Kaunitz were confident of success. They hoped for support from France, at least on paper the ally of the Habsburgs since 1756; and they expected that Catherine II would be too preoccupied by events in the Balkans and the Black Sea (see p. 238) to be able to give Frederick any effective help. On both counts they were wrong. Vergennes, the French Foreign Minister, wished to concentrate France's energies on the struggle with Britain in America which was now clearly imminent. He had no intention of helping to strengthen the Habsburgs in Germany, where he aimed, on the contrary, at the maintenance of an Austro-Prussian balance. In March 1778, therefore, he made it clear to the Austrian court that 'circumstances did not permit His Majesty to take any part but that of neutrality in the war which might break out in Germany'. Moreover the beginning of hostilities early in July was quickly followed by signs that Catherine was likely to support Frederick: by the end of the year negotiations were under way for the sending of a Russian auxiliary force for this purpose. The result was that though Prussia failed completely to win any significant military success the Austrian government was forced, in February 1779, to accept pre-

[1] *Maria Theresa und Joseph II. Ihr Briefwechsel*, ed. A. von Arneth (Vienna, 1867–68), vol. II, pp. 171–2.

liminary peace terms which gave it only a minor part of what had been hoped for in Bavaria. When peace was signed in May, at Teschen in Silesia under French and Russian mediation, Joseph had to abandon his Bavarian plans and to accept only the Innviertel (a relatively small area of eastern Bavaria) as a consolation prize. He also agreed not to oppose the eventual union with Prussia of the little South German principalities of Ansbach and Bayreuth, which were held by a junior branch of the Hohenzollern family now clearly on the verge of extinction. Frederick was thus justified in claiming that the war had ended in a victory, though by no means an overwhelming one, for Prussia, and that 'in the Empire we shall in future be thought of as a useful counterweight to the despotism of Austria'.[1]

Joseph was not slow in providing fresh evidence of an apparently implacable determination to dominate South and West Germany. His relations with the smaller States continued to show all the tactlessness and inflexibility which marked his entire life. When the Prince-Bishop of Passau died in February 1783, for example, those parts of his diocese which extended into Austrian territory were seized by the Emperor and incorporated into two new bishoprics of Linz and St. Polten—perhaps the grossest breach of the imperial constitution which Joseph ever perpetrated, and one which aroused violent antagonism in Germany, particularly in clerical circles by tradition often favourable to the Habsburgs. Fear and dislike of the Emperor thus continued to haunt Frederick II until his death in August 1786. The breakdown in 1780 of the alliance with Russia which had been the main prop of his foreign policy for sixteen years intensified these feelings, especially as Catherine II replaced it in the following year by an *entente* with Austria. In May 1782 he solemnly warned his nephew and heir that Joseph now threatened to become more powerful than any ruler since Louis XIV and would sooner or later attempt to destroy the Prussian monarchy. The last achievement of his life was the construction in July 1785 of the *Fürstenbund* (League of Princes). This united a number of important German rulers—the Elector of Saxony, the Archbishop of Mainz, George III as Elector of Hanover—with Prussia in opposition to the Emperor, and in particular to Joseph's scheme, now coming to a head, to acquire the whole of Bavaria in exchange for the Austrian Netherlands.

[1] *Politische Correspondenz*, vol. XLII, p. 420.

The growth of Austro-Prussian antagonism, of 'dualism' in Germany, was the most important development in the politics of eighteenth-century Europe apart from the emergence of Russia. Its significance for the future was great. By his victories Frederick laid the foundations of belief in the moral superiority of Prussia to the other German States, a belief whose wide acceptance is easy to understand but which was to have dangerous results. The achievements of his reign consolidated, though they could hardly intensify, the military character of the State he had inherited from his father, and established the Prussian army as one of the great factors in European politics. Above all, by challenging Habsburg leadership and weakening still further the Empire as an institution, Frederick made less likely the creation in the future of a unified 'Great Germany'. He thus helped (though many other factors entered into the process) to pave the way for the 'unity' achieved by Bismarck in 1866–71—a 'unity' which deliberately excluded from the newly created Reich the many millions of Germans then under Habsburg rule. Not until the days of Hitler was this effect of the events of 1740–63 overcome, and then only momentarily.

XI

Spain, Italy and the Mediterranean

The Peace of Utrecht, which in 1713 ended the War of the Spanish Succession, made great changes in the balance of power in the western Mediterranean. It deprived Spain of much territory; established Britain as an important factor in the politics of the area; and set up the Habsburgs, at least for the time being, as the dominant power in Italy. It disappointed long-cherished French hopes of obtaining control of the kingdom of Naples. It marked an important stage in the slow rise of the north Italian State of Savoy-Piedmont. Changes so great and so rapid inevitably generated a whole series of new ambitions and grievances in the States concerned; these emotions were to provide the driving force behind events in this area during the next generation.

Spain had been the main, indeed the only real, territorial sufferer by the war. Its close saw the loss of all her European possessions. The Spanish Netherlands, the Duchy of Milan, Sardinia and the Kingdom of Naples had been surrendered to the Emperor. Sicily had been lost to the Duke of Savoy. These losses were in many ways an advantage to the country. They relieved her of the obligation to protect distant and constantly threatened territories which her economic and demographic weakness

BIBLIOGRAPHY. On the specifically Mediterranean aspects of international relations less has been written than on the subjects of the previous two chapters. The following, however, may be mentioned: E. Armstrong, *Elizabeth Farnese* (London, 1892), which is thorough and objective and, in spite of its age, has not been superseded; S. Conn, *Gibraltar in British Diplomacy in the Eighteenth Century* (New Haven, 1942); A. Baudrillart, *Philippe V et la Cour de France* (Paris, 1890–1900), vols. III–V; and A. Mc.C. Wilson, *French Foreign Policy during the Administration of Cardinal Fleury* (Cambridge, Mass., 1936). P. Castagnoli, *Il Cardinale Giulio Alberoni* (Piacenza-Rome, 1929–32) is the best biography of this still in some ways enigmatic figure; while S. Harcourt-Smith, *Alberoni; or The Spanish Conspiracy* (London, 1943) is a lively semi-popular work.

All previous discussions of the internal structure of the Ottoman Empire are superseded by H. A. R. Gibb and R. Bowen, *Islamic Society and the West*, vol. I, *Islamic Society in the Eighteenth Century* (Oxford, 1950–57); while had, in the later seventeenth century, made it impossible for her to defend effectively.[1] They offered her an opportunity to reduce her financial and military commitments, to pursue a simpler and more realistic policy in international affairs. She could now, if she wished, concentrate her energies on the development of her own resources and those of her American possessions. However the Spanish government and the majority of Spaniards did not see the position in this light, and it was hardly to be expected that they should. The dismemberment of Spain's European empire, which in the later seventeenth century it had been the great object of Charles II (1665–1700) and his advisers to avoid, was accepted by most Spanish statesmen in 1713 as inevitable. It was nevertheless felt as a great blow to the country's international position and to the prestige of its ruler.

Worse still, Spain suffered the humiliation of being forced to surrender to her enemies, and to heretical enemies at that, parts of her metropolitan territory. Gibraltar had been seized in 1704 by an Anglo-Dutch fleet; and though it had never been regarded by the Spanish government as a fortress of great importance—its garrison when it fell consisted of only fifty-six regular soldiers and about a hundred militiamen—its retention by Britain at the peace was bitterly resented. The capture of Minorca in 1708 established Britain still more securely as a leading force in the affairs of the western Mediterranean: for the next half-century English statesmen and merchants cherished delusive hopes that the island might become a great commercial entrepôt comparable to Leghorn or Marseilles. The British Mediterranean squadron based on its capital, Port Mahon, was never in peacetime very large, while no men-of-war were regularly stationed at Gibraltar (where till 1766 dockyard facilities were poor and the roadstead exposed). Nevertheless the

C. von Sax, *Geschichte des Machtverfalls der Türkei* (Vienna, 1908) is still probably the best short narrative of its history during this period. Lavender Cassels, *The Struggle for the Ottoman Empire, 1717–1740* (London, 1968) is a readable though not very profound account of its subject; while Deena R. Sadat, 'Rumeli Ayanlari: the eighteenth century', *Journal of Modern History*, vol.XLIV, no. 3 (1974) discusses the social and political tensions in the European provinces of the Ottoman Empire and the breakdown to which they had led by the end of the century.

[1] At the beginning of the war of the Spanish Succession her army totalled no more than 20,000 men and some of her possessions, e.g. Sicily with a garrison of only 500 and Sardinia with one of only 200, were virtually defenceless. (C. Fernandez Duro, *La Armada Española* (Madrid, 1895–1903), vol. VI, pp. 15–16.)

strategic value to Britain of these bases was enormous. From them the ports of southern France and eastern and southern Spain could be observed, and in time of war blockaded. From them Britain could in wartime influence events in Italy far more effectively than ever before. By her possession of them she was brought into closer contact than hitherto with the Barbary States of North Africa, from which they imported a large proportion of their food. Most important of all, while she held them in force she could sever the Mediterranean squadrons of France and Spain, based on Toulon and Cartagena, from their Atlantic counterparts based on Brest, Rochefort, Corunna and Cadiz.

Both the loss by Spain of her European possessions and the acquisition by Britain of bases in the Mediterranean were probably inevitable. An imminent disruption of the Spanish Empire had been taken for granted throughout the tortuous negotiations over the Succession question from 1668 onwards. As early as the 1650s the Commonwealth government had established a navy agent at Leghorn and made the port a base for the squadrons it then maintained in the Mediterranean. The growth of Austrian power in Italy, which was in some ways the most important result of the treaties of 1713, was less easy to foresee. The partition treaties of 1698 and 1699 (agreed to by Louis XIV, the English and Dutch governments, and in the case of the first one the Emperor) would, if carried out, have given France a dominant position there on condition that a Bourbon ruler was not established in Spain. In the peace negotiations of 1712–13 the British government had proposed an arrangement by which Philip V, if he renounced the Spanish throne, would receive as compensation Sicily and all the possessions of the Duke of Savoy. Austrian dominance in Italy was thus the price Louis XIV had to pay for his success in maintaining his grandson as king of Spain. The fate of Austrian rule was, however, very different in the two regions of Italy which saw its establishment in 1713. In Naples it was never popular, achieved little, and lasted a bare two decades. In the Duchy of Milan it endured till the wars of the French Revolution, did much to increase the prosperity and improve the administration of the area, and eventually gained considerable popularity.

The gains made in 1713 by the ruler of Savoy, Victor Amadeus II, were not the result of victories he had won, or of the intrinsic strength of his dominions. They were rather the outcome of the strategic position near the meeting-point of French and Austrian influences in North Italy enjoyed by this minor State, and of the skill with which Victor Amadeus manœuvred between the competing great powers during the war (notably in his well-timed desertion of Louis XIV in 1703). Savoy continued throughout this period to be one of the most conservative and backward of the Italian States; until well into the century which followed very few people dreamt of her as the eventual leader of an Italian *risorgimento*. Nevertheless she was already showing both an appetite and a capacity for territorial expansion which no other State in the peninsula could equal.

Apart from Savoy those parts of Italy which remained independent were now of little account in international affairs. Venice was clearly a decadent State living on her past. Her political structure continued to enjoy, at least in the early decades of the century, a certain reputation for efficiency and stability; it was none the less increasingly weakened by factions within the Venetian nobility and by the growing discontent of the city's possessions on the Italian mainland and the Dalmatian coast. Moreover the stability of her constitution had now become a rigidity hostile to innovation of any kind: no government in Europe showed less sympathy with the ideas of the Enlightenment than that of Venice. Her industries suffered from the extreme tenacity with which guild privileges were maintained, and her commerce from the competition of Ancona, Trieste and Ragusa. As a result she found herself increasingly reduced to living on the profits of her position as a great tourist centre. The last real achievement of her armed forces was a successful defence of Corfu against the Turks in 1716 and that, significantly enough, was led by a German general. By the second half of the century her fleet was so little able to protect her commerce against the attacks of the Barbary corsairs that the British consul in Venice reported in 1766 that for many years past she had been able to send few ships to any port west of Malta. It is not surprising therefore that her territory attracted, in the later decades of this period, covetous glances from her powerful and aggressive neighbour, the Emperor Joseph II. A generation or more before her surrender to Napoleon Bonaparte in 1797 she was clearly marked as a victim-State. The peace with Turkey which she signed in 1718 was her last action of any importance on the stage of European affairs.

The other independent States of Italy were able to exert still less influence on the policies of the great European powers. Genoa, like Savoy but with much less success, attempted to safeguard and even improve her position by balancing between France and Austria. Her smallness, her vulnerability to attack, her failure to maintain control of her island possession of Corsica where serious rebellions broke out in

1729, 1734 and 1745, all weakened her. Though she retained much more of her former economic importance than Venice (see p. 91) she slowly degenerated into little more than a French protectorate. The Grand Duchy of Tuscany under its last Medici ruler, Gian-Gastone (1692–1737) remained a largely medieval State. In spite of its considerable wealth it played little part in European affairs under his Habsburg successors. The Duchies of Parma and Piacenza, the tiny Republic of Lucca, could never hope to have an active role of any significance.

The Barbary States in North Africa were even more on the periphery of European politics. Algiers, which had enjoyed a golden age as a centre of piracy and privateering (and also of legitimate trade) in the first half of the seventeenth century, was now quite unable to resist the pressure of great naval powers such as Britain and France. She was thus increasingly compelled to confine the attacks of her cruisers to the ships of weaker maritime States such as Sweden, the Netherlands, the Hanse towns and the Italian principalities. The city itself remained one of the greatest fortresses in the Mediterranean. It repulsed attacks by Spain in 1775 and by a combination of Spain, Portugal and the Knights of St. John in 1784: the British squadron under Lord Exmouth which bombarded it in 1816 lost more men than Nelson's fleet at Trafalgar. Nevertheless the Algerines were never, in the eighteenth century, more than a minor nuisance as far as the major States of Western Europe were concerned. Tunis, which had never been so great a centre of piracy as Algiers, concentrated increasingly during this period on legitimate trade, became richer and militarily weaker, and was captured by the Dey of Algiers in 1756 though she soon recovered her independence. Tripoli, small, poor, devastated by plague and possessing only a few insignificant cruisers, was little able to fire the ambitions or arouse the fears of any European power. Morocco, stronger and far less vulnerable to naval pressure than any other of the Barbary States, was in 1713 ruled by the Emperor Mulay Ismail, one of the strongest and most bloodthirsty characters in her bloodstained history. His death in 1727 unleashed a series of complicated civil wars which paralysed the country for a generation, while her weakness at sea meant that she could never play more than a minor role in the affairs of the western Mediterranean.

Far from the Barbary States being able to disrupt European commerce or terrorize the coasts of Spain and Italy as they had done in the sixteenth and seventeenth centuries, the boot was now increasingly on the other foot. Christian privateers and pirates (the distinction between the two often meant little in practice) based on Malta, Leghorn or the

Balearics, captured and plundered Turkish and Barbary ships and their crews on a large scale. They thus provided the basis for a considerable trade in Muslim slaves. Their activities may be one reason (though they were certainly not the only one, or the most important one) for the economic stagnation and even decline which is visible in some parts of the Arab and Turkish world in the eighteenth century.

The western Mediterranean after the Utrecht settlement thus presents the picture of a number of strong and ambitious powers—Spain, Great Britain, Austria, to a lesser extent Savoy—side by side with the smaller and weaker victim-States of Italy and North Africa.

The history of the area in the two decades which followed the peace of 1713 is dominated by the efforts of the newly established Bourbon dynasty in Spain to recover its lost influence and possessions in Italy. Strengthened by the final subjection of Catalonia and the French-inspired administrative reforms of the early years of the century (see p. 151) it was now able to contemplate a war of revenge against the Habsburgs. In spite of the many personal defects of the king a new spirit, a refusal to accept the losses of the war as permanent, a will to power unknown for decades, were all beginning to be felt in Madrid. These feelings were focused on Italian affairs by Philip's marriage at the end of the war to his second wife, Elizabeth Farnese, niece of the Duke of Parma. She was a woman of strong character and narrow out-look who very soon acquired great influence over her husband and Spanish policy. Her arrival led almost immediately to a reduction in the hitherto dominant French influences at Madrid and their partial replace-ment by Italian ones. Orry, the very able Frenchman who had done more than anyone to overhaul Spain's inadequate fiscal system, left the country. So did the very influential French *Camarera Mayor*, Madame des Ursins. Italians such as Cardinal del Guidice and above all the Abbé Giulio Alberoni began to play a great part in Spain's political life, notably in her foreign policy. Alberoni had originally come to Spain as the agent of a French commander, the Duc de Vendôme, during the Succession struggle. He remained there after his patron's death, as diplomatic agent of the Duke of Parma, and helped to arrange the marriage of Philip V and Elizabeth Farnese—his first great success in international affairs. Though he was never to hold any recognized Spanish administrative post or title his influence over the queen made him for several years the leading personality in the government of the country and a figure of European importance.

Alberoni undoubtedly felt a personal hostility to the Habsburg family and Germans in general, and may have dreamed of some form of political unity in Italy after their influence had been expelled from the peninsula. Moreover the Emperor Charles VI had stubbornly refused, in the settlement of 1713–14, to abandon his claim to be rightful King of Spain. This meant that relations between Madrid and Vienna were still those of an armed truce rather than of genuine peace. These factors, coupled with the imminent extinction of the Medici dynasty in Tuscany and the desire of Charles VI to acquire Sicily from the Duke of Savoy, to whom it had·been given in 1713, made the position in Italy extremely unstable. The neutrality of the peninsula in the future struggles of the major European States which had been declared in vague terms by the Treaty of Utrecht was clearly unlikely to last very long. Overshadowing all these questions was the possibility that if the sickly Louis XV should die Philip V might assert, as grandson of Louis XIV, his claim to the throne of France, in spite of the renunciation of it he had been forced to make as part of the settlement of 1713. The effort of George I and the Regent d'Orléans to consolidate in the Anglo-French alliance of 1716 (see p. 290) the *status quo* from which both of them benefited was a failure as far as the Mediterranean was concerned.

The spark which ignited this combustible situation was struck at the end of May 1717. The Grand Inquisitor of Spain, a man of over eighty, was arrested by the Austrian governor of Milan while returning from a visit to Rome and died soon afterwards in prison. In spite of the doubts of Alberoni, who realized only too well the real limits of Spanish resources, Philip V declared war on the Emperor in July. The struggle which followed was short and dramatic. Sardinia, whose Austrian garrison was extremely weak, was quickly overrun by a Spanish expeditionary force. The efforts of Britain and France to appease Spain by promising that Don Carlos, the elder son of Philip V by Elizabeth Farnese, should inherit the Italian States of Tuscany, Parma and Piacenza, were a failure. Alberoni demanded some more tangible satisfaction than a promise; while even a suggestion that Gibraltar might be restored failed to appease the queen. The summer of 1718 saw a rapid conquest of Sicily which, though a possession of the ruler of Savoy and thus neutral territory, the Spanish government hoped to use as a base for the invasion of southern Italy. An imposing edifice of Spanish power in the Mediterranean had thus been erected in less than a year. But it was fundamentally unstable. It depended on seapower, and Spanish seapower was still much inferior to that of Great Britain. When, on 11 August, a British squadron under Admiral Byng destroyed off Cape Passaro near Messina the fleet so painfully built up in the last four years, the whole structure collapsed.

Nevertheless Alberoni, who now hoped that Britain's difficulties in the Baltic (see p. 222) might weaken her position in the Mediterranean, at once declared war on her. The Jacobite Duke of Ormonde was provided with a Spanish squadron and some troops with which to attempt an invasion of England; and it became clear that only a land attack on Spain herself would force the government in Madrid to submit. As a result in January 1719, after considerable hesitation on the part of the Regent, France declared war and invaded the Basque provinces and Catalonia. From this hopeless position Philip V had no escape but by surrender. In December he dismissed Alberoni. A month later he announced his adhesion to the Quadruple Alliance of Britain, France, Austria and the United Provinces which had been signed at the beginning of August 1718. The evacuation of Sicily and Sardinia and a new renunciation by him of his claims to the French throne followed in due course. In return it was promised that Don Carlos should inherit Tuscany, Parma and Piacenza, though he was to hold these territories as imperial fiefs. Thus the only immediate territorial result of the crisis of 1717-19 was the transfer of Sicily from Savoy to the Emperor in exchange for the far less valuable Sardinia. The events of these years had shown that the provisions of the Utrecht settlement, backed by the great conservative powers of Britain and France, could easily withstand the pressure of discontented and ambitious Spain.

The defeats of 1718-19 did not, however, force Philip V to abandon all hope of improving his country's strategic and diplomatic position. He claimed, somewhat unrealistically, the fulfilment of the offer to return Gibraltar which had been made in 1718 before the outbreak of war with Britain. But for violent opposition in Parliament he might well have recovered the fortress, for neither George I nor his ministers attached much importance to its retention. As it was, Philip had to content himself with a letter of June 1721 in which the king of England promised to consider the surrender of Gibraltar 'with consent of my Parliament . . . at the first favourable opportunity'—which in fact meant never. In spite of this renewed check to her ambitions events were moving in Spain's favour in many ways in the early 1720s. Good relations with France had been restored by a convention of March 1721 which provided for the betrothal of Louis XV and the Infanta Maria-

Anna-Vittoria, the daughter of Philip V by his first wife. Simultaneously the efforts from 1722 onwards of Charles VI to establish a trade between his Netherlands dominions and the East Indies by the creation of a privileged Ostend Company caused acute friction with his British and Dutch allies. Nevertheless when in January 1724, after long delays, an international congress of diplomats met at Cambrai to work out in detail the settlement of Italian affairs reached four years earlier, France and Britain gave only half-hearted support to the demands of Spain. In particular she failed to secure her main objective, the occupation of the chief fortresses of Tuscany and Parma by Spanish troops, which she had demanded as a tangible guarantee of the eventual succession to these duchies of Don Carlos.

The result of this failure was perhaps the most remarkable diplomatic revolution of the century. Elizabeth Farnese, infuriated by the setback, resolved to attempt an alliance with the Habsburgs, an alliance which would blot out the antagonisms of the past decade. Through a Dutch adventurer and Catholic convert, Ripperdà, she proposed in Vienna a marriage between her sons Don Carlos and Don Philip and two Austrian archduchesses, daughters of Charles VI. The marriage negotiations, which dragged on till 1729, came to nothing. However in February 1725 the Duc de Bourbon, who had been chief minister in Paris since the death of the Regent in August 1723, broke off without warning the betrothal of Louis XV to the Infanta Maria and sent the unfortunate princess back to Madrid. He did this because she was still so young that there was no hope of her producing a Dauphin for many years, and because if Louis died childless the Crown would pass, by the terms of the Utrecht settlement, to the Orleans branch of the royal family who were Bourbon's personal enemies. His selfish and short-sighted action produced a natural outburst of resentment in Madrid. It threw Spain completely into the arms of the Habsburgs and led to the signature, on 30 April 1725, of an Austro-Spanish treaty of alliance. This was followed in November by a very secret offensive alliance which envisaged not merely the recovery of Gibraltar by Spain but even a dismemberment of France.

This new and unexpected combination of States proved less fragile than might have been expected. But it found itself faced almost immediately by the opposition of Britain, France and Prussia united in the so-called Alliance of Hanover, and collapsed after the outbreak of another Anglo-Spanish struggle early in 1727. This war, provoked partly by the Spanish desire to retake Gibraltar and partly by British resentment of commercial concessions which Philip V had granted to Austrian merchants, lasted only a few months. By June the pressure of France and Austria had forced the Spanish government to suspend the siege of Gibraltar which it had begun in February. Finally in November 1729, after another protracted and futile congress at Soissons, Britain and France agreed by the Treaty of Seville to the introduction of Spanish troops into the fortresses of Tuscany and Parma as a guarantee of the succession of Don Carlos; and in the following year they extorted the Emperor's consent to this. When at the end of 1731 an Anglo-French fleet disembarked 6,000 Spanish soldiers at Leghorn Elizabeth Farnese appeared to have triumphed.

However Italian politics had still problems in store for the statesmen of Europe. The confused struggle known as the War of the Polish Succession (1733–35) had, in its origins, nothing to do with the problems of the peninsula. The defeat of the French candidate for the Polish throne, Stanislas Leszczynski, by the nominee of Austria and Russia, the Elector Augustus of Saxony, nevertheless impelled the French government to look for compensation in Italy at the expense of the Habsburgs. In this search it had the support of Spain and Savoy. In 1734 the Austrian army suffered a series of defeats at the hands of the French and Spaniards, at Parma, Guastalla and Bitonto, and when peace terms were agreed in October 1735 (the definitive treaty was signed at Vienna only in 1738) the Habsburgs surrendered Naples and Sicily to Don Carlos. They received in exchange, however, Parma and Piacenza. Tuscany (whose last Medici ruler died in 1737) was handed over to Francis, Duke of Lorraine, the husband-to-be of the Archduchess Maria Theresa. The Duchy of Lorraine was given as compensation for his lost Polish throne to Stanislas Leszczynski and was to revert to France on his death, a provision which promised her a very important acquisition. This complicated series of territorial exchanges, so typical in many ways of the diplomacy of the period, had a certain logic. It therefore proved more durable than most of the treaties of the first half of the eighteenth century. It established in the southern half of Italy the power of the Bourbon dynasty which was to rule there for the next century and a quarter. It consolidated in Milan and set up in Tuscany that Habsburg domination which was to last almost as long. It paved the way for the formal incorporation in 1766 of Lorraine in France, the last important success of that forward movement of the country's eastern frontier which had been in progress for centuries. Above all it showed that the French and Spanish Bourbons were at last, after many vicissitudes, working in concert for their mutual advantage. The alliance between them which developed in the 1730s was to be a permanent factor in the politics of Europe for more than half a century.

After 1735 Italian questions, and particularly Spanish ambitions in Italy, no longer dominated international relations as they had done so often in the previous two decades. The War of the Austrian Succession which was opened by Frederick II's attack on Silesia in December 1740 had indeed, more than that of the Polish Succession, a Mediterranean aspect. All the major belligerents except Prussia devoted a good deal of their energies to a struggle for territory and influence in Italy. Though Cardinal Fleury was strongly averse to another conflict with Austria he was, as has been seen (p. 253), overruled by the more bellicose elements in Paris and Versailles. Spain, still dreaming of a further extension of her influence in Italy, was anxious to take advantage of the apparent weakness of the Habsburgs and allied herself with the opponents of Maria Theresa in the spring of 1741. The King of Sardinia, who hoped to obtain the Duchy of Milan and an outlet to the sea by the seizure of Genoese territory, was willing to side with anyone who would promise him these acquisitions. Above all the 1740s saw the entry of Great Britain into the complexities of Italian politics on a scale hitherto unknown.

The danger of Spanish domination of the peninsula seemed for a time very real. In 1742 only a British threat to bombard Naples forced Charles IV of the Two Sicilies (the former Don Carlos) to abandon his plans to attack the Austrians in north Italy in conjunction with the Spaniards. In January 1743 a Spanish army based in southern France occupied Chambéry, the capital of Savoy proper, which it held until the end of the war. In September of that year, however, Maria Theresa was at last prevailed on to purchase, with the promise of part of the Milanese, the help of Charles-Emmanuel III of Sardinia. Though he was never a reliable ally, even the lukewarm assistance he gave her was of vital importance at that moment. With the conclusion in the following month of an alliance of France and Spain directed against Austria and Great Britain the stage was set for a new outbreak of large-scale warfare in Italy.

The details of this struggle are unimportant. The British Mediterranean squadron maintained command of the sea, in spite of its failure to win any decisive victory and the continual shortage of small craft for scouting and blockade work from which it suffered. As a result Spain was unable, after 1741, to ship troops to Italy, and found it difficult to use effectively those she already had there. Moreover the Marquis d'Argenson, who became French Foreign Minister in November 1744, was no friend to the Spanish alliance. One of the most remarkable statesmen of the century, a visionary and an idealist, he dreamed of reorganizing Italy as a federation of independent States freed from both Austrian and Spanish influence. (The idea was not new: something similar had been proposed by Louis XIV's minister Pomponne in the 1690s, and schemes of this kind go back to the sixteenth century.) In spite of these difficulties the 'Gallispan' armies won considerable successes in 1745, though these were largely offset by defeats in the following year. Philip V, however, died in July 1746; and with his death the influence of Elizabeth Farnese on Spanish policy came to an end. His successor, Ferdinand VI, was almost as dominated by his wife as his father had been; but the wife in question was now Portuguese, favourable to Britain and little interested in Italy. The war in Italy thus petered out in stalemate. The Treaty of Aix-la-Chapelle, which ended it in November 1748, made only minor changes in the political geography of the peninsula. Don Philip, the younger son of Philip V and Elizabeth Farnese, received the Duchies of Parma and Piacenza (mainly through the support of his father-in-law Louis XV) while Charles-Emmanuel of Sardinia was given the slice of the Milanese promised him in 1743.

The balance of forces established in Italy by 1748 was to endure almost unchanged until Napoleon's campaigns of 1796–97. In 1752 Ferdinand VI, Charles-Emmanuel and Maria Theresa jointly guaranteed each other's possessions there; and the conflicts of the second half of the century left the peninsula untouched. After 1748 indeed the whole character of international relations in the western Mediterranean changed radically. Hitherto they had been dominated by a series of military struggles in Italy between France, Spain and Austria. Henceforth, with France and Austria united by the treaties of 1756–59 and the rulers of Spain little interested in Italian affairs, they were to centre on a series of naval conflicts between France, Spain and Great Britain.

These struggles had considerable repercussions on the balance of forces in the area. The Seven Years War saw British naval dominance in the Mediterranean carried to unprecedented heights, in spite of the capture of Minorca by a French expedition in 1756. The years which followed the Peace of Paris saw as a result a sustained effort by France to challenge that dominance. This effort expressed itself in the reconstruction and strengthening of the French navy, in the consolidation of the alliance of 1761 with Spain (see p. 302), and, most notable in this

context, in the purchase and annexation in 1768–69 of Corsica, hitherto an ungovernable and relatively valueless dependency of Genoa. The island failed to provide the naval bases and easily accessible timber for shipbuilding which had been hoped for in Paris. Nevertheless its acquisition, the last significant territorial gain made in Europe by the

France of the *ancien régime*, was accomplished without war in spite of the open hostility of the British government. It was thus widely and correctly interpreted as showing that domestic troubles and poor leadership were now making it difficult for Britain to maintain the international position which she had achieved during the Seven Years War. Moreover Spain, ruled from 1759 onwards by Charles III, a king of some ability and considerable energy, was now becoming a more serious threat than ever before to Britain in the Mediterranean. The war between them in 1761-63 had proved disastrous for Spain, but the losses she suffered by the Peace of Paris were relatively slight (see p. 301). After 1763 the improvement of her armed forces proceeded fairly rapidly, while in 1767 she helped to free her hands for action against Britain by a peace treaty with Morocco, with whom she had been intermittently at war throughout the century. An ambitious expedition against Algiers in 1775 was a humiliating failure, but none the less an index of the self-confident and even aggressive spirit which was once more, as in the days of Alberoni, gaining ground at Madrid.

The growing weakness of Britain's hold on the western Mediterranean was dramatically illustrated after 1778 during the War of the American Revolution. Faced by the most powerful hostile coalition she had yet had to meet, hampered by the Armed Neutrality of 1780, suffering heavy losses at the hands of enemy privateers, her position contrasted strikingly with that she had enjoyed two decades earlier. It is true that on this occasion Minorca did not fall until the last stages of the struggle, in 1782. But long before then Britain's naval power in the Mediterranean had been destroyed, and as a result her trade there had for the time being almost ceased to exist. Nevertheless she was able to maintain her most important foothold in the area. Gibraltar withstood the 'great siege' of 1779–82 by a powerful Franco-Spanish army and the blockade which accompanied it; while feeling in Parliament and the country at large made it impossible for George III and his ministers to accept, as they otherwise would have done, Spanish proposals to exchange it for Puerto Rico. The end of the war meant, though this was not fully grasped at the time, the end of any real hope of a Spanish recovery of the fortress. Britain while she retained it was always, even in defeat, potentially a Mediterranean power of the first rank.

The part played by the eastern Mediterranean in the politics of eighteenth-century Europe was as a rule little affected by what happened in the western part of that sea. In the Aegean and the Levant the course of events was dominated during this period by the decline, at first slow and intermittent, eventually catastrophic, of the Ottoman Empire. This decline had become unmistakable in the struggles of the Turks with Austria, Poland and Venice which were ended by the Treaty of Carlowitz in 1699. It was already giving rise, at the beginning of the eighteenth century, to projects for a partition of the decaying bulk of the empire. The belief that Turkey was on the verge of collapse seemed justified by the unmistakable and fundamental defects from which she suffered.

In the first place the composition and policies of the Turkish government were extremely unstable, above all in the early decades of the century. The Grand Vizier (the chief minister of State) was liable to lose his position and even his life as the result of some temporary setback in war or diplomacy or some whim of the Sultan (there were thirteen occupants of the position in the years 1703–18 when instability of this kind was at its worst). Even the Sultan himself was not safe from deposition, for Mustapha II was removed in this way in 1703 and Ahmad III in 1730. Moreover the empire lacked any real administrative unity or military efficiency. The emergence of powerful and virtually independent local warlords who were sometimes able to transmit their power to their descendants (the most important example during this period was the rise of the Karaosmanoglu family in western Anatolia from the end of the seventeenth century onwards) seemed both to illustrate and to intensify the incompetence of its rulers. The development of its economic life was impeded by a number of factors: misgovernment; religious conservatism; and not least the devastating epidemics from which the area continued to suffer as in the past (two-thirds of the population of Cyprus are said, probably with some exaggeration, to have died of plague in 1692, and a third or a half in 1759–60). Intellectual life was backward in the extreme. Constantinople had no printing press until 1726; and the activities of the one set up in that year (typically enough by a Hungarian renegade, not a Turk) were short-lived. Above all the definiteness of the distinction between Muslim rulers and Christian ruled, a distinction which was often strengthened by differences of language, increasingly undermined the foundations of the European parts of the empire as time went on. 'Other nations,' wrote a British ambassador in Constantinople, 'may suit and adapt their maxims to their circumstances, but the Turkish Policy and Government is so interwoven with their religion that they cannot make any alterations, and without them they can neither annoy their neighbours nor defend themselves.'[1]

The fate of the Balkan peoples under Ottoman rule varied very considerably. In a few areas, notably in Bosnia and much of Albania, the population had been converted *en masse* to Islam. In others, above all Bulgaria, almost all consciousness of belonging to a distinct national group had been lost. The Rumanian principalities of Moldavia and Wallachia remained Christian and retained a high degree of autonomy. They paid tribute to the Sultan and were ruled, or more usually misruled, by their hospodars (who from the early eighteenth century onwards were always Greeks appointed from Constantinople).

The relationship of the Greeks to their Turkish master was more complex and more important. The islands of the Aegean were perhaps less oppressively ruled than any other part of the Ottoman Empire; and in the barren and rocky Morea many Greek villages existed as virtually independent communities, having little contact with the Turkish administration. On the other hand the wealthy and educated 'Phanariot' Greeks of Constantinople (so called from the fact that they inhabited the Phanar or 'lighthouse' quarter of the city) played a leading, even a dominant, role in that administration. In particular their knowledge of languages and their contacts with foreign countries made them valuable in the conduct of Turkish diplomacy; from 1661 onwards the position of Dragoman (i.e. chief interpreter) of the Porte, an office of real power, was monopolized by them. From the ranks of the great Phanariot families, moreover—the Cantacuzènes, the Mavrocordatos, the Callimachis—were drawn the large majority of the hospodars of Moldavia and Wallachia during this period.

In general the Balkan peoples were becoming steadily more hostile to their Ottoman rulers during the eighteenth century. This was partly because the position of the peasantry was deteriorating in many areas as the *timar* system of land tenure (under which the peasant had enjoyed some security and fiefs had not been hereditary) gave way to the *chiflik* system (under which fiefs were hereditary and the peasants virtually serfs). At the same time the slow growth of trade tended to produce, especially in some seaports such as Salonika, a commercial middle class which was anti-Turkish in outlook; while by the end of this period contacts with Central and even Western Europe were beginning to stimulate national feeling in some parts of the peninsula (the

---

[1] Sir E. Fawkener to the Duke of Newcastle, 18 May 1736 (Old Style), Public Record Office, S.P. 97/30.

first Greek and Serbian newspapers were published at Vienna in 1790 and 1791 respectively).

In spite of its internal difficulties the military weaknesses of the Orroman Empire developed only slowly to their full extent. In 1711 the Turks were able to inflict a crushing and spectacular defeat on Peter I of Russia (see p. 233) though it was the result of the Tsar's rashness as much as of their own military virtues. In a renewed struggle with the Habsburgs in 1716–18 they were heavily defeated by the great Austrian commander Prince Eugène, saw Wallachia invaded by an Austrian army and lost Belgrade, a Turkish fortress for over two centuries. These losses, though substantial, were not crippling. They were partly offset, moreover, by the fact that a simultaneous war with the Venetians, begun in 1714, resulted in the recovery of the Morea (which had been ceded to Venice by the Treaty of Carlowitz). Here, as to a lesser extent in Serbia, the dislike felt by an Orthodox population for rule by often intolerant Catholic masters was a source of strength to the Turks.

The war which Turkey waged with Russia and Austria in 1736–39 was by no means unsuccessful. The Habsburg armies showed themselves little more competent than the Ottoman ones; and the final loss of Azov to Russia, when peace was made at Belgrade, was more than compensated for by the recovery from Austria of the territory ceded to her in 1718. The Austrian frontier, after a temporary advance to the south, had thus been pushed back once more to the line of the Danube and the Save, along which it still ran in 1914. Not until the disastrous struggle with Russia which began in 1768 did the extent to which the power of the Ottoman Empire had declined become fully visible to most observers.

Of the States of Western Europe France was the only one with important political interests in the Levant during the first half of the eighteenth century. Britain's trade with the area continued to flourish until about 1730, after which it rapidly declined; but from the political point of view she was interested only indirectly in the eastern Mediterranean. The British Ambassador at Constantinople continued to be the representative of the Levant Company almost as much as of the government. Spain for her part regarded herself, in the tradition of the Counter-Reformation, as the natural enemy of Turkish and Muslim power in the Mediterranean. She had no diplomatic relations with Turkey during this period; the first treaty between the two States was signed only in 1783. Eighteenth-century France inherited, by contrast,

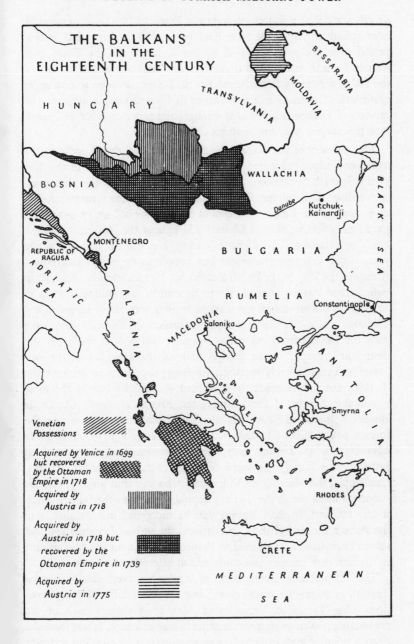

THE BALKANS
IN THE
EIGHTEENTH CENTURY

HUNGARY

TRANSYLVANIA

BESSARABIA

MOLDAVIA

WALLACHIA

BOSNIA

Danube

Kutchuk-Kainardji

BULGARIA

BLACK SEA

MONTENEGRO

REPUBLIC OF RAGUSA

ADRIATIC SEA

ALBANIA

RUMELIA

Constantinople

MACEDONIA

Salonika

ANATOLIA

EUBEA

Smyrna

Chesme

Venetian
Possessions

Acquired by Venice in 1699
but recovered
by the Ottoman
Empire in 1718

Acquired by
Austria in 1718

Acquired by
Austria in 1718 but
recovered by the
Ottoman Empire in 1739

Acquired by
Austria in 1775

RHODES

CRETE

MEDITERRANEAN
SEA

a well-established tradition tracing from Francis I (1515–47) of political interest and activity in the Near East. Her activity was inspired, in this period as in the past, above all by her desire to use the Turks as a weapon against Austria and thus divert the attention and resources of the Habsburgs away from the politics of Western Europe to a struggle against the Ottomans in the Balkans. In Constantinople alone of the capitals of Europe, significantly enough, the representative of France took precedence over his Austrian colleague.

The memory of the defeats she had suffered on the Danube in the 1680s and 1690s prevented Turkey from playing any part in the War of the Spanish Succession. She did nothing to support the Hungarian nationalists who, under Francis Rakoczi, maintained themselves in arms against the Emperors Leopold I and Joseph I in 1704–11. She gave little effective help to Charles XII against the Russians after the battle of Poltava and his flight to Turkey. Nor did she play any active part, as the French government had hoped, in opposing Austria and Russia in the War of the Polish Succession. Nevertheless her friendship with France was maintained, as can be seen in the sending to Paris in 1720 of a Turkish embassy, a mark of honour very rarely accorded any Christian State. Moreover a rapid expansion of France's commerce with the Levant from the 1720s onwards, which soon made her the dominant influence in the foreign trade of the area, bound the two States still more closely together. In the 1730s efforts to improve the Turkish army were made, with limited success, by one of the most remarkable figures of the century, the French renegade Comte de Bonneval (Bonneval Pasha) who also had considerable influence on the foreign policy of his adopted country. The peace of 1739, much more advantageous to Turkey than her achievements on the battlefield justified, was largely the work of the French Ambassador at Constantinople, the Marquis de Villeneuve, who was thus able to raise his country's influence at the Turkish capital to perhaps the highest pitch it ever attained. In the following year he succeeded in obtaining from the Porte a renewal of the Capitulations, the series of commercial and other concessions first granted to France by Suleiman the Magnificent in the sixteenth century and confirmed at intervals ever since.

The 'Diplomatic Revolution' of 1756, however, dealt Franco-Turkish relations the most severe blow they had suffered for generations. The Treaty of Versailles of May 1756 obliged each of the contracting powers to support the other in case of attack. It was from the French point of view essentially a weapon against Britain; but it meant nevertheless that if the Turks attacked the southern frontiers of the Habsburg territories France would find herself, in spite of her traditional friendship with them, compelled to support Austria. The Porte could not fail to see this, and protested strongly to the Comte de Vergennes, the newly appointed French Ambassador at Constantinople, against his government's failure to exclude the Ottoman Empire from the scope of the treaty. The Franco-Russian *rapprochement* which followed the events of 1756, though it was very fragile, did even more to weaken Turkish faith in French goodwill, and led some Turkish ministers to consider seeking safety in an approach to Prussia. A Prusso-Turkish treaty of friendship and commerce was signed after long negotiations in 1761, but the hopes of Frederick II that the Porte might intervene actively in the war against Russia or Austria were never realized. In the following year the death of the Empress Elizabeth and the coldness which came over Russo-French relations with the accession of Catherine II paved the way for a resumption of the friendship with France which had been so marked at Constantinople before 1756. From 1762 onwards France and Turkey were bound together by their mutual fear of Russia, as they had been in the past by their mutual hostility to the Habsburgs.

The role of France in bringing about the Russo-Turkish war of 1768 and its disastrous results for the Ottoman Empire have already been mentioned (see pp. 234ff). During the struggle France attempted more systematically than ever before to strengthen the Turkish army by supplying it with instructors and technicians of various kinds; and this policy was continued, though never on a really large scale, down to the 1790s. In spite of this, her inability to give the Porte substantial aid against Russia or to help it avoid the humiliating peace of 1774 could not fail to reduce somewhat her influence at Constantinople. In particular her powerlessness, in face of British hostility, to exclude the Russian fleet from the Mediterranean in 1770 did a good deal to shake Turkish faith in her value as an ally. Moreover in the decade which followed the Treaty of Kutchuk-Kainardji fear of Russia far more than friendship with France was the driving force behind the development of Turkish policy. As a result France, though represented at Constantinople by the very able Comte de Saint-Priest and still regarded by the Porte as its most reliable supporter, lost a good deal of the influence she had enjoyed in the 1760s. Vergennes, now Foreign Minister, had his attention fully occupied by events in America, by the war with Britain which broke out in 1778 and by the problem of the Bavarian Succession.

He was thus neither willing nor able to involve his country in heavy Near Eastern committments. He realized that the *entente* of 1781 between Austria and Russia exposed European Turkey to the risk of dismemberment by these rapacious neighbours, but could give the Porte little help except in the form of good advice. Even after France had made peace with Britain in 1783 his efforts to prevent the annexation of the Crimea by Russia, though they very nearly destroyed the thread-bare Austro-French alliance of 1756, did little to restrain Catherine II; while his insistence at Constantinople on the need to make further concessions to the Russians discouraged and antagonized the Turks.

The end of this period thus saw Russian influence in the Levant at the highest pitch it had hitherto reached. Intriguing in European Turkey through the consuls she had secured the right to maintain there in 1774 and through the contacts she kept up with local chieftains and religious dignitaries, expanding into the Crimea, laying the foundations of a powerful Black Sea fleet, exerting increasing pressure on the Caucasian as well as the European frontiers of the Ottoman Empire, Catherine II seemed about to dominate the whole area. Joseph II, though jealous of his new ally's power and success, had no intention of breaking with her and hoped increasingly to achieve in the Balkans the territorial gains which had so far eluded him in Germany. France, still overwhelmingly the greatest commercial power in the eastern Mediter-ranean, nevertheless now saw her political influence there threatened as never before during the century. Britain remained, as she had done throughout this period, uninterested in the Near East for its own sake and willing to intervene actively in its affairs only when they seemed to affect her position in Western Europe. Above all the decline of the Ottoman Empire, the source of most of the complexities and peculiari-ties of Near Eastern politics, continued. By the end of the eighteenth century some at least of the essentials of the 'Eastern Question' in the form in which Palmerston, Gladstone and Disraeli knew it were already in existence.

XII

The Anglo-French Struggle for Empire

The prolonged colonial struggle between Britain and France which began in 1689 and ended in 1815 was one of the dominant themes of eighteenth-century history. It was not, from a European point of view, of greater importance than the rise of Russian and Prussian power which has already been described. In some respects indeed it was less significant. It involved no changes of European political boundaries or of the political allegiance of European populations comparable to those brought about by Peter I, Catherine II and Frederick II. None the less it deeply influenced the history of the continent. It had important repercussions, which were clearly visible to contemporaries (see pp. 210–11), on the balance of power. It allowed Great Britain, even then to some extent outside Europe, to play in the politics of the continent a part far greater than her purely domestic resources justified. Above all it was the most important political link between Europe and the non-European world.

BIBLIOGRAPHY. The best general study of the Anglo-French colonial struggle is to be found in vol. I of the *Cambridge History of the British Empire* (Cambridge, 1929); from the French side H. I. Priestley, *France Overseas through the Old Régime* (New York, 1939), and H. Blet, *Histoire de la colonisation française*, vol. I (Grenoble, 1946) provide good starting-points. They may be supplemented by J. Saintoyant, *La Colonisation française sous l'ancien régime* (Paris, 1929), vol. II. For the Spanish Empire C. H. Haring, *The Spanish Empire in America* (New York, 1947) is an excellent general account. R. Pares, *War and Trade in the West Indies, 1739–1763* (Oxford, 1936) is a very thorough study of a crucial area of conflict. Anglo-French naval warfare can be followed in Admiral H. W. Richmond, *The Navy in the War of 1739–1748* (Cambridge, 1920) and Sir J. Corbett, *England in the Seven Years War* (London, 1907); and from the French side in J. Tramond, *Manuel d'histoire maritime de la France* (2nd ed., Paris, 1927). H. Dodwell, *Dupleix and Clive* (London, 1920) remains an excellent account of the critical years of the struggle in India. C. Fernandez Duro, *Armada Espanola* (Madrid, 1895–1903) is old-fashioned but still the only substantial history of the Spanish navy; vols. VI–VII are relevant to this period. On the Seven Years War there is much material in the unfinished work of

The colonies of the European States were now becoming to some extent parts of the European political system and were increasingly influencing the policies of some of the greatest of its members. The idea, so widespread in the previous century, that States might be in conflict in America or the East and still remain at peace in Europe, was now clearly outdated. Colonial events now no longer took place in a different political world as well as in a different continent. The Anglo-Spanish war of 1739 and the undeclared Anglo-French war of 1755, the first great struggles between European States to be provoked solely by commercial and colonial rivalries, showed unmistakably how things had changed in this respect.

In Europe the death of Louis XIV was followed by an unexpected and anomalous Anglo-French *rapprochement*. This was based, in both countries, on dynastic at least as much as national interests. In particular it was inspired by the wish of the Duc d'Orléans, Regent during the minority of Louis XV, to safeguard his position as heir to the French throne should the young king die and to exclude from the succession the rival claimant, Philip V of Spain. In other words, the government of France, for which the Treaty of Utrecht had been in many ways a defeat, as well as that of Britain for which it represented on the whole a victory, now desired to uphold the peace settlement of 1713–14. The result was an Anglo-French agreement in November 1716 which paved the way for the Triple Alliance of January 1717. By the latter Britain, France and the United Provinces combined to maintain the Utrecht settlement, the rule of the Hanoverian dynasty in Britain and the garrisoning by the Dutch of a number of 'barrier fortresses' in the Austrian Netherlands. The good, or at least officially good, Anglo-French relations thus created lasted, with some fluctuations, for well

R. Waddington, *La Guerre de Sept Ans* (Paris, 1896–1914), though this deals mainly with the fighting in Europe; and from the British side valuable insights can be found in R. Whitworth, *Field-Marshal Lord Ligonier* (Oxford, 1958). R. Pares, 'American versus continental warfare, 1739–1763', *English Historical Review*, vol. LI (1936) is the best brief discussion of the conflicting trends in British strategy during the middle decades of the century. The most recent study of the Peace of Paris is Z. E. Rashed, *The Peace of Paris, 1763* (Liverpool, 1952) but this does not supersede the detailed accounts to be found in the works of Pares and Corbett mentioned above. On the American Revolution two very useful general works are J. R. Alder, *The American Revolution* (New York-London, 1954) and J. C. Miller, *Origins of the American Revolution* (Stanford, 1959). Its international aspects are well covered in R. B. Morris, *The Peacemakers: the Great Powers and American independence* (New York, 1965) and R. W. van Alstyne, *Empire and Independence: the international history of the* over a decade. In 1719–20 the two powers combined to oppose Spanish ambitions in Italy, and in 1725–27 to counterbalance the newly-formed Austro-Spanish alliance (see pp. 275–6). Their co-operation, however, was always fragile and appeared to many contemporaries almost unnatural. With the death of Orléans in 1723 and the growth to manhood of Louis XV much of its original basis disappeared. By the 1730s, under Cardinal Fleury, French policy was once more acquiring much of its traditional anti-British colouring.

Nor could the tendency of the two States to combine in Europe during the years after 1716 conceal the fact that their interests and ambitions overseas now conflicted more violently than ever before. In 1713 the Treaty of Utrecht gave Britain a stronger position in America than she had hitherto possessed. Her acquisition of Acadia (Nova Scotia) did a good deal to protect New England from possible attacks by the French in Canada. That of Newfoundland consolidated her position in the valuable cod fisheries of the Gulf of St. Lawrence. That of Hudson's Bay, though less important, guaranteed her a share in the fur trade of Canada. Nevertheless Britain was still far from complete domination in North America and even farther in the Carribean. Her mainland colonies, though their population and wealth were rapidly growing, were still widely separated; not merely by geography but by their differing histories and outlooks. The majority of them were governed in a roughly similar way, by a governor appointed by the Crown and an elected assembly whose relations with the governor were often far from amicable. But in few other respects had they much in common. The New England colonies had for long periods of the seventeenth century been virtually independent republics. In some of them, notably Massachusetts, the assemblies even before the American Revolution were elected by something approaching manhood suffrage. They differed widely from the Carolinas, which had been founded under Charles II by a royal grant of lands and jurisdiction to a syndicate of noblemen and capitalists, and from Virginia. There, at least in the areas near the coast, aristocratic social traditions remained strong.

American Revolution (New York, 1965); and its military ones in P. Mackesy, *The War for America, 1775–1783* (Oxford, 1964). G. S. Graham, 'Considerations on the War of American Independence', *Bulletin of the Institute of Historical Research*, vol. XXII (1949) provides a brief but stimulating commentary on the struggle, as does R. B. Morris, *The American Revolution Reconsidered* (New York, 1967). V. T. Harlow, *The Founding of the Second British Empire*, vol. I (London, 1952) gives a somewhat discursive but penetrating account of the peace negotiations of 1782–83.

Pennsylvania, still dominated by the Quaker tradition of its founders, differed almost as much from New York, the most cosmopolitan of the colonies and one which included, in families such as the Livingstons and the Van Rensselaers, many of the greatest landowners in British America. Geographical dispersal, social and economic differences, and the parochialism which still distinguished the outlook of many of the colonists, meant that the British settlements never combined effectively against the French or Spaniards. Their contribution to the struggles of this period against the French in Canada was provided mainly by one or two of them, above all by Massachusetts and Connecticut.

Politically and socially French Canada was far better adapted to a military struggle for survival. Her society, dominated by *seigneurs* and priests, and her administrative system, controlled by the military governor and the intendant, had been modelled on those of France herself. Her outlook was far more authoritarian than that of any important British colony. Her population, though small (about 19,000 in 1713, rising to about 56,000 in 1740) was incomparably better organized for military purposes than the far larger one of the British mainland colonies. France's position moreover was strengthened by her alliances with the Indian tribes on the frontiers of her territories, and by her possession in Louisbourg on Cape Breton Island (built from 1720 onwards) of the most powerful of all North American fortresses. Her struggling colony of Louisiana, which became administratively separate from Canada in 1717, had less military significance. Already, however, her exploration of the Mississippi basin was beginning to threaten an eventual junction of her possessions on the St. Lawrence with those on the Gulf of Mexico, the hemming-in of the British colonies by a gigantic arc of French-held territory which would include the Great Lakes and the Ohio valley.

In the Caribbean also Anglo-French antagonism was constant and sometimes acute in the early decades of the century, notably over the possession of the four 'neutral islands' of St. Vincent, St. Lucia, Dominica and Tobago, which had been left in 1713 as a kind of no-man's-land. In this area, however, the position was complicated by the presence of other powers; the Dutch in Curaçao and St. Eustatius, the Danes in St. Croix (bought from France in 1733) and above all the Spaniards in Cuba, San Domingo and their vast Central and South American Empire. It was with Spain, not with the more powerful and aggressive France, that Britain first came into serious conflict in the western hemisphere after the peace of 1713.

The *Asiento* agreement which she had extorted from an unwilling
Spanish government in March 1714 provided for the sale each year by
the English South Sea Company to Spanish America of a specified number
of Negro slaves at a fixed price. It also permitted the company to send
each year to trade in the Indies one ship, the *navio permiso*. It is now
clear that this ship was not used as a cover for illegitimate trade on the
scale which some historians used to believe; but the breach which it
represented in Spain's traditional policy of confining trade with her
American possessions strictly to the mother-country made it deeply
suspect to the Spanish officials on whom the success of its voyages
depended. Only eight such voyages were in fact made in the period
1717–33. By the 1730s persistent illicit trading with Spanish America
by British ships and the often brutal efforts to prevent it of Spanish
guardacostas were straining Anglo-Spanish relations very severely. A
series of efforts to smooth over the situation had no success, largely
because of the increasingly aggressive and anti-Spanish attitude of
British public opinion. Attracted by dreams of the conquest of wealthy
Spanish colonies, the opening-up of new opportunities for British trade
and the capture of Spanish treasure-ships, an attitude summed up in
the slogan 'Take and Hold', many Englishmen were not only ready but
anxious for a war with Spain. This attitude was strengthened by disputes
over the boundaries between the new British colony of Georgia
and the Spanish possession of Florida, and over the right of British
subjects to cut logwood on the coast of Honduras. Its influence was
increased by the growing weakness and division of the Walpole
Cabinet. By October 1739 it had led to the outbreak of an Anglo-Spanish
war.

But for Frederick II's attack on Silesia, which revolutionized the
position in Europe, Britain would undoubtedly have found herself by
1741 engaged single-handed in a great naval and colonial struggle
against France as well as Spain. Only the outbreak of the War of the
Austrian Succession and France's resulting preoccupations in Germany
postponed an open breach between Britain and France till 1744. With
the formal outbreak of war between the two States in that year and the
resulting involvement of the Netherlands, the Anglo-Spanish conflict
which had been proceeding somewhat languidly since 1739 was transformed into the greatest colonial struggle hitherto known in European
history. Its results in America were none the less indecisive. The capture
of Portobello on the isthmus of Panama by Admiral Vernon in the first
weeks of the war stimulated great hopes in Britain; but disease, rum and

constant friction between military and naval commanders combined to stultify all other attempts to seize Spanish territory in the Caribbean. Two thousand miles to the north Louisbourg fell in June 1745 to a force consisting largely of New England militia. This was a striking reminder that the British colonies, in spite of their jealousies of each other and the intractability of their assemblies, possessed material resources which French Canada, once cut off from the mother-country, could not hope to equal. Nevertheless their achievement had no permanent result. When peace was made Louisbourg was returned to France.

This was done, much to the annoyance of the New Englanders, partly because France found herself in a strong position in Europe when the war ended. In 1745–48 her armies, under the Maréchal de Saxe, had overrun the Austrian Netherlands and defeated a combined British, Austrian and Dutch force in a series of battles at Fontenoy (1745), Raucoux (1746) and Lawfeldt (1747). By the spring of 1748, with the great fortresses of Bergen-op-Zoom and Maastricht in his hands, Saxe was threatening a conquest of the United Provinces. Such gains were sufficient to offset much heavier losses overseas than France had suffered, and more than compensated her for two considerable naval defeats at the hands of Britain in 1747.

Britain was also compelled to return Louisbourg by her failures on the other side of the world, in India. Here the British and French East India Companies, the former established in the subcontinent for over a century, the latter since the time of Colbert, had shown until the 1740s few signs of increasing their military or territorial power. In spite of the breakdown of the Mughal Empire, which had begun to be visible even before the death of the Emperor Aurangzeb in 1707 and was greatly accelerated after that date, they remained for long mere trading companies. Their possessions in India were confined to a few forts and trading-stations—Bombay, Madras and Fort St. George (Calcutta) in the case of the British Company; Pondicherry, Chandernagore and Mahé in that of the French one. Already Dumas, the French Company's *Commandant-Général*, had been forced in the later 1730s, in order to maintain France's position, to conclude political alliances with some of the independent rulers who were now emerging in South India. Mahé de la Bourdonnais, governor of the French islands in the Indian Ocean in 1735–40 and one of the greatest of French empire-builders, had dreamed of making Mauritius an important naval and privateering base. As yet, however, hardly anyone in London or Paris thought of a territorial empire in the East. Even in 1744, on the out break of war between Britain and France, Dumas's successor J.-F. Dupleix proposed that these countries' Indian possessions should take no part in the struggle.[1] The only important event of the conflict which followed the British Company's rejection of this proposal was the fall of Madras to a French force in September 1746; it was largely to secure the return of this valuable commercial post that Louisbourg was given up when peace was made.

That peace, embodied in the Treaty of Aix-la-Chapelle of October 1748 was, in its colonial as in its European aspects, a mere truce. From it Britain and France 'gained nothing but the experience of each other's strength and power'.[2] France in particular received a very inadequate return for her victories in Europe. The comparatively trivial claims of the South Sea Company against Spain were settled two years later; but the increasingly acute and incomparably more important Anglo-French rivalry was obviously insoluble without further conflict. On both sides the events of the 1740s had roused resentments and whetted appetites, so that within a very few years the two countries found themselves drifting into a state of undeclared war.

In North America the growing violence of the struggle can be seen in the capture by the British of Fort Beauséjour on the Chignecto isthmus in 1755 and the forcible deportation of 10,000 French-speaking and potentially disloyal Acadians from Nova Scotia. At the same time each power was seizing the other's ships in the Gulf of St. Lawrence and protracted negotiations were once more going on over the 'neutral islands' in the West Indies. More important were the conflicts now springing up around the forts which France was establishing in the Ohio valley. The danger that she might consolidate her grip on this area and thus prevent further expansion westwards by the British colonies seemed a very real one, with the building of Fort Presqu'île and Fort-le-Bœuf to the south of Lake Erie in 1749 and of Fort Duquesne on the Ohio in 1753. The British reply—the construction of Fort Necessity, also on the Ohio, and the unsuccessful efforts of expeditions under Washington in 1754 and Braddock in 1755 to shake French power in the area—meant that the two States were now in fact at war in America though still at peace in Europe.

Simultaneously a complex struggle between the British and French

---

[1] This was the last effort of any significance to assert the principle that events in Europe and those in America or the East could be kept in separate compartments, so that States at war in Europe could be de facto at peace overseas.
[2] W. Coxe, Memoirs of Horatio, Lord Walpole (London, 1802), p. 359.

East India Companies was developing in the part of South India known as the Carnatic, each power acting ostensibly as the supporter of rival claimants to the position of Nawab, or ruler of the area. In this struggle the French were defeated. This was partly because of lack of money (though Dupleix spent during the conflict over £350,000 subscribed by himself and his friends). It was also because neither the French government, which was weak and preoccupied with events in America, nor the directors of the French Company, to whom Dupleix gave no detailed explanation of his plans till October 1753, provided adequate backing. His recall in 1754 was a symbol as well as a result of his defeat. In the powerful State of Hyderabad, however, a French force under Bussy, the ablest of French soldiers in India, had achieved by 1750 a dominant position which it was to retain for the next eight years.

Thus in 1755 the balance seemed still fairly even in the two great areas of Anglo-French rivalry. In June of that year the British Admiral Boscawen, on the orders of the government, attacked without any declaration of war a large French convoy taking reinforcements to North America. He did not succeed in destroying it, as had been hoped in London; but he captured two French men-of-war and in the following months the British fleet seized over 300 French merchantmen. A declaration of war by France was thus made inevitable: only the weakness of Louis XV and his ministers delayed it till May 1756.

The struggle which followed began badly for Britain. At the outset of the war Minorca, her largest overseas naval base, fell to French attack. The government led, in so far as it was led at all, by the fussy and uninspiring Duke of Newcastle, was discredited by the defeat and driven from power in November. It was succeeded at the end of June 1757, after a period of weakness and confusion, by the most successful British Cabinet of the century, that led by Newcastle and the elder William Pitt. Pitt, who was soon to prove himself the greatest war minister in British history, had first achieved prominence by the violence of his attacks on Walpole in the 1730s. Disliked by George II, his abilities as an orator and the strength of his personality made him a figure of importance in the politics of the 1740s and early 1750s. Now the climax of his career was at hand. His irritability, his lack of any capacity for friendship, his obsessive francophobia, make him an unsympathetic figure. Yet he imparted to British policy at a critical moment an energy and determination which were soon to produce a series of splendid victories. This could not be foreseen, however, by observers in 1757, and the new government was formed just in time to see the defeat and capitulation

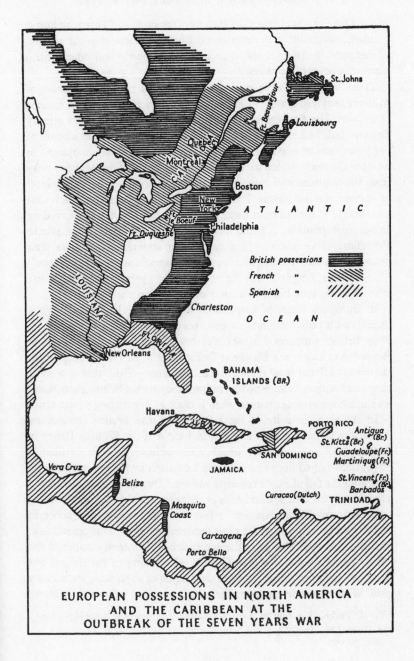

British possessions
French   "
Spanish   "

St. Johns

Ft. Beauséjour
Louisbourg

Quebec
Montreal
C A N A D A

Boston

New York

A T L A N T I C

le Boeuf
Ft. Duquesne
Philadelphia

L O U I S I A N A

Charleston

O C E A N

New Orleans

F L O R I D A

BAHAMA
ISLANDS (BR.)

Havana
C U B A

PORTO RICO
Antigua
(Br.)
St. Kitts (Br.)
Guadeloupe (Fr.)
Martinique (Fr.)

SAN DOMINGO

Vera Cruz

JAMAICA

St. Vincent (Fr.)
(Br.)
Barbados

Belize

Mosquito
Coast

Curacao (Dutch)
TRINIDAD

Cartagena

Porto Bello

EUROPEAN POSSESSIONS IN NORTH AMERICA
AND THE CARIBBEAN AT THE
OUTBREAK OF THE SEVEN YEARS WAR

of the Duke of Cumberland in Hanover (see p. 260). 'We are no longer a nation,' wrote the very experienced Lord Chesterfield in the autumn of that year, 'I never yet saw so dreadful a prospect';[1] and other British statesmen echoed his gloom.

These misgivings were excessive. France, apart from the capture of Minorca, enjoyed almost as little success as Britain in the first months of the war. Her finances were strained and some of her leaders already demoralized. Most important of all she was now involved, as a result of her new commitments to Austria, in a series of large-scale campaigns in western Germany which inevitably diverted much of her energies away from the maritime and colonial struggle with Britain. 'The great object of the nation [i.e. Great Britain],' wrote a very well-informed contemporary, 'is the American war . . . the probability of our succeeding in our main point is . . . much increased by the part the French take in the affairs of Germany, which turns their attention, as well as their money, from their marine, and . . . making expeditions to our Colonies.'[1] These factors, coupled with the new impetus given to the British war effort by Pitt, soon brought a complete change in the situation.

In Europe a series of amphibious attacks were launched in 1758, though with only moderate success, on the north coast of France. In 1759 British supremacy at sea was consolidated by the victories of Boscawen at Lagos and Hawke at Quiberon Bay. In 1761 the capture of the island of Belleisle off the south coast of Brittany illustrated once more the potentialities of 'combined operations' and gave the British government a valuable bargaining counter when it came to negotiating peace terms.

In America, in spite of the brilliance of the French commander Montcalm (who captured the British base of Fort William Henry in August 1757 and won two considerable successes at Fort Carillon in 1758) Canada had been severed from Louisiana by the end of the latter year after the fall of Fort Frontenac and Fort Duquesne. Simultaneously Louisbourg fell into British hands once more, this time for good. British troops captured Fort Niagara in July 1759 and above all Quebec in September, after perhaps the most remarkable amphibious operation in British history. A year later the surrender of Montreal completed the extinction of French power in Canada. The victory of Britain was one of numbers and material strength over equal or even superior military skill. Weakness at sea, an overwhelming numerical inferiority in North

[1] P. C. Yorke, *The Life of Lord Chancellor Hardwicke* (Cambridge, 1913), vol. III, p. 123.
[1] *Ibid.*, p. 157.

America and a constant threat of food shortage in Canada, made the defeat of France inevitable. In the West Indies, where some of the same factors operated, the valuable sugar island of Guadeloupe fell to a British expedition in the spring of 1759. In the same year the French possessions of Gorée and Fort Louis in West Africa were captured.

In India the course of events was complicated by the existence of powerful native States with policies and problems of their own, States capable of raising armies many times larger than Britain or France could send thither. But the fighting of the last decade had shown that European troops, if properly led, could more than hold their own against apparently overwhelming numbers of Indians; and this fact was soon to be driven home unmistakably. The capture of Calcutta in June 1756 by Siraj-ud-Daula, the ruler of Bengal (probably provoked by fear of the growing power of the East India Company) was merely a temporary setback. Six months later it was retaken by Robert Clive, who had already greatly distinguished himself in the Carnatic. This success was followed by the capture of the French station at Chandernagore and, in July 1757, by the complete defeat of Siraj-ud-Daula at Plassey. Though the French played little part in these events (their energies were diverted largely to the maintenance of Bussy's foothold in Hyderabad) Clive's victory fatally undermined their position in India. This was because it gave the British Company control through Mir Ja'far, their nominee as successor to Siraj-ud-Daula, of a great area of populous and fertile country whose revenues could be used to maintain powerful sepoy armies. By contrast the French forces farther south in the Carnatic, the main scene of direct conflict with the English, were now continuously and sometimes disastrously short of money. This contrast between the financial positions of the rivals does as much as anything to explain the defeat of France.

In India, as in America and in European waters, 1759 was a decisive year. The failure of the French, under the gallant but unfortunate Lally-Tollendal, to take Madras in February, and the British capture of Masulipatam in April, were the turning-point of the war there. Without control of the sea, weakened by the quarrels of their commanders, the French in India were now clearly fighting a losing battle. The defeat of Lally by Sir Eyre Coote at Wandewash in January 1760 and the fall a year later of Pondicherry, France's main stronghold in India, completed the British victory. An attempt by the Dutch to land troops in Bengal and supplant the British there had already been decisively defeated by Clive in November 1759: five years later the battle of Bakhsar led to the

British conquest of Oudh and by 1765 the Nawab of Bengal had become the mere figurehead of a British-dominated administration. When Clive secured from the Mughal emperor at Delhi in that year control of the finances of Bengal, Bihor and Orissa, the East India Company had been launched by force of circumstances and the initiative of its servants on a career of territorial conquest from which it could not draw back.

Against these massive and world-wide British successes France could place nothing but the capture of Minorca. Moreover tentative peace negotiations at The Hague in 1760 and Paris in 1761 showed that Pitt, supported by British public opinion and the Press, intended to drive a hard bargain when a treaty was signed. In particular it was clear that he wished to exclude the French from any share in the Newfoundland fishery and thus, by depriving them of a great source of experienced seamen, to prevent the revival of their navy. Nevertheless the Duc de Choiseul, who had replaced the incompetent Bernis as French Foreign Minister in November 1758, still had a card to play. Charles III, who had in 1759 succeeded his half-brother Ferdinand VI as King of Spain, did not share his predecessor's freedom from anti-British feeling. In particular he was genuinely alarmed by the growth of Britain's power in North America, which he feared might be the prelude to attacks on Spain's possessions in South America and the West Indies. Already in 1759, soon after his accession, he had unsuccessfully offered to mediate between Britain and France. Choiseul hoped, by playing on his fears, to bring Spain into the war as the ally of France and thus limit the losses which the latter must inevitably suffer when peace was made. The involvement of Spain in this way proved remarkably easy: indeed in 1761 the advances for a Franco-Spanish alliance came from Charles III, who feared the conclusion of a peace which sacrificed Spanish interests in America, rather than from France. The Family Compact of August 1761 which united the two States against Britain was thus, unlike previous agreements of this type made in 1733 and 1743, inspired by colonial rather than purely European rivalries. Its conclusion brought one immediate advantage to the French; in October Pitt, who demanded an immediate attack on Spain, resigned when the Cabinet failed to support him. Nevertheless from the military and naval point of view France's new ally achieved little. Pitt's colleagues, belatedly adopting the policy he had advocated, declared war on Spain at the beginning of January 1762; and the year which followed saw a series of British victories comparable to those of 1759. In the West Indies Havana, the greatest Spanish base in the western hemisphere, was captured, as was the very valuable French sugar island of Martinique. In the Pacific an expedition from India took Manila, the capital of the Philippines. A Spanish attack on Portugal was repulsed with British help; and in West Germany Ferdinand of Brunswick drove the French from Kassel and Göttingen.

In the peace negotiations of 1761–63 Britain did not exploit these successes fully. The Earl of Bute, who had been the leading minister since Pitt's resignation, was anxious for peace and completely unskilled in diplomacy. The Duke of Bedford, who also played a leading part in these negotiations and who signed the Treaty of Paris (February 1763) as the British plenipotentiary, was even less willing to push France to extremes. Moreover in one respect Choiseul occupied a favourable position, since he acted to some extent as an intermediary between Britain and Spain; this he was able to turn to advantage. The result was that the peace of 1763 was not for France the complete disaster of which Pitt had dreamed. Her losses were none the less severe. Canada was surrendered, and with it the vast undeveloped territory of which France had claimed possession to the east of the Mississippi. Grenada, St. Vincent and Tobago were ceded; and perhaps only the unwillingness of British sugar-planters to expose themselves to the competition in the home market of the more fertile French islands prevented the loss of Guadeloupe or Martinique as well. In India, though she retained her trading stations, France was now clearly unable to compete with Britain. In West Africa her forts in Senegal were surrendered to her rival. These losses, moreover, had been incurred as a result of defeats in the colonies themselves. In Europe France was not directly threatened, in spite of the mediocre performance of her armies in Germany. Apart from British raids on her coasts her territory had never to fear invasion. In spite of Pitt's well-known phrase, America was not 'conquered in Germany'. It was conquered in America and on the high seas; and even the complete defeat of Frederick II could not have restored it to France. Spain for her part ceded to Britain in 1763 the comparatively valueless province of Florida and in exchange recovered Havana. She also regained Manila; while as compensation for her losses and to strengthen the alliance of 1761 she received from France the latter's territories and claims in that part of Louisiana which lay west of the Mississippi.

The colonial wars of the middle decades of the century had thus changed the political face of much of the world. On the empires of Spain and Portugal, which except in a few frontier areas had long reached the limits of their growth, their impact was slight. That of France they reduced to a few islands—Guadeloupe, Martinique, the western half of San Domingo, Mauritius and the Seychelles—many of which were valuable producers of tropical products, above all of sugar, but none of which offered scope for territorial expansion. That of Britain they raised to the position of a world power. Nevertheless with all her victories Britain had not reduced France and Spain to the position of second-rate States: to do so was far beyond her ability. Moreover the collapse of her wartime relationship with Prussia (see pp. 263–4) left her isolated in Europe after 1763. Her enemies, by contrast, were united rather than divided by defeat; in the years which followed the war the alliance with Spain much more than that with Austria became the cornerstone of French policy.

It was not to be expected that France would accept the decision of 1763 as final. The terms of peace seemed lenient to many Englishmen, above all in allowing her to retain a share in the Newfoundland fishery and hence the possibility of resurrecting her navy. In Paris, however, they stimulated a natural desire for revenge. Before his fall Choiseul did much to rebuild French naval power and strengthen the Franco-Spanish alliance. In 1770 he was willing to support Spain, even at the risk of war, in a dispute with Britain over the ownership of the Falkland Islands; and perhaps only the timidity of Louis XV, which led to the minister's dismissal in December of that year, prevented the outbreak of a new imperial struggle. Choiseul had also realized that the best chance of humbling Britain lay in encouraging and stimulating the growing unrest which was now showing itself in her American colonies.

That unrest had many causes. The best known is the effort of the British government from 1763 onwards to force the colonies to contribute more adequately to the costs of their own defence against French, Spanish or Indian attack. This it attempted to do partly by enforcing the legal restrictions (many of them had been disregarded for decades) which limited the commercial freedom of the colonists in the interests of the mother-country (see pp. 317–18). Led by the efficiency-minded George Grenville, it tightened up in 1763–65 the hitherto very lax customs administration in the colonies and used vice-admiralty courts (which were independent of the colonial assemblies) to try smugglers. More serious, it attempted to tax the colonists, directly by the Stamp Act of 1765 and indirectly by the Townshend Acts of 1767. Almost simultaneously it tried, by a proclamation of October 1763, to restrict the westward movement of the frontier of settlement in North

America and thus avoid friction with the native inhabitants. (A considerable Indian rising known as the 'revolt of Pontiac', which lasted till September 1764, was just then showing how dangerous the position on the frontier might become). A few years later it reinforced colonial suspicions, above all in Calvinist New England, by passing the remarkably liberal and enlightened Quebec Act of 1774 which recognized the position of the Catholic Church in Canada (at least by implication, in that its priests were given the right to collect tithes). All these measures, in varying degrees, were unpopular in America. Restrictions on trade, however well-grounded in law, aroused a great deal of understandable ill-will in the ports of the eastern seaboard. The levying of taxation by the British government for revenue purposes was an innovation which seemed to emphasize the inferior and dependent position of the colonies. Since the Parliament which authorized such taxation included no colonial representatives it was easy for idealists or trouble-makers to raise the seductive cry of 'no taxation without representation'. Efforts to suppress smuggling and protect the Indians again seemed, or could be made to seem, tyrannical interference with colonial liberties by a corrupt and overbearing government.

Moreover there was already in existence by the 1760s a tradition of friction between the British government and the colonial assemblies over a number of issues. One of these was the right claimed by the latter to issue paper currency and thus lighten the weight of the debts owed by many colonists to British merchants. Such issues were prohibited in 1765, and the debt of about £5 million owed in Britain by American traders and planters has been considered by some writers as an important factor in the final break with the mother-country. Other long-standing disputes were inspired by the claims of many colonial assemblies to control the governors appointed by the Crown, and by the right often though not very effectively exercised by rulers of Great Britain to veto legislation passed by such assemblies.

Underlying all these specific grievances and drawing strength from them was a growing feeling in America that the colonies were no longer mere offshoots of the mother-country; that they differed radically from her in their social and political structure; that they were now beginning to form a separate nation. This profound though largely unconscious movement of separatist feeling in America is the real explanation of the American Revolution. It was this feeling (whose growth had been noticed by European travellers at least as early as the 1740s) which drove so many Americans to disregard legality, precedent and as it sometimes seemed common sense, in the pursuit of liberty. It was the emotions it generated, far more than any material grievance, which drove them to react against British rule; first by the Non-Importation Agreements of the 1760s (by which American merchants agreed not to purchase goods on which duties had been placed by Parliament); then by the stoning of British troops and the tarring and feathering of officials who attempted to enforce the law; and finally by armed rebellion.

It is true that even as late as 1775 only a minority, perhaps a fifth, of the colonists wished for independence, and that perhaps a third or even half of them disapproved of outright resistance to British rule. These 'loyalists' provided many of the most bitter opponents of the movement towards independence and often suffered exile and loss when it had triumphed. The war in which the colonies threw off British rule was therefore in a very real sense an American civil war. Nevertheless by the 1760s the temper of many of the most politically conscious and politically active Americans, above all in New England, was such that no concessions the British government could have made would have permanently satisfied them. As early as 1768 a Boston newspaper was talking of an appeal to France for aid in resisting British oppression.

The events of the later 1760s and early 1770s, as antagonism mounted between the colonists and the British government, need only be touched on here. The duties on stamped paper used for various legal documents in America, imposed by the Stamp Act of 1765, were repealed in the following year in response to colonial protests. Those placed by the Townshend Acts of 1767 on glass, paper, lead, tea and colours imported into the colonies were swept away, with the exception of that on tea, in 1770. As a result, tension relaxed somewhat in the following two or three years; but in 1773 the passage of the Tea Act (which gave the East India Company the right to export tea to America in its own ships and sell it there through its own agents) led to a new burst of colonial resentment. By allowing the company to dispose of a large stock of surplus tea at low prices it appeared to strike at the interests of both smugglers and legitimate traders in America. Events now moved swiftly to a crisis. The destruction by groups of colonists of supplies of tea, above all in Boston, was followed by British punitive measures directed against that city and the colony of Massachusetts. These in turn inspired the meeting, in April 1774, of the first Continental Congress, a gathering of representatives of most of the mainland colonies. This issued a Declaration of Rights, and by declaring its support of Massachusetts identified itself with rebellion. By 1775 fighting on a considerable scale between British troops and American militia had begun. In July 1776 another congress of colonial representatives meeting at Philadelphia declared the colonies independent of Britain.

When American discontent thus came to a head Britain was in a weaker position, both in Europe and overseas, than at any other time during the century. She had made efforts in the middle 1760s to escape from political isolation by adopting the Russian idea of a Northern System which was to include Russia, Prussia, Sweden and Denmark, as well as Great Britain (see p. 232). These efforts were a failure. So were more prolonged and more promising negotiations, which dragged on till 1773, for a treaty with Russia alone. The result was that Britain found herself in the 1770s, as in 1763, alone in face of a revengeful, envious or indifferent Europe. This isolation does much to explain her defeat in America.

She was also weakened by the unpopularity of the struggle in the colonies with great bodies of British opinion. It was opposed by merchants who saw their profitable colonial trade interrupted or destroyed. It was unpopular with Nonconformist groups who tended (with the notable exception of the Methodists) to sympathize with the largely Calvinist New England colonies and to suspect George III and his ministers as the representatives and tools of the aristocracy and the Established Church. These feelings moreover were used and played on by opposition politicians. Some of these (for example many of the Rockingham Whigs) were sincere believers in the rightness of the American cause, but others were animated merely by desire for office and in some cases personal hostility to the king. The good fortune which had provided the country with the leadership of Pitt during the Seven Years War was not repeated. The chief minister, Lord North (1770–82), had some administrative ability and considerable personal charm; but neither he nor any other statesman could symbolize the national cause and rally flagging energies in Britain in the way that the colonial leader George Washington did in America. As the seriousness of the struggle became more apparent, above all after the surrender of a British army to the Americans at Saratoga in 1777, hostility to the government increased. In 1779–80, as has already been seen (see p. 141) the discontent brought to a head by the war for a short time reached almost revolutionary proportions. In 1782, in the last days of the struggle, the threat of revolt in Ireland allowed its Parliament in Dublin to recover the legislative independence it had lost almost three centuries earlier.

The decisive event of the war was the entry of France on the anti-British side early in 1778. This was undoubtedly stimulated in part by a desire for revenge after the defeats of the Seven Years War: the French government had for some time been supplying the rebels with arms and equipment and sheltering American privateers. The ambitions of Vergennes, the French Foreign Minister, were however remarkably moderate. He had no desire to recover Canada or Louisiana and aimed much more at regaining the prestige which France had lost in the Seven Years War, and at expanding French trade, than at the mere acquisition of territory. French intervention, nevertheless, whatever its motive, made it extremely unlikely that Britain would be able to subdue her rebellious colonies. Its importance was seen when in 1778 the Americans rejected a series of very sweeping concessions offered them by the British government in the so-called Conciliatory Propositions. There seemed for a moment a chance that the British proposals might be accepted by the rebels, and some of the more extreme of the colonial leaders feared them as 'more dangerous to our cause than ten thousand of their [the British government's] best troops'. The availability of French support was a most powerful incentive to continue the struggle; and with the rejection of the British proposals the last real possibility of reconciliation with the mother-country vanished.

Britain's difficulties were greatly increased when Spain joined the ranks of her enemies in June 1779. Vergennes had proposed as early as January 1777 that she and France should jointly declare war on Britain and sign a treaty with the Americans, but it was only slowly and reluctantly that the Spanish government took the plunge. Unlike that of France, it was completely unwilling to recognize the independence of the thirteen British mainland colonies or to have any dealings with their representatives. This was inevitable: signs, though as yet relatively slight ones, of growing resentment of at least some aspects of Spanish rule were now beginning to show themselves in South America. A general reassertion of control from Madrid, after a century of inertia, set in motion by the reforming régime of Charles III from about 1765 onwards, partly explains this. So does the very marked rise in emigration from Spain (particularly from the southern provinces) to America in the later eighteenth century. This provoked bitter complaints from small businessmen, artisans and minor office-holders in the Spanish colonies, who resented the frequently greater energy and success of the new-comers. In 1771, in an early reflection of this attitude, the *cabildo* (town council) of Mexico City demanded that all government offices in Mexico be reserved for Mexicans and Spaniards treated as foreigners. With great problems of this kind slowly beginning to emerge in her own possessions Spain was bound to see the revolt of the thirteen British colonies in a very different light from France. Moreover possible territorial gains bulked much larger at Madrid than in Paris. Spain entered the war above all to recover Gibraltar. It was the refusal of the British government to contemplate the return of the fortress by peaceful negotiation which made a new Anglo-Spanish struggle inevitable. The declaration of war by Britain in December 1780 against the United Provinces, whose ships had for long been supplying the colonists with arms and supplies of all kinds, was an act of great boldness; but it made her position more difficult still.

She now found herself fighting against odds unparalleled in her history, and fighting moreover under the most unfavourable circumstances—poorly led, divided by bitter party rivalries, and deprived by the revolt in America, according to a contemporary estimate, of a third of her merchant marine and 18,000 seamen. The Armed Neutrality of 1780 (see p. 238) did her little real harm but it weakened still further her influence in Europe.

From this desperate position Britain emerged less ingloriously than might have been expected. Hostility to France and Spain, traditional enemies, did a good deal to unite popular feeling for the continuance of the struggle and to ensure that it would be prolonged; in this sense French intervention harmed as well as helped the colonists. The numerical superiority which the French and Spanish fleets possessed in the early stages of the war was never fully utilized: by 1782 Rodney had restored British predominance at sea and averted any possibility of the loss of Jamaica by a decisive victory over the French at The Saints islands in the West Indies. During the war, in the exchanges of naval prisoners which were then normal while hostilities were in progress, Britain sent to France at least 31,000 men and probably far more: she received in return only a little over 16,000 British prisoners taken by the French.[1] (Though against this it should be remembered that her losses of merchant ships to French, Spanish and American privateers were exceptionally heavy.) A very well-informed French ob-

[1] Public Record Office, Admiralty 98/14/319. I am indebted to my wife for this information. It is of course true that the number of prisoners exchanged was not necessarily the same as that taken. Nevertheless these figures show that Britain was more than holding her own against France at sea.

server spoke admiringly some years later of 'this so to speak miraculous struggle of the naval forces of England alone against those of the three greatest maritime powers in Europe'.[1] Moreover Gibraltar successfully withstood a siege of three years (1779–82)—by far the greatest military operation of the war. Canada and Newfoundland were retained, though this was partly because the French government had no desire to see the American colonists, by acquiring them, become strong enough to throw off its influence. Simultaneously the East India Company consolidated its position in the Deccan at the cost of a difficult and expensive war with the Sultan of Mysore. Most important of all in many ways, France was in no financial position to face a long war. By 1780, therefore, the desire for peace was strong in Paris; and during that year both Maurepas, the most influential of all the French ministers, and Necker, the Controller-General of Finance, made unofficial approaches to the British government. The negotiations of 1782–83, which ended the war, were conducted on the French side under the ever more imminent threat of financial collapse.

But the thirteen mainland colonies in North America were irretrievably lost. Even without the intervention of France and her allies their enormous area, their remoteness, their self-sufficiency in food and the great difficulties of moving a regular army within them, would have made them very hard to subdue. Britain's preoccupations in Europe made them unconquerable. With the surrender of Lord Cornwallis's army at Yorktown in October 1781 (a surrender compelled by France's temporary command of the sea in American waters) their independence was an accomplished fact. As late as the summer of 1782, in the peace negotiations at Paris, the British Prime Minister, Lord Shelburne, hoped that it might be possible to reunite them with the mother-country by conceding a high degree of self-government. It soon became clear that he had mistaken the temper of the colonists and that such ideas were totally impracticable. The Treaty of Versailles of September 1783, which recognized the independence of the thirteen colonies, also returned to France some of the West Indian islands she had lost in 1763 and her former strongholds in Senegal. Spain recovered Minorca (which had been taken from Britain by a French expedition in 1782) and East Florida. The United Provinces, whose part in the war had been almost uniformly unsuccessful, signed a definitive treaty with Britain only in 1784, at the cost of a promise not to prevent British

[1] A. M. Arnould, *Système maritime et politique des Européens pendant le dix-huitième siècle* (Paris, 1797), p. 322.

subjects from freely navigating the seas which the Dutch claimed to control around Indonesia.

Britain's influence and prestige in 1783 were perhaps lower than at any other moment in modern history. France had had her revenge, and had helped to create a new independent nation with unprecedented potentialities; but at a cost which ruined her finances and fatally undermined her system of government.

The colonial struggles of the eighteenth century faced both Britain and France with strategic problems of a hitherto unknown magnitude. Both States were, or were struggling to become, world powers. Both therefore had to work out a world strategy, at least of an embryonic kind. Both had to face the difficulties created by the interaction of events in Europe with those in America or the East.

In each country hostility to the other remained a dominant political emotion during this period. In France, however, its effects were tempered and diluted by a number of factors. Anti-British feeling had there to compete with an even more deeply ingrained hostility to Austria and the Habsburgs, at least in the first half of the century. It was further modified by the admiration which many educated Frenchmen increasingly felt for British intellectual life and constitutional methods. Above all the fact that France possessed long land frontiers in Europe, that she had a well-marked tradition of territorial expansion there and that her people settled overseas only reluctantly and in small numbers, meant that colonial expansion never possessed for her the exclusive and dominant interest which it had for many Englishmen.

In Britain anti-French feeling was more profound than anti-British feeling on the other side of the Channel. This was because France offered a more serious threat to Britain than Britain ever could to France. The latter's intrinsic strength was in most respects far superior to that of her rival. Her population was about three times as large as that of Britain and her taxable capacity, though no French government during this period could tap it effectively, was greater than the British one. Of more direct importance, she possessed a better and far larger army than Britain. As early as the war of 1672–78 Louis XIV had managed for a time to maintain under arms about 400,000 men, a force greater than any seen since the break-up of the Roman Empire in the fourth century. By contrast the Duke of Marlborough himself argued in the early eighteenth century that Britain could not afford to keep the total strength of her armed forces for any length of time at a figure of more than 70,000. This was certainly a gross underestimate: by the end of the War of the Grand Alliance, in 1697, the army alone had risen to about 90,000 men. Nevertheless the military inferiority of Britain to France continued to be marked. In 1760 the total number of soldiers voted by Parliament, including the very large foreign levies then in British pay, amounted to 170,000. This was the greatest exertion of British military strength at any time before the 1790s; but even so it represented little more than half the number of men then at the disposal of Louis XV's generals. During the Seven Years War an effort was made to provide more adequate forces for home defence by the passage of an important Militia Bill in 1757. Two years later, however, at the height of one of the most serious invasion threats of the century, only a little over 17,000 men had been raised under this very unpopular Act; and of these only a little over 6,000 were ready for service.

France's material strength threatened Britain's position in two ways. It might allow her to establish her hegemony on the continent, destroying British influence there and perhaps even excluding much of British trade from Europe by the organization of a 'Continental System' on the lines later attempted by Napoleon. Suggestions for action of this kind were put forward by more than one French writer during the Seven Years War. Much more serious, France, once in control of the Channel for a few hours, might invade and overrun Britain without encountering effective resistance. The successes won by a few thousand untrained and poorly equipped Highlanders during the Jacobite rebellion of 1745–46 lent point to such fears. Moreover the existence until the middle of the century of Jacobitism as a force to be reckoned with, at least in Scotland, was an additional inducement to French statesmen to risk a bold stroke against Britain, even across seas which the French fleet controlled imperfectly or not at all. It is not surprising therefore to find that British governments during this period were frequently alarmed by the spectre of French invasion and that their policies were influenced by their alarm. In 1739 Walpole, at the outbreak of war with Spain, was unwilling to send a really powerful fleet to the West Indies because of fears of this kind; while the capture of Minorca by the French in 1756 was made possible by the justified refusal of the government, for the same reason, to dispatch a large squadron to the Mediterranean.

None of the numerous plans and suggestions put forward in France during this period for an invasion of Britain had any success. Some were impeded by bad luck. Thus in March 1744 the Maréchal de Saxe had actually begun to embark troops in the Austrian Netherlands for an attack on England (with which France was still officially at peace) when bad weather brought his activities to a halt. Other invasion schemes failed because of lack of determination in their leaders—for example the small-scale landing made at Torbay in 1690, at a time when the French fleet was in control of the Channel. Others were stultified by a combination of both factors—above all in 1779, when the temporary superiority of the French and Spanish fleets in the Channel was not utilized and was soon lost when they were weakened by disease.

The chances of successful French invasion were enormously reduced by the strength of the British navy and its normal superiority to that of France. This more than anything else explains British's victory over her opponents in the colonial struggles of 1739–63. In no eighteenth century war was her navy effectively inferior for any length of time to those of France and Spain combined. Moreover its superiority to its rivals tended to increase as each of the struggles of this period progressed. This was partly because it lost fewer ships in battle than those of France and Spain (though since it spent much more time at sea it lost more by wreck, fire and other accidents). It was also because, by maintaining an effective blockade of French and to a lesser extent of Spanish ports, it could make it difficult for these countries to import naval stores from the Baltic. More important still, by reducing the activities of their merchant marines it restricted the supply of trained seamen on which their fleets could draw.

The responsibilities which fell on the British navy were extremely heavy. The country depended on it not merely for physical security from foreign attack but also for the maintenance of much of its economy and above all of its financial system. It was not until the 1770s that Britain began to be a net importer of food; but throughout this period much of her economic strength depended on her ability to import and export freely and to act as an entrepôt from which colonial and Oriental goods could be distributed over much of Europe. Any sustained interruption of her trade might well bring down in ruins the complex and sophisticated structure of public finance which was normally one of her greatest assets. In general the navy rose to its responsibilities with success, except to some extent during the War of American Independence. The French fleet, normally unable to challenge Britain openly for control of the seas, tended increasingly as the century went on to fall back on defensive tactics, on commerce-raiding by individual ships or small squadrons (see p. 195). This policy, though it sometimes caused much loss to British merchants, depended for ultimate success on France's ability to send out her fleets and win a clear-cut victory at sea, an ability which she never possessed. The result was that the outbreak of an Anglo-French war was usually followed by a temporary drop in Britain's seaborne trade as French cruisers and privateers got to work, but that this in turn gave way to a steady rise in both imports and exports towards the end of each struggle, as British naval superiority was increasingly asserted. Simultaneously French seaborne trade would fall, sometimes as in 1747–48 and 1759–62 to a mere trickle. France, however, was far less vulnerable to pressure of this kind than Britain. She could lose much of her fleet and trade and still remain one of the greatest European States, as she showed in the second half of the Seven Years War. Similar losses would reduce Britain almost overnight to the position of a second-rate power.

British superiority at sea had also profound repercussions on events in the British and French colonies. It meant above all that France could be prevented from translating her material superiority in Europe into a corresponding superiority overseas. She might possess enormous armies; but unless they, or adequate parts of them, could be transported to Canada, the West Indies or India, their existence could have little direct bearing on the outcome of the colonial struggle. In fact British seapower made it impossible for them ever to be deployed effectively outside Europe. In the Seven Years War, the real crisis of the Anglo-French conflict, very few of the 300,000 men whom France had under arms in Europe were sent overseas. The only French colonial expeditions of any significance during the war, those of Montcalm to Canada and Lally-Tollendal to India, mustered between them only about 10,000 fighting men. By contrast Britain had as early as 1757 over 70,000 regular troops in her North American colonies alone. Moreover some French possessions, at least in the West Indies, were very vulnerable to blockade—much more so than France herself. This fact was never adequately exploited, largely because British commanders in the West Indies were chronically short of light vessels suitable for blockade purposes. Nevertheless many French West Indian islands were prepared for British conquest by this means, both in the War of the Austrian Succession and the Seven Years War. More than once (notably in 1747–48) more rigorous and effective use of blockade might have led to the surrender through starvation of all France's possessions in the area.

Naval power was thus by far the sharpest weapon at Britain's disposal in her colonial struggles with France. Was it by itself sufficient to ensure victory? Could Britain, in spite of her great inferiority in numbers and resources, defeat her rival in single combat, unsupported and unencumbered by European allies?

The vast majority of Englishmen hoped and believed that the answer to both questions was 'Yes'. It was widely felt throughout this period that Britain should as far as possible fight only at sea and for objectives of some commercial value, potential if not actual. In other words, public opinion was heavily biased against 'continental' and in favour of 'American' or 'colonial' warfare. 'Sea war, no Continent, no subsidy,' wrote the Duke of Newcastle in July 1755 at one of the most critical moments of the Anglo-French struggle, 'is almost the universal language. It would be betraying the King to say otherwise, or to conceal the truth.'[1] For this attitude, with its undertones of hostility to and suspicion of Europe, there were various explanations. In part it was merely the result of the contempt and dislike for foreigners which was now more deep-rooted in Britain, or at least in England, than in most other parts of the continent. To a large extent it was also the product of a natural desire to wage war as cheaply as possible. Experience showed that continental allies had usually to be encouraged or bribed by British subsidies before they were willing, or sometimes able, to set their armies in motion against France. Sometimes it was necessary, to make sure of their support in wartime, to pay them subsidies in time of peace as a kind of retaining fee, a practice which was fiercely opposed by the majority of both politicians and public opinion in Britain. Moreover bitter experience showed that many of the rulers on whom subsidies were lavished, especially many of the smaller German princes, failed to justify the hopes placed in them or to make a military effort commensurate with the sums they received. Naval warfare on the other hand, it was widely believed, could be made to pay for itself, since it involved the capture of valuable enemy prizes and led to the acquisition of lucrative colonies and trading-posts. Finally the idea of maintaining the balance of power in Europe, which underlay much of the policy of subsidizing continental States against France, made little appeal to the ordinary Englishman. Many politicians, especially if they were out of office, tended to challenge the validity of the whole concept of a balance of power and to allege that it was being used by the government as a pretext to squander British money on foreign princes.

Opposition to 'continental' warfare was always stronger in Parliament

[1] C. W. Eldon, *England's Subsidy Policy towards the Continent during the Seven Years War* (Philadelphia, 1938), p. 17.

and among the general public than in the Cabinet. In the vital decades of the 1740s and 1750s ministers such as Henry Pelham (First Commissioner of the Treasury, 1743–54 and in many ways the most important influence in British politics during these years) tended to share the popular prejudice against continental entanglements; but others—Lord Carteret, the Duke of Newcastle and eventually Pitt himself—saw the advantages to be gained by pinning down a large part of France's energies and resources in Europe. 'A naval force,' wrote Newcastle in 1749, 'tho' carried never so high, unsupported with even the appearance of a force upon the Continent, will be of little use . . . France will outdo us at sea when they [sic] have nothing to fear by land . . . I have always maintained that our marine should protect our alliances upon the Continent; and they, by diverting the expense of France, enable us to maintain our superiority at sea.'[1] This was the formula which, backed by the energy and vision of Pitt, brought unprecedented and unrepeatable victory in 1759–62.

Moreover Britain could not in practice withdraw completely from Europe, however much she might wish to do so. She was linked to the continent, most unfortunately in the eyes of nearly all Englishmen, by the fact that her ruler was also, as Elector of Hanover, ruler of an important German State. Under George I and George II the connexion with Hanover was almost universally unpopular in England, and understandably so. The fact that both were interested in the Electorate at least as much as in Britain meant that British policy was often influenced by their desire to safeguard or extend their German territories. Thus Anglo-Russian relations in the last years of Peter I were affected very much for the worse by George I's territorial ambitions in North Germany and by Hanoverian fears of the Tsar's influence there. A projected Anglo-Prussian alliance in 1740 was stultified by George II's jealousy of Frederick II, while in the following year he seriously disorganized British policy by making an agreement for the neutrality of Hanover in the struggle which was then beginning (see p. 253).

More serious, the fact that Hanover was exposed to French attack could be used in wartime to put pressure on Britain and perhaps to extort concessions from her when peace was made. If the Electorate were overrun by France, Britain might be compelled, in order to recover it, to return conquests made overseas at the cost of British blood and money. But to abandon Hanover to its fate, though most Englishmen in their hearts would have been happy to do so, was hardly practical

[1] Yorke, op. cit., vol. II, p. 23.

politics. Such a step was certain to be most violently opposed by the king. Moreover the loss of the Electorate would greatly damage British prestige, while control of it would greatly strengthen France's influence in the Holy Roman Empire and Northern Europe. Thus Hanover could neither be safely abandoned nor easily defended. As long as it was associated with Britain, even by the somewhat slender bond of a personal union, British governments were willy-nilly involved in the politics of Germany. It was therefore impossible during this period for Britain to fight a purely naval and colonial war against France unless France herself were willing to fight on these terms.

Both in 1740 and in 1755 it seemed that this might be the case. In the former year Cardinal Fleury was actively preparing to support Spain in a struggle of this kind against Britain. In the latter British aggression at sea, though it led to proposals for a French attack on the Electorate, produced no immediate threat to Hanover. In neither case, however, did France in the event confine her war effort to the oceans and the colonies. By 1741 she had become involved in a struggle to destroy Habsburg power in Central Europe; and from 1756 onwards she played a part, though an ineffective one, in efforts to partition Prussia. To many French statesmen action in Europe still seemed the most effective means of redressing the balance, otherwise favourable to Britain, at sea and in America.

The disastrous experience of the Seven Years War shook this view severely. The maintenance in western Germany of a powerful French army, the payment to German princes of very large French subsidies, did little or nothing to strengthen France's position in the negotiations of 1761–63 or to reduce the losses which she suffered by the Treaty of Paris. The idea that Britain's colonial supremacy might be weakened by French action in Europe was not, however, abandoned. The Duc de Choiseul, for example, argued at the end of 1765 that in any future war with her France should seize the United Provinces, which could be set off, when it came to peacemaking, against any further losses of French territory overseas. He asserted that he would have proposed this course of action in 1763 if peace had not been made in that year. To the Comte de Vergennes, on the other hand, such ideas made little appeal. More influenced than almost any other leading statesman of the century by the humanitarian and pacifist aspects of the Enlightenment, he regarded another conflict with Britain as inevitable, and as necessary to weaken her preponderant position in the overseas trade and expansion of Europe. But he did not believe that France should gain territory in

Europe. Throughout his years as Foreign Minister (1774–87) he worked for peace and stability on the continent. The result was that the Anglo-French war of 1778–83 was the only one of the century which did not involve large-scale land warfare in Europe (apart from the 'great siege' of Gibraltar in 1779–82). For once French resources were not diverted to the Rhine, the Netherlands or Italy. This, combined with the help of Spain, the Dutch and the American rebels, allowed Vergennes to achieve his object. By the end of the struggle he had reduced Britain's power and prestige and established, as he hoped, the basis for a more stable relationship between her and France. The misgivings of New-castle and other British statesmen about their country's ability to win a purely naval and colonial war against France had been justified, though under conditions which were not likely to recur.

XIII

Europe and the Outside World

To the average European during the eighteenth century colonies were chiefly areas in which the commerce of the mother-country could develop. They were an outlet for trade, a source of raw materials, above all those which the mother-country could not produce for herself, and a market for manufactured goods. They were not primarily receptacles for surplus population or a gratification of national pride, far less the embryos of new independent States.

All the imperial powers had now embodied these ideas in complex legislation aimed at making the colonies complement and support the economy of the mother-country and thus contribute to the creation of an economically unified empire. The best-known of these bodies of legislation is the Navigation System in England. Originating with the Navigation Ordinance passed by the Commonwealth government in 1651, it was rapidly extended and consolidated, notably in 1663 and 1673. Though eighteenth-century statesmen altered and added to it in

BIBLIOGRAPHY. F. Mauro, *L'Expansion européenne, 1600–1870* (2nd ed.; Paris, 1967) and J. H. Parry, *Trade and Dominion: The European Oversea Empires in the Eighteenth Century* (London, 1971) are the most satisfactory general studies; G. Williams, *The Expansion of Europe in the Eighteenth Century* (London, 1966) is also useful. The ideas about the value and justifiability of colonial expansion current in the two most rapidly expanding European States can be studied in K. E. Knorr, *British Colonial Theories, 1570–1850* (Toronto, 1944) and C. L. Lokke, *France and the Colonial Question, 1763–1801* (New York, 1932). The former in particular gives references to a great mass of eighteenth-century printed material. The expansion overseas of the other States of Western Europe can be followed in detail in the somewhat old-fashioned C. de Lannoy and H. Vander Linden, *Histoire de l'expansion coloniale des peuples européens*; there are two volumes, *Portugal et Espagne* (Brussels-Paris, 1907) and *Néerlande et Danemarck* (Paris-Brussels, 1911). J. Godechot and R. R. Palmer, 'Le problème de l'Atlantique du XVIIIe au XXe siècle', in *X Congresso Internazionale di Scienze Storiche, Relazioni* (Florence, 1955), vol. v, is stimulating. The economic value of colonial possessions to their owners is discussed in E. E. Williams, *Capitalism and Slavery* (Chapel Hill, 1944), an interesting book various ways they made little fundamental change in it. This group of laws (for which, it must be repeated, parallels existed in every State with overseas possessions) aimed at giving the staple products of the colonies, such as sugar or tobacco, as far as possible a monopoly of the British market. In return the colonists were to supply goods (mainly raw materials and foodstuffs) which Britain could not herself produce. Certain valuable colonial products, the so-called 'enumerated commodities', were to be exported only to the mother-country (the severity of this provision tended to be modified as time went on, notably by the removal of sugar from the list in 1739). Trade between Britain and her colonies was to be carried on only in British or colonial ships and foreigners excluded as far as possible from commercial contacts with British possessions overseas. The system, at least at the time of its creation, had a certain symmetry and logicality and was never designed merely as an instrument of colonial exploitation. Throughout this period, in spite of conflicting pressures and propaganda from many different interest groups, British governments and public opinion adhered fairly steadily to its basic principles, though until the 1760s laws embodying them were often very poorly enforced in the colonies.

The value of a colony was therefore determined mainly by its commercial potentialities. There was a strong tendency to regard the wealthy islands of the Caribbean, or slave-trading stations in West Africa, or commercial bases in India or South-East Asia, as more important than great overseas territorial possessions, most of which made a less striking and immediate contribution to the wealth of the mother-country. Tropical or subtropical colonies might even be regarded as more valuable than her territory in Europe. Thus in 1738 a pamphleteer argued that every British settler in the West Indies, by the British goods he consumed and the employment he gave to British shipping, contributed twenty times as much to the national wealth as he would at home.[1]

[1] J. Bennett, *Two Letters ... on the Sugar Colonies and Trade* (London, 1738), p. 55. Forty years earlier Charles Davenant had claimed that one man settled in Virginia or the Carolinas was as profitable to Britain as seven who remained at home: *Discourses on the Public Revenues and the Trade of England* (London, 1698), vol. II, p. 224.

which overstates its case, and H. Furber, *John Company at Work* (Cambridge Mass., 1948). The growth of the British empire in India can be followed in the *Cambridge History of the British Empire*, vol. V (Cambridge, 1929), while P. J. Marshall, 'British expansion in India in the eighteenth century; a historical revision', *History*, vol. LX (1975) is a stimulating short analysis. The 'swing to the East' in the imperial interests of Britain and France in the 1770s and 1780s

Four decades later in September 1779, at one of the most critical moments in Britain's history, George III argued that 'our [West Indian] Islands must be defended even at the risk of an invasion of this Island. If we lose our Sugar Islands it will be impossible to raise money to continue the war.'[1]

These very high contemporary estimates of the degree to which Britain (as distinct from individual Englishmen or Scots) profited from her West Indian possessions were often exaggerated. The tariff preference given in the British market to sugar from the British islands meant that the consumer paid higher prices than he need have done; and the capital attracted by these preferences into sugar production in the Caribbean could probably often have earned higher returns in some other field, especially if the cost of defending these colonies is set off against the profits made. Nevertheless there is no doubt of the extent of the British economic stake in these islands: in the years immediately before the American Revolution there were about £37 million of British money invested in the West Indies. Moreover in both Britain and France the tendency to overvalue the sugar islands was strengthened by the loss of their main colonies of settlement, actual or potential— French Canada and Louisiana in the Seven Years War, the British mainland colonies in America two decades later. These losses made small overseas possessions of purely commercial value appear not only the most lucrative but also the most manageable type of colony; so that the idea of an empire as a mechanism for the development and protection of trade was perhaps more firmly established at the end of the century than ever before. 'It would be making a great mistake', wrote the French Minister of Marine to the Governor of Martinique in 1765, 'to think of our colonies as French provinces separated only by the sea

---

[1] *Correspondence of George III*, ed. Sir J. Fortescue (London, 1927), vol. IV. No. 2773.

is well discussed in V. T. Harlow, *The Founding of the Second British Empire*, vol. I (London, 1952). The very interesting subject of Chinese intellectual and artistic influences on eighteenth-century Europe is well analysed in A. Reichwein, *China and Europe* (London-New York, 1925), W. W. Appleton, *A Cycle of Cathay* (New York, 1951), and more recently in H. Honour, *Chinoiserie: the vision of Cathay* (London, 1961); while H. N. Fairchild, *The Noble Savage* (New York, 1928) and M. Kraus, 'America and the Utopian ideal in the eighteenth century', *Mississippi Valley Historical Review*, vol. XXII (1936) deal with different aspects of the influence of America on European thinking. The growing importance of the outside world in European intellectual life is also discussed in a number of the works mentioned in the Bibliography to the next chapter.

from the mother-country. They are absolutely nothing but commercial establishments.' Two decades later another French official made the same point more tersely—'nothing need be considered but trade; that is the real mine of wealth'.[1]

Such ideas were encouraged by the fact that the trade of all the great maritime powers with their colonies was increasing rapidly during the century, more rapidly than their overseas trade in general. Thus commerce with America made up 19 per cent (by value) of all British overseas trade in 1715, but 34 per cent in 1785. For France the corresponding figures are 13 per cent and 28 per cent (though in this case most of the increase was concentrated in the two decades after 1763). In the same way Britain's trade with Africa and Asia, which represented 7 per cent of her total commerce in 1715, rose even more spectacularly to 19 per cent in 1785. For France, defeated in the struggle for power in India, the increase was merely from 5 per cent to 6 per cent. In other words by the end of this period over half of all Britain's foreign trade and over a third of that of France was being done with areas outside Europe. The same position can be seen in Portugal, which by the end of the century carried on almost half of all her trade with America, Africa and Asia.[2] Europe was thus becoming less self-contained economically than ever before. An increasing proportion of her resources in manpower and capital was now employed in long-distance colonial trade. The distinction in wealth between the States of Western Europe which had important colonial possessions, and those of Germany, Italy, Scandinavia and Central Europe which had not, was becoming more apparent; while the efforts of the latter to redress the balance (for example by the creation of the Ostend Company in 1722 or of the Swedish and Danish East India Companies) had little success. Some countries, above all Britain and Portugal, now looked outwards towards America, Africa or the East, rather than inwards towards Europe. They were thus ceasing to be European States in the fullest sense of the term.

From the western hemisphere Europe received during the eighteenth century a wide range of commodities, most of them in steadily increasing quantities, in exchange for her textiles, hardware, tools, paper, glass and other manufactured goods. From Canada came furs which were valuable in themselves and also formed the basis of an important hat-

---

[1] Saintoyant (see Bibliography, p. 289), vol. II, pp. 439, 446.
[2] These figures are taken from Godechot and Palmer (see Bibliography, p. 317), pp. 196–7. Slightly different ones can be found in W. Sombart, *Der Moderne Kapitalismus*, 4th ed. (Munich-Leipzig, 1921), vol. II, Pt. 2, pp. 961–5.

making industry. From Newfoundland came inexhaustible supplies of salt fish. This formed a staple export to the Catholic countries of the Mediterranean, where there was a demand which neither local supplies nor Norwegian stock-fish could satisfy. The New England colonies, however—Massachusetts, Connecticut, Rhode Island and others— though in many ways the most highly developed overseas possessions of any European State, produced little that was of use to Britain or to Europe in general. They were therefore criticized and suspected by many publicists. Undoubtedly they provided Britain with a very important market for manufactured goods; but they had few products that the mother-country could profitably import. As a result, it was calculated by one contemporary, Britain had in 1700–73 exported to them nearly £14 million more than she received from them. They sent much timber to the West Indies; but a long series of efforts to make them a source of naval stores had disappointing results. They exported considerable quantities of provisions and horses, but again only to the West Indies; and their important shipbuilding industry gave them the means of carrying on a large-scale illegitimate trade with the colonies of France or Spain, even when Britain was at war with these countries. Above all the tentative industrial development of these colonies in the second half of the eighteenth century made it clear that they were now beginning to compete with as much as to supplement the economy of the mother-country. Right down to the American Revolution New England continued to fit awkwardly into the British colonial system.

Farther south, Virginia and Maryland produced large quantities of tobacco; but in the eighteenth century they failed to maintain the prosperity and rapid development which had marked the first generations of their existence. Their planters thus became increasingly dependent on the British factors who marketed their crops and supplied them with manufactured goods and capital. Farther south again, however, in South Carolina and Georgia, the production of rice and indigo was increasing rapidly. The former was exported on a considerable scale to the Mediterranean and the latter used in the textile industries of Europe.

Almost all the islands of the West Indies based their economies on the production of sugar, varied in some cases by the cultivation of coffee, ginger, indigo, cochineal or cotton. These crops were produced by slave labour used on a very large scale; and a steady supply of slaves at reasonable prices was essential to the economic life of the area. This meant that the economic connexion between the Caribbean and the slave-producing (or rather slave-exporting) parts of West Africa was very close. With the great slaving ports of Europe—Liverpool, Bristol and Nantes—these two areas formed the corners of the so-called 'triangular trade' which bulked so large in the pattern of West European activity overseas in the eighteenth century. This trade could take a variety of shapes. In its simplest form it involved the export from Europe to West Africa of 'trade goods' such as textiles, firearms, beads and mirrors; the purchase with them of slaves; and the sale of these in the West Indies for sugar or sugar products such as rum or molasses. The slave trade was thus one in which the interval between investment and return was long. It was also a risky trade—slaves were not always easy to come by in West Africa and losses by disease on the trans-atlantic passage could be heavy. As a result it fell more and more in every country in the later eighteenth century into the hands of a relatively small number of large merchant houses. It remained through-out this period, however, an important branch of European commerce, and one which bulked large in the calculations of governments.[1] It achieved this position not merely because it gave employment to ships and seamen and provided a rather minor outlet for manufactured goods; but above all because it was the basis of the whole economic life of the Caribbean and the southern colonies of North America, and to a lesser extent of that of Brazil and some parts of Spanish America as well.

Europe's trade with Latin America was quantitatively smaller than that with North America or the West Indies. It none the less remained of great importance. It brought to Europe dyestuffs and fine woods for cabinet-making from Central America and growing quantities of hides from the La Plata area. More important, it supplied her with gold and silver, as it had done for over two centuries; and from the 1730s onwards with a still more exciting though less important commodity, diamonds from Brazil. From Cadiz and Lisbon the precious metals of South America were diffused over Europe, mainly by British, French, Genevan or German merchants or bankers, partly by smuggling. Broadly speaking France relied for her supplies of bullion during this period mainly upon silver from the Spanish colonies, Britain mainly though by no means entirely upon gold from Brazil. The importance of

[1] It has been estimated that 610,000 slaves were imported into Jamaica in 1700–86, and that the total import to all British colonies in 1680–1786 was well over 2 million: F. W. Pitman, *The Economic Development of the British West Indies, 1700–1763* (New Haven, 1917), pp. 67, 69–70, 79.

precious metals from America indeed far transcended the political boundaries of Europe. They played a great part in European trade with China and until fairly late in the century with India; while the Austrian *thalers* or *pataques* which became the most important form of currency in the Near East in the second half of this period were coined from silver imported from the western hemisphere.

The position was sharply different where Europe's trade with Africa and the Far East was concerned. In America by the last decades of the century the number of European settlers (or settlers of European or part-European extraction) could be numbered in millions. In Asia resident Europeans were counted only in thousands, in some areas only in hundreds or even dozens. In British India there were in the 1780s about 5,000 of them protected by some 20,000 European soldiers; while in the princely States and the small settlements of the other European powers there were perhaps 2,000 more. At Canton, to which practically all European trade with China was confined, there were about 900–1,000 in 1720 and about 4,500 in 1785; but this was a constantly shifting merchant community without roots in the country. In 1745 there were only ninety resident European Portuguese (in a total population of 13,000) at Maçao, which had been a Portuguese possession for two centuries. Russia's vast Siberian colony, the only part of Asia in which large-scale white settlement was a practical possibility, remained throughout this period thinly peopled and neglected. Tentative efforts by Catherine II to increase its Russian population had little result, partly because of her unwillingness to see the existing social structure of European Russia weakened by a large exodus of peasants to the east. In Africa there were European trading establishments in the seaports of the Barbary States and Egypt, a few Spanish strongholds such as Ceuta and Oran on the coasts of Morocco and Algeria, slave-trading bases in the Gulf of Guinea, and decaying Portuguese fortresses on the coasts of Angola and East Africa (the most important of these, Mombasa, was finally lost to the Arabs of Oman in 1730). Apart from the Dutch colony at the Cape of Good Hope which was beginning to show important expansive tendencies (it had a white population of about 12,000 by the 1750s) there was no permanent European settlement. The majority of Africans still ended their lives without having seen a white man or been influenced by European ideas or techniques.

Again America provided a great and rapidly growing market for European goods while Asia and Africa consumed only small quantities of them: the Asian countries, above all China, because they were self-sufficient and unattracted by what Europe had to offer, Africa because she was so poor and inaccessible. Finally and most important of all, in Asia alone of the non-European parts of the world were there indigenous States capable of withstanding serious European pressure with the slightest hope of success.

The influence of these facts on Europe's trade with Africa and the East was immense. They meant in the first place that it was much smaller in volume than that with America. The British East India Company sent an average of only eleven ships a year to India in the early part of the century and only twenty a year in its middle decades. In spite of the legal monopoly which it enjoyed of Anglo-Chinese as of Anglo-Indian trade it sent only seven ships to Canton in 1751, only eight in 1776, and only twenty-one in 1789 when this aspect of its activities was increasing very rapidly. These figures, which are higher than the corresponding ones for any other European country engaged in these branches of commerce, contrast sharply with the hundreds of British ships which sailed westwards each year across the Atlantic. (In the 1730s it was claimed that trade with Jamaica employed 300 British merchant ships and that that with the little island of Barbados alone gave employment to a thousand seamen.) In the same way the Dutch East India Company sent on the average only about twenty-nine ships each year to all its eastern possessions in the first half of the century, a number which if anything fell slightly from the 1750s onwards; by contrast trade with the small Dutch South American colony of Surinam alone employed by the 1760s an annual average of sixty to seventy ships.

European trade with the East also differed from that with the Americas in that it was for the most part in the hands of a number of privileged trading companies. These were semi-official bodies which enjoyed great political influence, and their activities are fundamental to the history of Europe's relations with Asia in the seventeenth and eighteenth centuries. Companies of this kind were by no means unknown in trade with America. The Spanish government created a series of them during this period, of which the Caracas Company of 1728 was the most important and successful. Pombal made similar experiments in the regulation of Portuguese trade with Brazil. Nevertheless they had never in transatlantic commerce anything approaching the importance which they possessed in that with Asia. The British East India Company experienced during this period perhaps the strangest and most romantic turn of fortune which has ever overtaken any trading organization.

From the 1750s onwards it was drawn, without any conscious plan and often against the will of its directors in London, into military conquest and territorial expansion on an immense scale. Within a few years the enterprise of its servants made it the dominant power in a large area of South India and, more important, in the province of Bengal.

These developments, it must be stressed, were unforeseen and un-desired so far as both the Company and the British government were concerned. It was not until the last years of the century that both ceased to regard the British role in India as a primarily commercial one to be sustained by the use only of a minimum of military and naval force. Sometimes, therefore, opportunities of territorial gain were deliberately rejected: in both 1760 and 1784 areas in South India which had been occupied during struggles with native rulers were returned when these ended. Nevertheless by the 1760s the East India Company was ceasing, at least so far as its activities in India itself were concerned, to be primarily a trading organization. British pressure on the Indian States, partly to counter the French threat in the middle years of the century and partly in a simple quest for greater commercial privileges, was now undermining and destroying some of them—first Bengal in the decade after the battle of Plassey, then Oudh and the Carnatic. The economic basis of the Company's activities was ceasing to be trade and becoming the collection of taxes in the areas it dominated; while by lending money to local rulers and sometimes also supplying them with troops it was being drawn step by step into deeper territorial and political involvement in India. The personal interests of its representatives, war-like soldiers, ambitious governors, avaricious creditors of Indian potentates, pulled it constantly in the same direction—a fact of real importance since the very slow communications with England inevit-ably gave these representatives a great deal of independent initiative. Yet the Company was slow to transform itself into an effective political and administrative organism. For nearly a generation it remained an ineffective hybrid, unable to put its finances on a satisfactory basis, to make the large revenues it drew from taxation cover its administrative and commercial expenses, or to prevent a minority of its servants from making fortunes by dubious means. Not until the reforms under-taken by Lord Cornwallis in Bengal in the 1790s did it begin to lay the foundations of the great administrative structure of nineteenth-century British India.

To the French *Compagnie des Indes Orientales* the period brought a very different fate. Defeated by its British rival and heavily in debt, it went into liquidation in 1769. Revived in 1785, it continued to maintain a narrow foothold in India until its remaining factories fell to the British during the revolutionary wars and, freed from the cares of administering large territories, probably made a small but genuine profit. As a serious factor in the history of India, however, it had ceased to count. It sent one or two ships to Canton each year, and in 1778 a French consulate was established there to protect its trade; but here too it was decisively inferior to the British company. The Danish Asiatic Company and the Swedish East India Company managed to prolong their existence throughout the century and to maintain small trading-stations on the Indian coast. Neither had great economic importance and neither attempted to become a political or military force in the East. Nor had the Royal Philippine Company, founded by Charles III of Spain in 1785 on the ruins of the old Caracas Company, any great significance.

On the other hand the Dutch East India Company, the most success-ful trading organization of the seventeenth century, in some ways increased its importance in this period. Like its British counterpart it found itself drawn almost insensibly into the assumption of political control over wide and wealthy territories. In Java, the centre of its power in the East, a long and complicated series of struggles in 1740–57 consolidated its position. One of the two main Javanese States, Mataram, became its vassal after 1743. A revolt against it in the other, Bantam, was suppressed in the 1750s. In 1765 a war with the native ruler of Ceylon ended in the fall of his capital and gave the company control of the main sugar-producing areas of the island. Efforts at expansion in the comparatively inhospitable islands of Borneo and Sumatra had less success.

Like the British company, however, the Dutch one tended to become less effective as a trading organization as its territorial power expanded. Its outlook was excessively monopolistic and restrictive (until the middle of the century all trade between different parts of the Dutch empire in the East had to pass through Java) and it aimed consistently at selling small quantities of colonial products in Europe at the highest possible price. In the seventeenth century it had deliberately restricted the production of spices and sugar in order to keep up prices. From the 1730s onwards it extended this policy to the newly introduced crop of coffee, the production of which in Java was rapidly increasing. The rigidity of its structure, the conservatism of its ideas and the growing competition of the more enterprising British company, made its financial position steadily more difficult. In the last years of its life, before its final collapse in 1795, it was being maintained in existence only by the indirect aid of the Dutch taxpayer.

Europe's imports from Asia were important, but in a somewhat different way from those which she drew from America. From the East, as from the West, came raw materials for her industries and foodstuffs for her people—cotton from Bengal and the Near East, raw silk from Persia and China, sugar and spices from the East Indies, tea from China. In addition came manufactured goods, the only ones which Europe imported on an appreciable scale—fine textiles from India, silks and porcelain from China. These imports were small in quantity but had a psychological and artistic importance out of all proportion to their bulk. From them thousands of Europeans who had never set foot in Asia derived their ideas (often very misleading ones) of the East. Their beauty and the craftsmanship they displayed stimulated European manufacturers to imitate and finally in some respects to surpass them.

The rulers of Western Europe were well aware of the advantages given them by their overseas trade and colonial possessions. In particular they realized that the wealth thus placed at their disposal gave them an important superiority over the large but relatively undeveloped countries of the east and central parts of the continent. 'The House of Austria,' wrote the Duc de Choiseul in 1760, 'Russia, the King of Prussia, are only second-rate States, since they can make war only when they are subsidised by the commercial powers.'[1] This was an exaggerated statement of the position. The events of the next generation were to show that it was not necessary to possess maritime strength or colonial territories in order to have great, even dominant, influence in Europe. Nevertheless the profits of trade and empire gave the colonial powers, Britain in particular, the means of buying allies and hiring armies on the continent in a way that would otherwise have been impossible.

Nor were the peoples concerned indifferent to the significance of their overseas possessions. In Britain indeed public opinion if anything exaggerated their value and was excessively sensitive to any possible threat to them, while regarding almost with indifference great territorial changes in Europe. The excitement aroused in the 1730s by Spanish 'depredations' in the Caribbean, or in 1770 by a Spanish threat to the Falkland Islands, contrasts strikingly with the apathy which greeted the first partition of Poland. In the United Provinces also, increasingly

[1] A. Bourguet, *Le Duc de Choiseul et l'alliance espagnole* (Paris, 1906), p. 159.

dominated as the century wore on by the psychology of 'safety and three per cent', the preservation of the country's commercial and colonial position seemed more important than that of a largely mythical balance of power in Europe. Even in France attention and interest which in the reign of Louis XIV had been concentrated almost entirely on the affairs of Europe was now being increasingly diverted towards events in America and the East.

Both governments and peoples, when they turned their eyes outside Europe, looked first of all to the Americas, particularly in the first half of the century. There were a number of reasons why the western hemisphere should attract so much more attention than Asia or Africa. As has been seen, trade with it was far more extensive than with any other part of the non-European world. It had been for nearly two centuries a recognized field of international rivalry, rivalry whose importance was increasing as Anglo-French conflicts became more acute. Moreover communications with America, slow and imperfect though they might be, were far more rapid and reliable than those with the East. It was possible for a well-informed Englishman or Frenchman to have a knowledge of events in Canada or the Caribbean which was not hopelessly out of date. By contrast news from India, still more from China or Indonesia, seemed to come almost from another planet.

So close were the human and intellectual contacts between Western Europe and America in the later eighteenth century that a certain parallelism is visible, if not in their political development at least in their political aspirations. In each continent can be seen an increasing effort to modernize and rationalize administrative and financial methods. This was exemplified in British America by the legislation of the 1760s which attempted to enforce a more rigorous application of the Navigation System, and in Europe by the growth of Enlightened Despotism. In each continent these changes were powerfully opposed by vested interests and local patriotism, forces which disrupted the British Empire in the 1770s and had almost disrupted that of the Habsburgs by 1790. In each the importance of the Press, and of public opinion organized and mobilized for political purposes, was increasing rapidly. In some respects at least an Atlantic civilization now existed, uniting Western Europe with North and to a lesser degree South America. The ocean, far from being a barrier to the movement of men and ideas, positively facilitated their transmission, for until the coming of railways travel was normally swifter by sea than by land. It was usually far easier for a man or an idea to go from London to Boston or Philadelphia than to

Constantinople or Moscow, or even Rome or Berlin.

Above all America was now the home of great numbers of emigrants from Western Europe; and conflicts there were decided in the main by forces recruited in the West European States. Campaigns on the Hudson or in the Antilles were fought by Englishmen or Frenchmen and might influence directly and immediately the lives of tens of thousands of English or French colonists. Campaigns in the Deccan or Bengal were fought largely by sepoys under European officers; they seemed to affect only the power and profits of two great trading companies.

The result of this concentration on the western hemisphere was that until quite late in this period no government in Europe devoted much attention to territorial expansion in Asia. Not until the 1760s did it become clear that a great Indian Empire had for some time been within the reach of both Britain and France, while until the end of the century the rapidly growing weakness of the Chinese Empire passed unnoticed in the West. By the last decades of this period, however, the indifference with which the British and French governments had hitherto contemplated the possibility of expansion in Asia was slowly beginning to be replaced by a more interested and acquisitive attitude. The victories of Clive and Coote in India showed their countrymen what could now be achieved, and stimulated France to seek elsewhere for compensations for what she had lost there. The result was what one historian has called a 'swing to the East' in the colonial and commercial activities of both States. This did not mean that Asia replaced America as the main focus of European overseas expansion; but from the 1760s onwards it received more attention than ever before from the governments and public opinion of these countries.

This rising interest in Eastern affairs showed itself in a number of ways. It contributed to a new burst of speculation about the possibility of discovering a north-west passage, a practicable sea route uniting the Atlantic and Pacific round the north coast of America. Of this the most important and enduring result was the discoveries made by Captain James Cook on his last voyage in 1776–79. It also stimulated a great deal of detailed survey and exploration work in the Pacific and Indian oceans: no less than ten hydrographic expeditions were sent from France to the East in 1784–89.

The new attitude also led to more serious attempts than ever before to extend European influence to the States of South-East Asia, hitherto almost untouched by it. In Burma the British East India Company held the port of Negrais for a few years in the 1750s; while a French shipyard was in operation at Rangoon for a decade after 1766. Warren Hastings, the greatest of all English proconsuls in India, made a short-lived effort to establish commercial relations with Cochin-China in 1778–79. In 1787 Louis XVI, by a treaty signed at Versailles, promised its ruler, who had been deposed two years earlier, help in recovering his throne. Much more important, however, was the active interest which was being taken in Paris from the 1770s onwards in the possibility of annexing Egypt. Wealthy, populous, strategically placed and easily defended, the country seemed ideally suited to compensate France for what she had lost in India and the Caribbean. The growing weakness of the Ottoman Empire made it easy to argue that France should take Egypt as part of a general partition of Turkish territories among the States of Europe. The abominable misgovernment of its rulers, the Mamluk Beys, who were in theory vassals of the Sultan, meant that the country would be easy to conquer. The result of all these factors was a series of proposals from 1770 onwards for a French seizure of Egypt, proposals which paved the way for the Napoleonic invasion of 1798.

None of these British or French attempts at expansion in the East had much immediate success outside India. The trading stations which were set up soon fell into decay. The treaties signed with native rulers were broken or never carried out. Nevertheless a change had taken place in the colonial policies of the two States during the last decades of the century, one with important implications for the future of large parts of the world. The preoccupation with America as the greatest, almost the only, area of European expansion overseas, which had marked their policies in the first half of this period, had now been tempered by a realization of the opportunities available in the East. For the first time in history it was becoming possible for one or two favoured nations to think of themselves not merely as European or even Atlantic powers but as potential world powers.

Europe's relations with the outside world in the eighteenth century affected not only her economy and politics but also her intellectual and artistic life. Exploration and colonization, the publication of increasingly full and detailed accounts of newly discovered lands, gave Europeans more clearly than ever before a sense of the immense variety of human habits and customs and of the difficulty of judging them fairly. In particular contact with China, with its wealth, its apparently stable and enlightened government and its enormously long recorded history, challenged many received ideas and stimulated the growth of new attitudes. China was disturbing to Europeans in a number of ways. Efforts to reconcile Chinese and biblical chronology undermined hitherto unchallenged assumptions about the past. By the middle of the seventeenth century scholars were being forced to accept a date for the beginning of Chinese history much earlier than the traditional one for the Flood: in other words China had been inhabited before the days of Noah and the Flood had been a merely local event. More important, the Chinese had evolved a workable and indeed highly successful system of morality which was completely secular and even political and which did not depend at all on religion in any normal European sense of the term. Such an achievement threw doubt on the hitherto virtually unchallenged assumption that revealed religion was the only source of true moral ideas and the only barrier between society and the anarchy which must follow a breakdown in morals. Moreover the separation of morality from religion opened the way to the dangerous idea that morals might be relative, not absolute, that each people might have a different moral system which suited its particular history and needs. Finally China appeared to Europeans as a striking illustration of the fact that religious tolerance did not necessarily weaken or divide a State. The *Dictionnaire historique et critique* of Pierre Bayle (1697), a work which was to become one of the foundations of the eighteenth-century Enlightenment, provides plentiful evidence of the way in which Chinese achievements could be used by critics of European religious obscurantism and intolerance to support their case.

Europe's interest in China had been developing throughout the seventeenth century, in its later decades with increasing speed. The first attempt at a translation of Confucius appeared in Paris in 1687. Ten years later the great German scholar Leibniz provided, in his *Novissima Sinica*, not merely a compendium of up-to-date information about the country (drawn largely from Jesuit sources) but also a powerful plea for further study of so fascinating and important a society. In the two or three generations which followed this interest grew in scope and intensity. The philosopher Christian Wolff, the most important figure in German intellectual life in the first half of the eighteenth century, was an admirer of the Chinese. François Quesnay, the leading figure in the first generation of Physiocrats, was deeply influenced by what he thought to be Chinese practice in government and economic life: his followers referred to him admiringly as 'the European Confucius'. In the arts the same process is visible. The forty-nine volumes of Chinese paintings presented to Louis XIV by a Jesuit missionary in

1697 were only the most striking example of an influx which by the early and middle decades of the eighteenth century was beginning to influence seriously such artists as Watteau and Boucher. The German architect Fischer von Erlach, in his *Entwurff einer historischen Architektur* (1721) provided 'the first appreciative account of Chinese architecture to be published in Europe'; and by the middle of the century many rulers were building new palaces, or at least 'porcelain rooms' in existing ones, in what they or their architects imagined to be the Chinese style. This admiration for things Chinese reached its climax in Voltaire's *Essai sur les Moeurs* (1756), which presented Confucius as an anticipation of the *philsophes* of the eighteenth century and used China's alleged virtues, often rather unscrupulously, as a stick with which to beat the France of his own day. It is true that there were important figures in European intellectual life who did not share this uncritical admiration. In particular the more radical wroters of the Enlightenment in France—Helvétius, d'Holbach, Diderot, and most notably Rousseau—were all in varying degrees negative in their attitude to China. Nevertheless the dominant tone of European comment on the country and its government was during this period favourable, sometimes very strongly so. This comment was, however, still based on very limited and inadequate knowledge. In particular the widespread belief that China was dominated by rational and enlightened thought, that mysticism and superstition had no foothold there, was wildly untrue. The translation of Confucius nevertheless supported this misconception; while the works of the much more mystical and equally influential Lao Tzu, which would have done much to explode it, remained inaccessible to European readers.

The influence on European intellectual life of the rest of Asia was relatively unimportant. Mohammed had already been introduced to Europe through the interest of the seventeenth century in Turkish and Arabic studies. Zoroaster was made accessible by the translation of the *Zend-Avesta* which the French scholar Anquetil du Perron published in 1771. From the 1780s onwards Charles Wilkins and Sir William Jones made available English translations of the main Hindu classics—the *Bhagavad-Ghita*, the *Hitopadesa* and the *Sakuntala*. But the Ottoman Empire, Persia and India had no great intellectual influence on Europe. This was partly because they were easier of access than China and thus less likely to be the object of flattering misconceptions; but also because, unlike China, they were all politically weak. Their civilization lacked the prestige and attractive power which strength alone could give.

The artistic life of Europe, as well as her philosophical and political ideas, was influenced by the example of China. Some of the leading painters of the century—Boucher, J. R. Cozens, above all Watteau—drew inspiration from Chinese art. Chinese or pseudo-Chinese motifs became common in European architecture from the middle decades of the century onwards, though they usually influenced the decoration of buildings rather than their basic design. The immense popularity of porcelain, which has been called 'the typical material of Rococo art', was a result of the import on a large scale of Chinese ceramics and of efforts to imitate them in Europe. On a lower level of importance the manufacture of wallpaper and the use of water-colours in painting were further results of Chinese influence. Never before had Europe received so powerful and varied an artistic stimulus from a country outside her own frontiers.

The intellectual influence of America on Europe in the eighteenth century was quite different from that of Asia. It dates, as a factor of importance, only from the achievement of independence by the British colonies. Until then, although its aboriginal inhabitants attracted a certain amount of attention (mainly as exemplifying the 'state of nature' which was still a commonplace of political thought) the western hemisphere had no influence in Europe comparable to that of China. The emergence in the early 1780s of an independent though as yet unstable confederation of the former British colonies completely revolutionized this position. It was realized by some far-seeing contemporaries that the new State possessed material potentialities of a kind unknown and unattainable in Europe. It would become, wrote one, 'the Arbitress of the commercial, and perhaps . . . the Mediatrix of peace, and of the political business of the world, . . . the principal leading Power in Europe, in regulating the courses of the rest, and in settling the common centre of all'.[1] Of greater immediate importance was the stimulus which successful revolution in America gave to the forces making for change in Europe. Events across the Atlantic seemed a victory for liberty and natural rights, for the ideas which were increasingly challenging the *ancien régime*. Moreover this victory appeared to have been won by an egalitarian, predominantly agricultural and hence 'natural' society over the forces of tradition and social conservatism. It therefore appealed powerfully to emotions and prejudices increasingly widespread among the educated classes of Europe. In Spain, where 'enlightened' ideas were relatively weak, and in parts of

[1] T. Pownall, *A Memorial . . . to the Sovereigns of Europe* (London, 1780), pp. 77, 92.

Italy, this appeal aroused little response. But in Great Britain, the Netherlands, France and even Germany, the revolution in America aroused vast interest. The immediacy of its impact, the extent to which it gave vicarious expression to resentments and tensions bottled up in the old world, are symbolized in the reaction of Count Vittorio Alfieri, perhaps the greatest poet then alive. When he dedicated his play *Bruto Primo* to Washington, or wrote in 1781–83 the five great odes grouped under the title of *America Libera,* he was not merely expressing approval of the rebellion of the thirteen colonies (of which he had no particular knowledge). He was rather throwing down the gauntlet to the government of his native State of Savoy-Piedmont, one of the most conservative in Europe.

For all these reasons the independence of British America was recognized clearly and immediately as something new, as a social and political experiment which was adding a new element to the collective experience of humanity. As such it aroused in the 1780s and 1790s a great volume of comment and discussion. Much of this was favourable, sometimes uncritically so. Some was pessimistic, jaundiced by the cultural backwardness of America and the persistence of Negro slavery there. Some was well-informed and the product of direct observation; some by contrast was based merely on theories and *a priori* judgements. All of it, however, was convinced of the immense importance of the subject. Not for well over a century was North America again to receive such attention, it might almost be said such reverence, in Europe. The 'spiritual flight from the Old Régime' to which the achievement of American independence gave rise among radicals and reformers all over Western Europe was to be of great importance in the events of the next two decades there, though its exact significance is still very much a matter for debate.

The eighteenth century, which saw the bonds uniting Europe and her colonies drawn in most ways closer than ever before, also saw an unprecedented growth of hostility on moral grounds to overseas expansion. The argument that colonial empires as they developed were likely to involve injustice and oppression, an overriding of the rights of their aboriginal inhabitants by violent and unscrupulous conquerors, was of course far from new. In the eighteenth century it was more frequently advanced and more widely accepted than ever before. Montesquieu in his *Lettres Persanes* (1721), Swift in his *Gulliver's Travels* (1726), as well as many less well-known writers, satirized what they regarded as the immoral tendencies of overseas expansion. In

Spain the statesman Macanaz in his *Testamento de España* (1740) showed unmistakable signs of remorse for the methods by which the Spanish Empire in America had been acquired. In Britain the scandals of the East India Company's administration of its territories from the 1760s onwards produced a crop of protests which culminated in the protracted trial (1788–95) of Warren Hastings on charges of corruption and oppression. The attitude of many of his countrymen was summed up in Horace Walpole's remark, in a letter of 1783, that 'no man ever went to the East Indies with good intentions'. Such judgements, though often sharpened by envy of the wealth which lucky or unscrupulous 'nabobs' were able to bring home with them, were in part at least the result of a genuine repugnance for the methods by which this wealth had been gained. Similtaneously the anti-colonial feeling which had always been powerful in France, and which was now being fanned by the growing primitivist tendency to exalt the virtues of non-Europeans at the expense of an over-civilized and over-sophisticated Europe, was expressed in an extreme form in one of the most popular and influential books of the century, G. T. F. Raynal's *Histoire . . . des Établissements et du Commerce des Européens dans les deux Indes* (1770). Ideas of this kind were never powerful enough to dominate the policies of States. The emotions which underlay them were sincere; and the achievement of American independence stimulated widespread cynicism about the permanence of great colonial empires. Nevertheless at no time during the eighteenth century did any government propose to relinquish voluntarily an important overseas possession. On the contrary, the development and increasing ramifications of Europe's economic life were making it less and less practicable for her to relax her growing control over the extra-European world. The significance of that world in European life was by the end of this period greater than ever before, greater in many ways than it was to be during the first three-quarters of the century which followed.

XIV

Education and Cultural Life

Schools and universities developed comparatively little during this period. In some countries the quality of formal education may even have declined. At the school level, especially at that of the primary school, shortage of trained teachers and money was often a serious obstacle to improvement. A still more serious one was the widespread feeling that it was unnecessary and might be dangerous to educate men who must gain their living by manual labour, in other words the great bulk of society. This idea was put forward by writers so different as the cynical Bernard Mandeville in his *The Fable of the Bees* (1714) and the fervent Jean-Jacques Rousseau in his *Nouvelle Héloïse* (1762).

In Catholic countries the first of these difficulties was partially avoided, since there a high proportion of the teachers was normally provided by religious Orders. The control exercised by the clergy over the schools of Spain and Portugal was complete. In much of Italy

BIBLIOGRAPHY. J. W. Adamson, *A Short History of Education* (Cambridge, 1919) is a standard introduction with two chapters on the eighteenth century; and N. Hans, *New Trends in Education in the Eighteenth Century* (London, 1951) contains much information. S. D'Irsay, *Histoire des universités françaises et étrangères*, vol. II (Paris, 1935) has some informative pages on this period with very full references; and B. Fay, 'Learned societies in Europe and America in the eighteenth century', *American Historical Review*, vol. XXXVII (1931–32) is a good summary account. The growth of scientific knowledge can be followed in A. R. Hall, *The Scientific Revolution, 1500–1800* (London, 1954) and, in rather bewildering detail, in A. Wolf, *A History of Science, Philosophy and Technology in the Eighteenth Century* (2nd ed.; London, 1952). On literature and the arts a vast amount has been written: P. Lavedan, *Histoire de l'art*, vol. II (Paris, 1944) has much information and good bibliographies; A. Hauser, *The Social History of Art* (London, 1951), vol. II, is an interesting attempt to relate the artistic life of the period to its social and economic background; and M. Levey, *Rococo to Revolution* (London, 1966) is a readable general account. R. Wellek, *A History of Modern Criticism, 1750–1950*, vol. I (London, 1955) is a work of great penetration. N. Pevsner, *Academies of Art* (Cambridge, 1940) gives a good account of also their influence, though resented and challenged by many intellectuals and statesmen, was great. In France, where the majority of village schoolmasters werè laymen, clerics had by the end of this period come to dominate education in the towns. The monks, nuns and priests who played so great a part in forming the youth of Catholic Europe very often made no charge for their work (this was usually the case in France for example): with all their faults they provided a body of teachers, conscientious if often conservative in their methods, which at this level the Protestant States could hardly match.

Several governments made efforts during this period to develop primary education. In France Louis XIV ordered in 1698 that each rural community should establish a school which all children were to attend up to the age of fourteen, and should pay the salary of a master to teach in it. This order was repeated in 1724, when the parents or guardians of children who did not go to school were threatened with prosecution. These edicts, though strongly supported by the Church, were not effectively enforced. In 1762 an anonymous author, possibly Diderot, estimated that there were 2 million boys of school age (6–16) in France, of whom less than a tenth received an effective education. This was certainly too gloomy a view of the situation. By 1789 every parish in Champagne was said to possess a school; and in what later became the *département* of the Aube 72 per cent of men and 22 per cent of women could read. These figures, however, were above the average for the country as a whole; and a very large part of the population, above

its subject. On music P. H. Lang, *Music in Western Civilization* (New York, 1941) is a good general work; and the first half of F. Blume, *Classic and Romantic Music* (London, 1972) gives a close analysis in a brief compass of eighteenth-century developments, at least from the 1740s onwards. On literature useful works in English are: J. G. Robertson, *A History of German Literature* (Edinburgh-London, 1933); E. H. Wilkins, *A History of Italian Literature* (London, 1954); and on a larger scale the relevant volumes of the *Cambridge History of English Literature* (Cambridge, 1907–27). Geneviève Bollême, *La Bibliothèque Bleue: la littérature populaire en France du XVIᵉ au XIXᵉ siècle* (Paris, 1971); the same author's *Les Almanachs populaires aux XVIIᵉ et XVIIIᵉ siècles: essai d'histoire sociale* (Paris, 1969); and still more some of the essays in Geneviève Bolleme, J. Ehrard and others (eds.), *Livre et société dans la France du XVIIIᵉ siècle* (2 vols.; Paris-The Hague, 1965–70) are interesting and important correctives to any view based merely upon the reading of the educated and well-do-do. On French cultural influences L. Réau, *L'Europe française au siècle des lumières* (Paris, 1933) is a standard work, though one which exaggerates the extent of French dominance in this respect.

all of the female population, was still unable and often unwilling to acquire even the rudiments of education. In Russia, where the shortage of trained men of all kinds was more acute than in any other major European State, the first effort to develop a system of primary education was made by Peter I. In 1714 he ordered the establishment throughout the country of 'cyphering schools' to teach arithmetic and geometry, largely with the idea of producing the technicians needed to carry out his plans of military and economic development. The difficulties of realizing such a scheme were very great. Little more than forty such schools ever existed and in 1726, the year after the Tsar's death, only about 500 pupils were attending them. Under his immediate successors, though the idea of creating a system of primary education was not forgotten, very little was done to this end. Even Catherine II, whose last years saw a rapid expansion of educational facilities in the towns, could do little to solve the intractable problem of extending some tincture of education to the peasants.

It was in Prussia, Scotland and the Habsburg hereditary lands that primary education was made genuinely available to the mass of the population. Frederick II made it compulsory for his subjects in 1763; and although this order was not completely enforced, by the end of the century the inhabitants of Prussia were better educated than those of any other country. In Scotland an almost equally wide dissemination of basic education was achieved. This came about without legal compulsion or State action of any kind, through the influence of the Church and the pressure of public opinion. In Austria Joseph II made strenuous and largely successful efforts to establish a system of universal primary education for his subjects. In England by contrast education for the masses remained throughout this period comparatively backward. This was because the widespread distrust of strong central government made a State-controlled educational system impossible, because the position was complicated by the mutual antipathy of Established Church and Dissenters, and simply because popular demand for education was weak. The charity school and Sunday school movements made efforts, often devoted and not altogether unsuccessful, to spread a tincture of book-learning among the lower strata of society, above all in the towns. These attempts, however, were inspired by the desire to combat vice, drunkenness and irreligion, rather than by any belief in the desirability of knowledge for its own sake.

Primary education, like almost everything else in eighteenth-century Europe, thus varied enormously in scope and quality in different countries, from the relative efficiency of Prussia or Austria to the backwardness of Russia or Spain. Variations almost as marked can be seen in the continent's secondary schools and universities. The grammar and public schools of England, unadventurous in their teaching methods and still anchored to a curriculum dominated by the classical languages, contrasted strongly with the establishments for vocational training in such subjects as navigation, engineering and medicine established by Peter I in Russia and continued by his successors. These in turn were very different from the *collèges* to be found in every local capital in France, which were dominated by religious Orders, above all the Jesuits, and taught with greater efficiency a curriculum almost as narrow as that of the English grammar schools.

Secondary education developed and changed during this period more than its poor relation, the primary schools. From Locke and his followers it derived an emphasis (which increased as the century drew to a close) on education through the senses as well as through the printed word, on the importance of teaching practical accomplishments and developing useful abilities. Ideas and assumptions of this kind can be seen in such works as Saint-Pierre's *Projet de Perfectionnement de l'Éducation* (1728): they appear in their most extreme form in Rousseau's *Émile* (1762). Through pioneers such as Basedow, Pestalozzi and Froebel they were to influence the whole future development of educational techniques. From the scientific progress of the later seventeenth century secondary education also derived a high idea of the importance of mathematics and a perhaps exaggerated estimate of the subject's power to teach the art of logical reasoning. The development of Europe's economic life led to increasing demands for the teaching of such obviously useful subjects as book-keeping, navigation, geography and modern languages. These new ideas and pressures were not easy to reconcile with a system of education which was still, over most of the continent, based upon the study of the classics and dominated by clerical influences. To some extent they were met by the foundation of new establishments designed to provide a purely professional and technical training. Such were the schools of mining set up at Brunswick in 1745, at Fribourg in 1755, at Clausthal in 1775 and in Paris in 1778; or the school of architecture created at Berlin in 1799; or the commercial schools and schools of agriculture which began to come into existence, notably in Germany, in the second half of the century.

More important, however, was the influence of these new demands in modifying the curricula of existing colleges and grammar schools and in stimulating the creation of new ones designed to provide a broader education. In Prussia the study of French was introduced into the secondary schools in 1763. Almost simultaneously French schoolboys began to receive for the first time some instruction in their own language and literature. In Scotland the foundation of Perth Academy in 1760 was one of the first recognitions of the need for schools with a more realistic curriculum. The first *Realschule*, designed to provide an education which would include such subjects as modern languages, geography and book-keeping for boys intended for a career in business or commerce, was founded by J. J. Hecker at Berlin in 1747. The fact that Germany took the lead in adapting education to the needs of an age increasingly dominated by commerce and technology, and that France notably lagged behind, was of the highest importance for the future. In the second half of the century the schoolmasters of the German States were, for the most part quite unconsciously, helping to set their nation on the road to future greatness, indeed to leadership of Europe. In France by contrast can already be seen that intellectual rigidity and academic conservatism which was later to have profound repercussions on her political life and even her international position.

The universities of Europe differed at least as much as its schools— in their size, in the composition of their student bodies, in the ease with which they accepted new methods of teaching or recognized the importance of new subjects. On the one hand were a small group of institutions which were genuine centres of research and at which first-class teaching, at least in certain subjects, was to be had. These were among the most important factors in the intellectual life of the age. They included Leyden in the first half of the century and Göttingen, Edinburgh, and to a lesser extent Vienna, Halle and Glasgow in its later decades. Göttingen is of particular interest as the finest example of the new type of university which was now beginning to develop. In the emphasis it laid on the physical sciences, in the degree to which it was controlled by the Hanoverian State, and still more in its remarkably successful combination of teaching and research, it pointed the way, more than any of its contemporaries, towards the universities of the present day. The best index of its vitality and activity is the growth of its library. Though the university was founded only in 1737 the library, within less than a generation, included 60,000 books and 100,000 pamphlets, while the manuscript subject-index to it ran to eighty-six volumes. This was almost certainly the greatest university library of the century. At the other end of the scale were such places as Alcalá, where the chair of Greek was left vacant for over forty years (1693–1734); or Santiago, where in 1779 of the thirty-three chairs twenty-nine were un-filled or occupied by underpaid deputies appointed by the titular holders; or Gräz, which in 1781 had only twenty-three matriculated students.

Between these extremes were to be found a large number of institu-tions which continued to provide teaching of a tolerable standard with-out making much contribution to the age's stock of knowledge and ideas. Such were the twenty-two universities of France, the thirty in the Holy Roman Empire, the numerous though somewhat declining Italian colleges, and those of England and Scandinavia. Some of these, such as Paris and Oxford, remained important because of their size, their traditions and their political significance: few of them played a great part in Europe's intellectual life. The efflorescence of French political and scientific thought during this period owed as little to the French universities as Burke or Priestley did to the English ones. Giambattista Vico, the most original mind produced by Italy during the century, held a poorly paid post at the University of Naples but was largely self-educated.

The universities of the eighteenth century can also be classified in terms of the social origins of their students. From this point of view the essential division was that between a group whose clientele was drawn exclusively or mainly from the aristocracy or wealthy bourgeoisie, and a larger group access to which was relatively free. The first included Oxford and Cambridge (whose exclusive character was probably inten-sified by the increasing cost, especially in the first half of the century, of maintaining a student there) as well as Strasbourg, Göttingen and a number of other German universities. The second was composed of the Scottish universities, most of the French and Italian ones, and, sur-prisingly at first sight, the University of Moscow, the first to be estab-lished in Russia. Whatever their social background, however, students were not a factor of the slightest political importance in this period. No eighteenth-century government paid or needed to pay any attention to student political activity or demands; for such activity and demands did not exist. Nevertheless there were beginning to be visible by the 1790s the first hopes and fears that the universities, or some of them, might become centres of political radicalism. It was not until well into the following century that this began to happen on any significant scale; but in the early 1790s a leading Austrian Jacobin was envisaging a revolution which would begin with the seizure of Vienna by 3–4,000 student radicals who were then to kill army officers, aristocrats and eventually the emperor himself.[1] Totally unrealistic and completely ignored at the time of their formulation, these dreams were none the less a pointer to the future.

Most European universities, however they might differ in other respects, found themselves compelled during this period to pay increasing attention to the physical sciences and medicine, the departments of knowledge whose frontiers were advancing most rapidly. Opposition from theologians and classicists tended to hamper this change of emphasis, especially in Catholic Europe, and very few of the greatest scientific discoveries of the century were made by university teachers. Nevertheless a good deal was achieved. In 1702 the first university textbook to be based on the principles of Newtonian physics and mathematics, David Gregory's *Astronomiae, Physicae et Geometriae Elementa*, was published at Oxford. The first continental scholar to base his teaching on Newton's discoveries was W. J. s'Gravesande, professor of astronomy and mathematics at Leyden from 1716 onwards. It was above all in physics and astronomy, and to a lesser degree in mathematics, that new ideas and new techniques filtered into the intellectual world of the universities. Leyden had an observatory of its own as early as 1706, and Uppsala acquired one in 1738. Even in Spain the government ordered in 1770 the drawing-up of new university curricula which emphasized the importance of mathematics and physics.

Medical teaching also developed with remarkable rapidity during this period. From Leyden, which by the beginning of the century had replaced Padua as the leading medical school of Europe, new methods and a new spirit, largely the work of the great professor Hermann Boerhaave, spread slowly to the rest of the continent. The important medical school which developed at Vienna after the middle of the century was created largely by a pupil of Boerhaave; while the Edinburgh medical school, whose fame was at its height in the last years of this period, also owed much to the example of Leyden. In medicine, however, as in the physical sciences, a high proportion of the most important discoveries were made by men who had no direct connexion with the universities—for example the work of Réaumur (1752) and Spallanzani (1780) on digestion, or the better-known studies of respiration by Priestley and Lavoisier. The gap between teaching and research, which had been opened by the Renaissance in almost every branch of

---

[1] P. P. Bernard, *Jesuits and Jacobins* (Urbana–Chicago–London, 1973), p. 166.

intellectual activity, was still as wide as ever in the eighteenth century.

Nor did the scientific and learned societies of the age make much contribution to the progress of knowledge. New organizations of this kind were indeed founded in considerable numbers. Academies of Science came into existence in Sweden (1710) Russia (1725) and Denmark (1742); and societies of a less ambitious kind were founded in many large cities of Western Europe. Few of these however added much of importance to Europe's stock of scientific ideas, while their predecessors in England, France and Italy were even less effective. The Royal Society in London during most of this period was little more than a gentleman's club, and the *Académie des Sciences* in Paris was almost as moribund.

The interest in the physical sciences which was slowly taking root in some of the universities was reflected in the attitude of the educated public. In particular the discoveries of Newton, which seemed to lay bare the inmost workings of the universe, appealed to the spirit of the age, and particularly to the love of intellectual and artistic symmetry which was so well developed in the early and middle decades of the century. They thus aroused the greatest interest and admiration. In France national pride and a resulting unwillingness to abandon the cosmology of Descartes, hitherto generally accepted there, delayed for decades the final acceptance of Newtonian physics. In 1742 the astronomer and mathematician Maupertuis published his *Discours sur la Figure des Astres*, the first scientific work in French to accept completely Newton's discoveries; but as late as 1759 the *Académie des Sciences* was still struggling to reconcile the Newtonian and Cartesian systems. Nevertheless the victory of Newton in France, though delayed, was absolute. A host of admirers headed by Voltaire used his name (often without having understood or perhaps even read his works) to symbolize the triumph of light over darkness, of knowledge over ignorance, and by implication of 'rational' and 'natural' religious belief (see pp. 390-1) over ecclesiastical tradition. The work of the mathematicians d'Alembert and Lagrange completed the acceptance of Newtonian principles and gave them, by the use of more analytical mathematical techniques, more precise and systematic expression. In 1796 Laplace was able to provide, on the basis of their work, the most complete description hitherto produced of the universe as it appeared to the astronomer. His *Système du Monde* is in effect a hymn of praise to the physical sciences, or at least to physics, astronomy and mathematics, a kind of scientific poem. The almost arrogant self-confidence, the delight in the essential simplicity and logicality of the structure of the universe which it radiates, sum up one side of eighteenth-century science. They make the book a landmark in the history of philosophy, of religion and of ideas in general.

The refinements of Newtonian physics and mathematics remained beyond the reach of the ordinary man, even of the ordinary educated man. They none the less influenced, often without his knowledge, his attitude to the world around him and to the society in which he lived. A feeling of having at last acquired full understanding and hence potential control of his physical environment; a new consciousness of power; a belief in the ability of human reason to make even the most complex mysteries simple and comprehensible; a faith in deductive argument from general principles; a tendency to distrust tradition—all these were stimulated by the work of Newton and his followers.

The other sciences lagged far behind physics and astronomy in their development. The great biological discoveries of 1660–80 had no adequate sequel in the eighteenth century. This remains true in spite of the remarkable work of the Swedish botanist Linnaeus, who by the end of his life (he died in 1778) had come to see that new species might arise by crossings between existing ones, and the French scholar Buffon, who realized that the earth was far older than was usually believed and that existing biological types were not fixed. Chemistry also was slow to develop. This was not merely because it was hampered by the mistaken 'phlogiston' theory (that of a substance with negative weight which was present in all other substances and was released by combustion). Advance was impeded far more by the fact that, until the work of Priestley and above all Lavoisier at the end of this period, the need for rigorous quantitative methods was hardly at all understood. Electricity moreover remained throughout the eighteenth century a completely mysterious subject, though one highly interesting to the ordinary man. Even the distinction between conductors and insulators was not clearly established until the 1730s. Nevertheless the general picture of eighteenth-century scientific life is one of progress, however uneven. One of the most important illustrations of this is the development of more elaborate and exact scientific vocabularies and systems of terminology (for example those created for botany by Linnaeus and later by Lavoisier for chemistry). Moreover mistaken theories and inadequate knowledge did little to shake the interest which the educated public increasingly took in the physical sciences and the faith which it increasingly felt in scientific progress.

This increasing interest is visible in a number of ways. The first and most obvious is the fact that works on scientific subjects make up an increasingly large proportion of total book publication as the century progresses. This has been most convincingly demonstrated for France;[1] but there is no doubt that the same development took place at least in all the more developed parts of Europe. Another is the increasingly wide use in ordinary speech and writing of scientific and mathematical terms and even of metaphors drawn from the sciences. Another is the success of popular works on scientific subjects such as the Abbé Pluche's *Spectacle de la Nature* (1732) or Priestley's *History and Present State of Electricity* (1767) and the interest aroused by the courses of public lectures on elementary science which were now becoming increasingly common (the most famous is that given in Paris by the Abbé Nollet in 1734). Yet another is the unprecedented extent to which prominent figures of the political, intellectual and even religious worlds dabbled in the sciences. Thus George III took some interest in botany, Victor Amadeus III of Savoy performed the course of experiments prescribed by Nollet, Samuel Johnson dabbled in chemistry, Montesquieu wrote papers on drunkenness, fever, tides and the causes of echoes, and both Rousseau and Diderot took a semi-serious interest in mathematics.

Most of this public interest in science was very superficial. The lectures and writings of Nollet and his fellow-vulgarizers were designed to provide amusement as much as solid instruction; they had to be made palatable to an audience which was still in the main uneducated in scientific matters. The drawing-room experiments in physics or electricity which delighted so many people were a game or a social accomplishment rather than a serious exploration of nature. Even in the universities the primitive and undeveloped state of many of the physical sciences is clearly illustrated by the ease with which dilettanti could not merely obtain appointments but often hold them very successfully. Richard Watson, for example, knew nothing whatever of the subject when he became Professor of Chemistry at Cambridge in 1764; but

[1] F. Furet, 'La "librairie" du royaume de France au 18e siècle', in G. Bollême and others, *Livre et société dans la France du XVIIIe siècle* (Paris-The Hague, 1965); for German figures which suggest a similar conclusion see A. Ward, *Book Production, Fiction and the German Reading Public, 1740–1800* (Oxford, 1974), p. 47.

within three years he was able to publish what at once became a standard academic work on metallurgy. Nor was there, at least over most of Europe, any effective application of science to the development of new industrial processes or the improvement of existing ones. In the more developed parts of the continent, Britain, France, the United Provinces or Sweden, it is true, there was a growing understanding of the new possibilities of this kind. Thus in 1692 a committee of the *Académie des Sciences* produced, at the request of the French government, a detailed report on the proportions required in an optically satisfactory printing type. Two generations later the chemical laboratory in the Ashmolean Museum at Oxford was being used in the production of Worcester china. The work of John Dollond in the 1750s in improving the telescope shows a certain union of scientific knowledge with traditional techniques; Joseph Black did important work in industrial chemistry though he was a university professor; and in 1759 the great engineer John Smeaton made the first attempt to measure accurately the efficiency of different types of watermill and windmill. Lavoisier himself, the greatest chemist of the century, was employed in the 1780s as a government consultant in efforts to improve the manufacture of explosives in France. The Industrial Revolution in Britain developed against an intellectual background marked by the increasingly widespread dissemination among manufacturers and artisans of scientific knowledge and, equally important, scientific attitudes. Nevertheless the importance of all this in a European context should not be exaggerated. Over most of the continent technology, like so many other aspects of life, continued to be dominated by tradition, habit and rule-of-thumb. A Platonic separation of science from the mundane processes of everyday life continued to prevail.

Nevertheless something had been gained. Scientific experiments, even of the most dilettante kind, were an advance on the cabinets of 'curiosities' (fossils, coins, shells, etc.) which had been popular in the previous century (and which continued to be so in this period). Public interest in science at least showed a more widespread realization than ever before that the physical world was governed by laws, that the phenomena of which it was composed could be logically classified and that these laws and classifications could be discovered by intelligent observation and careful measurement.

How far did this interest in the physical sciences promote the scepticism and the declining faith in religious dogmas which are visible in many parts of Europe during the eighteenth century? This is a complex question; but it seems clear that the importance of science in this respect, and indeed in the general development of radical thought during this period, has often been exaggerated. In Britain, which made through Newton the greatest single contribution to the century's stock of scientific ideas, scarcely anyone as yet thought of science as dangerous to faith. One historian has gone so far as to speak of 'that peculiarly English phenomenon, the holy alliance between science and religion'.[1] To all British scientists natural phenomena, however much they might be studied, however closely observed and subtly classified, had still their first cause in God. They were still manifestations of His being and nature. Many of the most popular writers and lecturers on science were themselves clergymen. The undermining of the intellectual foundations of revealed religion which was undoubtedly though very slowly taking place in Britain (see p. 392) was only indirectly the work of the mathematicians or astronomers. It owed at least as much to moralists such as Mandeville, historians such as Gibbon, and above all philosophers such as Hume. It was Hume, not any of the scientists, who was first willing to argue openly against the credibility of miracles.

In France the position was similar. There the assault on traditional faith and the religious establishment was led, not by Maupertuis, Buffon or Lavoisier, but by philosophers, historians and publicists, by La Mettrie, Helvétius, Morellet, above all Voltaire. The books and pamphlets produced by such authors were repeatedly condemned and criticized by the Assembly of the Clergy from 1765 onwards; but scientific writings as such were never attacked in this way. Not until the last years of the century did a scientist, Laplace, produce a description of the universe in which no place was allotted to God; whereas as early as 1770 the writer Holbach in his *Système de la Nature* had revived the Lucretian concept of the universe as the mere result of a fortuitous combination of atoms, and thus by implication ruled out the idea of a creator. Scepticism and materialism were certainly rife in the *salons* of Paris. As in England, however, they were the product of a philosophy hard to reconcile with traditional religious assumptions, of an increased knowledge of the peoples of the extra-European world which bred moral relativism, and of an intensified study of history which threw doubt on many clerical claims and traditions. The development of the physical sciences undoubtedly helped to create an atmosphere in which a widespread turning away from religion became possible; but it did little directly to stimulate such a movement.

[1] B. Willey, *The Eighteenth Century Background* (London, 1940), pp. 136–7.

The development of literature during the eighteenth century is usually described in terms of a transition from classicism or neo-classicism to romanticism. The description is over-simplified and the terms it employs are vague; but some change of emphasis of this kind undoubtedly occurred. The neo-classicism which still dominated aesthetic theory almost everywhere in Europe at the beginning of this period aimed at the imitation of Nature; but this was a Nature of a somewhat special kind, generalized, universal and unchanging. The writer was to concern himself with these aspects of his subject rather than with the more individual, intimate and fluctuating ones. Associated with these theories was the belief that literature, or at least the higher forms of literature, should be essentially if not overtly didactic, that art should be 'a mere intellectual statement of moral precepts,'[1] and that the various literary *genres*—tragedy, comedy, epic, lyric—were each governed by rules which could not be infringed without lowering the quality of the resulting work. The conventionality and rigidity, not to say dullness, of so much of the poetry of the first half of the century was produced by the influence of these ideas. This system of criticism moreover was suited to, and the product of, an aristocratic society. It presupposed on the part of the reading public some acquaintance with the literature of classical antiquity and a certain detachment from the mechanical processes of contemporary life.

Theories so rigid and so abstract were never completely dominant in the literature of any European country, even in the early decades of the century. They were strongest of all in France, where classical traditions were deeply ingrained. There literature was still little influenced by the slowly growing current of romanticism and sensibility. Even in France, however, the *Réflexions critiques sur la Poésie et sur la Peinture* of the Abbé du Bos (1719) has been acclaimed as an important step in the development of a new attitude towards the literary expression of the emotions. Simultaneously in the hands of Lesage and Prévost the realistic novel reached a high pitch of development; while the plays of Marivaux show not merely wit but a psychological subtlety and realism uncommon in any period. In England acceptance of classical literary theories had always been limited to an educated upper class in which French influences were strong. Below this social level the old national writers uninfluenced by classical aesthetics, such as Shakespeare, remained widely read. Moreover the appeal of classicism was further limited by its association with pagan antiquity, and by a lingering

[1] Wellek (*see* Bibliography, p. 283), p. 23.

popular preference for themes inspired by Christianity or at least drawn from the history of the Christian era. A moderate reaction against classical aesthetics can be seen as early as 1712 in Addison's series of essays 'On the Pleasures of the Imagination', which appeared in the *Spectator* of that year. As in France, the novel, with which classical aesthetics was hardly at all concerned, sometimes assumed a highly realistic and popular form—for example in Defoe's *Moll Flanders* and *Colonel Jack*. In Italy also the beginnings of a reaction against classical or neo-classical literary standards can be seen from the beginning of the century. It is clearly visible in L. A. Muratori's *Della Perfetta Poesia Italiana* (1706) and in the rediscovery of Dante (the greatest of all medieval poets, whose works had been virtually ignored for generations) by G. V. Gravina. In Germany the slowness with which a national literature developed meant that classical ideals and standards were seen, as in England, largely as imports from abroad, in particular from France. Thus the new ideas on the importance of emotion and imagination which began to enter the country in the second quarter of the century, notably through the activities of the Swiss critics Bodmer and Breitinger, fell on comparatively fertile ground.

The middle decades of this period saw classicism in literature under increasingly heavy attack almost everywhere from a number of directions. Its adherents found themselves faced by a growing demand for greater naturalism, signs of which can be detected even in the writings of essentially conservative critics such as Diderot and Johnson. Novels or plays which dealt with recognizable individuals against a realistic and often middle-class background—Lessing's *Miss Sara Sampson* (1755) and Diderot's *Le Père de Famille* (1758) are good examples—now won increasing popularity. Established critical ideas were also being undermined by the growing cult of 'sensibility', of high-minded emotion and undeserved suffering. In England this tendency can be seen gaining strength from the 1720s onwards in the works of such writers as Thompson, Shenstone and Young. Its full potentialities were first revealed in the prodigious success of Samuel Richardson's *Pamela* (1740) and later, in a somewhat different form, in the popularity of such books as Henry Mackenzie's *The Man of Feeling* (1771), Goethe's *Sorrows of Werther* (1774), and Bernardin de St. Pierre's *Paul et Virginie* (1789). Most important of all was the growth of a more historical and relativist and less absolute attitude towards literature. Literary history of a modern kind, stressing the elements of growth ,and development inherent in every great literature, can be found in Italy as early as 1698, in G. M. Crescimbeni's *Istoria della volgar Poesia*. As this period drew to a close an increasing element of historicism, an effort to escape from absolute judgements divorced from any historical context, is visible in many critical works, notably in Thomas Warton's *History of English Poetry* (1774–81).

This trend bore fruit most noticeably in the tendency to revalue (and often overvalue) the literature of primitive peoples or of the non-classical past which is usually referred to as 'primitivism'. This is seen most clearly in the amazing success all over Europe of James Macpherson's *Works of Ossian*, a collection of allegedly ancient Celtic poems (mostly the work of Macpherson himself though including genuine elements) published in 1765. It is also visible in the interest taken by such people as Bishop Percy in England, and above all J. G. Herder (see pp. 385–7) in Germany, in the collection and publication of folk-songs. The new attitude was clearly expressed in works such as Richard Hurd's *Letters on Chivalry and Romance* (1762) which claimed that the feudal period was more favourable to the production of great poetry than the Homeric one because of 'the improved gallantry of the feudal times' and 'the superior solemnity of their superstitions', and argued that by the victory of neo-classical taste 'we have lost ... a world of fine fabling'.[1] These anti-classical influences, typified by the growing taste for wild natural scenery and for natural 'English' gardens as opposed to the highly artificial arrangements of *parterres*, topiary and statuary which French influence had done so much to popularize in the first decades of this period, continued to gain strength as the century drew to a close. Classical models still had great influence on literature and aesthetic theory in its second half, an influence strengthened by the admiration for the classical past which was an important element in the Enlightenment in France (see pp. 369–70). But this influence was now declining and changing its character. Europe, led by England and Germany, was now escaping from the rigidities and limitations of the French-dominated classicism of the age of Louis XIV. The changing meaning for Europeans of classical models in the later eighteenth century can be seen most clearly in Germany. There, by way of such books as J. J. Winckelmann's *Thoughts on the Imitation of Greek Works in Painting and Sculpture* (1755) and above all Lessing's *Laocöon, or the boundaries between painting and poetry* (1766) they came to be seen as illustrating the triumph of art, and the inner serenity which art can

[1] 1911 edition, pp. 108–13, 154.

bestow, over the tragedy of human life, rather than as examples of style to be assiduously imitated.

The literature which has been described in the preceding paragraphs was that of the educated, of the reasonably affluent, of the town-dweller with at least partly developed tastes and fairly easy access to books. It was therefore quite untypical of the reading of the ordinary peasant, artisan or wage-earner, who enjoyed none of these advantages. We know very little indeed about the reading habits of the 95 per cent or more of Europeans in this period who were not well educated or well-to-do and who did not possess libraries of which there is some surviving record in wills or inventories; but what fragmentary information there is suggests strongly that the reading of this vast majority (or of those members of it who could read at all) remained highly traditional. In France, the one area in which popular reading habits have been seriously studied, there had since the early seventeenth century been a large output of small, cheap and often badly printed booklets for an unsophisticated mass market. During the eighteenth century there were about 150 printers producing literature of this kind (mainly in northern France, where peasant and working-class literacy was much more widespread than in the south). Almanacs; collections of prophecies and works on astrology; collections of traditional and often very ancient tales (notably of Charlemagne and his paladins); manuals of practical advice on aspects of everyday life, health care, etc.—such appear to have been the staple reading of the ordinary man (in so far as that phrase has meaning) in France during this period.[1] It was the reading of the uneducated: astrological predictions appear to have bulked large in it precisely because they could be expressed in conventional signs rather than in words and thus 'read' by the illiterate or partly literate. It was the reading of those who wished to escape, however briefly, from a life often mercilessly hard; such feelings underlie the taste for the marvellous and the exotic which this type of literature so often expresses. It was the reading of men to whom change was more often than not something to be resisted and novelty an object of mistrust; hence the way in which works of this type could be reprinted for generations, even centuries, without alteration. (A poem giving general advice on health, *L'Escole de Salerne, en vers burlesques*, first published in 1474, had gone, without change, through almost three hundred editions by 1846.) It was, in the

---

[1] The bulk of Geneviève Bollême, *La Bibliothèque Bleue* (*see* Bibliography, p. 337) consists of extracts from these booklets.

last analysis, a literature of submission, the reading of men in the grip of physical and social forces against which they felt it vain to struggle.[1] No other part of Europe produced anything quite similar; but if popular reading in other countries were studied in the same way it is hard to believe that this would not yield at least some similar conclusions. We must not forget that underlying the world of literature in the textbook sense of the term, the world of enlightenment, of scientific discovery and cosmopolitan high culture, was another intellectual universe, dark and barely penetrable by the historian but none the less inhabited by the overwhelming numerical majority of Europeans.

In architecture and the visual arts changes of a kind very roughly similar to those in literature can be traced. The Baroque styles of the age of Louis XIV, with their highly developed plastic values, their efforts to impress and uplift rather than to amuse or attract, their occasional heaviness, were slowly transmuted by the new tendencies which developed during this period. The decorative style known as Rococo, which evolved in France towards the end of the seventeenth century and later enjoyed enormous popularity and influence in Germany, can be regarded as an offshoot of Baroque or even a degenerate form of it. Nevertheless it differed in a number of ways from its predecessor. The stress which it laid on curves and its general dislike of geometrical patterns, the fondness which it often showed, at least from the end of the 1720s, for asymmetry, its frequent use of newly discovered materials such as porcelain and later stucco, the way in which it was influenced in some of its forms by Chinese models—all these distinguish it from the art of the seventeenth century.

It was essentially a decorative style and little more: its influence on the structure and plan of the buildings which it ornamented was inconsiderable. Italian architects, still in some ways the leaders of the profession, continued until the middle of the century to be dominated by Baroque ideas and traditions, though the exuberance which that style had displayed in seventeenth-century Italy was now somewhat modified in the work of Juvara, Galilei and Vanvitelli. In France pseudo-classical Renaissance and 'Palladian' styles showed greater powers of resistance than in Italy and Baroque influence on architecture was limited, as can be seen in the work of Robert de Cotte or J.-A. Gabriel. In England Palladianism, and the ideas of regularity, sym-

[1] See the discussion of this type of writing in R. Mandrou, *La France aux XVIII*[e] *et XVIII*[e] *siècles* (Paris, 1967), pp. 141–5.

metry, and restraint in external ornament associated with it, continued to be almost completely dominant in the early eighteenth century: Baroque models except in the design of furniture had little influence there.

The painting of the early eighteenth century is hard to describe briefly, but is perhaps best regarded as a continuation of the Baroque art of the later seventeenth century with its stress on movement and colour, on visual rhetoric and (except in England) on religious and mythological subjects. Even as late an artist as the Venetian Tiepolo (1692–1769) has been acclaimed as 'the epitome and the perfection of Baroque art'.[1] Already, however, such unity as the Baroque style and tradition still possessed was breaking down in the paintings of Watteau, one of the most difficult of all great artists to classify satisfactorily, and in the different types of realism exemplified by Hogarth in England and Chardin in France.

The middle decades of the century saw the pace of change accelerate. Like poetry, though in a rather different way, the visual arts were now becoming more and more historically-minded. The art of Greece and Rome was suddenly being made more accessible than ever before, partly by the excavation of Pompeii and Herculaneum from the 1740s onwards and partly by the publication of the first accurate descriptions and drawings hitherto available of the great buildings of classical antiquity, particularly of Greece. In architecture this flood of new knowledge stimulated the growth of a conscious and often highly elegant neo-classical style. First developed in England by the Adam brothers from about 1759 onwards, this had spread to France by the 1770s; later it inspired the construction of the Brandenburger Tor in Berlin (1778–91) and had considerable influence even in Russia. In interior decoration and the design of furniture it not merely popularized classical or pseudo-classical motifs (well illustrated in the pottery produced in Staffordshire by Josiah Wedgwood from the 1760s onwards) but also gave rise to the often exaggerated and fanciful 'Etruscan' and 'Egyptian' styles of the later decades of the century.

In painting the influence of newfound classical models and neo-classical theories can be seen even more clearly. It is visible in the distrust felt by artists such as Sir Joshua Reynolds for mere manipulative skill, and in a tendency to exalt form at the expense of colour, draughtmanship at the expense of decorative effect, repose at the expense of

---

[1] Lavedan (see Bibliography, p. 283), vol. II, p. 368.

movement. Moreover the typical neo-classical belief in the educative effect of great art, and in the artist's obligation to select from and generalize Nature in order to produce this effect, were now becoming almost as influential in discussions of painting as they had been in literary theory a generation or more earlier.

The past to which the art and architecture of the later eighteenth century returned was, as in the case of literature, medieval as well as classical, Gothic as well as Greek. In England an interest in Gothic architecture had begun to develop even before the end of the seventeenth century, one which both stimulated and was stimulated by the formation of the Society of Antiquaries in 1718. The slow growth of a taste of this kind in the decades which followed is illustrated by the publication in 1742 of Batty Langley's *Ancient Architecture Restored ... in the Gothic Mode*, and above all by the building and rebuilding by Horace Walpole of his house at Strawberry Hill (1750–76). The *dilettanti* of the eighteenth century were still far from a genuine understanding of or sympathy with medieval architecture. Strawberry Hill, as has often been pointed out, was really a ridiculous and anachronistic jumble of styles; and to the end of this period Gothic continued to have much less influence on the development of architecture in England than Palladianism and neo-classicism. 'The Saxon and Gothic antiquities', wrote a commentator in 1798, 'tho' justly objects of curiosity and even of admiration, are still the remains of society in its infancy and therefore barbarous and false.'[1] Even in continental Europe, however, where classical traditions were in general stronger than in England, Gothic art attracted some interest. As early as 1741 the great French architect Soufflot published a defence of it in his *Parallèle des églises Gothiques avec les églises modernes*, and in 1776 the Prince of Anhalt can be found building for himself at Wörlitz a palace in the Gothic style. But in neither France nor Germany was it an important element in the artistic life of the age.

The painting of the later eighteenth century, like its literature, was powerfully influenced by the ideas of sensibility and Nature. The influence of the former is seen most clearly in the work of Greuze, who was praised by Diderot and is known to have been influenced by the writings of Rousseau. His scenes of family life, with their emotional and moralistic overtones and their lack of humour, are one of the best visual reflections of the spirit of the decades before the French Revolution: a similar attitude can be found, in slightly different forms, in the work of

[1] W. Jackson, *The Four Ages* (London, 1798), p. 4.

many painters active during the same period—Madame Vigée-Lebrun, Fragonard, perhaps Gainsborough.

The eighteenth century, or at least its middle and later decades, was thus a period of rapid aesthetic and stylistic change. In architecture and decoration Baroque and Palladian traditions struggled with the influences of Rococo and neo-classicism, while the position was further complicated by an appreciable admixture of Chinese or pseudo-Chinese influences (see p. 333). The stylistic confusion which resulted, and which was at its height just after the middle of the century, is well reflected in the pattern-books of Thomas Chippendale and other cabinet-makers. In painting Baroque slowly gave way to a style, or rather a group of styles, which were more realistic and above all more intimate and more sensitive. In literature the classical taste of the early part of the century (which had in any case been largely confined to poetry and tended to ignore prose as beneath serious criticism) was steadily eroded and transmuted by the growth of sensibility and by a more generous and realistic view of the literature of the past.

No art was in the eighteenth century more widely appreciated and practised than music. It attracted the interest, often a keen and well-informed interest, of some of the most important writers and scholars of the period. Rousseau was the author of an opera (*Le Devin du Village*) and his *Lettre sur la musique francaise* (1753) was one of the most influential critical works of the century. Voltaire in the 1730s played a leading role in the controversies between the French composer Rameau and his critics. An enormous quantity of music, most of it now totally neglected and forgotten, was written in the eighteenth century; in some parts of Europe at least it was more accessible than literature to the ordinary man. (Twelve hundred operas were produced in Venice alone during the century and in the 1780s one observer claimed that the Papal States possessed forty opera-houses). Its sheer abundance, however, makes it difficult to describe or analyse briefly. Moreover music is by its very nature the most abstract, the most timeless of the arts, that least influenced by the climate of ideas surrounding it.

Parallels between its development and that of literature and the visual arts are thus hard to draw with any certainty. Some nevertheless can be suggested. The Rococo art of the early decades of the century has, it can be argued, an analogy in much of the music (or at least the instrumental music) of the same period—music which was highly decorated, designed to please, melodically often somewhat impoverished and often rather lacking in both lyricism and architectural sense. From the 1740s on-wards, as the true classical musical style begins to take shape, there is a much greater emphasis than before on melody; and by the later decades of the century a growing stress on making music simpler and more comprehensible to the ordinary man is visible. This led to a considerable infusion of folk elements even into some of the greatest achievements of the period: Mozart's *Magic Flute* (1791) is the supreme example of this. Such a development is in marked contrast to the early decades of the century, when folk music had attracted no attention at all from pro-fessional composers. The same movement towards simplicity, com-prehensibility, a wider and less aristocratic audience, it has been argued, underlies the tendency in the second half of the century towards the use only of a limited range of simple keys (D, F, G and B flat) and its marked preference for major rather than minor ones. It is tempting to see such developments as a parallel in musical life to the movement towards naturalism and sensibility which has already been seen in novels, plays and painting. Some other analogies can be tentatively suggested. For example the rationalism, the taste for firmness and clarity, which made up another strand in the intellectual life of the early eighteenth century and were strongest in France, are perhaps reflected in the music of Jean Philippe Rameau, the greatest French composer of this period. His *Traité de l'harmonie reduite à ses principes naturels* (1722), the most important and systematic work of the century on the theory of composi-tion, reflects the faith in rules and systems, the belief that success in any of the arts is above all a matter of correctness, of choosing a suitable model and taking it as a guide, which was so powerful in the Europe of Louis XIV. In the same way the neo-classicism which becomes so powerful in the visual arts in the last decades of this period is echoed in a sterner and more masculine tone in the remarkable operas of Gluck—particularly *Orfeo ed Euridice* (1762) and *Alceste* (1767)—which made their effect by placing on the stage 'monumentally simplified character types which led . . . back to the classical tragedy of antiquity'.

These analogies, however seductive, cannot be pressed too far: they break down when applied to the greatest composers of the age. To classify J. S. Bach, whose most important works were in a quite different tradition, that of the church music of Protestant Germany, in terms of the well-worn and somewhat shapeless concepts of Rococo, Baroque or classicism is pointless as well as impertinent. Like the other towering musical geniuses of the century—Mozart and perhaps Handel—he transcends all classifications and cannot be confined to any of these battered pigeon-holes.

Eighteenth-century music was none the less a function of society where its forms if not its spirit were concerned. Like every other art it had to adapt itself to a given political and economic structure. This is seen most clearly in the domination of much of it by the needs and tastes of rulers and the greater nobility. Monarchies and aristocracies, the leading social and political institutions of the period, provided the most lucrative market for music as for so many of the arts. The great importance of opera as a musical form, especially in the first half of the century, was largely a result of this position. In the seventeenth century operas, often mounted on the most lavish scale and combined with ballets, aquatic spectacles, firework displays and other extraneous elements, had been a means by which the rulers of the Italian States displayed their wealth and their patronage of the arts. By the early decades of the eighteenth century a taste for opera was spreading from Italy, by way of the Habsburg court at Vienna, to many parts of Germany. By the middle years of the century it had penetrated even as far as St. Petersburg. The result was the creation at many of the courts of Europe of opera-houses served by professional musicians and singers and often, in the larger States, with composers and librettists permanently attached to them. Thus for example a line of Italian composers of real eminence—Galuppi, Traetta, Paisiello, Cimarosa—were associated with the development of opera in St. Petersburg in the last generation of the century.

Opera-houses of this type, created by princes, were generally accessible to the ordinary man in Italy and South Germany. In the main, however, they were closed to him in North Germany and other parts of Europe. The type of work which they produced, the *opera seria* normally by Italian composers, drew heavily upon classical mythology for its subjects and was usually designed to give the utmost scope to the singers. (In no other period have supremely accomplished singers been so numerous or so lavishly rewarded.) It therefore tended to become somewhat stereotyped, and as the century progressed encountered increasing competition from new and more realistic operatic forms, especially in countries whose cultural life was less dominated by courts and princes than that of Germany. In England the ballad opera (the most famous example is John Gay's *Beggar's Opera*, produced in 1728), in France the *opéra comique* which developed from the 1750s onwards, in Spain the *tonadilla* (a kind of intermezzo often based on popular tunes), in Austria the *Singspiel* which culminates in Mozart's *Magic*

Flute, even in Italy itself the realistic *opera buffa*, can all be considered as different forms of this reaction against the *opera seria* inherited from the previous century.

Thus in spite of the fact that so much music was written for courts and so many composers depended for employment on monarchs and nobles, music was not an art designed purely for the enjoyment of the privileged classes. This was especially the case where a large educated bourgeoisie existed. It was in such areas that the concert open to the public, which can be regarded as a declaration of middle-class cultural independence, had its origins. A series of public concerts was founded at Hamburg in 1722 and the first concert organization of a modern type, the *Concerts Spirituels*, was set up in Paris three years later. With the concert-hall and the anonymous audience came the first printed music criticism, originally in periodicals such as the *Mercure Galant* and the *Spectator*, later on a more professional scale in books such as J. Matteson's *Critica Musica* and J. A. Scheibe's *Der Critische Musicus*. It is important, however, to remember that much eighteenth-century music, like a good deal of eighteenth-century poetry, was written for a small and relatively expert audience, not for the common man. Unless this is grasped neither its strengths nor its limitations can be completely understood.

It would be quite wrong to imagine, from what has been said above, that the opera was the only important musical form in Europe even in the first half of the century. On the contrary instrumental music of various types continued to be produced in great quantities, and the demand for chamber works for performance by groups of amateurs was very considerable. Some of this instrumental writing—Bach's Brandenburg Concertos and Handel's Concerti Grossi are obvious examples—was very fine. In the later decades of this period the balance began to tilt more and more towards instrumental music, a development clearly illustrated by the emergence of orchestras bigger and more highly disciplined than any hitherto seen. This was essentially a German development. It was at Mannheim under the Bohemian Stamitz and at Stuttgart under the Italian Jomelli that the first great European orchestras took shape; and by the end of the century the largest might include a hundred or more players. Combinations of this size, properly trained and controlled, opened to composers a whole new world of possible symphonic effects.

Germany's leadership in the development of the orchestra warns us not to overestimate, in spite of the enormous prestige of Italian composers and performers, the importance of Italy in eighteenth-century music. Even in the first decades of the century Bach owed little, at least directly, to Italian influences; and in France an important and active school of native musicians struggled with some success against the threat of Italian dominance. With the advantages of two hundred years or more of hindsight, indeed, it is clear that the 1740s saw the beginning of a German leadership of the musical world (in large part the work of Bohemian composers of whom Gluck was the greatest) which has lasted until well into our own century. Even England was able to retain a distinct musical tradition of her own; though her relative backwardness is shown by the survival there until the end of this period of forms such as the concerto grosso, the organ concerto and the French-type orchestral overture long after they had been discarded elsewhere in Europe. Nevertheless the first half of the century saw an Italian, above all, Neapolitan, pre-eminence which lasted to a considerable extent until the 1780s or even later. Lulli, who had founded the French school in the 1660s and 1670s, was a Florentine: Handel was profoundly influenced by a visit to Italy. Not until the end of this period did Haydn become the first German composer to achieve a truly international reputation (and incidentally the first great European musician to have his works performed in the new United States of America).

How far is it justifiable to speak, as many writers have done, of French cultural domination in eighteenth-century Europe? One of the period's main intellectual currents, that of romantic sensibility, owed little to French influence or example. In music France's influence, as has just been pointed out, was less than that of Italy. In many respects, none the less, it is possible to consider the century as one of French cultural leadership. During its early decades in particular the example and enormous prestige of Louis XIV stimulated the creation of a whole galaxy of imitations of Versailles—by Philip V of Spain at La Granja, by John V of Portugal at Queluz, by the Dukes of Parma at Colorno, by the Dukes of Modena at Rivalta, by Charles of Naples at Caserta, by Frederick I of Prussia at Charlottenburg, and by many of the minor German rulers. Even in Russia one of the pavilions in the park at Peterhof, the palace begun by Peter I, was called *Marly* and others *Mon Plaisir* and *l'Hermitage*, while great Russian and Polish noble families built themselves vast country houses in whose construction the example of Versailles played some part. Many of these palaces were designed by French or French-trained architects; almost all of them owed something to the work of French painters, sculptors or cabinet-makers. Throughout this period, moreover, the development not merely of the content but of the formal teaching of art was greatly influenced by French example. The rules of the Academies of Art founded at Berlin in 1697 and Vienna in 1705 were drawn almost word for word from those of the *Academie Royale de Peinture et Sculpture* in Paris.

The eighteenth century also saw the complete dominance of French as the language of European scholarship, culture and polite society. As early as 1697 a writer could claim that 'the French language has succeeded the Latin and Greek languages . . . it has become so general that it is spoken today throughout almost the whole of Europe and those who frequent society feel a kind of shame if they do not know it'.[1] A natural result of this position was that educated Frenchmen developed a contempt for the languages of other peoples. 'We entertained so high an idea of ourselves and of our language,' wrote one in 1792, 'that we looked upon foreign idioms as the jargon of barbarians: accordingly we neglected to learn them.'[2] France's linguistic dominance, like her influence on the arts, was particularly marked in countries such as Poland, Russia (see p. 239), Sweden and the German States, which had as yet little native literature and whose languages were sometimes only beginning to take shape as literary media. The uncritical acceptance of French by their ruling classes and the contemptuous rejection of the native language which it often involved are seen in their most extreme form in the attitude of Frederick II of Prussia. Born and growing to manhood in an age in which the attraction of French models was at its height, he remained till his death a wholehearted admirer of French literature and, as his own works show, of the strictest and most arid classicism. Despising German as a barbaric dialect, he used it only when he had to, and ordered in 1743 that the papers read to the Academy of Sciences at Berlin should be published in French.

Even in the first half of the century, however, French cultural influence was much weaker in countries such as England and Spain, which had well-established literatures of their own, than in the less developed States of Central and Eastern Europe. The generation which followed the Seven Years War saw moreover a tendency for this influence to decline in many areas. The decline was most marked in

[1] Janssaeus, *La Véritable Clef de la Langue Française*, quoted in H. Kohn, *The Idea of Nationalism* (New York, 1945), p. 194.
[2] J. P. Rabaut de Saint-Etienne, *The History of the Revolution of France* (London, 1792), p. 15.

Germany, where the growth of a great and original national literature was now under way. Thus the Academy of Sciences began after Frederick II's death in 1786 to transact business in German as well as French, while Herder and Lessing published attacks on the artificiality and lack of natural feeling which they considered the main characteristics of French literature. In Spain distrust of the sceptical and irreligious character of so much French writing raised a further barrier in the way of any widespread adoption of ideas or literary models from beyond the Pyrenees, while even in Russia there were faint signs in the last years of the century of a reaction against French cultural dominance.

Moreover France herself was now being influenced to a degree unknown for at least a century by foreign books, buildings, paintings and ideas. The English novel, represented notably by Richardson, enjoyed a considerable vogue there. It was largely from England that neo-classical architectural styles were popularized in France. By the 1760s there were even signs that German poetry was beginning to attract some attention in Paris. In the years before the Revolution French cultural influence in Europe was still much greater than that of any other State; but France was rapidly becoming a mere *primus inter pares* in this respect and was no longer the unchallenged leader of the whole continent.

XV

The Enlightenment and its Competitors

The small minority of Europeans who were educated and responsive to currents of intellectual change were conscious during much of the eighteenth century of living in an age of 'Enlightenment'. What did this term mean?

In the first place the Enlightenment meant very different things in different parts of the continent and even as between different individuals in the same country. In some areas and in the work of some writers it took a form which was radical, aggressively critical of existing political and social structures, contemptuous of the past and particularly of the religious assumptions which had done so much to shape the history of Christian Europe. In others it was more moderate. Sometimes its influence, at least on the educated and opinion-forming sections of society, was very great. Elsewhere, where such groups were smaller and weaker, or where they were protected against radical intellectual challenge by social stability or powerful religious influences, it had much less purchase. The thinkers of the Enlightenment were never a unified school, a disciplined intellectual phalanx, even in any single European

BIBLIOGRAPHY. The best single book on the Enlightenment in English is N. Hampson, *The Enlightenment* (The Pelican History of European Thought, vol. IV: Harmondsworth, 1968) which is concise, clearly written and very informative. A. B. Cobban, *In Search of Humanity: the role of the Enlightenment in modern history* (London, 1960) is penetrating and suggestive. Two works by P. Gay are stimulating though slightly idiosyncratic: *The Enlightenment: an interpretation. Vol. I, The Rise of Modern Paganism* (London, 1967); *Vol. II, The Science of Freedom* (London, 1970) and *The Party of Humanity: studies in the French Enlightenment* (London, 1964). E. Cassirer, *The Philosophy of the Enlightenment* (Princeton, 1951) is an older but still classic account. P. Hazard, *The European Mind, 1680–1715* (London, 1953), though the French edition appeared as long ago as 1935, still remains the best account of the 'pre-Enlightenment'; and the same author's *European Thought in the Eighteenth Century: from Montesquieu to Lessing* (London, 1954) is a work of importance.

state. In so far as they were united at all it was merely by a generic or family likeness; and many of the most original thinkers of the age largely escaped from or even reacted against what are usually considered typical 'enlightened' influences. It would not be a great exaggeration to say that there were several different Enlightenments in eighteenth-century Europe, reacting with and influencing one another in complex ways; while outside this circle of intellectuals, important above all in France, the great bulk of European society, traditional and resistant to all new influences, remained largely unaffected.

Moreover the vitality and influence of the Enlightenment fluctuated sharply as between different parts of the century. Most of its basic ideas and assumptions had taken shape before the death of Louis XIV, even before 1700. But it was not until the 1740s that it emerged as a clearly identifiable movement of ideas with recognizable leaders and a certain degree of internal coherence. This was the decade of Diderot's *Pensées philosophiques* (1746) and *Lettre sur les aveugles* (1749), and above all of the most radical and iconoclastic philosophical work of the century, David Hume's *Enquiry concerning Human Understanding* (1748). The 1760s and early 1770s see the Enlightenment at its height: by the middle and later 1770s it was in decline. Of its greatest figures Voltaire, Rousseau (if he can justly be considered a man of the Enlightenment at all), Diderot, Condillac, d'Alembert and Mably all died in the years 1778–85. Well before the outbreak of the French Revolution, therefore, it had shot its bolt and was increasingly challenged and undermined by new intellectual and emotional currents—romanticism, sensibility, incipient nationalism and various forms of more or less unconcealed irrationalism.

None of this, however, means that this remarkable intellectual cur-

F. Venturi, 'The European Enlightenment', in his collection *Italy and the Enlightenment: studies in a cosmopolitan century* (London, 1972) is an interesting essay which attempts to relate the intellectual developments of the century to its political and social history. R. Pomeau, *L'Europe des lumières: cosmopolitisme et unité européenne au dix-huitième siècle* (Paris, 1966) provides much interesting background to the intellectual and cultural life of the period. The outstanding attack on the totalitarian tendencies implicit in some aspects of the Enlightenment in France is J. L. Talmon, *The Origins of Totalitarian Democracy* (London, 1952). Several authors have discussed in great detail particular aspects of French intellectual life: L. G. Crocker, *An Age of Crisis: man and world in eighteenth-century French thought* (Baltimore, 1959); R. Mauzi, *L'Idée du bonheur dans la littérature et la pensée françaises au XVIIIᵉ siècle* (Paris, 1960); and J. Ehard, *L'Idée de nature en France dans la première moitié du XVIIIᵉ siècle* (Paris, 1963). On individual figures a long list of books could be given. R. Shackleton,

rent, however confused and complicated by eddies and even counter-currents, was unimportant. Both its partisans and its enemies were conscious of its power. By the 1760s, when the Enlightenment was at the peak of its influence, the intellectual life of Europe was very different from what it had been half a century earlier at the death of Louis XIV. This change, however violently it was later to be denounced, even vilified, in the aftermath of the French Revolution, could never be undone.

What historians have generally agreed to regard as the central strand in the Enlightenment, its critical, rationalistic, intellectually liberating element, suspicious of tradition and received ideas, scornful of what were seen as the destructive follies of the past, was predominantly French. It was from Paris that ideas and attitudes of this kind spread, with widely varying effect in different parts of the continent, to the rest of Europe, The intellectual style of the French Enlightenment—and it was, it must be emphasized, a style, a set of attitudes, much more than a systematic body of doctrine—is embodied above all in the writings of Voltaire. In a series of brilliant and piercingly amusing stories or short novels: *Zadig* (1747); *Micromégas* (1752); *Candide* (1759), as well as in his *Dictionnaire philosophique* (1764) he attacked conventional attitudes, most of all conventional religious beliefs and prejudices, with unparalleled effect. Savage irony, sarcasm raised to the level of devastating intellectual and political criticism, became in his hands weapons with which to attack churches, clerics and their allegedly stultifying effects on human liberty and happiness. This attack he launched with a cultivated ferocity, a venomous elegance, never seen before. No one did more than he to spread the ideas of 'natural religion' and deism, the

---

Montesquieu: a critical biography (Oxford, 1961) and A. M. Wilson, *Diderot, the Testing Years* (New York, 1957) are both excellent. On Voltaire there are A. Besterman, *Voltaire* (London, 1969) and P. Gay, *Voltaire's Politics: the poet as realist* (Princeton, 1959), both somewhat uncritical in tone, and R. Pomeau, *La Réligion de Voltaire* (Paris, 1956). Rousseau is discussed in R. Derathé, *Le Rationalisme de J.-J. Rousseau* (Paris, 1948) and *Jean-Jacques Rousseau et la science politique de son temps* (Paris, 1950); and in R. Grimsley, *Jean-Jacques Rousseau: a study in self-awareness* (Cardiff, 1961). There is a large literature on both Vico and Herder: perhaps it is sufficient to mention here H. P. Adams, *The Life and Writings of Giambattista Vico* (London, 1935) and F. M. Barnard, *Herder's Social and Political Thought: from Enlightment to nationalism* (Oxford, 1965). Some aspects of the reaction against the Enlightenment are briefly and brilliantly discussed in R. Darnton, *Mesmerism and the End of the Enlightenment in France* (Cambridge, Mass., 1968).

opposition to religious intolerance, which are briefly discussed in the last chapter of this book (see pp. 390ff). He was not a man of great intellectual depth. His range of sympathies was in many ways narrow. But within his own limits he was the most brilliant and persuasive of all propagandists of ideas.

The second great symbol of the French Enlightenment is the *Encyclopéaie: ou dictionnaire méthodique des sciences, des arts et des métiers* which appeared in Paris in thirty-five volumes in 1751–80, and for the production of which Denis Diderot, in many ways the most radical and interesting of all French thinkers of the century, was mainly responsible. This famous work, which had enormous success and influence in France and was the largest single publishing venture of the period, attempted to summarize the whole of human knowledge as it then existed. But besides its function merely as a vast assembly of information it had another, a more dynamic one—that of popularizing and disseminating attitudes which, in spite of variations bteween different contributors, in all essentials epitomized the Enlightenment.

The intellectual currents which, in rather different ways, Voltaire and the *Encyclopédie* represented, had a largely non-French ancestry. In particular the English contribution to them was very great. Newton had shown more dramatically and on a larger scale than any other scientist the existence in nature of fundamental regularities, basic laws of the widest scope which gave coherence and meaning to otherwise shapeless masses of facts. His example strengthened and gave force to a fundamental Enlightenment belief, that in the possibility of transforming, by the use of human reason, a world of apparent chaos and contradiction into one of intellectual unity, one comprehensible to and therefore controllable by the intelligent man of good will. Even more important, from John Locke, in his *Essay concerning Human Understanding* (1690) and *Thoughts concerning Education* (1693) can be traced the Enlightenment belief that the human mind is formed by the sense impressions which it receives from the outside world, in other words by experience and environment. Man was thus seen as highly teachable. His mind, when this line of argument was pushed to its logical conclusion, became merely a *tabula rasa* upon which, through education, enlightened ideas and beliefs could be imprinted. In one sense such a view was, by implication at least, pessimistic. If all knowledge were limited by man's sense perceptions, then he could know only the external aspects of the universe; knowledge of essences and final causes, for which so many philosophers and mystics had striven in the past, was forever beyond his reach. The French writer Condillac, whose *Traité des sensations* (1754) is the most extreme statement of this type of sensationalist psychology, frankly admitted as much. On the everyday level, however, the implications of this view of the human mind were highly optimistic. Man might, it seemed, be made virtuous merely by providing him with the right environment, the appropriate set of stimuli both positive and negative. This meant, in practical terms, subjecting him to simple, just and comprehensible laws and, most important of all, appropriate education. It is from the Enlightenment and its inheritance from Locke that there stems that faith in the power of systems of education to reform man and society, a faith sometimes noble though often deluded and even pathetic, which has continued to inspire radicals of different types down to our own day.

But if the Enlightenment in its French, or French-centred, form depended heavily on English ingredients, it transformed them into something distinctively its own. What then did it, as seen at full maturity, involve?

The most famous answer to this question is that given by the German philosopher Immanuel Kant, a strong partisan of the Enlightenment and later for a time of the French Revolution, in his article, 'Beantwortung der Frage: Was ist Aufklärung' (An answer to the question: What is Enlightenment), published in the *Berlinische Monatschrift* in December 1784. In this he identified the essential characteristics of the great intellectual change as 'man's leaving his self-caused immaturity'. Hitherto he had been in intellectual tutelage, unable to use his mind freely without outside control and guidance. Now he had grown up. His unrestricted search for knowledge, his achievement of intellectual autonomy, would lead him to discard his former prejudices and bring him to a new freedom and the full realization of his potentialities. '*Sapere aude!* Dare to use your own intelligence! That is the motto of the Enlightenment!' Kant summed up. This well expresses the most fundamental aspect of the Enlightenment; its search for freedom. Man, guided by reason, was now to make his own way in the world without relying as in the past on the supports offered him by revelation and religious tradition, supports which had crippled even while they appeared to aid him. His newfound freedom was to be very largely the product of criticism, criticism of the past, of custom, of received ideas of any kind which could not stand the test of reason. From this criticism was to come man's power to make sense of the world and hence to control his own destinies. Philosophy was to become 'disciplined aggression against concrete problems'.[1]

The purpose of this aggression was human happiness. Overwhelmingly the greatest single emotional drive behind the Enlightenment was that towards making men happy in the here and now; and as it progressed it became more and more easy to believe that no other objective really counted for very much. The potentially explosive idea of happiness as a right, something to which all men were entitled and which only ignorance and external obstacles—bad government, archaic laws, worst of all cramping and irrational religious influences—denied them, was now for the first time in history gaining wide acceptance. Such an idea, impossible to reconcile with traditional Christian faith, was still challenged by one or two thinkers of real stature (the most important was the Marquis de Vauvenargues, the greatest moralist of the century). But these were increasingly regarded as perverse and unworthy of serious attention. The general happiness so eagerly sought could be ensured by correct engineering of government and society.

The methods by which Newton had explained the physical universe and Locke and Condillac that of the mind and the emotions could be applied to political and social problems. Such an application would make possible for the first time a just and virtuous, and therefore happy, society. This society would be just, virtuous and happy because it was natural, no longer distorted by unfairness and irrationalities sanctioned merely by time and tradition. Its members would enjoy natural rights, be ruled by natural law and practice the natural religion of which God had implanted an instinctive consciousness in their hearts. They might even enjoy, according to some of the more extreme advocates of such ideas, natural equality, though what this could mean in practice was seldom spelt out in any detailed or satisfactory way. The Enlightenment faith in the potentialities of intellectual freedom, in the application of reason and intelligence to the problem of human life, was therefore profoundly optimistic. Few thinkers of the period had any naïve belief in the inherent or absolute goodness of human nature; but almost all were deeply hopeful about what could be achieved even with very imperfect human beings through the workings of science, education and good government, and through the rebuilding of society along lines dictated by reason. Social usefulness, the maximization of human happiness, must become the criterion of morality.

It must be emphasized once more that the Enlightenment was a complex and in many ways disorganized intellectual movement which

[1] Gay, *The Rise of Modern Paganism* (*see* Bibliography, p. 362), p. 183.

extended over a considerable period of time. What has been given in the preceding paragraphs is merely a highly simplified account of its main attitudes and beliefs. The full reality was much more complex; for different writers inevitably stressed different aspects of the set of ideas and attitudes which was shaking French intellecual life by the middle of the century. Voltaire represents its fierce anticlericalism and its demand for religious toleration; but in political terms he was a moderate, a believer in efficient monarchical government. His view of society (perhaps this is not surprising in a man who was both extremely wealthy and also well into middle age by the 1740s) was markedly conservative. Diderot, both politically and socially, was a far more genuine radical; he was one of the few *philosophes* who consistently displayed an open dislike for any form of despotism. In the secondary figures of the period a wide range of different forms of extremism can be seen. La Mettrie, in his *L'Homme machine* (1748) represents the materialist currents which the Enlightenment inherited from the seventeenth century carried to dogmatic and almost ludicrous lengths; d'Holbach, in his *Le Christianisme dévoilé* (1767) and *Système de la nature* (1770) shows anti-religious feeling expressed as explicit atheism; Morellet in his *Code de la Nature* (1755) and Mably in his *De la Législation* (1776) exemplify the visionary and utopian aspects implicit in the whole system of 'enlightened' ideas.

The attitudes and beliefs of the *philosophes*, though they were often held with great force and sincerity, were in many ways unrealistic. This was partly because, while so sweeping and grandiose in some respects, they were surprisingly limited, even narrow, in others. They were concerned with Man in the abstract rather than with specific societies or communities; underlying them was a frequent assumption that the problems of government and society were at bottom much the same everywhere, that policies did not need to be carefully adapted to varying conditions or to the differing feelings, traditions and potentialities of those affected by them. What was required for good government, it was assumed, was a firm grasp of correct principles, not detailed study of particular problems and conditions. This attitude underlies the contempt with which so many writers of the Enlightenment regarded mere erudition and their indifference or even hostility towards scholarship and minute knowledge. 'Details', wrote one of them, 'can take care of themselves; in fundamentals everything is to be seen in relation to general principles, simple but unchanging. It is of the highest importance to understand them, and this is the main study of the statesman.' Much important work was done during the eighteenth century in accumulating knowledge of non-European societies, in laying some of the foundations of modern anthropology and sociology.[1] But the extent to which this over-lapped with or influenced political and social speculation was in many ways surprisingly small. (The only important exception to this generalization is the interest in China as an example of good government and a well-organized society referred to on pp. 331-2.) Moreover Enlightenment theorizing was weakened by the indifference or contempt with which it tended to regard history, or at least most of what had happened since the great days of the Roman Empire. Good government and the just and happy society were to be achieved by analysis, criticism of what already existed, the use of reason, rather than by trying to deduce lessons from the past. What had existed proved nothing about what might, far less what should, exist in the future. 'The rights of men in society', wrote Turgot, who more sincerely than anyone else during the century attempted to give ideas of enlightened government practical effect in France, 'are based not on their history but on their nature.'[2] In particular the Middle Ages, permeated by the Catholic Christianity which the *philosophes* regarded as their greatest enemy, aroused widespread contempt and revulsion. Kant spoke of them as 'an incomprehensible aberration of the human mind', a phrase no more severe than many other thinkers of the period used. Such an attitude grossly overestimated the extent to which men could escape from their past and the speed and ease with which radical change of any kind could be introduced. It therefore contributed substantially to the optimism which many *philosophes* felt about the possibility of rapid political and social progress.

In so far as the Enlightenment appealed to history, it was to that of Greece and Rome. In so far as it looked for models in the past they were models of classical grandeur and urbanity, those to be found in Virgil and still more in Horace and Cicero, the most popular Latin authors of the period. 'Nature and the ancients' was a slogan frequently used by the *philosophes*; and it is clear that many of them saw themselves as the heirs of classical antiquity fighting once more the struggle which 'the ancients' had lost against Christian bigotry and repression. To them the classical tradition offered an alternative to Christianity which most

[1] The *De generis humani varietate nativa* of the German scholar J. F. Blumenbach, which was published in 1775, is sometimes described as the earliest genuine work of physical anthropology.
[1] *Oeuvres*, ed. G. Schelle (Paris, 1922), vol. IV, p. 575.

of them were glad to embrace. 'All over Europe and America', as a recent historian has put it, 'for all philosophes alike, the ancients were signposts to secularism.'[1] Even the physical condition of the city of Rome in the eighteenth century, brokendown, dirty, with perhaps a third of the population of its greatest imperial days, seemed visible testimony to the conflict between classical antiquity and Christian belief. It was this contrast, symbolized by 'bare-footed friars . . . chanting their litanies in the temple of Jupiter' which in 1764 inspired Edward Gibbon (the only great English scholar of the century who can be considered as fully in the mainstream of the Enlightenment) to begin his *Decline and Fall of the Roman Empire* (1776–88).

There were other, and equally serious, ways in which the *philosophes* and the Enlightenment showed their limitations. So far as effective social change was concerned, as distinct from mere speculation or the construction of paper Utopias, their radicalism was often a sham. Violence in words, especially when religion and established churches were being attacked, coexisted easily with a marked readiness in practice to accept with little or no demur society as it existed. The possibility of sweeping change through the application of reason might be envisaged; but the most daring speculation was almost always underlain by a comfortable conviction that society as it stood was in essentials unchangeable. The *philosophes* were well aware that they wrote only for a small educated élite. They took it for granted that the great majority of Europeans would continue, as in the past, to be outside this charmed circle, largely uneducated and perhaps ineducable. Some of them (Voltaire is the best known example) actively opposed the education of the masses since this might make them unwilling to perform the routine manual labour, harsh and badly paid, on which the existence of society depended. It is possible to find works by *philosophes* which can in some general and theoretical sense be called socialist. But these (the best examples are Morellet's *Code de la Nature* and Mably's *De la législation*) were utopian schemes, not a response to immediate and specific grievances. They enunciated vast and far-reaching theories of social and legal equality, of the collective ownership of property, of the restriction or abolition of rights of inheritance; but this was a very different thing from a practicable programme of social change. A truer pointer to the

[1] Gay, *The Rise of Modern Paganism* (*see* Bibliography, p. 362), p. 44: Book I, Chap. i of this book is the best account of the debt of the Enlightenment to classical antiquity.

future in many respects was the *Théorie des lois civiles* of S. N. H. Linguet, which appeared in 1767. This attacked the claim of Locke and his followers that property originated from man's 'mingling' his labour with material objects and was therefore a natural right. On the contrary, Linguet argued, property had its roots merely in force and was at bottom nothing but the right of the stronger. Law and government, which existed to protect property rights, were thus 'a conspiracy against the most numerous part of the human race'. It is not surprising to find these assertions quoted with approval by Marx a century later. But Linguet was one of the most individual and idiosynrcatic writers of the century, difficult to classify and in many ways quite untypical of the Enlightenment.

Moreover the genuine liberalism, the real concern for freedom (or at least for the intellectual freedom of the educated minority) which inspired so much of the work of the *philosophes* did not exclude from the Enlightenment significant elements of intolerance, even of fanaticism. On one level this found expression in relatively trivial acts of personal self-seeking and group exclusiveness. Thus Diderot, while employed as a government censor, can be found demanding the suppression of a play (the *Satirique* of Palissot de Montenoy) which poked fun at enlightened ideas; while the publication of the Abbé d'Expilly's great statistical dictionary in 1762–70 seems to have been delayed by the influence of the Physiocrats, since it dared to contradict their dogmatic belief that the population of France was declining. More important was the fact that by the end of the 1760s or the early 1770s the *philosophes* had gained complete control of organized intellectual life in France. The Academy in Paris, the numerous provincial academies, the literary societies, all were dominated by them; and they used this position to impose the ideas of the Enlightenment (in a moderate and watered-down form) as a kind of official orthodoxy. This cliquishness aroused much resentment among those denied the official posts and the publication opportunities which the dominant group monopolized.[1]

But far more significant than these rivalries was the absolutism and intolerance inherent in many of the very assumptions of the Enlightenment when they were pressed to their logical conclusion. In their more extreme form these postulated an ideal type of society and government which could, indeed must, be attained by the free workings of human

[1] On this see the very interesting article of R. Darnton, 'The high Enlightenment and the low-life of literature in pre-revolutionary France', *Past and Present*, No. 51 (May, 1971).

reason. All existing political and social systems, the products merely of history and of the selfishness and obscurantism of rulers, aristocracies and churches, were thus destined to be replaced by a natural and rational order. This would come into existence when all the irrational and unnatural features of existing societies had been swept away. In such a society men would at last be free; but this would not lead to the emergence of differing opinions and parties among them. On the contrary, unfettered reason would produce complete harmony and unanimity. Such a society would also be one of perfectly virtuous men; and the idea of virtue (conceived of in narrow terms of asceticism and intolerance of 'luxury') was one which was gaining ground in radical circles in France during the 1770s and 1780s. Side by side, therefore, with the mocking, critical, worldly, sometimes cynical spirit represented so brilliantly by Voltaire there lurked within the Enlightenment another which was utopian, messianic and at least potentially totalitarian. In the works of Mably, and even more through those of Rousseau, this was to have considerable influence during the French revolution. Later it was to become one thread in the complex intellectual fabric of European radicalism in the nineteenth and twentieth centuries.[1]

The most impressive characteristic of the Enlightenment, however, it must once more be emphasized, was its complexity, its many-sidedness. To every generalization about it qualifications, sometimes serious and important ones, must be made if any fair picture is to emerge. Certainly many of the *philosophes* were buoyed up by a belief in the rationality of man and in his ultimate perfectibility if he were placed in the correct environment and subjected to the correct form of education. Yet at the same time there was in the thinking of others a distinct vein of scepticism, even pessimism, a consciousness that consistent and cumulative human progress over a long period of time might in fact be difficult to achieve. In the middle of the previous century the great philosopher and scientist Pascal, in opposition to Descartes, had claimed to set distinct boundaries to the potentialities of human reason; and his successors a century later had not really disproved the claim. It is true that in the 1790s, when the Enlightenment proper was over, Condorcet in his *Esquisse d'un tableau historique des progrès de l'esprit humain* (1795) restated the doctrines of human perfectibility and inevitable social and intellectual advance in their most extreme form. But by then this was a mere survival of earlier attitudes, attitudes which in

[1] The classical discussion of the messianic and intolerant side of the Enlightenment is that in the first chapters of J. L. Talmon (*see* Bibliography, p. 363).

any case had never been fully accepted by most *philosophes*. It has been argued with a good deal of force that, apart from Condorcet, Turgot alone of eighteenth-century thinkers possessed 'a fully articulated theory of progress'.[1] Again, most writers of this period thought of nature as helpful to man, as something to be understood and then used by him. Yet Buffon, the French scientist whose *Histoire naturelle* (1749–88) was by far the most influential description of the natural world produced during the century, became, as its thirty-six volumes appeared, increasingly inclined to see the natural world as hostile to man, an obstacle which he must overcome or even a foe which he must conquer. Here again pessimism crept into the picture.

Nor were the *philosophes* always uninterested in other ages than their own and unwilling to realize that human societies were the distinctive products of specific times and places. Voltaire himself, in his *Essai sur les moeurs* (1756) made a remarkable pioneering effort to see the social development of humanity in historical and comparative terms. Moreover the Enlightenment, hard though it might try, could never completely cut itself off from its Christian intellectual roots. What it did, in essentials, was to erect a new orthodoxy, humanist and pseudo-scientific, to challenge that which had preceded it. To Christian, and above all Catholic, universalism it opposed its own, more liberal and optimistic. But what it preached was none the less a form of universalism; and this necessarily limited the genuineness of any claim it might make to be truly empirical in its outlook and methods. The contributors to the *Encyclopédie*, its greatest monument, clearly owed much to a legacy of Catholic orthodoxy of which they were the beneficiaries.[2]

Perhaps the greatest difficulty of all in the way of any simple account of the Enlightenment, however, is the fact that the two most original and important French thinkers of the period, Montesquieu and still more Rousseau, stand in varying degrees apart from it and are difficult (in Rousseau's case impossible) to fit into any conventional Enlightenment mould.

Rousseau may not be the greatest of eighteenth-century writers on political and social problems. But he has certainly been the most

[1] P. Gay, 'The Enlightenment in the history of political theory', *Political Science Quarterly*, vol. LXIX (1954), p. 380.
[2] On this see R. Hubert, *Les Sciences sociales dans l'Encyclopédie* (Lille, 1923), pp. 358ff.

influential. For this there are two reasons. He created a new view of
the State; indeed he was the only writer of the period to put forward
any significant theory of the State. He also went far towards creating
a new sort of political and social consciousness, a new psychology. To
the intellectual style of the mid-century Enlightenment typified by
Voltaire and Hume, sceptical, witty, at least within certain limits
genuinely liberal, he opposed another which was earnest, often intro-
spective, deeply distrustful of the cosmopolitan high culture of the
period, of wealth, great cities, sophistication of any kind. In political
terms his greatest and most lasting achievement was to elevate the
State to a position higher and powers more all-embracing than any of
his predecessors had contemplated. Its functions in his eyes went much
further than the mere protection of the individual and his property
which Locke had assigned to it. On the contrary it was the fact that
men lived in societies, and societies which were also States, which really
distinguished them from the animals. In his emphasis on this fact
Rousseau can be seen, in a very general sense, as a major precursor of
modern sociology; his exaltation of the State and its creative functions
also gives his political philosophy some general affinity with that which
Hegel was to popularize in Germany, with such far-reaching effect,
half a century later. It was the State, according to Rousseau's theory
in its mature form, which made men fully human. That theory was
embodied in a famous work, the *Contrat social* (1762). This envisaged
men deciding to create a society, but none the less retaining in their
own hands ultimate sovereign power which they would exercise by
meeting periodically to legislate for their needs. The ideal, in other
words, was direct democracy of a sort practicable only in a small State;
Rousseau remained always deeply suspicious of any sort of representative system, which in his eyes must mean that the ordinary citizen
would lose interest in and control over public affairs. This attitude owed
something to admiration of the city-states of antiquity and still more
to Rousseau's upbringing in the little state of Geneva, an early experience which deeply influenced his ideas. The citizen of his ideal State,
when as a body they took decisions, declared the General Will, which
must, by definition, always work for the advantage of society as a whole.
It was nothing so mechanical as the mere will of a numerical majority.
On the contrary, it expressed the 'real will' of every individual citizen,
what each would desire if he were fully informed on the issues at stake
and acted in accordance with the dictates of his higher nature. To the
General Will factions and parties must give way; indeed groups and

sectional interests of this kind were a grave danger to the State and must as far as possible be suppressed. There are very obvious totalitarian possibilities inherent in such a view of political life and Rousseau recognized and welcomed this. To the State he assigned enormously far-reaching functions. It must enforce a high degree of economic equality between individuals (since this was essential for the preservation of society as Rousseau envisaged it). Even more important, it must control the private morals of citizens, must determine the education they received and must if possible be supported by a State religion systematically preaching patriotism and civic virtue.

All this is separated by a great gulf from the main stream of Enlightenment thought. Where the latter had little theory of the State and in general little interest in political philosophy as such, Rousseau made the State one of the cornerstones of his thought. Where the Enlightenment in general moved, though slowly and unevenly, towards greater economic liberalism, Rousseau demanded strict and pervasive economic controls (sumptuary laws; restriction of the right of inheritance; measures to preserve agriculture, the foundation of liberty and virtue, against the potentially corrupting effects of industry and finance). Where the Enlightenment was cosmopolitan, Rousseau showed a deep feeling for exclusive patriotism. Yet it must be stressed that he retained always a profound belief in the value and rights of the individual. It was to safeguard these, in his eyes, that the State and its machinery existed; they had no other justification.

The State of the *Contrat social*, as Rousseau himself admitted, was an ideal. It was not intended to bear any direct relationship to the facts of everyday experience. He agreed that it could be realized only in small, geographically coherent societies—Geneva, Berne, perhaps Corsica for which he attempted in 1764 to draw up a constitution. His only attempt at practical constitution-making for a large territory, his *Considérations sur le gouvernement de Pologne* (written in 1771 though not published until 1790) was by contrast remarkably moderate, almost conservative. In it he stressed that it was desirable 'to change nothing, either for retrenchment or addition, unless it is necessary', and envisaged the freeing of the Polish serfs only by stages and the continued exclusion of the mass of the population from any political power.

The puzzles and inconsistencies of his political doctrines by no means exhaust the interest of Rousseau for the historian. He was very much more than a merely political thinker. He was also the writer who, more than anyone else, popularized and indeed to a large extent created a new kind of consciousness, almost a new kind of man. His whole deeply unhappy life can be seen as a continuous effort to be himself, to realize his own potentialities without compromising with the world as it was, without succumbing to the longing for wealth, for worldly success, for the approval of the great and powerful. 'He provided', writes his most recent biographer, 'an exemplary instance of the power of absolute integrity in a man whose life and thought were in perfect harmony, and of the tremendous impact, far-ranging effect and truly revolutionary value of that integrity.'[1] His struggles, his hopes and fears, his successes and failures, he revealed to the world with unprecedented frankness in his *Confessions*, the autobriography of which the first six volumes were published in 1782, four years after his death. This book is the greatest single monument of the later eighteenth-century cult of sensibility. In its revelation of the most intimate details of his private life, its preoccupation with feeling and emotion, its passionate response to natural scenery and its deep distrust of urban and intellectual society, it offers a revealing contrast with the *Memoirs of my Life and Writing* by Edward Gibbon (1796). Restrained, reticent, elegant, often ironic, Gibbon's book is the quintessence of many aspects of the Enlightenment. Rousseau's is both more and less. In it the Enlightenment in its rational and Roman aspects does not appear at all; but the *Confessions* points the way, as Gibbon does not, towards a new state of mind, a new set of psychological values. These also suffuse totally the most popular of all Rousseau's writings during his lifetime, his novel, *La Nouvelle Héloise* (1761).

Throughout his life Rousseau was tormented by the need to choose between values good in themselves but apparently irreconcilable with one another. Could liberty really be combined with the progress of the civilization which both attracted and repelled him? Would the native virtues of the good heart be corrupted by the growth of knowledge? How was the patriotism which meant so much to him to be reconciled with a love of humanity in general? The fact that he was well aware of these questions and struggled to find answers to them is one source of his continuing fascination for generations of later historians and commentators.

Montesquieu was the most many-sided, the most productive of stimulating ideas, of all the major writers of the eighteenth century on politics and society. In these respects he had had no superior, perhaps

[1] J. Guéhenno, *Jean-Jacques Rousseau* (London–New York, 1966), vol. I, Preface, p. xvi.

no equal, since Aristotle himself. Of all the thinkers of the age he is in many ways the one whose methods of thought seem most modern, most relevant to the present day and its problems. He is also the only important figure amongst them who can be reasonably described as a conservative. His greatest work, *De l'esprit des lois* (1748) restated with great effect traditional ideas of 'mixed' government. In a well-regulated State one power would be balanced by another and no authority able to override all competitors. To the formation of this attitude both the practical example of the British constitution, which Montesquieu greatly admired, and his own position as a member of an important family of the *noblesse de la robe* and the holder of high office in the *Parlement* of Bordeaux certainly contributed. The monarch (whom Montesquieu distinguished very clearly from an arbitrary despot of the Asiatic type) must be limited in his actions by a powerful and responsible nobility and by laws which he could not override. In an age of increasing political absolutism Montesquieu therefore stood, though in a limited, traditional and classbound way, for freedom. From the dogmatism and universalism, the tendency to generalize widely on the basis of *a priori* assumptions and scanty or even non-existent evidence which marked much eighteenth-century political writing, he did not escape. His discussion, in the *Esprit des lois*, of the essential characteristics of monarchical, aristocratic and republican forms of government is an example of this. It is based on the description of 'ideal types' of each of these, to a large extent divorced from time and place, rather than on the discussion of specific historical examples. Nevertheless his work (his earlier *Considérations sur les causes de la grandeur des Romains et de leur décadence* (1734) as well as the *Esprit des lois*) is unique in the writing of his own age in its effort to base analysis and explanation on a great body of detailed information. From the facts of history, from information about non-European peoples and their organization and achievements, Montesquieu tried to evolve laws which ruled the evolution of human societies. 'It is not Fortune that governs the world', he wrote. 'There are general causes, either moral or physical, which operate. . . . In a word, the dominant trend carries with it all particular incidents.' This attitude, in effect an effort to write a pioneering work of sociology on the largest scale, is Montesquieu's supreme claim to importance. It led him, against the dominant current of Enlightenment thinking, to think of morality and government as relative, the product of specific times and places, and thus to be judged fairly only in their own context. It also strengthened his conservatism; for the result of his work was usually to justify whatever customs or habits existed at any given moment in any particular society. Moreover the laws which he attempted to formulate—notably his, in modern eyes, naïve theory of the effects of differing climates on human psychology and hence on institutions, a theory which was not even at all novel—had little permanent value. Yet there is no denying the greatness of the effort; and Montesquieu's work at its best has a combination of realism and intellectual scope which puts it in a different class from almost anything else produced by the French Enlightenment. It is significant that his relativism, an attitude which gained increasing support from many writers during the later decades of the century, seems to have appealed particularly to statesmen and diplomats, men with direct experience of government and its problems. Thus Tanucci (in many ways no friend to the Enlightenment) agreed that 'universal laws in moral and political matters do not exist; laws arise from the position of the country and its people'.[1] In the same vein the Neapolitan ambassador in Paris, the Abbé Galiani, himself a voluminous writer on economic and social problems, proclaimed that 'good legislation is always that which corresponds to the constitution, strength and nature of each country'.[2] Montesquieu, then, had no simple panacea for all social and political ills. More clearly than any other major writer of the century he realized that good government was difficult to achieve and maintain; this alone gives him a claim on the sympathies of our own age

What has been said in the preceding pages is concerned almost entirely with the Enlightenment in France. It is inevitable that she should bulk very large in any discussion of the subject. It was in Paris that this whole movement of ideas appeared, between the 1740s and the 1770s, in its most concentrated and intellectually convincing form. It was French books, far more than German, Italian or even English ones, which were translated into other languages during this period. It was French writers and scholars who found themselves invited by rulers elsewhere in Europe to visit their courts and to accept posts as advisers or as members of academies of sciences. Voltaire's unsuccessful visit to Prussia in 1750–53, the mathematician Maupertuis's years as President of the Berlin Academy in 1745–53, the fruitless journey of Diderot to Russia in 1773–74, are obvious examples of this. In so far as Europe

[1] Quoted in H. Holldack, 'Der Physiocratismus und die absolute Monarchie', *Historische Zeitschrift*, vol. CXLV (1932), p. 521.

[2] *Dialogues sur le commerce des blés* (Berlin, 1795), pp. 121, 475.

was a single intellectual world in the eighteenth century it was a world of which France was the leader (see p. 360). Nevertheless it would be a great mistake to imagine that the Enlightenment elsewhere in Europe was merely a copy of that in France. On the contrary; everywhere it was deeply influenced by local traditions, values and preferences. Nowhere is this more clearly seen than in England. There increasing political stability, sustained economic growth and remarkable success in the building up of a great overseas empire meant that criticism, discontent and hankering after change, so strong in intellectual circles in France by the middle of the century, was relatively muted. Neither the support for Wilkes in the 1760s nor the movement for parliamentary reform in the later 1770s and 1780s (see pp. 141, 143) owed much to the type of radical political speculation so widespread in France. Gibbon, the one great figure whom England contributed to the Enlightenment, spent much of his life abroad and remained in his own country isolated and untypical. Later in the century the country produced a group of writers—Jeremy Bentham, Richard Price, William Godwin and Thomas Paine—who stood squarely in the main continental 'enlightened' tradition of rationalism and anticlericalism. But most of these did not become significant until the 1790s, in an environment quite different from that of Voltaire and the *Encyclopédie*.

The failure of the country which led Europe in economic and technological development during the century to be seriously affected by the Enlightenment is perhaps the strongest of all grounds for rejecting the frequently repeated Marxist view of the latter as essentially the ideology of a developing middle class. Moreover the lack of any serious 'enlightened' impulse in England is thrown into sharper relief by the development of a very interesting and important Scottish Enlightenment. Its leading figures, Adam Ferguson, in his *Essay on the History of Civil Society* (1767), and John Millar, in his *Observations concerning the Distinctions of Ranks in Society* (1771), clearly inhabit the same intellectual world as the leaders of French intellectual life during these years. Perhaps an Enlightenment of this type, critical and hostile to many aspects of the status quo, can develop only in societies where modernity and backwardness confront each other at close quarters. Such stark discontinuities stimulate questioning and discontent. The contrasts in France between the high intellectual life of Paris and the ignorance of so much of the population in general, or in Scotland between the world of Adam Smith and David Hume and the archaic poverty of the Highlands, very recently emerged from tribalism, had this effect.

In England, by contrast (and for that matter in the Dutch Republic also) society, in spite of gross inequalities and many regional disparities, was too well integrated for such an effect to be possible.

This argument is supported by the experience of Italy during this period. There also there were gross disparities, above all in intellectual development and achievement, between different parts of the peninsula. The stagnation in this respect of Savoy or Venice contrasts sharply with the growth in Naples, during the later decades of the century, of a remarkable group of thinkers on political and economic questions: Genovesi, Galiani, Filangieri. The government of the Papal State, one of the most backward-looking and hostile to change in Europe, confronted the enlightened régime of Leopold in Tuscany. The country where clerical conservatism was stronger than anywhere else in Europe outside the Iberian peninsula and possibly Bavaria produced, in the *Delle delitti e delle pene* of Cesare Beccaria (1764), the book which began the development of modern penology, one of the key works of the Enlightenment as a movement of practical reform. The Italian Enlightenment, though it was in part a response to Italian conditions and problems, can none the less be seen as essentially an aspect of the great European movement of intellectual development, of questioning and criticism, of striving for liberty and rationality, which had its centre in France. The greatest single figure in the intellectual history of eighteenth-century Italy, however, Giambattista Vico, stands quite outside this tradition and had done all his work before it came to fruition. His whole cast of mind was profoundly historical: he has been described as 'one of the most historically minded men who ever lived'.[1] In this alone he differs radically from almost all the great figures of the French Enlightenment. Moreover he is important chiefly because of a quality of creative imagination lacking in their thinking. The central idea of his greatest work, the *Scienza nuova* (first published in 1725; the final version appeared in 1744, the year of his death) is that the true history of humanity is the history of its mental states. But only by an immense effort of the imagination, a struggle by the historian to project himself into an intellectual environment quite foreign to that of his own day, can these be understood. The history of an age must therefore be approached not merely through documents and inscriptions but even more through the study of its poetry and its use of language, and through the interpretation of its mythology. This attitude clearly fore-

---

[1] H. P. Adams (*see* Bibliography, p. 364), p. 164.

shadows nineteenth-century developments and entitles Vico, more than any other thinker, to be called the founder of the philosophy of history. But it sets him apart from (many historians would now say above) the main stream of the French Enlightenment.

It is most clearly that in Germany that we see an Enlightenment which owed little to France and to the intellectuals of Paris. Some debt there undoubtedly was; but it was incurred mainly towards the great untypical figures of the French movement, Montesquieu and Rousseau, both of whom achieved widespread popularity and influence east of the Rhine. The *Aufklarung* in Germany was based on foundations different from those of the Enlightenment in France. Essentially its tone and style were very different. Empiricism, materialism, the sensationalist psychology which stemmed from Locke, utilitarianism with its simple and direct emphasis on happiness in the here and now; none of these became a leading element in German intellectual life during the century in the way that they did in France. While the dominant strains in French thought became increasingly hostile to ambitious metaphysical systems, which seemed merely to confuse simple issues and bamboozle honest men, in Germany thinking of this kind remained supreme. The prestige of the great German scientist and philosopher Leibniz, still enormous for long after his death in 1716, was one of the bases of this attitude his idealism, his belief in a personal God and transcendental moral values, made a powerful appeal to German intellectual tastes. The leading *Aufklarer*, such as Christian Thomasius and Christian Wolff, sternly rejected empiricism. Even Kant, a radical liberal and deeply interested in the physical sciences, thought it inadequate as a method for the understanding of either science or morality. No significant German thinker of the century ever advocated that men should be guided by principles derived from the study of physics or astronomy rather than by those drawn from their own insights and intuitions.

In practice this contrast between France and Germany showed itself most clearly in the great and continuing intellectual importance and appeal of religion in the latter. 'While French philosophes leaped into unbelief', one historian has written, 'their German brethren were seduced into it, step by reluctant step.'[1] Even this overstates the case; most of the *Aufklarer* managed to resist seduction more or less completely. Wolff, the most powerful figure of the century in German

---

[1] Gay, *The Rise of Modern Paganism* (*see* Bibliography, p. 362), p. 331.

intellectual life, never abandoned his belief in the possibility of reconciling reason with the revealed truths of Christianity. Nor did the significance of religion and religious controversy in Germany show much sign of declining as the century drew to a close. 'When all other nations have given up respect for religion', wrote the Frenchman Chateaubriand in 1797, 'it will find a haven among the Germans.'[1]

The generally un-French and strikingly moderate character of the *Aufklarung* in Germany was to have enormous long-term importance for the country's history. It helps, in particular, to explain the weakness throughout the nineteenth century of German liberalism as a political force. In the shorter term, however, it also had significance in one important respect outside Germany. Whereas the Enlightenment in Italy and Spain drew sustenance from the fountain-head in France, that in Russia was very largely German in inspiration. Though French cultural influences were very powerful in Russia from the 1750s onwards and the prestige of French literature and the French language very great, German philosophical and scientific influences were more important there than those stemming from France. The roots of the Enlightenment in Russia (in so far as it ever took root there) lay, it now seems clear, in the German universities which had been deeply influenced by Pietism, such as Halle, Marburg and Leipzig, rather than in France. Well before the end of the eighteenth century, therefore, the higher reaches of Russian intellectual life were being cast in a German rather than a French mould. This development was to be continued and intensified in the century which followed.

The intellectual currents which have been discussed in this chapter were among the most important legacies bequeathed by the eighteenth century to the future. Nevertheless it must be emphasized that their effect in their own day was in many ways limited. When we talk about the Enlightenment we are, as almost always in discussion of intellectual history, talking about a small intellectual élite. In France, the centre of the movement, with a total population in the later decades of the century of 26 million or more, the entire 'enlightened' public probably did not number more than 30–50,000 people. This was the tip of a social pyramid still based almost everywhere on unthinking routine and the ignorance of the uninstructed masses. The vast numerical majority of Europeans, the peasant at the plough, the artisan at his loom or forge, the

[1] Quoted in G. P. Gooch, *Germany and the French Revolution* (London, 1920), p. 71.

ordinary man everywhere still often compelled anxiously to scan the latest food prices, were totally unconscious of living in an age of enlightenment. To them government and society as they existed were something given and unchangeable, something to be endured. Revolt against specific acts of oppression was conceivable; fundamental change in traditional power structures was not. But even within the minority with enough leisure to read books and enough education to absorb abstract ideas the Enlightenment was never without serious competitors. 'In this century of reason', writes a recent historian, 'people never ceased to delight in superstition.'[1] The remark is justified. Sometimes feelings of this kind took the more or less respectable form of adherence to the more esoteric kinds of Freemasonry or to extreme religious mysticism or ritualism (see pp. 398-9). On a different intellectual level there existed everywhere a dense undergrowth of deeply rooted popular belief in portents, miracles, good-luck rituals, a complex body of peasant belief, many aspects of which were older than Christianity itself. But besides these there was an unmistakable willingness, indeed eagerness, throughout the century, even among the educated and in the highest ranks of society, to embrace relatively sophisticated forms of superstition. Henri, Comte de Boulainvilliers was one of the most radical thinkers of its first decades. His *Vie de Mahomed*, published posthumously in 1730, was an important contribution to the growth of religious scepticism and rationalist criticism in France. Yet he found it possible to believe in astrology, one of the most ancient of all forms of superstition. In 1711, in his *Astrologie mondiale*, he attempted to prove its validity by drawing up parallel tables of historical events and astrological conjunctions in order to demonstrate the influence of the latter upon the former. In rather the same way a few years later the terrible plague which devastated Provence in 1720 (the last great outbreak of the the disease in Western Europe) was attributed by some doctors to the malign influence of the stars.[2]

To a considerable extent the progress of the physical sciences undermined belief of this kind. The spectacular advance of astronomy meant that by the seond quarter of the century astrology was increasingly ridiculed by the educated. (Though the much slower development of

[1] L. Trenard, *Lyon de l'Encyclopédie au préromantisme* (Paris, 1958), vol. I, p. 175.

[2] For these two examples see Ehrard (*see* Bibliography, p. 363), pp. 42-3; the first chapter of this book is the best discussion of irrationalism in France during the early decades of the century.

chemistry made it difficult to oppose alchemy, belief in the possibility of transmuting metals, of finding an universal solvent or even the elixir of life, with the same certainty.) However scientific progress was a two-edged weapon. On balance it encouraged a rationalist, analytical and materialist view of the world. But it also made it more intellectually respectable than in the past to see the universe as pervaded by forces beyond man's comprehension. The discovery of gravitation, of the fact that air and water, hitherto regarded as elements, were not simple substances, above all the attention attracted by the still incomprehensible power of electricity, added to the mystery and wonder of the world for many. Science, it could be argued, pointed in this direction as much as in a rationalist one. 'Above science is magic', claimed a writer in the 1780s, 'because magic follows it, not as an effect, but as its perfection.'[1] Attitudes of this kind, combining a taste for the marvellous with scraps of half-understood science, may well have been becoming more common over much of Europe in the 1770s and 1780s, as the dynamism and self-confidence of the Enlightenment rapidly ebbed. Certainly striking instances of a crude belief in magic can be found in the very highest reaches of society. Gustavus III of Sweden for example, in many of his policies an important exponent of Enlightened Despotism, was deeply attracted by the occult. He had his horoscope cast and consulted a female seer who claimed to foretell the future. Round his neck, in a gold box, he carried a magical powder intended to ward off evil spirits.[2]

In France, the source of the Enlightenment in its most radical and uncompromising form, the growth of mysticism and irrationalism was especially remarkable. The German pseudo-scientist F. A. Mesmer, who claimed to effect miraculous cures through the powers of the 'universal fluid' which permeated and bound together the entire natural world, enjoyed immense success and popularity in Paris for a time in the early 1780s. So did the wonder-working Count Cagliostro, an adventurer who claimed to be a thousand years old, to have access to the mystic lore of the ancient Egyptians and to be able to transmute base metals into gold. Simultaneously L. C. de Saint-Martin, 'the unknown philsopher', was preaching an almost unintelligible but emotionally satisfying mysticism which, in its explicit rejection of the specific and the measureable, its assertion that the material world was subordinate to a more real spiritual one, had great appeal in many parts of Europe.

[1] R. Darnton (see Bibliography, p. 364), p. 38.
[2] A. Viatte, *Les sources occultes du romantisme* (Paris, 1928), vol. 1, p. 183.

By the 1780s the Enlightenment was dying in the city which more than any other had given it life, its deathbed surrounded by a whole family of loosely interrelated exotic mysticisms. 'Never, certainly,' wrote one Parisian mesmerist in 1788, 'were Rosicrucians, alchemists, prophets, and everything related to them so numerous and so influential. Conversation turns almost entirely upon these matters; they fill everyone's thoughts; they strike everyone's imagination. . . . Looking around us, we see only sorcerers, initiates, necromancers and prophets. Everyone has his own, on whom he counts.'[1]

This turning away from rationalism and materialism, this search for a mental diet which nourished the emotions as well as the intellect, is clearly connected with the growth of the cults of sensibility and primitivism and with the whole complex movement of early romanticism, which has already been briefly alluded to (see pp. 349–50). It has been said that 'the romantic mentality is the mentality of miracles' and certainly the phrase expresses one important aspect of the early stages of the romantic movement. More than anywhere else it was in Germany that many aspects of romanticism came to their fullest fruition in the later eighteenth century. It was German writers above all who propagated the belief, deeply hostile to the assumptions of Parisian *philosophes*, that the merely rational is weak and impoverished whereas the primitive is creative and strong. This attitude was first put forward in the 1760s by one of the strangest and most enigmatic writers of the century, J. G. Hamann, 'the Magus of the North', a figure who defies categorization. It finds its supreme expression in the work of J. G. Herder, whose most important book, *Ideen zur Philosophie der Geschichte der Menscheit*, appeared in 1784–91. Herder, more than any other writer of the century except Rousseau, was to shape the mind, indeed the whole history, of Europe in generations to come. His supreme contribution to the future was to make the happiness of the individual and the full realization of his capacities depend absolutely on his membership of an organic and historically based community, a nation. This community was to be defined above all in terms of its language, the language in which Herder believed 'the whole heart and soul' of a nation were to be found. This view of humanity, with its complete rejection of universalism, of cosmo-

---

[1] Darnton (*see* Bibliography, p. 364), pp. 70–1. There is an important discussion of the growing taste for the irrational and the miraculous in Prussia during the last years of the century in H. Brunschwig, *La Crise de l'état prussien a la fin du XVIIIᵉ siècle et la genèse de la mentalité romantique* (Paris, 1947), Pt. III, Chap. i.

politan and supranational standards of judgement, was impossible to reconcile with the main stream of the Enlightenment as it had developed in France. Herder's whole cast of mind, indeed, his love of all that is natural and deep-rooted and his deep dislike of uniformity and distrust of abstract reasoning, were quite foreign to the dominant intellectual style of the French Enlightenment. So were his view of history, his passionate belief that a man must be of his own age and his own nation, that every historical moment and situation is unique and different from all others. It followed from this that different civilizations and cultures could never be fairly compared with one another. But to rule out comparisons of this kind, to reject the widespread Enlightenment belief in the inferiority of the Middle Ages and the superiority of Augustan Rome or Periclean Athens, was to abandon the search for an ideal State and an ideal man. This in turn meant giving up any easily optimistic idea of the inevitability of progress once man's intellect had been freed from artificial restrictions. Herder believed in the possibility of progress; but to him it was to be measured in terms only of a specific society and a given historical epoch, not in those of some utopian ideal. Assertions of this kind amounted to a revolution against the whole drift of much of European thinking for most of the last hundred years. Moreover although Herder himself was in political terms far from conservative (he opposed hereditary rule, serfdom, despotism and censorship) it was a revolution whose implications were, in the long run at least, to be conservative as much as radical. Its importance in the history of ideas was enormous. It is Herder more than any other thinker who links the often vague and utopian political idealism of the eighteenth century with the orgnized and powerful liberalism of the nineteenth, a set of aspirations with a great political movement. Most important of all, he is the first and most constructive prophet of nationalism. He did not, of course, create or in his own lifetime do much to intensify, national and patriotic feeling. This had been slowly taking shape, at least in parts of Western Europe, for many generations. It was clearly becoming more powerful in the second half of the eighteenth century quite independent of anything intellectuals did to bring this about. The disasters of the Seven Years War, which faced the *philosophes* in France with a difficult choice between cosmopolitanism and national pride, had considerable effect in accelerating this development; while the palace revolution of 1762 which placed Catherine II on the Russian throne was in part an expression of national resentment of apparently predominant German influences in St. Petersburg. But it was Herder, far more than anyone else, who provided nationalism with an organized and convincing ideology. He thus provided the intellectual foundations for the most dynamic political emotion, the most seductive political style, of the world which was taking shape by the time of his death in 1803. No writer illustrates better the fecundity and variety of the intellectual life of eighteenth-century Europe and the impossibility of forcing it into a purely French, a rationalist and universalist, mould.

XVI

Religion and the Churches

The geographical distribution of the major Christian communions in Europe altered little during this period. Lutheranism, normally of a highly orthodox and conservative kind, held sway over Scandinavia and much of North Germany. Anglicanism, though subjected to increasingly serious competition from the various dissenting sects and from the Methodists, remained dominant in England. In Scotland, the United Provinces, a few German States and some of the Swiss cantons, Calvinism maintained the ascendancy so painfully won in previous generations, while an important Calvinist minority existed in Hungary and appreciable ones in France, Poland and Bohemia. Catholicism retained its hold on the Iberian peninsula, Italy, France, and most of the Habsburg Empire and South Germany. In the East the Orthodox Church, dominant in Russia, continued to claim the allegiance of large groups in eastern Poland and parts of the Habsburg Empire. In the Balkans, where its hierarchy was almost entirely Greek, it was, except

BIBLIOGRAPHY. The most recent work on the Catholic Church during this period is E. Préclin and E. Jarry, *Les Luttes politiques et doctrinales au XVII*[e] *et XVIII*[e] *siècles*, Pt. 2 (vol. XIX of *Histoire de l'église depuis les origines jusqu'à nos jours*) (Paris, 1956). The relevant volumes of L. von Pastor, *History of the Popes* (London, 1941–) provide an immense amount of information interpreted from a Catholic point of view. On Jansenism A. Gazier, *Histoire générale du mouvement janseniste* (Paris, 1922) is a standard work; E. Préclin, 'L'influence du Jansénisme français a l'étranger', *Revue Historique*, vol. CLXXXII (1938), is a useful sketch. On the suppression of the Jesuits P. Dudon, 'De la suppression de la Compagnie de Jésus, 1758–73', in *Revue des Questions Historiques*, vol. CXXXII (1938), is a useful account. Four works on a national scale deserve mention: N. Sykes, *Church and State in England in the Eighteenth Century* (Cambridge, 1934), and B. C. Poland, *French Protestantism and the French Revolution* (Princeton, 1957), which are balanced and accurate; A. L. Drummond, *German Protestantism since Luther* (London, 1951), which is pedestrian but useful; and R. R. Palmer, *Catholics and Unbelievers in Eighteenth-Century France* (Princeton, 1939), which is brilliant. There is a good general discussion in a few areas such as Bosnia and Albania, the Church of the great majority of the people.

The dream of a reconciliation of Catholic and Protestant, or at least of some co-operation between the rival Protestant Churches, continued to attract both clerics and laymen in Western Europe, especially in the first half of the century. The great Lutheran scholar Leibniz corresponded in 1692–94 and 1699–1701 with the greatest living Catholic apologist, Bossuet, Bishop of Meaux, about a possible union of Catholicism and Lutheranism. A few years later William Wake, Archbishop of Canterbury, embarked on protracted negotiations for a modified form of union between Anglicanism and the Catholic Church in France. Frederick William I of Prussia, the Calvinist ruler of a largely Lutheran State, attempted unsuccessfully to reconcile the two great Protestant communions; while during his reign negotiations were carried on for some form of union between the Protestant Churches in Prussia and the Church of England. More unexpected, the non-juring ministers of the latter (i.e. those who had refused to take an oath of loyalty to William III after the revolution of 1688) made a series of efforts from the 1690s onwards to enter into communion with the Orthodox Church in Russia, with which they had doctrinal affinities. None of these attempts at inter-Church unity or co-operation had any success; and after the first decades of the century hopes of this kind were less frequent and less influential. The idea of restoring the formal and organizational unity of Christendom continued to attract the devout; but the proposals they put forward— for example those of Rouvière (1756), Martinowitz (1781) and Dutens (1798)—had even less practical effect than those of their predecessors.

Almost everywhere in Western Europe, moreover, above all in Britain and France, established Churches and the systems of belief for which they stood were being subjected to a process of intellectual erosion. Increasingly their self-confidence and their hold over the minds of educated men were being eaten away by the growth of new assump-

of the position of the Orthodox Church in Russia in P. Miliukov, *Outlines of Russian Culture* (Philadelphia, 1942), vol. I, and an important specialized study in J. Cracraft, *The Church Reform of Peter the Great* (London, 1971). Different aspects of eighteenth-century irrationalism and superstition are well covered in J. M. Roberts, *The Mythology of the Secret Societies* (London, 1972), and F. Venturi, 'Enlightenment versus the powers of darkness', in his collection *Italy and the Enlightenment* (London, 1972).

tions and the development of new attitudes. The theological systems inherited from the past, well attuned to the conditions and intellectual ambience of the Reformation and Counter-Reformation, became from the later seventeenth century onwards increasingly out of harmony with the spirit of the age; they were, it has been said, 'a Gothic shrine in a Palladian basilica'.[1]

Traditional forms of religious belief were challenged during this period from a number of directions. 'Infidelity' and outright atheism probably became somewhat more common, and were certainly more openly expressed than ever before. They continued, however, almost as much as in the past, to be confined to tiny groups of eccentrics and *esprits forts*. In spite of the alarm they aroused in the ranks of the faithful, they had little practical importance. With few exceptions (Holbach is almost the only important one) even the most radical thinkers of the period were not prepared to advocate atheism or a purely secular State. Nor were theological deviations such as Arianism and Socinianism[2] a real threat to established belief except in a few parts of the continent. (The most important of those was England, where Socinianism developed in the later eighteenth century into a Unitarian movement small in the number of its adherents but strong in their intellectual quality.) Pure scepticism, in the sense of a denial of the possibility of certainty in answering religious problems, was very rare indeed throughout this period. More important than any of these was the challenge to belief now being offered by the development of techniques of criticism which stressed the improbabilities and inconsistencies of the Bible from a historical point of view. Against this challenge scholars such as Hardouin and Berruyer attempted to defend Catholic orthodoxy by stressing the importance of tradition, an unbroken tradition embodied in the teachings of the Church as it actually existed.

By far the most profound and widespread threat to existing systems of belief in Western Europe, however, was that provided by 'natural religion'. This was based on two assumptions. Firstly its adherents took it for granted, like all believers, that the universe was divinely constructed, the work of God. More particularly, they believed that

[1] B. Willey, *The Eighteenth Century Background* (London, 1940) p. 169.
[2] The heresies propounded respectively by Arius, a presbyter of Alexandria in the fourth century who denied that Christ was consubstantial with God, and by Laelius and Faustus Socinus, two sixteenth-century Italian theologians who denied the divinity of Christ.

its divine authorship was manifested by the symmetry and regularity of its workings, by the fact that it clearly obeyed certain simple and universal laws. Scientific discoveries, above all those of Newton, helped to strengthen and disseminate this assumption. They did much to spread the feeling that the study of the physical world, rather than of the works of orthodox divines or even the Fathers of the Church, was the passport to a knowledge of true religion. Secondly, and perhaps more important, belief in natural religion involved the assumption that there were certain religious ideas innate in every man, ideas which were intuitive and universal. Such were the knowledge that God existed; that man would be rewarded or punished in a future life for his behaviour in this one; and that he owed certain fundamental duties both to God and his neighbour.

Beliefs of this kind, though often very vaguely formulated, had considerable influence within the established Churches of Western Europe during this period. In France in particular they were pressed to remarkable lengths by a number of Jesuit scholars. Nevertheless they cut at the roots of orthodoxy, both Catholic and Protestant. God's continual manifestation of himself through a universe which science could describe and measure seemed to reduce, even to destroy, the significance of any special act of revelation. Natural religion was therefore by implication hostile to revealed religion, and even to the idea of a personal God. Thus the Jesuit Abbé Camier could argue, in a textbook published in 1769, that 'Natural Law has binding force independently of the existence of God,' and that 'moral principles impose obligation independently of the existence of God'. It was also hostile to the claims of the various Churches to the possession of exclusive truth. The Provost of Berlin Cathedral could claim towards the end of this period that the Jews were 'true Christians', since they believed in God, virtue and immortality. Many contemporaries would have accepted the assumptions behind these phrases, even if they shied at the clarity with which they were expressed. Moreover, if man came into the world with all the beliefs essential for salvation already imprinted on his heart, of what real value were the theological systems and dogmatic complexities, the liturgical and ceremonial elaborations, with which nearly all existing Churches were in varying degrees encrusted? Natural religion thus tended to be indifferent to the externals of belief and worship. It was also hostile to traditional theology, which it could easily regard as a mere breeding-ground of meaningless and unnecessary disputes. A Christianity cleansed of the corruptions which it had accumulated in the course of centuries and restored to primitive purity, a Christianity whose dogmas should be very few and very simple, a Christianity freed from priestly power and arrogance and from the theology which priestly power had created—this was a vision very attractive to many thinkers of the eighteenth century.

Feeling of this kind was strengthened by the growing interest in, and frequent admiration of, non-European peoples which was so marked during this period. The innate religious emotions and aspirations postulated by natural religion were the same for all men. All of them stood in the same relationship to God. Why then should a virtuous Brahmin or Confucian be considered the spiritual inferior of a Christian? Did they not all worship the same God? Was it not possible that Christians might learn something from a study of the holy books of other religions which were now beginning to be translated into European languages? (see p. 332).

Natural religion and the Deism and Latitudinarianism which it generated had during this period more influence in England than anywhere else in Europe. In the early decades of the century a galaxy of able writers—Samuel Clarke, Thomas Woolston, Matthew Tindal and others—by expounding its ideas undermined dogmas and assumptions which had for generations been the common currency of Anglicanism. Later the Unitarian Joseph Priestley, himself a great scientist, proposed in his *History of the Corruptions of Christianity* (1782) to purify Christian belief by stripping it of what all orthodox believers thought of as its essential doctrines—the Trinity, Original Sin, the Atonement and Predestination among others. In Germany the ideas of the philosopher Christian Wolff, the most influential figure in the intellectual life of the first half of the century, had considerable affinities with those of his Deist contemporaries in England: they led to his expulsion by Frederick William I from his chair at the University of Halle. Above all the writings of Voltaire must be considered, from the religious point of view, as a sustained plea, usually superficial but often brilliantly effective, for Deism and natural religion.

Underlying all these new and sometimes radical attitudes to religion were the forces of social change and development. The religion practised by the masses everywhere was still traditional, unintellectual, emotional and life-pervading. The more intellectual, self-conscious, limited and even sceptical forms of belief which have been described in the previous paragraphs were the faith merely of an educated minority, though an increasingly active and vocal one. Men of this stamp lived in a world increasingly dominated by ideas of accurate measurement and exact calculation, a world slowly but surely moving towards our own day and succumbing to the rule of statistics and balance-sheets. For them it was thus increasingly difficult to accept miracles, mysteries and legends, in fact much of the structure of belief with which traditional forms of religion were encrusted. Physics and astronomy had discovered laws by which the universe was ruled and which God himself, it was claimed, could not infringe. His power thus lost some of its total and awe-inspiring character and became almost contractual. An increasing emphasis on practical virtue and good citizenship meant that the overwhelming theologigal distinction between the saved and the damned became in practice less important than that between the man who did his duty in this world and the man who did not. Even the religious view of labour as the penalty exacted from the descendants of Adam in retribution for his sin was probably undermined by the growth in the amount of interesting and rewarding work which accompanied and underlay the slow emergence of the modern professional classes. Social forces of this kind, in their blind and almost unconscious workings, may have done more than the writings of the *philosophes* to undermine traditional religious attitudes. Certainly it is striking that natural religion, Deism, and hostility to religious tradition and dogma were the product of a few West-European States—Great Britain, the United Provinces, France and parts of Germany. In Spain, Portugal, the Habsburg territories and most of Italy they developed much more slowly and had far less influence. In Orthodox Christendom they were weaker still. In other words they were characteristic of States experiencing the intellectually liberating effects of scientific and geographical discovery, of societies which possessed a substantial educated middle class or at least a certain element of liberal-minded aristocracy. Where these factors were weak or absent such radical ideas found it almost impossible to take root.

The desire for a form of belief which should be simpler, more rational, more in tune with the leading currents of secular thought, also provided the foundations for the growth of Freemasonry, or at least the most widespread type of Freemasonry, during this period. From its foundation in England (the Grand Lodge there was set up in 1717) it spread rapidly to the continent. The first French and Italian lodges were opened in 1726. Frederick II founded a lodge at Charlottenburg in 1740 and became Grand Master of one in Berlin in 1744. In spite of condemnations by the Papacy in 1738 and 1751 its growth was rapid in many parts of Catholic Europe; and it attracted the support of many intellectuals, nobles, clerics and even rulers. In the second half of the century it began to be influential in Poland and Russia (where the statesman Count G. Chernyshev and the great journalist N. I. Novikov were among its leading adherents).

Many factors contributed to the popularity of Freemasonry. Its vague stress on reason and virtue as opposed to tradition and dogmatic subtleties; its equally vague but not always ineffective emphasizing of human brotherhood and the necessity to transcend national divisions;[1] the fact that it could, at least to a limited extent, bring together in its lodges people of widely differing social class; all these help to explain its rapid growth. It could appeal, in other words, to ideals and emotions which traditional forms of religion were increasingly failing to satisfy. Nevertheless it should be remembered that masonic lodges almost certainly differed a good deal in different parts of Europe in their outlook and character. In some areas at least neither the role played in their work by ideology nor their ability to transcend class differences should be overestimated. Often they seem to have been merely sociable gatherings of men interested in nothing higher than banqueting, conversation and the drinking of toasts.[2] Sometimes at least they were quite as class-conscious as society in general. Thus the constitution of the Peace lodge at Toulouse declared that 'no one may be received as a Mason or an officiate who is not of a profession nearly equal to that of most brothers in the lodge'.[3]

The liberalizing currents in eighteenth-century religious life which have been described above also aided the growth of religious toleration.

---

[1] In 1782 the French lodge *De la Candeur* proposed that the freemasons of France should provide by subscription a ship for the navy, then engaged in a critical struggle with that of Britain. The *Contrat Social* lodge of Paris, however, turned down the proposal as opposed to masonic ideals of peace and brotherhood, though it offered to contribute to relieve the widows and orphans of French sailors killed in the war. (G. Clement-Simon, 'La loge du *Contrat Social* sous le règne de Louis XVI', *Revue des Questions Historiques*, May 1937, pp. 12–13). One reason for Catherine II's growing hostility to Russian Freemasonry in the 1780s was the closeness of its relations with that of Prussia and Sweden.

[2] M. Agulhon, *Pénitents et Francs-Maçons de l'ancienne Provence* (Paris, 1968), pp. 203–10.

[3] L. R. Berlanstein, *The Barristers of Toulouse in the Eighteenth Century* (Baltimore-London, 1975), p. 126.

Thus in England the laws which discriminated against Protestant Dissenters were either repealed (as were the Occasional Conformity and Schism Acts passed by the Tories in 1711 and 1714) or if they remained on the statute book were usually enforced laxly or not at all for much of this period. (Catholics had to wait till 1778 for the first step towards any alleviation of their legal disabilities.) In France the persecution of the Huguenots (the French Protestants), which had produced a serious revolt in the Cevennes in 1702–04, continued far into the century. It became, however, steadily less severe and less wholehearted. Many French bishops, though remaining attached in principle to the idea of religious intolerance, were by the second half of the century ready to restore normal civil rights to the Huguenots. The edict of 1787 which partially effected this restoration was issued by a Cardinal, Loménie de Brienne, while one of the greatest dignitaries of the French Church, the Archbishop of Narbonne, congratulated Louis XVI on such a display of enlightenment.

It can scarcely be emphasized too strongly, however, that what has been described in the preceding pages was only one side of eighteenth-century religious life. Man does not live by reason alone; and natural religion, toleration and the faiths of the Enlightenment in general proved too meagre and unsatisfying a diet for many people, even many educated people, in this period. Everywhere religious literature of varying intellectual quality but of a quite traditional kind—printed sermons, collections of saints' lives, catechisms—continued to be sold in greater quantities than almost any type of secular writing. Even in England, the fountainhead of natural religion, the best-seller of the century was a devoutly conventional tract, Bishop Sherlock's *Letter from our Lord Bishop of London to the Clergy and People of London on the Occasion of the Late Earthquake* (London, 1750), of which over 100,000 copies were sold or given away by the author's admirers. Traditional forms of popular belief—in the efficacy of relics and pilgrimages; in fasting and other forms of mortification of the flesh; in the cult of the Virgin—flourished as they had done for centuries over the whole of Catholic and Orthodox Europe. The faith of the humble, of people who published no books, compiled no memoirs and did not normally even write letters, is inherently a difficult subject to discuss with precision or to measure in any clear-cut way. The extent to which belief in sorcery and witchcraft still flourished is particularly obscure, since the ending of the witch trials so common over much of Europe until the second half of the seventeenth century deprives us of the evidence which they provide for earlier generations. There is no doubt at all, however, of the persistence in the eighteenth century of widespread popular fear and hostility towards witches, at least in rural areas, even in some of the more developed parts of Europe. In western France in 1780, for example, a woman suspected of having bewitched animals had her feet burned by frightened and infuriated peasants and was then drowned in a pond. Two years later another was burned as a witch in one of the Swiss cantons. Nor was it very difficult, at least in parts of the continent, to find educated men prepared to give some support to such beliefs. A book published in Milan in 1742, which denied the existence of the magic arts in general, aroused a good deal of suspicion because of its alleged religious unorthodoxy; while in Bavaria (the most intellectually undeveloped of all the major German States) an attack on belief in witchcraft published by a priest in 1761 provoked sharp controversy.

The savagery which could underlie some aspects of popular and traditional religious feeling is well seen in the very frequent punishment by death of mothers who killed a young child, or allowed it to die, before it had been baptized. (It was, it must be emphasized, the failure to have the child baptized and thus safeguard its soul, rather than the killing itself, which aroused such revulsion.) Thus when in Anjou (admittedly one of the more backward areas of France) a young girl, illegitimately pregnant, killed herself in 1718, the body was exhumed and dragged face downwards through the town where the suicide had taken place. The public executioner then extracted the foetus from the body; and it was buried in a churchyard where unbaptized children were normally interred. The mother's corpse was hung up by the feet for an hour, bearing a written denunciation of her crime, and then burnt and the ashes scattered to the winds.[1] This brutal incident was at least as typical of religious attitudes in general in the early eighteenth century as the writings of English free-thinkers or French rationalists. We should not forget that in religion, as in every aspect of life, the growing rationality, tolerance and moderation which was a real characteristic of eighteenth-century Europe co-existed with a great body of deep and sometimes bitter popular conservatism.

Travellers from the more intellectually developed parts of the continent were frequently shocked and even frightened by the intensity with which such feelings were given expression in Spain, Portugal,

[1] F. Lebrun, *Les Hommes et la mort en Anjou aux 17e et 18e siècles* (Paris–The Hague, 1971), p. 422.

most of Italy and much of Catholic Germany and Switzerland. John Wilkes, at least ostensibly a radical and a freethinker (see p. 143), was impressed in this way by the behaviour of the Neapolitans in 1765, when the liquefaction of the blood of St. Januarius (San Gennaro), the most famous ritual miracle in all Europe, was delayed. As the cardinal conducting the ceremony vainly agitated the phial containing the miraculous fluid 'the people grew quite outrageous. The women shriek'd hideously, beat their breasts and tore their hair. The men seemed equally frantic. They began the most frightful yelling, and several were cutting themselves with knives.'[1]

Nor were beliefs of this kind confined to the lower strata of society. In Spain the Duchess of Alva, a member of one of the greatest grandee families, attempted to cure the illness of her son by making him swallow, in powdered form, what was alleged to be a mummified finger of St. Isidore. Even in Britain and France faith in the efficacy of the touch of a legitimate ruler as a cure for scrofula lingered on to the end of this period. Queen Anne was the last English ruler to 'touch for the King's Evil'; but the Jacobite pretender Prince Charles Edward and his brother, Cardinal York, kept up the practice till the latter's death in 1807. Over 2,000 sufferers came to be touched by Louis XV on the day before his coronation at Rheims in 1722, while over 2,400 came to beg the help of Louis XVI on the same occasion half a century later.

Apart from the persistence of traditional beliefs of this kind there was a growth in the most intellectually advanced parts of Europe of new sects, often of a mystical or semi-mystical kind. This growth was largely a reaction against the rationalism and Deism which were now increasingly influential in these areas, and became more rapid from the 1760s onwards.

The most important example of this tendency can be seen in the development of the Methodist movement in England. Methodism, which began to evolve a separate organization in the 1740s though its final break with the Anglican Church did not come till after John Wesley's death in 1791, was not mystical in the full sense of the word. Nevertheless it was explicitly hostile to religious liberalism and distrustful of some aspects of the physical sciences. Wesley himself doubted 'whether any man on earth knows either the distance or the magnitude, I will not say of a fixed star, but of Saturn or Jupiter, yea of the Sun or Moon', and complained that 'the infidels [i.e. rationalists and liberals]

---

[1] Quoted in C. Hibbert, *The Grand Tour* (London, 1974), p. 155.

have hooted witchcraft out of the world'.[1] He is known greatly to have admired a number of Catholic mystics, notably St. Francis de Sales. A similar distrust of many leading ideas of the age, a similar insistence on religion as a mode of experience rather than a system of thought, is to be found in the growth of Pietism in Germany. Here too the religion of the heart and the idea of a 'second birth' of the convert were central. The doctrines of the great Pietist writers of the previous century, Boehme and Spener, revived and adapted by Count N. L. von Zinzendorf, provided the basis for the Moravian movement, one of the most remarkable of this period. Many of the forms it took—for example its exaggerated and sometimes macabre use of traditional Christian symbols such as the lamb and the wounds of Christ—seem bizarre and even repulsive to modern eyes. Nevertheless its vitality was shown by its ability, like Methodism though on a smaller scale, to gain adherents. From its original strongholds at Bethelsdorf and Herrnhut, on Zinzendorf's estate in Lusatia, it spread not merely over much of Germany but also in North America. Pietism differed from Methodism in a number of ways. In particular it received a good deal of encouragement from various German nobles and even some rulers of minor German States, while few members of the English ruling class showed much sympathy for Wesley and his followers. Nevertheless the two movements had to a very large extent a common psychological basis, which revealed itself in a similarity of methods. Both laid great emphasis on the part to be played by music in arousing religious emotion. More significant, the adherents of both were often guided, in making difficult decisions, by drawing lots, or by opening the Bible at random and drawing inspiration from the first text to offer itself. Such methods were an implicit rejection of the idea of man as an autonomous individual, a reassertion of his position as a mere instrument of God.

Freemasonry also developed in the later eighteenth century, particularly in Germany and Russia, a markedly mystical and irrational side. Its most extreme and even bizarre form, the Strict Observance, which claimed to drive its origins from the medieval order of the Templars, showed marked tendencies of this kind and in political terms was, at least by implication, strongly conservative. I. G. Schwarz, a German from Transylvania who held a chair at the University of Moscow in 1779–83 and imported into Russian Freemasonry a large element of

---

[1] Quoted in R. A. Knox, *Enthusiasm* (Oxford, 1950) pp. 518–19.

mysticism and irrationalism, is a good example of tendencies of this sort. Side by side with the masonic lodges, moreover, there grew up in the second half of the century secret societies which carried mysticism, secrecy and a taste for exotic rituals to extreme lengths. The best known is that of the Illuminati, founded in 1776 in Bavaria by Adam Weishaupt, whose organization and ceremonies had some affinities with Strict Observance Masonry. The Rosicrucians, founded in Regensburg in 1755, went even further in this direction, for the leaders of the order were believed by their followers to possess divine powers and within it astrology and sorcery seem to have been fairly widely practised. It would be a mistake to regard these bodies as possessing great political or social influence (though Frederick William II of Prussia and two of his closest advisers were members of the Rosicrucians and their policies were affected by this). But their growth is yet another warning against any easy overestimate of the rationalism and 'enlightenment' of the eighteenth century.

Nor was the movement towards religious toleration universal or unchallenged. It is understandable that in Spain, where the identification of Catholicism with the country's history and aspirations was closer than anywhere else in Europe, one leading cleric could refer to the ideas of the Enlightenment as 'a vile prostitute misnamed philosophy' and another could refuse to learn French because of all the dangerous books written in the language.[1] But even in the most advanced states of Western Europe popular prejudice and intolerance was still very much alive.

The movement towards religious toleration was neither continuous not very profound. In England the penal laws against Protestant Dissenters might no longer be enforced; but a series of efforts to secure their repeal in 1787–90 ended in complete failure. The legal disabilities of English Catholics began very slowly to be whittled away in the last years of the century; but the Gordon Riots of 1780 (a great outburst of violence directed mainly against Catholics which for a few days placed London at the mercy of the mob) showed how great and how near the surface was the hostility to them which still existed. In France the Assembly of the Clergy was urging Louis XVI as late as 1775 to enforce more rigorously the very severe legislation against Protestantism. More serious was the position in Germany, Hungary and Poland. In all of these, generations of religious strife had left a legacy of mistrust, of

[1] C. C. Noel, 'The clerical confrontation with the Enlightenment in Spain', *European Studies Review*, vol. V (1975), pp. 116–17.

sensitivity on religious matters and of readiness to persecute. Thus in 1719 the action of the town council of Torun in Poland in putting to death a number of Calvinists found guilty of riotous behaviour led to a minor European crisis and provoked protests from several Protestant States. In Hungary, where there was a tendency to regard Protestantism as a relic of the long years of Turkish domination in the sixteenth and seventeenth centuries, this period saw systematic persecution of the Calvinists, in spite of the guarantees given them by the Peace of Szatmár (1711). In 1728 the Archbishop of Salzburg expelled 20,000 Protestants from his dominions at three days' notice. In Switzerland also the efforts of the Abbots of St. Gall to foster Catholicism in the Toggenburg, an area under their jurisdiction, provoked friction between the Catholic and Protestant cantons which led to open warfare in 1712 and did not finally die down till 1759.

By the later 1770s and 1780s, moreover, traditional and more or less unthinking prejudices against religious minorities were being sharpened, in many parts of Europe, by a more explicit and vocal clerical hostility to the Enlightenment than ever before. In France the royal edict of 1787 which granted civil rights to Protestants was widely unpopular. Two *parlements*, those of Dôle and Douai, refused to register it, while efforts were made to exclude Protestants from the electoral assemblies which chose members of the States-General in 1789. In Prussia an Edict Concerning Religion of July 1788 ordered all Protestant preachers to adhere strictly in their sermons to the orthodox Lutheran or Reformed creeds; any who indulged in rationalistic speculations or practices were threatened with severe punishment. Even the myth of a great anti-monarchical and anti-Christian conspiracy, international in scope and the work of Freemasons and perhaps Protestants, a myth to which the French Revolution was to give vitality and longevity, was beginning to be put forward in the 1780s.[1] The last years of the old régime, in fact saw a kind of clerical counter-revolution which antedated the Revolution itself.

There is another and quite different way, minor but not without interest, in which the persistence of traditional modes of thought in

---

[1] e.g. in the Abbé Lenfant's *Discours . . . sur le projet d'accorder l'État Civil aux Protestants* (1787). The first important French attack on Masonry as a dangerous movement for liberty and equality directed against all existing authority had been launched forty years earlier in an anonymous work, *Les Francs-Maçons écrasés* (1747); but hostility of this kind did not become widespread until the 1780s.

religious matters can be illustrated. This is the continuing production of proposals, at least during the earlier decades of the century, for some union of the European states to crusade against the traditional external enemy—the Turk. In political terms this idea had lost all real meaning generations, indeed centuries, earlier. From many Europeans, however, at least in the first part of this period, it could still arouse some response, though a faint and intermittent one; and a number of proposals of this kind continued to be made. Nor were they products merely of Catholic Europe; the third volume of Defoe's *Robinson Crusoe* (totally unknown to the general reader) which was published in 1720 contains a scheme of this kind.[1]

In religion then, as in most other departments of life, the eighteenth century bore within itself the seeds of an immense change. These seeds, however, had not yet sent down very deep roots. The liberal and rationalist tendencies which bulk so large in the works of most of the better-known writers of the period had not yet had much effect on the ordinary man. They were to be weakened and even reversed by the reaction which accompanied and to some extent antedated the French Revolution.

During this period the Catholic Church succeeded in maintaining the appearance of unity better than many of its reformed rivals. It suffered no overt external challenge, in the areas which it dominated, comparable to that which the Methodists, almost in spite of themselves, came to offer to the Church of England. It nevertheless had to face dissensions within its own ranks and pressure from the secular powers of Catholic Europe on a scale unparalleled since the days of the Council of Trent. It was weakened, at least in some areas, by the fact that its higher ranks were recruited mainly or exclusively from the aristocracy, a fact which opened a profound social and even intellectual gulf between its bishops and archbishops and the parish priests under their control. The latter, drawn for the most part from the peasantry and often very poorly paid, had in many cases little in common with their superiors. This position was seen at its worst in France, where the episcopate during this period was entirely aristocratic in origin and often scandalously worldly in outlook. Even in the Papal States themselves an increasing assimilation of the higher ranks of the Church to the secular aristocracy may perhaps be detected in the reconstitution of the Roman nobility as a closed caste of 187 families by Benedict XIV in

[1] The best known is *Cardinal Alberoni's Scheme for reducing the Turkish Empire to the Obedience of Christian Princes* (London, 1736).

1746. Elsewhere, however, this process was much less noticeable. In Spain particularly (though the Primate, the Archbishop of Toledo, was said to be the richest prelate in Christendom) comparatively few great ecclesiastics were of noble birth and the episcopate observed high standards in such matters as residence in their dioceses and the giving of charity. Morover the distinction between a wealthy episcopate recruited from the aristocracy and an underpaid and sometimes discontented parochial clergy was by no means peculiar to Catholicism. It could be found also in many parts of Protestant Europe, above all perhaps in England.

Much more important were the divisions provoked by the question of Jansenism. This was originally a theological dispute concerned with one of the most obscure yet important parts of Christian theology—doctrines of grace, free-will and predestination. Jansen, Bishop of Ypres, who gave his name to a movement which did not come into existence until a generation after his death in 1638, restated traditional Augustinian doctrines on these issues in a remarkably rigorous form. His assertion that every man was irreversibly predestined to heaven or hell minimized by implication the importance, as roads to salvation, of virtue, reason and good works. From the ideas which he formulated (in varying forms and expressed with varying degrees of rigidity they had long formed a part of Christian belief) developed an imposing structure of Puritan idealism, an intense preoccupation with the idea of sin and a denial of the assumptions of natural religion.

Jansenism gained the support first of a group of Paris theologians and from the mid seventeenth century onwards of the great French convent of Port-Royal. By the end of the century it was arousing interest among much wider circles in France, lay as well as clerical. In 1693 Pasquier Quesnel restated its central doctrines, in his *Nouveau Testament en francais avec des réflexions morales*, in terms which seemed to call in question the ultimate authority in matters of faith of the hierarchy of the Church. However the closer relations between Louis XIV and the Papacy which dated from this very year, as well as Jesuit opposition, led to a sustained effort by the French government to stamp out the movement. Port-Royal was destroyed in 1710; and in 1713 a number of errors alleged to be present in Quesnel's book were condemned by Clement XI in the bull *Unigenitus*.

With the promulgation of this bull the eighteenth-century phase of the controversy began. In the generations which followed Jansenism ceased to be what it had hitherto remained, an essentially theological question which interested in the main only a small intellectual class. Henceforth it became increasingly involved with almost every aspect of French life. Around it crystallized patriotic opposition to Papal claims and the growing hostility of the *parlements* to some aspects of absolute monarchy (since Louis XV, breaking with the traditions of his ancestors, tended to support the Papalist and Ultramontane party in the French Church) as well as the frustration and resentment felt by many of the lower clergy in face of the power and wealth enjoyed by the higher ranks of the Church.

Though they were given a good deal of official support during the Regency period, the Jansenists were greatly weakened by the accession to power of Cardinal Fleury in 1726. Two years later, when Noailles, the Archbishop of Paris who had been their supporter for over a generation, was at last forced to abandon them, they lost their last influential adherent within the French hierarchy. Increasing persecution led to the growth of a mystical and even hysterical wing of the movement, which was associated with the alleged miracles performed at the tomb of the deacon Pâris in the cemetery of St Médard and which helped to bring into disrepute the more disciplined majority of Jansenists. The latter, however, were protected by the *Parlement* of Paris during a long series of struggles with Fleury (1730–33), published a successful clandestine periodical, the *Nouvelles Ecclésiastiques* (1728–1803), and even thought of founding in Indo-China a mission independent of the Papacy. So great was their popularity in the capital that the lawyer and diarist Barbier estimated in the 1730s that two-thirds of the people of Paris were Jansenist in sympathy. By the middle decades of the century the movement, though driven underground to some extent by official pressure, was exerting extensive influence on French society. It now tended increasingly to stress the rights of the parish priest against his ecclesiastical superiors, and even to some extent those of the layman against the priest. In many parts of France, moreover, liturgical and ceremonial changes (for example greater use of the vernacular in services and communion in both kinds) had now been introduced by Jansenist *curés*. From 1749 onwards on number of prelates, notably de Beaumont, Archbishop of Paris, attempted to force penitents in danger of death, as a condition of receiving absolution, to prove their orthodoxy by producing a certificate signed by an orthodox priest. This effort to stamp out Jansenism aroused widespread opposition, an opposition which showed that the movement still retained much popular sympathy. By the 1760s, however, Jansenism in France had shot its bolt. In the later decades of the century it ceased to be a real danger, or even a serious nuisance, to either Church or State; though it has been argued that the Civil Constitution of the Clergy introduced by the revolutionaries in 1791 owed something to Jansenist tradition.

The influence of eighteenth-century Jansenism was in many ways as great outside as inside France. In the Catholic States of Germany, as in Spain and Portugal, it was never of importance. In the Habsburg Empire, on the other hand, it received a considerable amount of official encouragement. Maria Theresa's confessor, the Abbé de Tesme, was a Jansenist; and Jansenist books were allowed by the censorship to enter the Habsburg dominions freely. In the Netherlands Utrecht was a notable centre of Jansenist teaching. Above all in Italy Jansenism was widespread and influential, stimulating hostility to the Jesuits and the Papacy and sometimes assuming (notably in Lombardy) a radical and even democratic form. It has been claimed that its ideas were one element in the Neapolitan revolution of 1799, and that the hostility to the Papacy of Mazzini, the greatest prophet of nationalism in nineteenth-century Europe, was in part the product of the Jansenist influences he absorbed as a child in Genoa. In Tuscany it was even possible, in 1786, to hold a Jansenist synod at Pistoia; though its decisions were condemned by the Pope in 1794 and its leader, Scipione de Ricci, the greatest figure in the history of the movement in Italy, submitted to the Papacy in 1805.

More spectacular than the threat of Jansenism, though less dangerous to the unity and existing character of the Catholic Church, was the wave of hostility to the Jesuits which reached a climax in the 1760s and led to the dissolution of the Order by the Pope in 1773. The exaggerated hatred and fear felt for the Jesuits everywhere in Protestant Europe had always been echoed, sometimes with equal intensity, in many parts of the Catholic world. Their wealth (sometimes grossly exaggerated by rumour), the great influence they normally possessed at Rome and in many of the courts of Europe, above all the unity and discipline which made them appear a kind of secret society, aroused widespread envy and dislike. By the middle of the century it was becoming difficult for the governments of Catholic Europe, increasingly centralized and efficient, to tolerate the activities or even the existence of a body so Ultramontane and, by implication at least, so hostile to the existence of genuinely sovereign States.

The first overt action against the Society came in Portugal. There Pombal in 1757 drove from the court the Jesuits who had hitherto acted as the confessors of the royal family. Two years later he accused the Society, almost certainly without justification, of complicity in an attempt to murder the king; and in September 1759 its members were expelled from Portugal. These drastic attacks on Jesuit influence set off a chain reaction elsewhere in Catholic Europe. In France popular hostility to the Order, stimulated by the dissemination of Jansenist ideas, was particularly acute. There matters were brought to a head by the bankruptcy of a leading Jesuit, Père Lavalette, who had hitherto been a leading figure in the trade of Martinique, the wealthiest of France's West Indian islands. Sued by his creditors in the consular court of Marseilles, the French Jesuits unwisely appealed from its decision to the *Parlement* of Paris, which had a long tradition of hostility to Ultramontane influences. The *Parlement* seized the opportunity to demand that the statutes of the Order be submitted to it for approval, condemned them on a number of grounds, and in spite of the feeble opposition of Louis XV demanded in August 1762 the dissolution of the Society of Jesus in France. In this demand it was followed by most of the provincial *parlements*, though some (notably those of Aix and Toulouse) tended to oppose such a policy. The King, though he was supported by the great majority of the French bishops in his desire to maintain the Order in existence, gave way to this popular and institutional pressure. In November 1764 he issued the decree which ended its life in France (and thus produced a severe though temporary crisis in the country's educational system).

In Spain the Society was little more popular than in France. There riots in Madrid, Barcelona and other cities in 1766 were officially attributed to its machinations and were followed in the next year, after careful preparation, by the arrest and deportation of its members. This very drastic action was supported by the majority of the Spanish bishops. Finally, encouraged by the action of the French and Spanish governments, Naples, Parma and even the Order of St. John in Malta expelled the Jesuits from their territories in 1767.

Pope Clement XIII had not hesitated to declare his support for them (notably in the bull *Apostolicum Munus* of January 1765). He had also attempted unsuccessfully at the end of 1768 to put pressure on the Duke of Parma, the weakest of the secular rulers who had expelled them, by excommunicating his ministers. His successor Clement XIV, who became Pope in May 1769, was a weaker man; it has been conjectured that he may, before his election, have given the French and Spanish governments a promise to suppress the Society completely if he were chosen as head of the Church. After his accession he tried for several years to evade a decision on this point by asking for time to consider the question and by promising to call a general council. However in face of pressure from France, which occupied the Papal enclave of Avignon, from Naples, which seized a similar enclave, Benevento; and above all from Spain, whose ambassador in Rome secured by bribery the support of many members of the Curia, Clement had to give way. In July 1773 the brief *Dominus ac Redemptor* abolished the Society of Jesus throughout Catholic Europe. It was not applied everywhere with the same degree of severity, for both Louis XV and Maria Theresa wished to treat the Jesuits with moderation, while in Poland and some parts of Italy and Germany there was considerable opposition to their disappearance. Some of them, moreover, were able to find refuge in the dominions of Frederick II and Catherine II, non-Catholic rulers ostentatiously tolerant in matters of religion. By consenting to destroy the Society, however, Clement XIV had swept away the greatest institution of the Counter-Reformation. He had destroyed the one Catholic order which might have been able to reconcile traditional forms of authority in the Church with the new ideas, based on philosophical speculation and scientific discovery, which were now gaining so much ground in Europe. He had both illustrated and accelerated the decline in the real power of the Papacy which was one of the main facts of the religious life of this period in Western Europe.

This decline had become clearly visible long before 1773. As a factor in international affairs the Papacy had for several generations counted for little. It was represented in the negotiations of 1713–14 which led to the signature of the Treaties of Utrecht and Rastadt, but had not the slightest influence on the peace terms. The negotiations of 1748 which culminated in the Treaty of Aix-la-Chapelle were attended merely by its semi-official agent, the Vicar-General of the Bishop of Liège, who was kept in complete ignorance of what was going on. Already Clement XII had seen his Italian territories invaded, plundered, and used without his permission as recruiting grounds by the Spanish and Austrian armies in the wars of 1733–35 and 1741–48. His suzerainty over the Duchies of Parma and Piacenza, always shadowy, had in effect ceased to exist in 1731. With no real army, ruling one of the most backward and impoverished States in Europe, the Papacy had lost by the middle of the century most of its claims to be an effective force in warfare or diplomacy.

Its position, moreover, was now being threatened even more seri-

ously by the growing hostility of governments and large bodies of
their subjects to the powers which it continued to exercise, or at least
to claim, throughout Catholic Europe. This hostility was by no means
new. Resentment of Papal claims had been felt for centuries by both
rulers and people in many parts of Italy: the Republic of Venice for
example had been notoriously anti-Ultramontane during much of the
seventeenth century. When the Archbishop of Taranto in 1788 wrote of
'Papalism, the perpetual enemy of this kingdom', he was thus expressing
an attitude deeply ingrained over much of the peninsula. Similarly in
France Gallicanism (the belief that the French Church was autonomous
and that its internal organization should be free from Papal control)
retained much of the great popular appeal it had possessed in previous
generations. Jansenism with its anti-Papal implications was able to
draw strength from the still flourishing Gallican tradition. The *parlements* were solidly Gallican. Louis XV seriously damaged his own popularity and the position of the monarchy by the support he gave to the
opponents of Gallicanism. Even in ultra-Catholic Spain there was a
strong tradition of independence of Rome where the government and
organization of the Church were concerned; and royal control over
it steadily increased during the century. In 1765, for example, the
official printers to the government published a book asserting the right
of the king to set bounds to its acquisition of land

The growing demand that kings and princes must be masters in their
own houses—a demand which underlay the attacks on the Jesuits—
forced the Papacy in the second quarter of the century to make a series
of important concessions to the secular authorities of Catholic Europe.
By a number of concordats—with Spain in 1737 and 1753, with Portugal
in 1740, with Sardinia and Naples in 1741—the Popes surrendered to the
rulers concerned rights which Rome had hitherto possessed in theory
if not always in fact, notably over Church appointments. These sur-
renders did little to appease the enemies of the Papacy. The spread
of 'enlightened' ideas and the general movement towards more
effectively centralized administrative systems were alike hostile to
its traditional powers and position. Both brought clerical privileges
under increasingly heavy fire and intensified suspicion of the Popes as
the symbols and defenders of these survivals of the past. Moreover
rulers increasingly conscious of their own powers and responsibilities
were increasingly reluctant to accept interference with their actions by
any international authority. Feelings of this kind were stimulated in the
capitals of Catholic Europe by a series of able anti-Papal writers—

Giannone in Naples, Van Espen in the Netherlands, Febronius (i.e. J. N. von Hontheim, Vicar-General of the Archbishop of Trier) in the Habsburg dominions and South Germany. In many areas indeed the Catholic hierarchy itself played a leading part in opposing Papal and Ultramontane claims. Bishops who believed themselves to have received their powers directly from Christ and often enjoyed a high degree of administrative autonomy in their own dioceses (as in France for example) were usually willing to obey the instructions of the Papacy on spiritual matters but were otherwise frequently almost independent of it. This attitude was intensified by the aristocratic character of the episcopate in many countries. 'The Pope has his rights,' said the Bishop of Lombez towards the end of the century, 'and we have ours.' The remark summarized a point of view increasingly widespread during this period.

The last decades of the century saw a series of attacks on the position of the Papacy and even of the Church in general more open and more violent than any of those hitherto mentioned. In 1776 the Neapolitan government, still influenced by the anticlerical Tanucci, refused to continue the payment to Rome of the traditional tribute of the *Chinea* (a white horse richly caparisoned and 7,000 ducats in gold) in acknowledgment of the feudal subjection of the kingdom to the Pope. In several States of Catholic Europe—in Naples and Sicily during the 1760s and 1770s, in Lombardy during the last years of Maria Theresa, in France from 1765 onwards—decayed or superfluous religious houses were swept away. Almost everywhere efforts were made to reduce the number of appeals to Rome, to control the enforcement and even the publication of Papal bulls, and to reduce the economic privileges of the Church in such matters as mortmain and exemption from taxation. In Spain, where Catholicism was stronger than in any other major State, the power of the Inquisition declined rapidly (the last man to be burnt alive for a religious offence was executed at Seville in 1781, though others were put to death in the Indies even later than this) and those of other Church tribunals were steadily reduced. By the end of the century proposals were being made for the partial expropriation of the Spanish Church and the devotion of some of its wealth to secular purposes.

Above all a great offensive against clerical power and Papal claims was now under way in the Habsburg dominions. Even in the first decades of the century there were signs that the atmosphere at the Habsburg court was becoming less intolerantly Catholic than in the past. Both Joseph I (1705-11) and Charles VI (1711-40) married princesses of

Protestant origin; while a long series of disputes with the Papacy, the result of the territorial gains made by the Habsburgs in Italy during the Spanish Succession struggle, helped to strengthen liberalizing tendencies in Vienna. Under Maria Theresa, one of the most sincerely Catholic rulers of the century, efforts at reform, and hence interference with religious institutions, began on a considerable scale. Thus in Lombardy a new body, the *Giunta Economale*, was set up in 1767 to supervise clerical affairs: later the Inquisition was prevented from acting in the province, the number of monasteries was halved and their income reduced by two-thirds, and the judicial privileges of the Church were reduced in various ways. During her reign, however, its purely spiritual powers were left more or less unchallenged. In his religious policy as in all other respects Joseph II (though he remained to his death a practising and believing Catholic) was more wholehearted, more dogmatic and less patient than his mother. To him the Church as it existed was a parasite on the State, a useless consumer of resources which might otherwise be applied to constructive secular purposes. Worse still, by its intolerance and by the superstitions which it fostered it was the positive opponent of social and intellectual progress; while as an international institution it was a check on the sovereignty of secular rulers. Soon after his accession these ideas began to find legislative expression. In October 1781 religious liberty was granted to his non-Catholic Christian subjects in the hereditary provinces, Galicia and Transylvania. In the following year a limited degree of toleration was extended to the Jews; and the Inquisition, which had long ceased to have any practical importance, was formally abolished in the territories under his rule. Simultaneously religious houses were suppressed and their property secularized unless they maintained schools, relieved the poor, or engaged in scholarly work of some kind. A life of religious contemplation was, to Joseph, a life wasted. The funds provided by the dissolution of over 400 religious institutions were used to extend education, notably to create five new seminaries designed to produce priests who would carry out the Emperor's policies.

Most striking of all to contemporaries was the conflict with the Pope which was now clearly developing. Visits to Vienna by Pius VI in 1782 and by Joseph to Rome in the following year, even the signature of a concordat in 1784, did little to bridge the gulf which was opening between them. From 1784 onwards a litany in German, and not the traditional Latin one, began to be used in many churches in the Habsburg dominions. Moreover the religious policies of the Emperor were now being imitated in Catholic Germany, in some parts of which they had considerable influence. (The Elector Friedrich-Karl of Mainz, for example, when he abolished all legal discrimination in his territories against the Jews in 1783–84, was clearly following in the footsteps of Joseph II: Habsburg influence in the electorate was traditionally strong.) As early as 1769 the Electors of Mainz, Trier and Cologne, meeting at Coblenz, had asserted forcibly the rights, as they saw them, of Catholic bishops against the Papacy. Only a General Council, they claimed, possessed supreme legislative and judicial power over the Church. Secular power was directly instituted by God and thus independent of spiritual power. A bishop's administration of his diocese could not be interfered with by the Papacy. In 1785 the same three clerical electors, with the Archbishop of Salzburg, jointly protested against the appointment of a Papal Nuncio to Bavaria. In the following year, in a meeting at Ems, they demanded that the publication of Papal bulls in any part of Catholic Germany should depend on the consent of the bishops concerned, that appeals to Rome should be limited and that Papal nuncios should no longer be appointed to any of the German States. By the later 1780s, therefore, 'Josephism', apart from its importance in the Habsburg territories themselves, was a factor of significance in relations between the Papacy and the whole German world.

The movement was in the long run a failure. It was weakened by the stubborn resistance to Joseph's efforts to extend his schemes of religious reorganization to the Austrian Netherlands and later, more fundamentally, by the reaction against the French Revolution. For the next half-century or more, however, Josephist ideas continued to be important in the religious life of the Habsburg Empire and in its relations with the Papacy.

The Orthodox Church underwent during this period a series of organizational disputes and to a lesser extent intellectual challenges in some ways comparable to those which had to be faced by Catholicism and the Protestant sects. In the Balkans considerable controversy was provoked in the middle decades of the century by the assertion of Auxentios, Archdeacon of Galata, that converts to Orthodoxy from some other branch of the Christian faith must be rebaptized before being admitted to the Church. The suppression in the 1760s by the Ottoman government of the Patriarchates of Ipek and Ochrida, which deprived the Serbs and Bulgars of any remnant of ecclesiastical independence and subjected them to the control of the Greek Patriarchs of Constantinople, was to have considerable influence on the development of Balkan nationalism in the nineteenth century. In particular it did much to stimulate the resentment of Greek intellectual and commercial dominance which was already growing in the Slav areas of the peninsula. These developments, however, were all of essentially local importance and passed almost completely unheeded in Western Europe.

In Russia very important changes took place in the organization of the Church. The death in 1700 of the Patriarch Adrian brought to an end the high degree of independence of the State which it had hitherto enjoyed. No successor to him was appointed by Peter I; and during the first two decades of the eighteenth century Church property and Church-State relations in Russia were controlled by a government department, the *Monastyrskii Prikaz*. This was used by the Tsar as a means of diverting Church revenues, first of all to the needs of the war with Sweden and then to some extent to charitable and educational purposes. Many of Peter's attitudes in religious matters—his dislike of the contemplative and inward-looking aspects of traditional Orthodox piety; his efforts to prevent monks and priests becoming too numerous in his dominions; most of all his hostility to clerical wealth used, as he saw it, unproductively—clearly anticipate those of later rulers in Western and Central Europe. They are well illustrated by the new oath which Russian bishops, from 1716 onwards, had to take before consecration. This bound them not to increase the number of clergy in their dioceses or to build superfluous churches; to make sure that monks under their jurisdiction did not travel without their written permission, which was to be given only in exceptional cases; and in general not to interfere in secular affairs and legal proceedings. In 1721 the *Monastyrskii Prikaz* was replaced by a body of churchmen, the Most Holy Directing Synod, which was intended to act in religious matters as the equivalent of the Senate established a few years earlier for the supervision of secular administration. The lines along which it was to work were prescribed by the Tsar in a very detailed *Dukhovnyi Reglament* (Spiritual Regulation) issued in the same year, which again provides plentiful evidence of his desire to make the church in Russia an agency of secular improvement. (Fully a fifth of the Regulation dealt with education; and a supplement to it ordered that each priest should keep a register of births, marriages and deaths in his parish, though this never worked in practice.) By the time of Peter's death in 1725 the administration of the Church had become in effect merely a department of the centralized bureaucratic machine to which all Russians were now subject. A great secularization of Church lands by Catherine II in 1764 continued and consolidated this process, which encountered throughout remarkably little effective resistance from the Orthodox hierarchy.

From the intellectual point of view the main interest of this period in the history of the Russian Church is that it sees a complicated triangular struggle between Protestant ideas imported from Western and Northern Europe, Catholic tendencies from Poland and the Ukraine, and a strain of native mysticism which was hostile to all foreign beliefs. The reign of Peter I saw the victory of the Protestant and 'enlightened' influences typified by Feodor Prokopovich, the Tsar's main agent in Church affairs, over the Catholicizing trends represented by Stefan Yavorskii, Metropolitan of Ryazan. During the half-century which followed, a number of Lutheran doctrines—for example on original sin and justification by faith—made considerable headway, at least among the higher ranks of the Church. The last decades of this period, however, saw a pietist, mystical and ascetic reaction, typified in different ways by St. Tikhon Zadonskii and the monk Paissy Velichkovskii. This marked a return to Orthodox tradition and an increasing rejection of foreign doctrinal innovations. Russian mysticism was seen in a more extreme and spectacular form in the growth during the same period of a number of very radical noncomformist sects—the *Dukhobortsy*, the *Khlysty* and the *Skopsty*.

For the Jews the eighteenth century, or at least its later decades, held important developments. They remained, above all in Eastern and much of Central Europe, a despised, distrusted and often persecuted group. The myth of their ritual murder of Christian children was still repeated and often credited, in spite of the efforts of Popes Benedict XIII and Clement XIV to combat it. The early years of the century saw the publication of the most influential piece of anti-Semitic propaganda ever produced, J. A. Eisenmenger's *Das entdeckte . . . Judenthum* (Amsterdam, 1711). In England an effort in 1753 to make it possible for Jews to become naturalized met with so much popular resistance that it had to be abandoned. On a deeper level, the hostility of many of the *philosophes* in France to Christianity led them to attack Judaism, from which so many of what they regarded as the worst features of Christianity, in its intolerant and puritanical Old Testament form, had been derived. Voltaire's antagonism on these grounds to the Jews and what they appeared to stand for is particularly marked: one of his most important legacies to later generations was 'the fundamentals of the rhetoric of secular anti-Semitism'.[1] Nevertheless in many areas their

[1] A. Hertzberg, *The French Enlightenment and the Jews* (New York, 1968), p. 286.

position was improving, even rapidly improving, in the latter part of the century. In France they were exempted from the payment of a special poll-tax to which they had hitherto been liable. In the Habsburg territories Joseph II allowed them, under certain conditions, to settle in Vienna where, as in many other German towns, they had previously been forbidden to live or own houses. In Prussia they came to enjoy a high degree of equality with their Christian neighbours, though complete legal equality was achieved only in 1811–12. Moreover they too were now being influenced, at least in Western and parts of Central Europe, by the rationalism, optimism and universalism of the Enlightenment. Figures such as Moses Mendelssohn and his disciples were beginning to tear down the intellectual barriers which had for so long cut Judaism off from the life and thought of Europe. In this they were helped by the foundation in the later decades of the century of the first Jewish periodicals, at Königsberg and Dessau, and by that of the first modern Jewish school at Berlin in 1778. The sceptical and assimilationist attitude which they represented was still that of a small minority of European Jewry, and was opposed by powerful and deeply-entrenched forces of conservatism and orthodoxy. It was becoming an increasingly widespread Jewish attitude, however, even before the cataclysm which began in 1789.

It is impossible to regard the eighteenth century as a great age of religion. Nevertheless it was not an age of religious stagnation or indifference. It saw a considerable development of Christian, above all Catholic, missionary activity in America and the East. Catholic missions continued to be active in China, and to a lesser extent in India, Indo-China and Persia. They remained the most important channel through which Oriental art and philosophy was introduced to the life of Europe. Across the Atlantic the conversion of the native inhabitants of Central and South America continued; and in 1791 a Vicar-Apostolic was appointed to the United States. On the Protestant side the foundation in England of the Society for the Propagation of the Gospel in Foreign Parts in 1701 and the missionary activities of Methodists, Moravians and even Lutherans, showed similar forces and ideals at work.

Even more important, to the ordinary man everywhere in Europe religion continued to be of fundamental importance. He continued to find consolation, reassurance, often aesthetic pleasure, in the rituals to which habit had accustomed him. Above all he continued, with few exceptions, sincerely to desire to know God, to wish for a religion which would satisfy his feelings and his moral sense. Sometimes these desires took the form of mysticism, emotionalism and superstition. The age of the Enlightenment was also the age of the Jansenist excesses at St. Médard, of the Moravians, of the Methodists, of the obscurantist movement of Jewish pietism known as Hassidism. It was against this background of strong emotions and traditional beliefs that the structure of 'rational' or 'natural' religion, so impressive in the number and ability of its literary advocates, was erected. Nevertheless this structure was of great importance. The controversy which the new ideas aroused was generally conducted at a high intellectual level (much higher than that at which contemporary political ideas were discussed). Many of the arguments of the advocates of natural religion were superficial; but after they had done their work it was difficult for an educated layman, at least in Western Europe, to think of God or the universe quite as he would have done a century earlier. Science and rationalism had not destroyed religious belief. In some respects they had strengthened it. But they had wrought in it a qualitative change of fundamental importance, and had helped to produce a great wave of hostility among the educated to traditional dogma and ecclesiastical organization.

XVII

Conclusion

The period covered by this book saw in Europe a mixture of change, sometimes violent and drastic, and stability which sometimes verged on stagnation. The forces of progress and movement were affecting the continent, but their influence was fluctuating and uneven.

Politically, the European State-system and the balance of power were altered fundamentally by the dramatic rise in the international significance of Russia after 1709 and in that of Prussia after 1740. These developments involved a great eastward extension of the geographical scope of European diplomacy and the domination of international relations by East European problems to a quite unprecedented extent in the generation after 1763. Simultaneously the degree to which a European State could be strengthened economically and hence politically by the possession of colonies, the fact that the balance of power on the continent depended increasingly on events thousands of miles away from Europe, began to be fully grasped for the first time. In both these ways a political system whose scope and components had remained on the whole remarkably stable since the Renaissance was rapidly remodelled; from this point of view the changes seen during the eighteenth century were more important than those in any comparable period of European history.

In intellectual life also the age was in many ways one of change and development. The ideas of the Enlightenment grew from seed sown well before the end of the seventeenth century. Nevertheless they had produced in Western Europe by the middle decades of this period an intellectual climate which Descartes, or for that matter Newton himself, would have found almost unrecognizable and in many ways repugnant. Religious impulses, though they were not seriously weakened by the Enlightenment except among a small educated class, had in many areas to find new institutional forms; while systematic religious persecution became increasingly difficult to carry out or justify. In some ways more important, romanticism, whether in literature, in art, or in political ideas, was introducing by the 1750s not so much new ideas as new attitudes and a new scale of intellectual values. These were to modify profoundly though indirectly many sides of European life, as from the 1760s or 1770s the more analytical and classical aspects of the Enlightenment lost some of their vigour and were increasingly challenged by other values—those of sensibility and even of outright irrationalism.

Some aspects of European life, however, showed themselves until near the end of this period remarkably resistant to change. The economic structure of the continent, though it developed fairly rapidly in some respects, remained as far as the majority of Europeans were concerned essentially what it had been for generations or even centuries. The sophistication of some eighteenth-century systems of banking and public finance had been to a considerable extent foreshadowed by the Italian bankers of the later Middle Ages. The great extension of seaborne trade during much of the century was a quantitative rather than a qualitative change. Technology, little influenced by scientific discovery, advanced on the whole slowly and erratically. As late as 1776 Adam Smith could base his *Wealth of Nations* on the tacit and still unchallenged assumption that the economies of all European States were relatively static; the problems of an economic structure based on rapid growth and revolutionary technological change did not and could not engage his attention. Only in the very last years of this period did radically new methods of production or economic organization begin to be of fundamental importance even in Great Britain, now establishing herself as the most economically advanced country in the world.

The stability of Europe's economic life during this period meant almost inevitably that European society (if this question-begging term is permissible) was also relatively stable. The erosion of traditional lines of division between classes and the erection of new ones, the decay of some social groups and the rise of others, none the less proceeded more rapidly than the growth of factories and the modernization of agriculture. Even before the industrial revolution had got properly under way the growth of trade and towns had gone some distance, at least in the more advanced parts of Western Europe, towards replacing a society of communities, 'orders' and traditionally-organized groups by a more modern social structure based mainly though by no means entirely on wealth. Since in Russia a society like that of Western Europe had never really existed, it was chiefly in the central areas of the continent, above all in the German States, that the social heritage of the Middle Ages was transmitted on any considerable scale to the nineteenth century.

The end of the period covered by this book is much more clearly and sharply defined than its beginning. By the 1780s a few favoured areas on or near Europe's western seaboard were beginning to develop a type of economic organization so different from anything hitherto known, so complex, rational and productive, that its growth constitutes the most revolutionary change in the human condition since Neolithic times. Simultaneously the American revolution, in a series of European repercussions whose scope and depth are still incompletely understood, was helping to generate dreams, ambitions and grievances more far-reaching than any since the days of the Anabaptists and the Fifth Monarchy Men. They were dreams and ambitions, moreover, whose popular appeal was potentially almost unlimited. This made them far more important and far more of a challenge to the existing state of things than the restricted sectarian radicalism of the past. The age of large-scale factory production, of mass armies, of popular government, was not yet. Nevertheless it is possible, without an excessive use of the hindsight which is the historian's privilege and temptation, to see faint, and sometimes not-so-faint, portents of its approach. By the 1780s modern history in the genuine as opposed to the textbook sense of the term was beginning.

Appendix I

BIBLIOGRAPHICAL NOTE

It may be convenient to mention here a short selection of general histories of eighteenth-century Europe, and of histories of the major States during this period, which do not fit easily into the short bibliographies given at the beginning of each chapter. The three relevant volumes in the 'Rise of Modern Europe' series edited by W. L. Langer —P. Roberts, *The Quest for Security, 1715-40* (New York-London, 1947); W. L. Dorn, *Competition for Empire, 1740-63* (London-New York, 1940); and L. Gershoy, *From Despotism to Revolution, 1763-89* (New York-London, 1944)—are wide in scope and contain very full bibliographies. E. Préclin and V. L. Tapié, *Le XVIIIe Siècle* (Paris, 1952) which constitutes vol. VII, Parts II and III of the French series *Clio: Introduction aux Études Historiques*, contains a vast amount of information in somewhat summary form. The very large bibliographies are spoilt by frequent misprints. Other general works are: *The New Cambridge Modern History*, vol. VII, *The Old Régime, 1713-1763*, ed. J. Lindsay (Cambridge, 1957); vol. VIII, *The American and French Revolutions, 1763-93*, ed. A. Goodwin (Cambridge, 1965); R. Mousnier and E. Labrousse, *Le XVIIIe Siècle. Révolution intellectuelle, technique et politique, 1715-1815* (Paris, 1953) in the series *Histoire Générale des Civilisations* (excellent on some aspects of intellectual and social life; the chapters relating to this period were written by R. Mousnier); and the two relevant volumes in the French series *Peuples et Civilisations*— P. Muret, *La Prépondérance Anglaise, 1713-1763* (Paris, 1937) and P. Sagnac, *La Fin de l'Ancien Régime et la Révolution Américaine, 1763-1789* (Paris, 1941). The two last are in some ways more conventional than the *Clio* and *Histoire Générale des Civilisations* volumes and more concerned, especially the former, with diplomatic history. Both are balanced and reliable studies. P. Chaunu, *La Civilisation de l'Europe classique* (Paris, 1966) is a recent single-volume work which concentrates on economic and social history; it covers both the seventeenth and eighteenth centuries. A. Cobban (ed.), *The Eighteenth Century: Europe in the Age of Enlightenment* (London, 1969) is a magnificently illustrated collection of essays by experts on different aspects of the period. Other recent general works of merit are R. Mousnier, C.-E. Labrousse and M. Bouloiseau, *Le XVIIIe siècle: l'epoque des 'lumières'* (*1715–1815*) (Paris, 1967); and G. Rudé, *Europe in the Eighteenth Century: Aristocracy and the Bourgeois Challenge* (London, 1972).

The best histories of England for this period are Basil Williams, *The Whig Supremacy, 1714–1760* (revised ed., Oxford, 1962) and J. Steven Watson, *The Reign of George III, 1760–1820* (Oxford, 1960). They form part of the 'Oxford History of England' series and contain very comprehensive bibliographies. For France older works, now in some ways outdated, are H. Carré, *Le Règne de Louis XV* (Paris, 1911), and H. Carré, P. Sagnac and E. Lavisse, *Le Règne de Louis XVI* (Paris, 1911) which are respectively vol. VIII, Part II and vol. IX, Part I of E. Lavisse (ed.) *Histoire de France des Origines jusqu'à la Révolution.* R. Mandrou, *La France aux XVIIe et XVIIIe siècles* (Paris, 1967) P. Goubert, *L'Ancien Régime,* vol. I, *La Societé* (Paris, 1969) and A. Soboul, *La Civilisation et la Révolution francaise,* vol. I, *La Crise de l'Ancien Régime* (Paris, 1970) are stimulating recent single-volume works. All are focused mainly or entirely on social history. W. H. Bruford, *Germany in the Eighteenth Century* (Cambridge, 1939) is important for social history. On Austria the most recent general work is H. Hantsch, *Die Geschichte Oesterreichs,* vol. II (Vienna, 1950) and for Prussia O. Hintze, *Die Hohenzollern und ihr Werk* (9th ed. Berlin, 1926) is still perhaps the most satisfactory account. The best general works on Russia in western languages are P. Milyukov, C. Seignobos and L. Eisenmann, *Histoire de Russie* (Paris, 1932–33), vols. II–III and V. Gitermann, *Geschichte Russlands* (Zürich, 1944–49), vol. II. In English, G. Vernadsky, *A History of Russia* (New Haven, 1929) and B. H. Sumner, *A Survey of Russian History* (London, 1944) are useful short discussions. The standard large-scale history of Spain is A. Ballesteros y Beretta, *Historia de España y su Influencia en la Historia universal* (Barcelona, 1918–41): vols. V and VI are relevant here. The best general work in English is J. P. de Oliviera Martins, *A History of Iberian Civilization* (London, 1930). Good general works on Italy are not very numerous; F. Valsecchi, *L'Italia nel Settecento* (Milan, 1959) is written on a large scale and lavishly illustrated. In English the relevant chapters of L. Salvatorelli, *A Concise History of Italy* (London, 1940) are worth attention. On Poland the standard large-scale work in English is *The Cambridge History of Poland,* ed. W. H. Reddaway and others, vol. II (Cambridge, 1941). On Sweden and Denmark there is B. J. Hovde,

The Scandinavian Countries, 1720–1865 (Boston, 1948), vol. I, which has much information on economic and intellectual life but does not deal at all with foreign policy. The history of the United Provinces is covered by the somewhat old-fashioned P. J. Blok, *A History of the People of the Netherlands*, vol. V (New York, 1912) and the briefer B. H. M. Vlekke, *The Evolution of the Dutch Nation* (New York, 1945).

The most useful historical atlas for the student of this period is probably *Grosser Historischer Weltatlas*, vol. III, ed. J. Engel and others (Munich, 1957). The most comprehensive bibliography of eighteenth-century Europe is to be found in the relevant sections of J. Roach (ed.), *A Bibliography of Modern History* (Cambridge, 1968).

Appendix II

CHRONOLOGICAL LIST OF THE MAIN POLITICAL EVENTS MENTIONED IN THIS VOLUME

INTERNATIONAL EVENTS

1696 Peter I takes Azov from the Turks.

1699 Treaty of Carlowitz signed by Austria, Poland, the Ottoman Empire and Venice.

1698, 1700 First and Second Partition Treaties attempt to allocate the Spanish inheritance between the rival claimants.

1700 Outbreak of Great Northern War. Charles XII of Sweden forces Denmark to make peace (Treaty of Travendal) and defeats Peter I of Russia at Narva.

1702 Outbreak of War of the Spanish Succession.

1704 England takes Gibraltar.

1709 Battle of Poltava.

1711 Pruth campaign: Peter I restores Azov to the Turks.

1713 Peace made at Utrecht by France, Britain, Spain, the United Provinces, Savoy, and Portugal.

1717 Triple Alliance of Britain, France, and the United Provinces (becomes the Quadruple Alliance when joined by the Emperor in the following year). Spanish conquest of Sardinia.

1718 Battle of Cape Passaro. Anglo-Spanish war.
Treaty of Passarowitz (ends Austro-Turkish war in progress since 1716).

1719 France declares war on Spain.

1720 Savoy obtains Sardinia from the Emperor in exchange for Sicily.

1721 Treaty of Nystadt signed by Sweden and Russia.

1725 Treaty of Vienna signed by Austria and Spain.

1731 Second Treaty of Vienna signed by Britain, the United Provinces, Spain, and Austria.

1733 First Family Compact signed by France and Spain.

1733-35 War of the Polish Succession (formally ended by Third Treaty of Vienna in 1738).

1735   Outbreak of Russo-Turkish war (Austrian participation on the Russian side from 1737).

1739   Russia, Austria, and the Ottoman Empire sign Treaty of Belgrade.
Outbreak of Anglo-Spanish war.

1740   Prussian invasion of Silesia.

1742   Treaty of Berlin signed by Austria and Prussia.

1743   Treaty of Äbo ends Russo-Swedish war in progress since 1741.
France and Spain sign Second Family Compact.

1744   France declares war on Great Britain.

1745   Treaty of Dresden ends new Austro-Prussian struggle which had broken out in the previous year.
British capture of Louisbourg.

1746   French capture of Madras.

1748   Treaty of Aix-la-Chapelle signed by France, Britain, Spain, and the United Provinces.

1755   Outbreak of undeclared war between Britain and France. (Fighting in America had begun in the previous year.)

1756   Convention of Westminster signed by Britain and Prussia, Treaty of Versailles by Austria and France. Outbreak of Seven Years War.

1757   Second Treaty of Versailles signed by Austria and France (modified by a third treaty signed in 1759).
Battle of Plassey.

1759   British capture of Quebec.

1761   Third Family Compact signed by France and Spain.

1762   Break-up of Anglo-Prussian alliance.

1763   Peace of Paris signed by Britain, France, and Spain: Treaty of Hubertusburg by Austria and Prussia.

1764   Russo-Prussian alliance to control Poland.

1766   Duchy of Lorraine incorporated in France.

1768–69   French purchase and conquest of Corsica.

1768   Outbreak of Russo-Turkish war.

1772   First Partition of Poland

1774   Treaty of Kutchuk-Kainardji signed by Russia and Turkey.

1776   American Declaration of Independence.

1778   France enters the War of American Independence (followed by Spain in 1779).
War of the Bavarian Succession breaks out (ended in the following year by the Treaty of Teschen).

1780 Armed Neutrality formed. Britain declares war on the United Provinces.

1781 British surrender at Yorktown. Austro-Russian alliance against the Ottoman Empire.

1783 Treaty of Versailles signed by Britain, France, Spain, and the United States.
Russian seizure of the Crimea.

GREAT BRITAIN

1689 Bill of Rights.

1694 Triennial Act.

1701 Act of Settlement.

1702 Death of William III, accession of Anne.

1707 Union of England and Scotland.

1714 Death of Anne, accession of George I.

1715-16 Jacobite rising.

1716 Septennial Act.

1720 South Sea Bubble bursts.

1722 Robert Walpole First Lord of the Treasury (remains chief minister till 1742).

1727 Death of George I, accession of George II.
First Indemnity Act in favour of Nonconformists.

1745-46 Jacobite rising.

1757-61 Coalition ministry led by William Pitt and the Duke of Newcastle.

1760 Death of George II, accession of George III.

1763 Wilkes case arises. Friction with American colonies begins to be serious.

1769 Wilkes expelled from Parliament, twice re-elected.

1770-82 Lord North chief minister, personal influence of George III at its height.

1782 'Economical Reform' legislation.

1783 William Pitt the younger becomes chief minister.

FRANCE

1713 Bull *Unigenitus* condemns Jansenist doctrines.

1715 Death of Louis XIV, accession of Louis XV. (Philip of Orléans Regent till 1723.)

1720 Collapse of 'Mississippi Bubble' and financial schemes of Law.

1723–26 Duc de Bourbon chief minister.

1726–43 Cardinal Fleury chief minister.

1749 New tax, the *vingtième*, imposed by Controller-General Machault d'Arnouville.

1751 Failure of Machault's attempts to improve the government's financial position.

1758–70 Duc de Choiseul chief minister.

1764 Expulsion of the Jesuits.

1771 *Parlement* of Paris exiled by Maupeou.

1774 Death of Louis XV, accession of Louis XVI.

Fall of Maupeou and recall of the *parlements*.

Vergennes Secretary for Foreign Affairs (till his death in 1787)

1774–76 Turgot Controller-General of Finances.

RUSSIA

1689 Tsarevna Sophia (Regent since 1682) overthrown.

1695–96 Peter I begins the creation of a fleet for use against Azov and on the Black Sea.

1697–98 Peter's journey to Western Europe.

1703 Building of a Baltic fleet and of St. Petersburg begun.

1711 Creation of the Senate.

1718 Murder of Tsarevich Alexis. Creation of administrative colleges begun.

1722 Table of Ranks issued.

1725 Death of Peter I, accession of Catherine I.

1727 Death of Catherine I, accession of Peter II.

1730 Death of Peter II, accession of Anna. Failure of attempt to impose restrictions on the power of the monarchy.

1740 Death of Anna. She is succeeded in 1741, after several palace revolutions, by Elizabeth.

1762 Death of Elizabeth; accession, deposition, and murder of Peter III; accession of Catherine III.

Abolition of compulsory State service for the landowning class.

1767 Legislative Commission meets.

1773–75 Great peasant revolt led by Pugachev.

1775 Reorganization of local government.

1785 Charters to the nobility and towns issued.

SPAIN

1714 Capture of Barcelona by Philip V.
1719 Fall of Alberoni.
1743-54 Ensenada chief minister.
1746 Death of Philip V, accession of Ferdinand VI.
1759 Death of Ferdinand VI, accession of Charles III.
1767 Expulsion of the Jesuits.
1779-82 Unsuccessful siege of Gibraltar.

THE HABSBURG MONARCHY

1711 Death of Joseph I, accession of Charles VI.
     Hungarian revolt ended by Peace of Szatmár.
1713 Pragmatic Sanction issued.
1740 Death of Charles VI, accession of Maria Theresa.
1749 *Directorium in Publicis et Cameralibus* set up.
1753 Kaunitz becomes Chancellor.
1760 Council of State set up.
1765 Joseph II becomes Holy Roman Emperor and co-ruler with his mother of the Habsburg territories.
1780 Death of Maria Theresa. Joseph II in sole control of the Habsburg territories.
1781-85 Numerous reforms introduced by Joseph II (most notable his efforts in 1781 to improve the position of the peasantry).

BRANDENBURG-PRUSSIA

1713 Death of Frederick I, accession of Frederick William I.
1722 General Directory established.
1728 Foreign Ministry (*Kabinetsministerium*) established.
1733 Modified form of conscription introduced.
1740 Death of Frederick William I, accession of Frederick II.
1766 New excise introduced.
1786 Death of Frederick II, accession of Frederick William II.
1791 New law code issued.

OTHER STATES

1702-20 Heinsius leading political figure in the United Provinces.
1718 Death of Charles XII of Sweden.

1720 New constitution greatly reduces the power of the Swedish monarchy.

1747 Orangist revolution in the United Provinces.

1750–77 Pombal chief minister in Portugal.

1759 Jesuits expelled from Portugal.
Tanucci in power in the Kingdom of the Two Sicilies (till 1776).

1764 Stanislaus Poniatowski, last king of Poland, elected.

1765–90 Grand Duke Leopold ruler of Tuscany.

1771–92 Gustavus III king of Sweden.

1772 He re-establishes absolutism with French support.

1770–72 Struensee introduces reforms in Denmark.

Index

For rulers the dates given are those of their reigns; for other persons those of their birth and death. These dates are not given in a number of cases where the individual concerned is unimportant or where they are difficult to establish.

427

count (1678–1751), English states-
man and writer, 135
Bombay, 294
Bonneval, Claude Alexandre de (Bon-
neval Pasha) (1675–1747), French
soldier, 286
Borda, Charles (1733–99), mathe-
matician, 193
Bordeaux, *parlement* of, 147
Boscawen, Edward, Admiral (1711–
61), 296, 297
Bosnia, 283
Bossuet, Jacques Bénigne, Bishop of
Meaux (1627–1704), 4, 389
Boston, opposition to British rule in,
304
Boswell, James (1740–95), Scottish
writer, 174
Boucher, François (1703–70), French
painter, 332, 333
Boulainvilliers, Henri, Comte de
(1658–1722), French writer, 385
Boulton, Matthew (1728–1809), Brit-
ish industrialist, 52
Bourbon, Louis Henri, Duc de, 276
Boyarskaya Duma, in Russia, 120
Braddock, James, General, 295
Brazil, diamonds from, 322
Breslau, Treaty of (1742), 254
Brest, 196
Bristol, 322
Brittany, nobility in, 49; merchants
in, 55; agriculture in, 67; difficulty
of land communications in, 75;
seigneurial courts in, 114
Brühl, Heinrich, Count von (1700–
63), Saxon statesman, 246
Bucharest, peace congress at (1772–
73), 237
Buffon, George Louis Leclerc, Comte
de (1707–88), French naturalist,
347, 373
Bulgaria, 283
Burma, European activity in, 329–30
Bussy-Castelnau, Charles-Joseph
Patissier, Marquis de, French
soldier, 296, 299
Bute, John Stewart, 3rd Earl of (1713–
92), British statesman, 263, 301
Byng, George, Viscount Torrington,
Admiral (1663–1733), 275

Cadiz, 322

Cagliostro, Alessandro, Count (1743–
95), adventurer, 384
Caisse d'Escompte, in France (1776), 90
Calas, Jean (1698–1762), case of, 115
Calcutta, 294, 299
Cambrai, Congress at (1724), 276
Camier, Abbé, French theologian, 391
Campomanes, Pedro Rodriguez
(1723–1803), Spanish statesman,
154, 165
Canada, French society in, 292;
British conquest of, 298–99, 301
Canton, trade at, 323–24
Capitation, in France, 102, 107
Caracas Company (1728), 324, 326
Caribbean, Anglo-French rivalry in,
292, 299
Carillon, Fort, 298
Carlowitz, Treaty of (1699), 219, 282,
284
Carnatic, Anglo-French struggles in,
296, 299; growth of British power
in, 325
Carteret, John, Viscount (1690–1763),
British statesman, 254, 256, 314
Catalonia, 151
Catherine I, Empress of Russia (1725–
27), 137, 225, 227
Catherine II, Empress of Russia
(1762–96), 18, 41, 109, 113, 135,
155, 187, 190, 200, 203, 226, 323,
338, 386, 406, 411; and society in
Russia, 37–38; and serfdom in
Russia, 40, 161; and Rusisan nobility, 46; and Russian towns, 50;
administrative achievements of,
122; as an enlightened despot, 159–
63; continues policies of her predecessors, 161–62; and Poland, 230,
236; and the Ottoman Empire, 324–
28; and the Bavarian Succession,
265–66
Catholic Church, divisions within,
401
Census of population, attempts at,
96–7
Ceuta, 323
Cevennes, Huguenot revolt in (1702–
04), 395
Chambéry, 278
Chamlay, Jules-Louis Bolé, Marquis
de (1650–1719), French soldier, 178
Chandernagore, 294, 298

Chapman, Fredrik Hendrik af, Swedish naval architect, 193
Chardin, Jean-Baptiste-Siméon (1699–1779), French painter, 353
Charles II, King of Spain (1665–1700), 1, 269
Charles III, King of Spain (1759–88), 106, 166, 178, 300, 306, 326; monarchy of in Spain, 152, 154, 165
Charles IV, King of the Two Sicilies (1735–59) (formerly Don Carlos), 47, 278
Charles V, Holy Roman Emperor (1519–56), 198, 199
Charles VI, Holy Roman Emperor (1711–40), 74, 124, 203, 228, 276, 408; and Prussia, 249–50; and Spain, 274
Charles VII, Holy Roman Emperor (1742–45), 244; and War of Austrian Succession, 252, 254–55
Charles XII, King of Sweden (1697–1718), 130, 178, 233, 286; victories of, 220–21; defeat and death of, 221
Charles Edward Stewart, Prince (1720–88), Jacobite pretender, 397
Charles-Emmanuel III, King of Sardinia (1730–73), 254, 278, 279; reforms carried out by, 164
Charles Frederick, Margrave of Baden (1771–1811), 156
Charlottenburg, palace at, 359; masonic lodge at, 393; Treaty of (1723), 249
Chateaubriand, Francois-René, Vicomte de (1768–1848), French statesman, 382
Chauvelin, Germain-Louis de (1685–1762), French statesman, 46
Chemnitz, 83
Cherbourg, 150
Chernyshev, Count G., 394; Count Z. G. (1722–84), Russian statesman, 231
Chesmé, battle of (1770), 191, 235
Chesterfield, Philip Dormer Stanhope, 4th Earl of (1694–1773), British statesman, 297
Children, changing attitudes to, 24, 27
China, intellectual influence of over Europe, 330–32, 369; artistic influence of, 332–33

Chippendale, Thomas (d. 1779), cabinetmaker, 355
Choiseul, Étienne-François, duc de (1719–85), French statesman, 19, 145, 189, 202, 207, 211, 300, 302, 315; on importance of colonies, 327
Churches, efforts to reconcile, 389; missionary work by, 413
Cimarosa, Domenico (1749–1801), Italian composer, 357
Clarke, Samuel (1675–1729), English freethinker, 392
Clement XII, Pope (1730–40), 406
Clement XIII, Pope (1758–69), 405
Clement XIV, Pope (1769–74), 405
Clive, Robert, Baron (1725–74), soldier in India, 299–300, 329
Cocceji, Samuel von (1679–1755), Prussian jurist, 158
Cochin-China, 330
Codex Theresianus (1766), 113
Coke, Thomas (afterwards Earl of Leicester) (1752–1842), agriculturist, 65
Cologne, 76; social tensions in, 54
Colonies, valued for economic reasons, 317–20; trade of Europe with increasing, 320; economic importance of, 319; trade of in North America, 320–21; in Caribbean, 321–22; in Latin America, 322–23; in Asia and Africa, 323–24; British opinion on, 327; European guilt over, 334–35
compagnonnages, in France, conservatism of, 87–88
Conciliatory Propositions (1778), 306
Condillac, Étienne Bonnet de (1715–80), French philosopher, 363, 366, 367
Condorcet, Marie, Marquis de (1743–94), French philosopher, 372, 373
Confucius, 332
Connecticut, 292, 321
Constantinople, 200, 206, 237, 286; printing in, 282; Treaty of (1700), 219–20
Contemporary accounts of eighteenth-century history, 14–15
Cook, Capt. James (1728–79), British explorer, 329
Coote, Sir Eyre (1726–83), British soldier, 299, 329

tions of, 306; ideas of on policy,
315-16
Vernon, Edward, Admiral (1684-
1757), 192, 293
Versailles, First Treaty of (1756),
257-58; Second Treaty of (1757),
259-60; Third Treaty of (1759),
261, Treaty of (1783), 308; palace
at, imitations of, 359-60
Vico, Giambattista (-), Italian
philosopher, 341; ideas of, 380-81
Victor Amdeus II, Duke of Savoy,
King of Sicily and later of Sardinia
(1675-1730), 10; territorial gains
achieved by, 270-71
Vienna, Turkish attack on (1683), 1;
pamphlets published in (1781-82),
169; Treaty of (1725), 250; Treaty
of (1738), 277; newspapers published in, 284
Vigée-Lebrun, Elizabeth (1755-1842),
French painter, 355
Village communities, importance of,
42-43; conservatism of, 43-44
Villeneuve, Louis Sauveur Renaud,
Marquis de, French diplomat, 286
Virginia, 291, 321
Voltaire, François Arouet de (1694-
1778), French writer, 4, 11, 15, 22,
29, 115, 154, 159, 160, 165, 239, 343,
347, 363, 370, 372, 378; as an historian, 16, 373; and China, 332;
and music, 355; and the Enlightenment, 364-65, 368; and Natural
Religion, 392; and the Jews, 412

Wake, William, Archbishop of Canter-
bury (1657-1737), 389
Wallachia, 234, 235, 283
Walpole, Horace (1717-97), English
man of letters, 335
Walpole, Sir Robert (1676-1745),
English statesman, 142, 189, 296,
310
Wandewash, battle of (1760), 299
Warfare, growing mildness of, 174-
75; but not in Eastern Europe, 179
Warrington, 83
Warsaw, Treaty of (1717), 230
Warton, Thomas (1728-90), English
literary historian, 350
Washington, George (1732-99),
American statesman, 295, 334

Watson, Richard, professor of chemis-
try, 345-46
Watteau, Antoine (1684-1721),
French painter, 332, 333
Webster, Alexander (1707-84), statis-
tician, 96
Wedgewood, Josiah (1730-95), Eng-
lish industrialist, 353
Weishaupt, Adam (1748-1830), Ger-
man mystic, 399
Wencker, family of, in Strasbourg, 57
Wendel, de, family of, 52
Wesley, John (1703-91), Methodist
leader, hostility of to liberalism, 397
Westminster, Convention of (1756),
257, 258
Wetzlar, Reichskammergericht in, 242,
244
Wieland, Christoph Martin (1733-
1813), German writer, 20, 158
Wiener-Neustadt, military academy in,
185
Wilkes, John (1727-97), English
politician, 106, 379; controversies
associated with, 143; and supersti-
tion in Naples, 397
Wilkins, Sir Charles (1749?-1836),
translator, 332
Wilkinson, John (1728-1808), indus-
trialist, 52, 81
William III, Stadtholder and King of
England (1689-1702), 133, 140,
178, 389
William IV, Stadtholder of the United
Provinces (1747-51), 133
William V, Stadtholder of the United
Provinces (1751-95), 133
William Henry, Fort, 298
Winckelmann, Johann Joachim (1717-
68), German writer, 158, 350
Witchcraft, belief in, 395-96
Wolff, Christian (1679-1754), Ger-
man philosopher, 331, 381, 392
Women, improvements in the position
of, 26-28
Woolston, Thomas (1669-1731), Eng-
lish Deist, 392
Woolwich, military academy at (1741),
185
Wörlitz, Gothic palace at (1776), 354
Worms, 243; Treaty of (1743), 255
Württemberg, Duke of, 243; estates
in, 245

446